Student Guide to IFPS®

Student Guide to IFPS®

(Interactive Financial Planning System)

PAUL GRAY
Southern Methodist University

McGraw-Hill Book Company

New York St. Louis San Francisco Auckland
Bogotá Hamburg Johannesburg London Madrid
Mexico Montreal New Delhi Panama Paris
São Paulo Singapore Sydney Tokyo Toronto

To Robert E. Machol

STUDENT GUIDE TO IFPS®

67890 SEMSEM 898765

ISBN 0-07-024322-0

The editor was Charles E. Stewart;
the production supervisor was Joe Campanella.
Semline, Inc., was printer and binder.

IFPS is a Registered Trademark of Execucom Systems Corporation of Austin, Texas.

Library of Congress Cataloging in Publication Data
Gray, Paul, date
Student guide to IFPS (Interactive Financial Planning System)

Includes index.
1. IFPS (Computer system) I. Title. II. Title:
Student guide to I.F.P.S. (Interactive Financial Planning System)
HG4012.5.G7 1983 658.1'5'0285425 83-778
ISBN 0-07-024322-0

CONTENTS

Preface ix

I. Introduction 1

1.1 What This Book is About 3
1.2 Modeling 4
1.3 Decision Support Systems 15
1.4 Overview of IFPS 20

II. Basic Elements of IFPS 29

2.1 How to Obtain IFPS at Your Terminal and Begin Work 31
2.2 Creating and Solving a Simple IFPS Model 36
2.3 Multiple Models (The MODEL,FILE, and CATALOG commands) 41
2.4 How to Get Out of IFPS (The QUIT Command) 42
2.5 Correcting Mistakes (The Edit Commands) 44
2.6 Obtaining a Listing at the Line Printer (The RECORD Command) 47
2.7 The New Product Model -- An Example 49
2.8 Some Principles and Rules In Writing Your Model 54
2.9 Example--Pro Forma Profit and Loss Statement 56
2.10 What To Do if You Need Help (The IFPS HELP Commands) 64

III. Useful Features of IFPS 67

3.1 Using IFPS to Ask Questions About the Model 69
3.2 Built-In Functions (Financial, Forecasting Mathematical) 80
3.3 Built-In Subroutines (Depreciation, Amortization) 93

IV. Advanced Capabilities of IFPS 99

4.1 SOLVE Options 101
4.2 WIDTH and OPT 105
4.3 Plotting Results Graphically 107
4.4 Useful Calculational Features (L, MATRIX, SUM, IF, COLUMN) 113
4.5 Useful Command Features (', ! ,RESEQUENCE, COPY, COMPILESAVE, CROSSREF, EXPAND) 118
4.6 Data Files 122
4.7 Generating Formatted Reports (GENREPORT) 129
4.8 Consolidation 138
4.9 An Example Involving Data Files, Reports, and Consolidation 145
4.10 Additional Editing Commands 151

V. Monte Carlo Simulation (Risk Analysis) 157

5.1 The Rationale and Use of Simulation 159
5.2 IFPS Approach to Simulation 165
5.3 Built-In Probability Distributions 165
5.4 Defining Your Own Probability Distributions 168
5.5 Choosing The Same Random Number for All Periods or a New Value for Each Period 169
5.6 Example: The Simple IFPS Model with Uncertainty 170
5.7 Generating Scenarios (HIGH, LOW, MEAN, MOSTP) 171
5.8 Running a MONTE CARLO Simulation 174
5.9 The STOP Command (What To Do If You Make an Options Mistake) 179
5.10 Interpreting MONTE CARLO Results 180
5.11The POOL Command 182
5.12 Example: The New Product Model with Uncertainty 183
5.13 Example: A Risk Analysis Model 186
5.14 Example: Testing the IFPS Random Number Generator 191

VI. Applications in Finance 199

6.1 Introduction 201
6.2 Net Present Value 201
6.3 Present Value of Bonds and Stocks 205
6.4 Alternative Criteria for Investment Decisions 215
6.5 Optimal Timing for Selling an Asset or Making an Investment 219
6.6 A Larger Example--The Guano Project 221
6.7 Mean and Variance of the Return from a Portfolio of Two Stocks 226
6.8 Capital Asset Pricing Model 228
6.9 Analyzing Project Proposals: Break-Even and Sensitivity Analysis 231
6.10 Using Scenarios to Evaluate Project Proposals 239

6.11 Using Simulation to Evaluate Project Proposals 241
6.12 The Black-Scholes Formula for Call Options 244
6.13 Financial Ratio Analysis 248
6.14 Cash Management Model 253
6.15 Pro Forma Financial Forecast Models 255
6.16 Addendum: Year 0 vs. Year 1 261

VII. Applications In Statistics 265

7.1 Summary Measures --Mean, Variance, Standard Deviation 267
7.2 Permutations and Combinations 278
7.3 Probability Distributions 280
7.4 Chi -Square Tests of Goodness of Fit and Independence 283
7.5 Linear Regression 289
7.6 Multiple Regression 296
7.7 Time Series and Forecasting 301
7.8 Index Numbers 314

VIII. Applications in Production and Operations Management 319

8.1 Break-Even Analysis 321
8.2 Aggregate Scheduling 326
8.3 Inventory 333
8.4 Material Requirements Planning 349
8.5 Equipment Replacement 353
8.6 Quality Control 359

Appendix I. HELP Commands 367
Appendix II. IFPS Commands 372
Appendix III. Reserved Words 385
Appendix IV. 20 Most Common Error Messages in IFPS 388

Index 393

PREFACE

The Interactive Financial Planning System (abbreviated IFPS) was originally developed in the early 1970's by Dr. Gerald R. Wagner (at that time a Professor at The University of Texas at Austin) and his students. Its original impetus came from the desire to model risk in a way which could easily be understood by executives. The implementation which resulted proved to be a general purpose financial planning language that is particularly "user friendly". In the years since then, IFPS has been marketed through Execucom Systems Corporation of Austin, Texas, and has been widely adopted in both industry and universities. Until now, the only study material available has been that supplied through Execucom.

The purpose of this book is to provide a way for both students and professionals to learn the IFPS language. The book is intended for both the beginner and the experienced user. The beginner can learn the language by following the text and the many examples step by step. The more experienced user will find many new uses for the capabilities of the language.

In writing this book we have assumed that the reader has access to IFPS at a computer terminal. We also assume that the reader is either a student or a professional in business, engineering, economics, computer science, or related field (or is currently working in some area of business). We have tried to make the book accessible even to the novice with no prior computer experience by starting with the elementary operations of getting on and off the computer. The examples shown use ordinary English names (such as INVESTMENT, SALES, INCOME) rather than abstract symbols. Mathematical concepts are explained as they are needed.

In preparing this book we have selected those commands and features which we believe are the most widely used and which do not require professional programming skills. We have omitted a number of advanced features which, although extremely useful, are designed more for the computer professional.

This book is the outgrowth of using IFPS at Southern Methodist University. When we first introduced IFPS, MBA students were required to learn a conventional programming language. We found that students could learn IFPS much more easily and could use it directly in their work. The dissemination of the language through the University was student-driven; that is, the students started using it in many of their classes and faculty began learning the language to keep up with their students. In the fall of 1982, we changed our requirements and now teach only IFPS to MBA's. This *Student's Guide to IFPS* serves as the text. The language is taught as an integral part of a required first-semester course.

We find that although many of our students have no prior computer experience, they are all able to learn the language quickly. Typically, we offer a 90-minute introductory lecture that leads students through Chapter II and some of Chapter III of this book. Thereafter the students are asked to write models of increasing complexity as part of their regular course work. Formal instruction is given from time to time as new features are needed; for example, when we discuss simulation we spend some time discussing the simulation capabilities of IFPS.

IFPS Versions

This book is based on Release 8.0 of IFPS, which was issued in 1982. It is fully compatible with Release 9.0, and should be compatible with later versions as they are issued. The book can also be used by those who have IFPS MINI. The primary difference is that IFPS MINI is a subset of IFPS that does not have the simulation capability discussed in Chapter V.

A number of computer software packages compatible with IFPS are available. The packages include:

IFPS/SENTRY for data entry in a form directly compatible with IFPS.

IFPS/DATASPAN for converting data bases in arbitrary format to a form directly usable by IFPS.

IFPS/GRAPHICS for presenting IFPS results on color graphics displays.

IFPS/OPTIMUM for finding optimal solutions of IFPS models by linear, nonlinear, or integer programming.

These additional packages, which increase the capabilities of IFPS significantly, are not discussed in this volume.

Organization of This Book

CHAPTER I. This chapter introduces the basic ideas of modeling and decision support systems. These ideas are fundamental to understanding the IFPS modeling language. The discussion includes the reasons for using models, their advantages, and the pitfalls to be avoided. The chapter concludes with a description of the features of IFPS, particularly those that distinguish it from conventional computer languages.

CHAPTERS II THROUGH V. The purpose of these four chapters is to serve as a text from which to learn successively more and more about IFPS.

Chapter II is the starting point for the novice. It focuses on creating simple models. It shows how to obtain IFPS at a terminal, how to write a very simple model, and how to use elementary commands for manipulating the model and obtaining output. This chapter contains three models of increasing complexity. Each model is described step by step, including the statement of the problem, explanation of the model, and presentation of the results. The simple models of Chapter II appear again in later chapters in expanded form and are used to illustrate more advanced concepts. The chapter concludes with a discussion of the extensive HELP commands available on-line in IFPS to assist in case of difficulty.

Chapter III focuses on the capabilities built into IFPS for supporting decision making. It shows how to ask questions of models (What if...? How sensitive...? If my goal is...?) that help clarify their implications. It also describes the financial, depreciation, amortization, statistical, and mathematical functions available.

The purpose of Chapter IV is to introduce the features of IFPS that allow communication within the organization. In particular, Chapter IV discusses the graphical presentation of results, the use of data files for dealing with large data-driven problems, the creation of output in whatever format is used within an organization, and the the consolidation of the results of two or more models. Chapter IV also describes advanced calculational, command, and editing features available in IFPS.

Chapter V explains how to model uncertainty and perform risk analysis. Included is a discussion for the rationale for assessing risk by simulation and the use of fixed-time-interval simulations in general. The chapter shows how to generate scenarios and how to run a statistically significant number of iterations and obtain output statistics. The chapter includes three example simulations; other simulations are included in later chapters.

The major features of IFPS have been described by the end of Chapter V. That is, Chapters II through V are a text on IFPS. You, the reader, can work your way through the material sequentially to learn the language. You should then keep the book and use it as a reference that you consult when you encounter specific questions.

CHAPTER VI THROUGH VIII. The purpose of these chapters is to illustrate the wide range of applications for which IFPS can be used. The applications have been taken, respectively, from three fields:

- finance
- statistics
- operations management.

Each chapter is keyed to the typical course required to be taken by MBA students. In fact, the problems discussed are based on standard texts; however, the chapters are self-contained so that they can be followed without consulting these specific texts.

The emphasis in these three chapters is on formulating the application as an IFPS model. Therefore, the models presented involve only small amounts of data and do not use advanced formatting and report features. With the exception of a few sections describing simulations, these chapters can be read immediately after Chapters II and III. Thus, access is provided to applications early in the study of IFPS. Chapters VI, VII, and VIII are independent of one another and can be read in any order.

APPENDICES. The appendices contain reference information that is useful in working with IFPS. Specifically:

Appendix I contains a listing of the output of the various HELP commands available in IFPS.

Appendix II contains a listing of all the commands available in IFPS. Not all the commands are covered in this book. Section numbers are indicated for those commands which are discussed in the text. This is a reference guide.

Appendix III lists the "reserved" words in IFPS. These words have specific meanings in IPFS and there are restrictions on how and where they can be used.

Appendix IV contains a list of the twenty most frequently encountered IFPS error messages and explains their meaning.

Acknowledgments

This book had as its beginnings a small directed study in the summer of 1981 by Kevin L. Roper. Roper prepared a 10-page report that described how to obtain IFPS and use it on the SMU computer. He created the Simple IFPS model of Chapter II to illustrate some of the ways the language can be used.

As this book has evolved, a number of my colleagues at SMU, including Julius Aronofsky, Jay Aronson, Richard S. Barr, Christopher B. Barry, James Collins, David A. Goodman, Richard Helgason, Thomas E. Perkins, Marion G. Sobol, and Michael Van Breda, have read the book, commented on it, and used it in their classes.

I am particularly grateful for the editorial help I have received. Professor Martin K. Starr of Columbia University, editor of the McGraw Hill Series in Quantitative Methods for Management, reviewed the entire manuscript with great care and his comments helped shape it to its present form. The book has been checked for correctness in detail by a number of people at Execucom Systems Corporation; however, I should be held responsible for any errors that may still remain. In particular, Dr. William O. Cain and David Clark at Execucom provided invaluable assistance. Catherine Clark served as copy editor and assured consistency of style, format, and notation throughout.

Finally, a word of appreciation to my wife, Muriel, who spent many an evening listening to my word processor as this manuscript was written.

Paul Gray

CHAPTER I
INTRODUCTION

1.1 What This Book is About

1.1.1 Financial Planning Languages
1.1.2 The Approach Used

1.2 Modeling

1.2.1 The Nature of Models
1.2.2 EXAMPLE: The Value of a Savings Account
1.2.3 Example: Market Models
1.2.4 Steps in Model Building
1.2.5 Some Pitfalls and How to Avoid Them

1.3 Decision Support Systems

1.3.1 The Decision Process
1.3.2 Characteristics of Decision Support Systems
1.3.3 Situations in Which a Decision Support System is Useful
1.3.4 The Role of Assumptions in Decision Support Systems
1.3.5 Typical Uses of Decision Support Systems
1.3.6 Group Decision Making

1.4 Overview of IFPS

1.4.1 Basic Features of IFPS
1.4.2 What Occurs in an Interactive IFPS Session
1.4.3 The Structure of IFPS

CHAPTER I
INTRODUCTION

1.1 WHAT THIS BOOK IS ABOUT

This book is about an important new invention in methodology. For over 40 years, major strides have been made in the development of new computer-based technology as the computer has become pervasive in business, industry, science, and even the home. We have all become accustomed to the continual outpouring of innovation in technological devices. However, the pace of change in the ways we communicate with computers has been much slower. FORTRAN was developed over 25 years ago and, although ingenious refinements have been made since then, the basic way of telling the computer what to do, that is, computer programming, has remained relatively unchanged since then. A large software profession developed to fill an ever-increasing need for specialists who have programming skills. The net effect was that until recently executives had to rely on others if they wanted to communicate with the computer and obtain its power for answering important business questions. The rapid development of financial planning languages during the 1970's (the invention in methodology described in this book) had a major impact in that these languages allowed a change in the way executives work. Specifically, these languages ALLOW EXECUTIVES TO BUILD MODELS WITHOUT INTERMEDIARIES.

1.1.1 Financial Planning Languages

If you think about this change in executive work patterns for a minute, you will see how truly remarkable it is. Computers have previously required individuals either to develop programming skills or to hire professionals who would do the programming for them. With only a handful of exceptions, executives used programmers and other intermediaries to communicate with the computer because of the large amount of time, effort, and special skill required to obtain needed answers. Financial planning languages, however, allow executives to sit down at a terminal and rapidly create models that support their decision making process.

The Interactive Financial Planning System (IFPS) described in this book is one of a number of planning languages developed in recent years. These languages provide a new way for managers, analysts, and staff to work directly with the computer. No longer is the language of the computer seemingly reserved for high priests (that is, professional programmers) with specialized knowledge. Rather, the financial planning languages provide a simple, natural language way of communicating with the computer. Furthermore, most of these languages are interactive. That is, they allow you to sit at the terminal and obtain essentially instant feedback. Thus, new models can be created and "what if " questions can be asked, with answers obtained quickly and at low cost. With these characteristics, financial planning languages have enlarged the number and scope of the alternatives that executives can consider in arriving at a particular decision. In short, the quality of decision making has been improved.

Although called financial planning languages because of the original reason for their development, these languages turn out to be much broader than their name implies. They can be used in creating models in a wide variety of applications in business, in science and engineering, in mathematics and statistics, and many other disciplines. In this book, you will find chapters using IFPS for problems in finance, in statistics, and in operations management. These chapters merely hint at the range of applicability. As you read them and use their results, your imagination should be stirred and you will find innovative new ways to use financial planning languages. Remember that you now need no longer depend on others for formulating and solving your problems on the computer. You have obtained a new freedom.

1.1.2 The Approach Used

This book is really divided into three parts. This introductory chapter is the first part. It describes the role of models and the underlying ideas of decision support systems, both of which are fundamental to understanding what IFPS is about. The second part (Chapters II through V) teaches you the technical aspects of IFPS. It introduces you to the basics and then leads you through successively more advanced capabilities. The third part (Chapters VI through VIII) is devoted to applications of IFPS.

Throughout this book we show you complete IFPS models and their solutions. You will find over 100 different models, ranging from simple ones involving only a few lines to illustrate specific features of the language to much more complex ones that illustrate approaches to problems found in real life. We also include exercises throughout the text which are designed to extend your knowledge and to give you "hands on" experience in using IFPS. These exercises are not difficult; they build on what you see in the text. You will find that if you sit down at a terminal and solve the exercises as you proceed through the text, you will learn IFPS more quickly and will retain the concepts.

This book covers the essentials of IFPS. It is based on Release 8.0 of IFPS, issued in 1982. As its title implies, it is an introduction. If you master it you will be proficient in IFPS. However, it does not cover every feature available in the language. If you want to find out about these additional features or want additional information beyond what is in this book, you should consult the *IFPS USER'S MANUAL*, published by EXECUCOM Systems Corporation, P.O. Box 9758, Austin, TX. 78766.

1.2 MODELING

1.2.1 The Nature of Models

Most of your education and much of what you do on the job involves using models. Whether you are considering the financial status of a firm by studying its balance sheets, the value of goods in terms of money, the appropriate size of an order to replenish inventory, the appropriate competitive bid to make on a new oil lease, or the flow of goods from factory to customers, you tend to work with an abstraction of the process, that is, a model.

Models are abstractions of systems. They can be regarded as substitutes for the real system which capture the essence, but not necessarily all of the detail, of the real system. The advantage of a model is that it is usually possible to experiment with a model more quickly, at lower cost, and with less risk than to experiment with the real system. From the point of view of decision making, a model allows the consequences of alternative proposals and the anticipated effects of different contingencies to be evaluated.

Like all abstractions, models involve a large number of assumptions -- assumptions about the nature of the environment in which the system works, about the operating characteristics of its components, and about the way people behave. These assumptions must be fully understood and should be continually reevaluated. For example, it is easily possible to wind up producing an Edsel by assuming that consumer tastes will be the same three to five years from now as they are today.

The models considered in this book are quantitative. We may write such a model as a set of relations that represent the behavior of all or part of real systems under a variety of environmental conditions. The type of model needed to solve a problem will depend on the question to be resolved. In some cases, answers could be obtained from the proverbial "back of the envelope" calculation. In other cases, a large, logically consistent set of relations is required. In still other cases, mathematical or probability representation is needed. As models grow larger, a computer is needed to keep track of the relations and to perform the computations.

Models can be characterized in terms of a continuum of:

complexity:	from one variable to many
degree of uncertainty:	from deterministic to probabilistic
time:	from static to dynamic.

There are eight combinations, which are represented by the eight corners of Figure 1-1. (If you think about it, Figure 1-1 is itself a model.) Corner 1 represents the simplest situation, a deterministic model that involves only one variable, and does not involve time. For example,

TOTAL COST = UNIT COST * NUMBER OF UNITS

is a static, deterministic, one variable model (where unit cost is a given constant), that belongs at Corner 1. As we move away from Corner 1 to Corners 2, 3, or 5, we are still dealing with only one variable but either time or uncertainty or both are introduced. The following are examples of these one-variable problems:

Corner		
2	Deterministic, dynamic	Present value of a savings account
3	Probabilistic, static	Sales this month
5	Probabilistic, dynamic	Price of a share of stock

Corner 4 is the first place where complexity in the form of more than one variable comes in. Corner 4 corresponds to situations which can be modeled by simultaneous equations in many variables. The complexity of many variables is compounded if consideration either of time or uncertainty is added to the model. The most difficult problems and, unfortunately, the ones encountered most frequently in real business decision making, are the ones at Corner 8; that is, problems with many variables, much uncertainty, and rapid variation with time. Although you can often solve problems at Corner 1 and at a few corners adjacent to Corner 1 with relatively simple models, those at Corner 8 require the deepest understanding of the problem and the most sophisticated models.

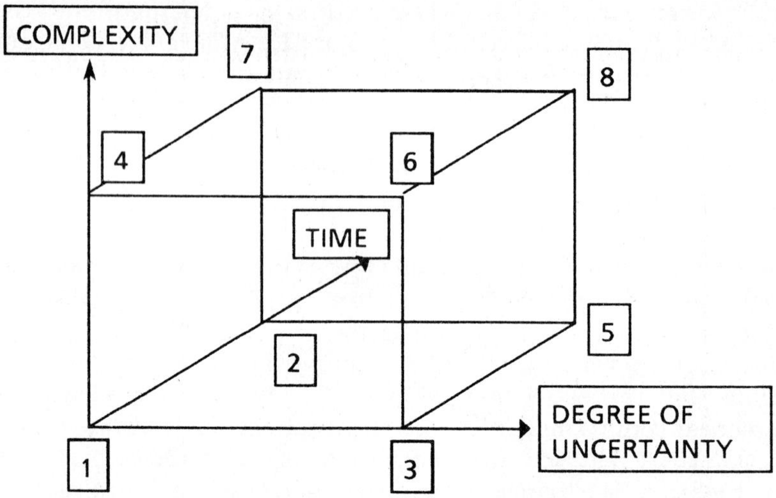

FIGURE 1-1. THE PROBLEM SPACE

Very often, a particular problem will best be solved by using a hierarchy of models, ranging from great aggregation to extreme detail. Many times the degree of detail depends on the level within the organization; the further up the organization, the greater the aggregation. The choice of model detail is important; too much aggregation can result in losing a detail that is critical, whereas attempting to model everything results in high costs and overwhelming amounts of data that hinder rather than help decision making.

Typically, as you work on a problem, your models of the situation proceed from coarse to medium to fine detail. This sequence is consistent with the amount you know about the problem as time progresses. As shown in Figure 1-2, when beginning a major project, because you know relatively little about the problem, your model will be relatively simple and have very little detail in it. Furthermore, your level of uncertainty will be greatest. If the uncertainties in the results based on the simple model are tolerable, you may stop at the initial level. In most cases, however, you will refine your models. For example, in a corporate financial model you may begin by considering only a few of the major product lines and aggregating the rest. As time goes on, you will typically increase the level of detail about company operations. You may also move from a deterministic, accounting model to a probabilistic forecasting model. If, however, the primary purpose of the model is to estimate total revenue of the firm for next year, you may find that an aggregated model is sufficient for your purpose

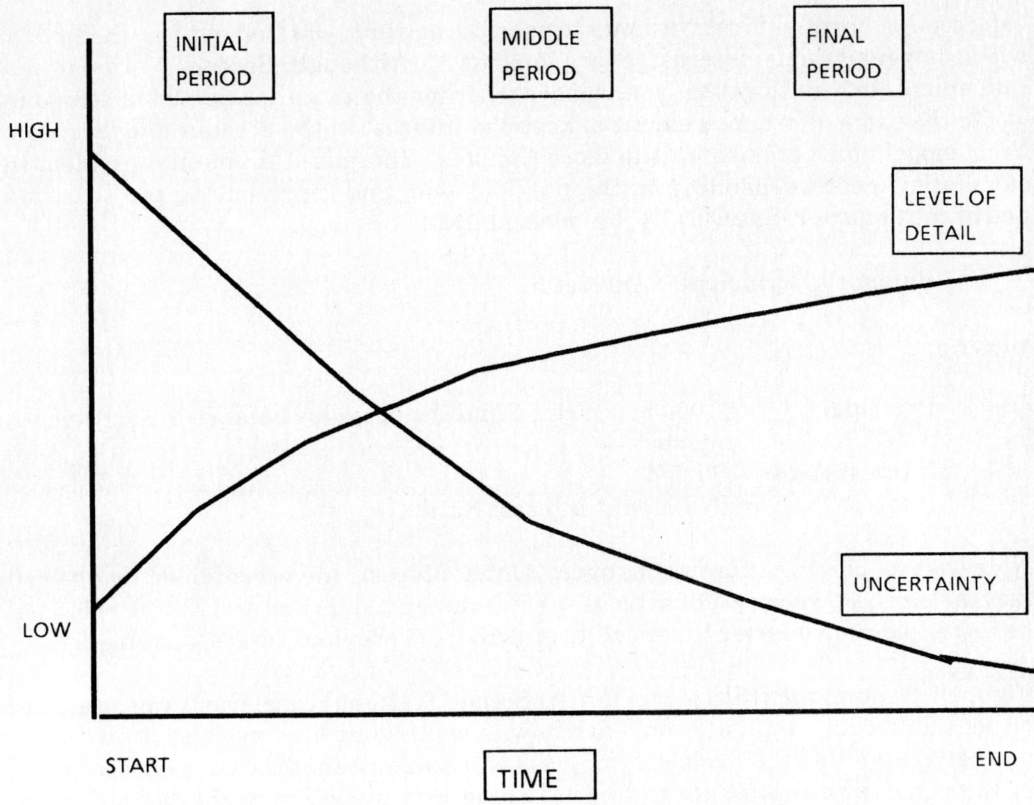

FIGURE 1-2. PROGRESS IN UNDERSTANDING THE PROBLEM

The level of aggregation that can be accepted is a critical choice that you make when you model. Although there is a natural tendency to want to model everything immediately, such an approach is highly risky. Evolving from a coarse model to a fine model is usually much wiser.

1.2.2 EXAMPLE: The Value of a Savings Account

As a simple example of modeling consider the options you might face in deciding on selecting a bank for your checking account. Suppose you expect to keep a minimum balance of $1000 over the next year. First National offers 5.25% simple annual interest on the minimum balance for the year. The model for this situation is:

Balance = Principal + Interest

where:

Principal	=	1000
Interest Rate	=	0.0525
Interest	=	Principal * Interest Rate

This is a model you can solve in your head. The 5.25% interest rate results in a payment of $52.50 on $1000 and your balance at the end of the year will be $1052.50. However, before going down to First National to open an account, you find out that Second National will compound your interest every quarter. Although Second National is not as convenient for you to get to, you wonder whether the extra income from compounding is worth the extra effort. You expect to keep the interest in the account and let it compound. Your model now becomes a little more complex. You might divide the problem into four calculations, each depending on the previous one, and representing the situation at the end of each quarter. Specifically, for each quarter:

Balance = Principal + Interest

where

Principal = $1000 in quarter 1 and the previous balance in each subsequent quarter
Interest Rate = .0525/4
Interest = Principal * Interest Rate

Note that we had to make two changes: (1) the interest rate was divided by 4 to reflect the fact that we receive only a quarter of the interest in a quarter, and (2) the principal had to be increased each quarter to reflect its growth from previous interest payments.

Figure 1-3 shows the IFPS model for the Second National case. Don't worry about how we wrote this model, you will soon learn how to write your own models. However, see that you can really read the models as long as you recognize that the first number on the right of the equal sign represents the initial value and the relation shows how the numbers build up. You should be able to hand check the results shown.

```
MODEL SECONDNATL  VERSION OF  12/30/82  15:53
10 COLUMNS 1-6
20 BALANCE=PRINCIPAL + INTEREST
30 PRINCIPAL = 1000,PREVIOUS BALANCE
40 INTEREST RATE =0.0525
50 INTEREST = PRINCIPAL*INTEREST RATE
END OF MODEL
? solve
MODEL SECONDNATL VERSION OF 12/30/82  15:53 -- 6 COLUMNS 4 VARIABLES
ENTER SOLVE OPTIONS
? all

                     1       2       3       4       5       6

BALANCE           1053    1108    1166    1227    1292    1359
PRINCIPAL         1000    1053    1108    1166    1227    1292
INTEREST RATE    .0525   .0525   .0525   .0525   .0525   .0525
INTEREST         52.50   55.26   58.16   61.21   64.42   67.81
```

FIGURE 1-3. SIMPLE INTEREST MODEL IN IFPS

Real life becomes more complicated as new alternatives are presented to you involving different rates or different interest payment rules (e.g., daily compounding, average rather than minimum balance). You can respond to these situations by building your own model and then asking "what if" questions that reflect the changes in the marketplace.

1.2.3 EXAMPLE: Market Models

If you took economics in college, you may recall that in the simplest model of the market for a commodity, it is assumed that:

1. As the price decreases, the demand for the commodity will increase.
2. As the price increases, the supply of the commodity available will increase.
3. The supply will equal the demand.

We can represent this model in terms of the following relations:

$$\text{DEMAND} = \text{A} - \text{B*PRICE} \tag{1-1}$$

$$\text{SUPPLY} = \text{C} + \text{D*PRICE} \tag{1-2}$$

$$\text{SUPPLY} = \text{DEMAND} \tag{1-3}$$

where A, B, C, and D are constants. These three relations form the market model. For this model to match the assumptions, the constants B and D must be positive so that supply goes up and demand goes down as price increases. Furthermore, A must be positive so that if price becomes high enough, the demand goes to 0. Figure 1-4 shows the results for this model for the following values of the constants:

$$A = 500, \quad B = 1000, \quad C = -40, \quad D = 800$$

When supply equals demand, the equilibrium price can be shown to be:

$$\text{PRICE} = (\text{A} - \text{C}) / (\text{B} + \text{D}),$$

which for our example values implies that the equilibrium price is 30 cents. At this price, according to equations (1-1) and (1-2), supply and demand are 200.

If you think about it, this model is at Corner 4 in Figure 1-1.

EXERCISE: Substitute the values of A, B, C, and D into Equations 1-1 and 1-2 and check that equilibrium occurs at 200 units.

This simple model has several interesting characteristics:

1. It represents a situation in quantitative terms
2. It contains major assumptions that have to be justified.
3. It neglects the effects of time.

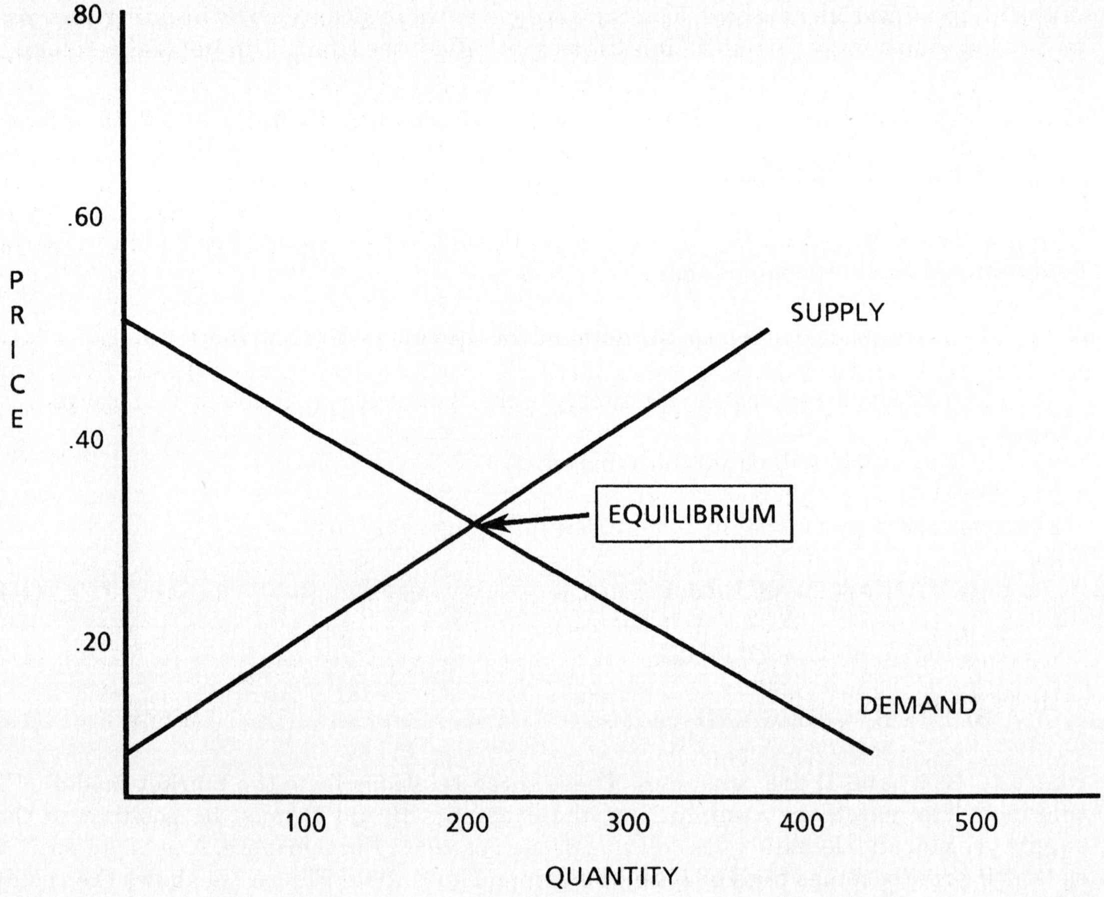

FIG. 1-4. SUPPLY-DEMAND RELATIONS; LINEAR CASE

A more realistic model would recognize that in real markets, information lags the current situation. That is, if we move from Corner 4 to Corner 7 of Figure 1-1. Additional realism is introduced if it is assumed that the supply produced in a given period is based on the price in the previous period. Agricultural markets, for example, might be thought to behave in this way with a period of one year. To introduce this change, we would modify our assumptions about the supply. Specifically,

$$\text{DEMAND} = \text{A} - \text{B*PRICE} \tag{1-4}$$

$$\text{SUPPLY} = \text{C} + \text{D*(PREVIOUS PRICE)} \tag{1-5}$$

$$\text{PRICE} = (\text{A} - \text{C} - \text{D*PREVIOUS PRICE}) / \text{B} \tag{1-6}$$

where PREVIOUS PRICE is the price one period ago. Note that these equations assume that the market is cleared; that is, the price in the marketplace each period is adjusted so that the demand just equals the supply produced.

Is the model given by Equations (1-4) through (1-6) a satisfactory model? Although it represents how we feel about prices intuitively, it fails to be complete on important issues. For example, it neglects the possibility that producers may base their current production on more historical data than just the last period. It assumes that all production and sales occur in the same period; thereby neglecting the possibility that merchants who maintain inventory will come into the market. Although there are situations where inventory cannot be retained for future sale (e.g., seats in an airplane that just took off) such situations are the exception rather than the rule. These two factors can be taken into account in a more complex version of the model.

In judging the model, recognize that it is a descriptive model. As such it can serve as an aid in decision making. However, descriptive models such as this one do not include the capability for finding the best solution (under the assumptions) for use by the decision maker.

1.2.4 Steps in Model Building

Model building is an interative process. You typically begin with a very simple model. Then, as your understanding of the system increases, you refine the model and introduce increasing sophistication into it. Even though you may back-track and redo parts or all of the model several times, there is a well-defined progression of steps that are followed. These steps are:

1. Formulate the problem
2. Define the environment
3. Identify the relevant variables
4. Build the model
5. Solve the model

In many respect, formulating the problem is the most difficult part of the job. You have to be clear in your own mind as to what decisions are to be made. Often the problem that is stated by management is not necessarily the problem that needs to be solved. The management science literature abounds with examples in which management asked for one thing and the real problem turned out to be something else. You want to make sure that you do not produce a solution for which there is no problem.

An important way of thinking about problem formulation is to analyze the decisions to be made. What alternatives are available and what choices have to be made? Your model should be such that it can be used to evaluate the alternatives and support the decision process. We will discuss the concept of decision support further in Section 1.3.

Having defined the problem to be solved in terms of the decisions to be made, you must next distinguish between what constitutes the system to be modeled and what constitutes the system's external environment. Particular elements may be within the system for some decisions and outside the system for others. For example, the going interest rate is part of the environment for a bank; for the Federal Reserve it is a basic decision to be made. The environment affects the system in ways that are usually uncontrollable and can be thought of as belonging to nature; in other words, the effects of the environment are exogenous. Typical factors that are in the environment for a firm are the general state of the economy, interest rates, raw material costs, the law, governmental regulations, social forces, and consumer tastes. In many cases, the principal use of a model is to examine contingencies that can result from changes in the environment (e.g., how do I change my capital construction plans if the interest rate goes up by three points? Goes down by three points? What happens if my industry is deregulated?). Typically, such studies of environmental effects involve building a model based on assumptions about what are the most likely outcomes and then running analyses in which one or more exogenous factors are changed. Such analyses are referred to as sensitivity analyses.

In some models, the interactions between the system and the environment must be taken into account. For example, if you change your pricing structure you may affect the competitive environment. Competitors, after all, are not devoted to your well being. As a result, your actions may cause them to respond in some way (i.e., change the environment) and your model must be sufficiently flexible so that you can determine what to do, depending on their response.

Parsimony is a basic principle of modeling. That is, a model should include only those things that are important to the decision to be made. Although a particular situation may involve many variables, only a few of them affect the outcome, and even fewer are under your control. The more variables that are included in the model, the more data need to be obtained and the greater the complexity of the model. Identifying which variables are relevant to the decision ensures that the model includes the elements that are needed but excludes peripheral considerations. In understanding the waiting lines in a business, for example, the rate at which customers arrive and the time required to serve them are relevant variables; however, customer heights or their shoe sizes are usually irrelevant.

What variables are relevant also depends on the level of the organization at which the model is to be used. At the lowest levels, only a few variables are important because only a few can be controlled at that level of the organization. The production supervisor can affect schedules and can attempt to reduce cost; however, product prices, product design, and delivery dates are normally out of the production supervisor's control. For the decision maker higher up in the organization, many more variables are controllable. The more complex the decision the greater the possible dimensionality of the model. In terms of Figure 1-1, we move from Corner 1 to Corner 8 as we move up the organizational ladder. Not only does the number of potentially relevant variables increase, but the variables become more heterogenous. That is, at low levels in the organization you may be able to express everything in terms of a single, easily measured unit, such as cost. At higher levels, complex trade-offs among cost, risk, image, and other factors are involved. The problem is further complicated by the increasing aggregation of details that occurs as you move up the organizational hierarchy (see Section 1.2.1). Fortunately, in most practical management situations only a few variables are considered relevant for a given organizational level. It is part of the modeler's job to build the model to focus on these variables.

You are now ready to build the model. The model building process usually goes through the steps shown in Figure 1-5 a number of times. The real world is, of course, given. The modeler begins by establishing the objectives of the model in terms of the decision to be made and then builds the initial model. This initial model may or may not be satisfactory. The only way to tell is to use the model to predict what happens under different input conditions. Here judgments have to be made. Does the model "match" the real world? Are the objectives established for the model met? In many cases, the match is not exact because of the simplifying assumptions made. The question really is whether the model is sufficiently close to reality to permit decision making. If the model does not match reality adequately or meet the objectives, the model must be revised and the process repeated.

The sequence of building, testing, and revising the model are the essence of the iterative process that is model building. As they are repeated, the belief in the validity of the model improves until you are ready to implement the model and use it to solve the problem at hand.

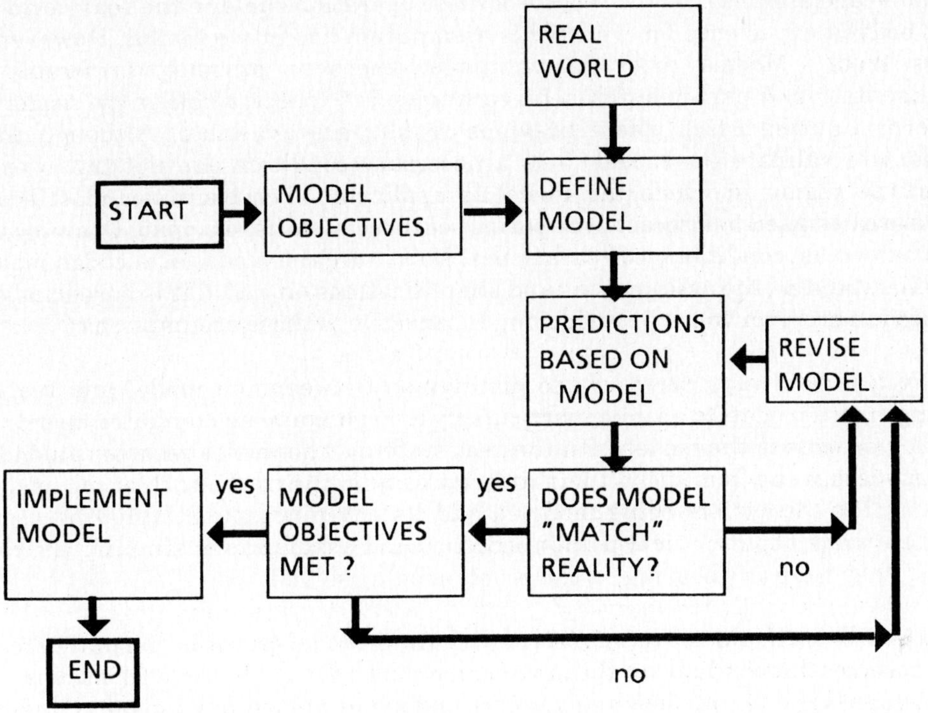

FIGURE 1-5. THE MODEL BUILDING PROCESS

If you observe the following three principles in building the model, your job will be made easier:

1. *Relevance.* The model should only include those elements that affect the decision to be made. If, in modeling profitability, the objective is to compare the effects of different financing methods, the hiring practices of the firm need not be modeled explicitly.

2. *Accuracy.* The accuracy required for input data depends on the decision to be made. Since in most cases, obtaining increased data accuracy implies increased cost, you should try to work with the minimum level of data accuracy that you need to make a decision.

3. *Aggregation.* Aggregation involves grouping a number of individual quantities into a larger quantity. For example, it may be perfectly adequate in a particular model to consider explicitly the seven products that constitute 85% of your sales and to lump the remainder into a product labeled "other".

1.2.5 Some Pitfalls and How to Avoid Them

Modeling is fraught with many pitfalls. In this section, we describe some of these pitfalls and discuss what can be done to avoid them.

FIRST, no model ever perfectly matches what happens in reality. The standard technique is to formulate a model, operate on the model (e.g., with sensitivity and "what if" questions) and assume that the results of these operations hold in the real world. There is a vast body of experience for which this assumption has proven valid. However, it is not always true! Models must be validated wherever possible, preferably through experimentation. A particularly useful technique is to check whether the model is true in simple or limiting cases where previous results are available. Although this is not sufficient to validate the model, it is a necessary condition. Do not try to extrapolate beyond the region in which the model is applicable. For example, most econometric models are designed to forecast over periods of three months to a year. Don't try to run the model to forecast conditions 10 years hence. Do not use the model in decision making until you understand all the assumptions and simplifications on which it is based and can check whether the problem you are considering is sensitive to these assumptions.

SECOND, it is always necessary to distinguish between the model and reality. After working with a model for a while, particularly a large complex computer model, there is a tendency to confuse the model with the real system. The model becomes an end in itself, and members of the firm spend their time working in the framework of the model instead of examining the system being modeled and its environment. Simplifying assumptions are often made about critical points because such assumptions simplify the model, not because they have any bearing on the problem being solved.

THIRD, models should not remain fixed over time. Models must be permitted to evolve as more becomes known and as the environment changes. Discredited models should be buried quietly, no matter how much effort and pride went into developing them. As new information becomes available that conflicts with the present model, use it to modify and improve the model.

FOURTH, to be useful, a model must serve practical purposes, rather than be an exercise in academic elegance. The point of a model is to help you understand problems and reach decisions. The purpose of technology and nomenclature in a model should be to enhance insight and to facilitate computation, not to impress or confuse. Introducing elegant names for simple ideas (e.g., waste management costs for janitorial) neither solves nor illuminates the problem.

FIFTH, models should not be a substitute for thinking. Too often, results are taken at face value. After all, the numbers came out of the computer. Remember, the fundamental value of the model is to clarify and lay bare the implications of the underlying assumptions that are often implicit rather than explicit.

FINALLY, models should not attempt to over-quantify. Some things cannot really be reduced to numbers. They are externals that should be handled qualitatively. For example, attempts to attach an absolute monetary value to loss of life or loss of wilderness area are generally not accepted by decision makers or by the public at large.

1.3 DECISION SUPPORT SYSTEMS (DSS)

IFPS and other planning languages are a key element of modern decision support systems. In this section we present a brief introduction to such systems that highlights some of the key points. In reading this section recognize that IFPS provides a way of creating the models that managers can use directly to support their decisions; that is, IFPS is a basic building block for a variety of decision support systems. If you would like to know more, consult the references given in the notes at the end of this chapter.

1.3.1 The Decision Process

The general structure of decision processes is shown in Figure 1-6.

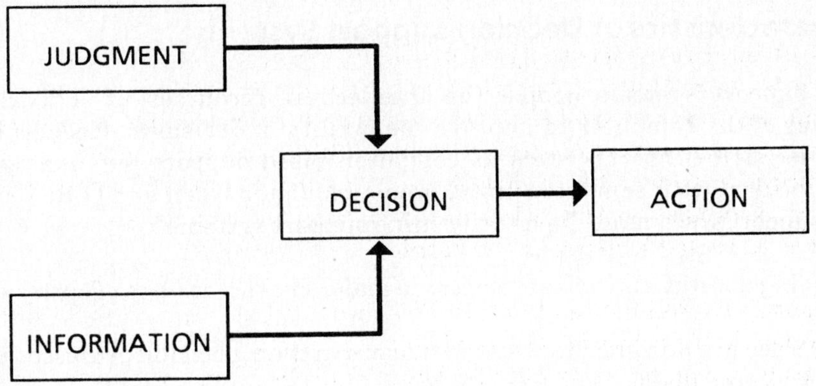

FIGURE 1-6. MAJOR ELEMENTS OF DECISION PROCESS

A decision involves combining information and judgment into a course of action and then implementing that action. The way in which this sequence occurs for a particular decision maker depends on the style of the individual. Peter Keen and Michael Scott-Morton[1] define five styles of decision making.

- The Rational Manager
- Satisficing
- Organizational Procedures
- Political
- Individual Differences

The rational manager attempts to be a single, informed decision maker. He is continually looking at alternatives and seeks to find the best possible alternative for the criterion or criteria that he has set. He will typically try to find the maximum profit or minimum cost solution to problems. Such a manager uses optimizing methods wherever possible. Few such managers are believed to exist in practice.

In the satisficing approach, optimal solutions to the problem are not required. Rather, the search is for "good enough" answers. The solution methods are typically heuristic (i.e., approximate methods that are known to give good results most of the time). For a manager using the satisficing approach, the role of the decision support system is to improve existing solutions.

The manager concerned with organizational procedures uses the company's standard procedures to reach decisions. The rules of such an organization are precisely laid down and the manager feels that following these rules is the most important aspect of his job. Here, a decision support system tries to find ways of improving the procedures.

In political decision making, the manager tries to reconcile the views and objectives of the different organizational subunits. The decision process involves bargaining between the units, with the decision maker acting as referee.

In the individual differences approach, each decision maker is seen as unique. Support is provided to each manager so that he or she can make best use of their personal strategies and abilities. It is this view which is *central* to decision support systems.

1.3.2 Characteristics of Decision Support Systems

Decision support systems couple the intellectual resources of individuals with the capabilities of the computer to improve the quality of decisions. Keen and Scott-Morton define a decision support system as computer-based support for management decision makers who deal with semi-structured problems. Peter Keen and G.R. Wagner [2] refer to decision support systems as " executive mind support systems".

The foregoing definitions indicate the three major characteristics of such systems:

1. They are designed to assist managers in their decision processes in semi-structured tasks.

2. They support, rather than replace, managerial judgment.

3. Their objective is to improve the effectiveness of the decisions in solving problems, not the efficiency with which decisions are made.

An important concept here is that of a "semi-structured" task. Tasks can be divided into structured, semi - structured , and unstructured. In a structured task, the procedures for obtaining correct answers are known. In a sense the manager is not needed at all. Whether the problem involves rules for reordering inventory or using linear programming for managing a refinery or deciding on plant location, the objectives are of the simple profit maximum or cost minimum variety and the manager can use the support of clerical, data processing, or management science people and models. In an unstructured task, human intuition is still the basis for decision making. Typical unstructured tasks include selecting the cover of the annual report, hiring a subordinate, or choosing a set of research and development projects for next year. The semi-structured tasks fall in between and involve a combination of both structure and intuition. Keen and Scott-Morton give such examples as trading bonds, setting marketing budgets for consumer products, and performing capital acquisition analysis. Here a decision support system can improve the quality of the information on which the decision is based by providing not only single solutions of models but also providing a range of "what if ", sensitivity, and risk analysis that allows the manager to understand better the nature of the problem and the range of options available.

It is important to recognize that decision support systems (DSS) are different, both quantitatively and qualitatively, from management information systems (MIS) and from management science (MS) models. Table 1-1 compares these three approaches.

TABLE 1-1

COMPARISON OF MIS, MS, AND DSS

MANAGEMENT INFORMATION SYSTEMS	MANAGEMENT SCIENCE MODELS	DECISION SUPPORT SYSTEMS
Structured Tasks	Structured Tasks	Semi-Structured Tasks
Higher Efficiency	Better Solutions	Higher Effectiveness
Provides Reports, Access to Data	Provides Recommendations on Optimal Decisions/Actions	Provides a Supportive Tool to the Manager

Decision support systems attempt to provide higher effectiveness and deal with semi-structured tasks. Management information systems provide reports and access to data; too often they provide so much information in reports that the reports are never used. They also provide access to data through various retrieval systems including inquiry systems and data base management systems. Their focus is on the past, that is, on what happened and on what was true. They involve record keeping, transaction processing, and business reporting. One of their main objectives is to present information in a consistent manner. Management science models provide recommendations on the optimal action once there is agreement on the assumptions and on the objective to be optimized.

Both management information systems and management science models tend to be slow, with emphasis on large computational efforts that are typically not on-line. Both management information systems and management science models can be, and are, key elements of a decision support system. However, they do not by themselves constitute a decision support system. Decision support systems focus on the present and the future and emphasize flexibility and ad hoc utilization. Their main role is to expedite the processes by which people make decisions about the future and communicate those decisions through the organization.

1.3.3 Situations in Which a Decision Support System is Useful

Decision support systems are designed to be used for complex problems that involve large masses of data and which often involve the expenditure of large sums of money. Because of the size of the problem, manipulation of the data base and extensive computations are needed to solve the problem. There are time pressures for reaching a decision; the problem is so urgent that it is not feasible to set a study team to work for six months or a year. Judgment is needed to:

- recognize or decide what are the objectives
- create alternatives

- choose a solution.

In most situations, much of the argument will be around the assumptions (see Section 1.3.4).Once the assumptions are agreed upon, finding a solution becomes a much more straightforward task.

The level of support provided by a decision support system can range from providing access to facts to providing useful models for the manager. Typical levels of support in increasing order of complexity are:

1. Access to facts for information retrieval

   Usually based on a data base management system that allows on-line inquiries to be made for specific items.

2. Pattern Recognition Capability in Data Retrieval

   Inquiry systems that aggregate information.

3. Simple computations, comparisons, projections

   Operations are performed on the data that allow individuals to assess the implications of the assumptions.

4. Useful models for the manager

   Here the manager is provided with models and their solutions. He or she can interrogate each model and investigate the implications of changes in assumptions about the external environment (e.g., anticipated sales, price of raw materials).

1.3.4 The Role of Assumptions in Decision Support Systems

In building a model for the manager that represents the elements of a business decision, you make a number of assumptions about the nature of the present and the nature of the future. You make choices as to what are the important variables, what present and past data are applicable, and how the variables are related to one another. You also make assumptions about the effects of time. More interesting, as Keen and Wagner point out, your assumptions encode your beliefs, hopes, and dreams about the future, your fears about what the future may bring, and your habits of thought from the past on how the world works. The role of a decision support system is to allow the decision maker to deal with assumptions. The sequence of steps that is gone through involves:

- externalizing
- understanding
- challenging
- exploring
- communicating
- believing
- owning

the assumptions of the models. Once the assumptions are believed and owned by the decision maker, the actual decision is, in most cases, relatively straightforward.

1.3.5 Typical Uses of Decision Support Systems

Decision support systems have been used in a large number of industries and for a variety of purposes. Various surveys of such systems have appeared. The following are typical of the types of applications found.

- Financial planning models. Here cash flows, returns, budgets, and similar information are produced. A financial planning language such as IFPS is used.

- Market models. Analyses are provided of advertising effectiveness, marketing strategy, product planning, and price decisions.

- Distribution and location models. These models support branch location, work force staffing, and transportation decisions.

- Portfolio management systems. These systems are designed to assist investment decision makers in institutions (e.g., bank trust departments, pension funds) in selecting a portflio mix.

- Geodata analysis systems. Graphical systems to show map and map-like information for city planning, police beat design, and school district boundary setting.

Other applications reported in the literature include corporate planning, insurance underwriting, budgeting and planning, to name just a few.

EXERCISE: Go to your company or college library and find a description of a decision support system. Prepare a short summary of the article. Indicate the decisions supported, the nature of the assumptions, the models used, and the perceived change in effectiveness from using the system. (Look up Decision Support Systems or DSS in the annual index of journals such as DATAMATION and the MIS Quarterly. Many books on Decision Support Systems also contain case studies).

1.3.6 Group Decision Making

In most organizations, major decisions involve consultation and agreement among many people. The concept of a single decision maker implicit in what we have discussed thus far is a simplification. If the organization as a whole is not behind a particular decision, it becomes difficult to implement even if it is the correct course of action. Thus, decision making is a group process. Typically one or more meetings are held that involve both the proposers of a project and the people who will have to implement the decision. You can think of such a meeting as a group of people sitting together around a conference table and holding a discussion. (With modern technology, however, other alternatives such as electronic mail, computer conferences, video conferences, and computer-aided decision rooms can be used for meetings.)

Consider the typical characteristics of such a meeting:

1. The meeting involves the joint activity of a group of five to 25 people who are of near-equal status in the organization. One person may, however, be in charge.

2. The activity as well as its outputs are intellectual in nature.

3. The product depends in an essential way on the judgmental contribution of the participants.

4. The meeting may begin with a formal presentation by a staff or line group outlining the problem, listing the alternative solutions considered, and presenting recommendations.

5. A discussion follows in which the participants ask questions, suggest new alternatives, and present viewpoints based on their own interests. (For example, marketing wants many products, finance wants small inventories, and production wants long production runs.) The discussion often involves bargaining and negotiation among the participants.

6. At the end of the meeting, a decision is (or is not) taken. If reached, the decision may be by vote or it may be by edict from the senior person present. If the decision goes against the concensus around the table, the manager who takes the decision knows that he or she will have a difficult time implementing it.

Although the research and implementation of decision support systems has focused on the single decision maker, many such systems can be used to support group decisions. By making the decision support system available on-line during the meeting, a richer set of "what if " questions can be answered and a broader set of assumptions explored. The meeting need not degenerate into discussions based on the memories and biases of the people present. In the group meeting setting, the decision support system provides a way of making the implications of the assumptions available to all the participants. For example, if the outputs of an IFPS model are used as the basis for the discussion, then as various alternatives are proposed the implications of these alternatives can be explored by using the model and displaying the results to all the participants.

1.4 OVERVIEW OF IFPS

1.4.1 Basic Features of IFPS

IFPS provides you with a complete modeling language. Its versatility is based on the many built-in features it contains. In this section we describe some of the major features available to you.

NATURAL LANGUAGE. You write the relations in your IFPS model in the same form as you think about them or talk about them. For example, you might write:

```
VARIABLE COST = VOLUME * UNIT COST
```

or

```
TOTAL INVENTORY COST = HOLDING COST + ORDER COST +
                       SHORTAGE COST - SALVAGE COST
```

That is, you can refer to variables in the model by the same names you use in everyday speech in English or any other language. This natural language capability makes it possible for you easily to communicate assumed values and relationships.

NO ORDER RESTRICTIONS. You can write ideas down in the order in which they occur to you or in the order in which you are used to thinking about them. In conventional computer languages such as BASIC or FORTRAN order is important. The computer will interpret the following example differently in IFPS or BASIC or FORTRAN

```
INVENTORY COST      = HOLDING COST + ORDER COST
   ORDER COST          = 200
   HOLDING COST        = 1000
```

IFPS will compute the inventory cost as being 1200. On the other hand, writing the same information in that order in BASIC or FORTRAN would result in the computer telling you that the inventory cost was either 0 or undefined, depending on which computer you used. In short, IFPS takes care of putting the statements in the correct order for you. The only thing you have to do is make sure that every variable (such as HOLDING COST) which appears on the right of an equal sign is also defined once on the left of an equal sign.

The technical term for such a language is "non-procedural". You will find many arguments in the literature, pro and con, about "procedural" languages such as BASIC or FORTRAN versus "non-procedural" languages. There are advantages and disadvantages to both. The advantages of non-procedural languages are user friendliness and ease of use; the cost is the larger computer memory required to solve a given problem.

SPREAD SHEET SOLUTION. In IFPS you write a series of lines (called a "model") that describe your problem and IFPS creates a spread sheet (or, if you prefer a more technical term, a matrix) for you. The following is a simple IFPS model and its spread sheet output:

Model:

```
10 COLUMNS 1983-1986
20 SALES =1000,1100,1200,1300
30 COST OF GOODS = .8* SALES
40 PROFIT = SALES -COST OF GOODS
```

Output:

	1983	1984	1985	1986
SALES	1000	1100	1200	1300
COST OF GOODS	800	880	960	1040
PROFIT	200	220	240	260

Note how easy it is to read the model. You will see that you first specify the column headings you want (Line 10) and that these are then printed out on top of the spread sheet. The next three lines of the model specify the row names on the left hand side of the equal sign. The calculations are defined on the right-hand side and can be specified either as numerical values (e.g., Line 20 for SALES) or as relationships (e.g., for COST OF GOODS and PROFIT). You receive a neat printout in spread sheet format automatically.

WHAT IF. IFPS's strength as a decision support tool comes from its built in "what if" capabilities. Given a set of assumptions, there is always the need to explore what happens should conditions change. WHAT IF sales are, say, double those estimated? WHAT if they are half? The WHAT IF feature allows you to explore what happens when one or a combination of assumptions changes. IFPS also allows you to perform sensitivity analysis on individual variables. For example, you can ask for a the effect on NET PROFIT AFTER TAX and CASH if the SELLING PRICE varies from −5% to +15% in steps of 5%.

GOAL SEEKING. Often management will set a goal and your problem is to determine what has to be done to meet this goal. For example, you may have a goal of NET PROFIT AFTER TAX =60000 and you want to find the VOLUME needed to achieve this goal.

CONSOLIDATION. Most firms have cost centers and many have multiple branches. A commonly encountered requirement is to consolidate two or more individual reports into a single report in a standard company format. IFPS contains commands which make such consolidations simple. It also has the needed data file handling and report generating capabilities to deal with the large volume of data and the formatting required.

RISK ANALYSIS. The future is uncertain. Although we can make plans and forecasts based on our best estimates and we can explore the effects of specific changes from a model's assumptions through WHAT IF and sensitivity analyses, these approaches do not weigh the risks explicitly. For example, we can perform sensitivity analyses for sales decreasing by 20% and by 40%. However, in interpreting the meaning of the results we have to be careful to weigh the likelihood of a 20% decrease occurring in a different way from that of a 40% decrease. In risk analyses, the probabilities of outcomes are included explicitly. IFPS allows you to perform risk analyses by providing a MONTE CARLO (i.e., simulation) capability. You specify probability distributions for variables that are uncertain and then tell IFPS to solve the model a large number of times. For each solution, IFPS picks a value at random from each probability distribution, giving a different scenario. IFPS then provides you with statistics (mean, variance, distribution) on the outcomes. (The use of IFPS for risk analysis is discussed in detail in Chapter V.)

BUILT-IN FUNCTIONS. IFPS contains a large number of financial, statistical, and mathematical functions that perform standard calculations for you. For example, financial functions include net present value, internal rate of return, amortization, and a number of depreciation options. Forecasting functions allow you to obtain moving averages, trend extrapolation, and regression analysis. (Each of the functions and their meaning are discussed in Chapter III.)

PREVIOUS and FUTURE. At any point in your IFPS model you can refer to events that happened in previous time periods or will happen in future time periods. For example, you might say:

```
SALES = 1000, PREVIOUS SALES * 1.06
```

to model an initial value of 1000 followed by a 6% growth in sales from period to period, or you might say:

```
ESTIMATED TAX PAYMENT = .2 * FUTURE PROFIT
```

Note that here the estimated tax payment depends on the value of a different variable, namely profit, that will occur in the future. PREVIOUS and FUTURE are powerful tools because they allow you to use data from throughout the spread sheet.

REPORTS AND DATA FILES. To make IFPS useful as a management tool for large-scale problems, it contains built-in capabilities for creating reports and data files. By specifying a report format, you can obtain output in any format you desire in addition to the spread sheet format provided automatically. Furthermore, by creating data files you can use the same IFPS model with a variety of inputs. The data file feature is particularly useful when you have several products or groups in an organization and want to process data about them in a uniform way.

1.4.2 What Occurs in an Interactive IFPS Session

When you sit down at a terminal to use IFPS, you are one of many time-sharing users of a computer. The typical sequence of steps that you follow are illustrated in Figure 1-7.

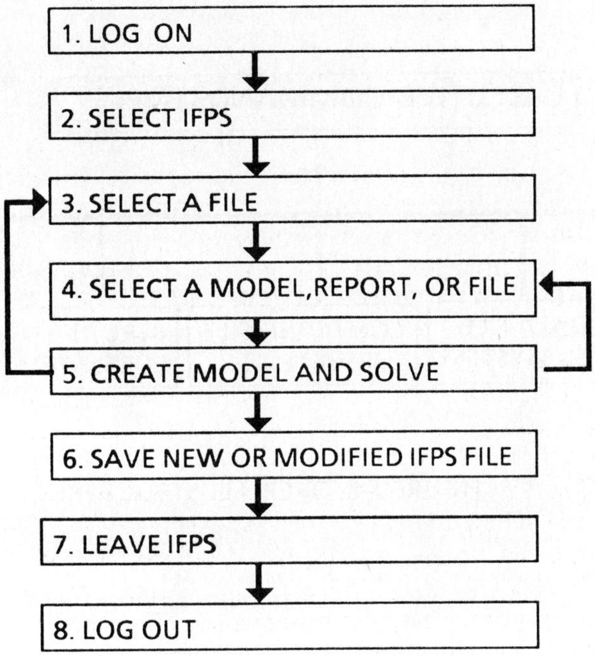

FIGURE 1-7 TYPICAL SEQUENCE OF STEPS DURING AN IFPS SESSION

You begin by telling the computer who you are. This is called logging on. Typically logging on involves typing your computer number and your computer password. (Step 1). REPORT You then tell the computer you want IFPS. Usually, this requires only typing the letters IFPS (Step 2). Because IFPS works with files stored in the computer's memory that contain the models and report formats that you create, you have to tell IFPS which file you want (Step 3) and then which model, report, or data file you want within the file that you selected (Step 4). At this point you can create, solve, modify, or delete (Step 5). Typically you move between Steps 4 and 5 many times during a session. Occasionally, you may go from Step 5 back to Step 3 if you keep several files. Once you have finished your work, you tell IFPS that you are done and IFPS asks you whether or not you want to save the new or modified file that you have created (Steps 6 and 7). Finally, when you are finished with your work, you log out from your computer by following the standard procedure for your machine (Step 8).

1.4.3 The Structure of IFPS

The purpose of this section is to explain briefly how IFPS is organized internally. On first reading of this book, this section will be principally of interest to the computer professional or computer science student who wants to know how the system works. You can safely turn to Chapter II and know that you have not missed anything required to understand the rest of this book. Once you have become proficient at creating and solving IFPS models you will find it helpful to come back to this section to obtain a deeper understanding of how IFPS works.

The over-all structure of IFPS is shown in Figure 1-8.

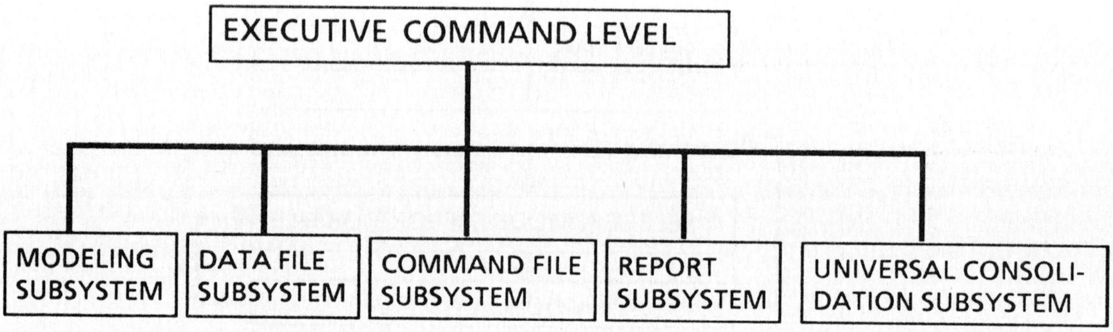

FIGURE 1-8. OVER-ALL STRUCTURE OF IFPS

At this level of abstraction, the system consists of an executive command level that coordinates the entire system and five subsystems that deal with models, data files, command files, and reports. Figures 1-9 and 1-10 and the descriptions in the following paragraphs provide more detailed views of the executive level and the five subsystems.

EXECUTIVE COMMAND LEVEL: When you enter IFPS you start at the top level, the executive command level. The role of the executive command level is to control the sequence of events that occur. At this level, you have access to

- file manipulation
- execution control
- subsystem selection

File manipulation commands allow you to create files, select which files you want to work on, and to manipulate information within the file in terms of listing, copying, deleting, merging, consolidating, referencing, and selecting specific models and reports. Execution control refers mostly to features that assist in running IFPS. The most often used execution control is the RECORD feature that allows you to obtain a paper copy of an interactive session if you are working at a video terminal that only presents data on a screen. As its name implies, subsystem selection lets you pick a subsystem to work on and to move from one subsystem to another.

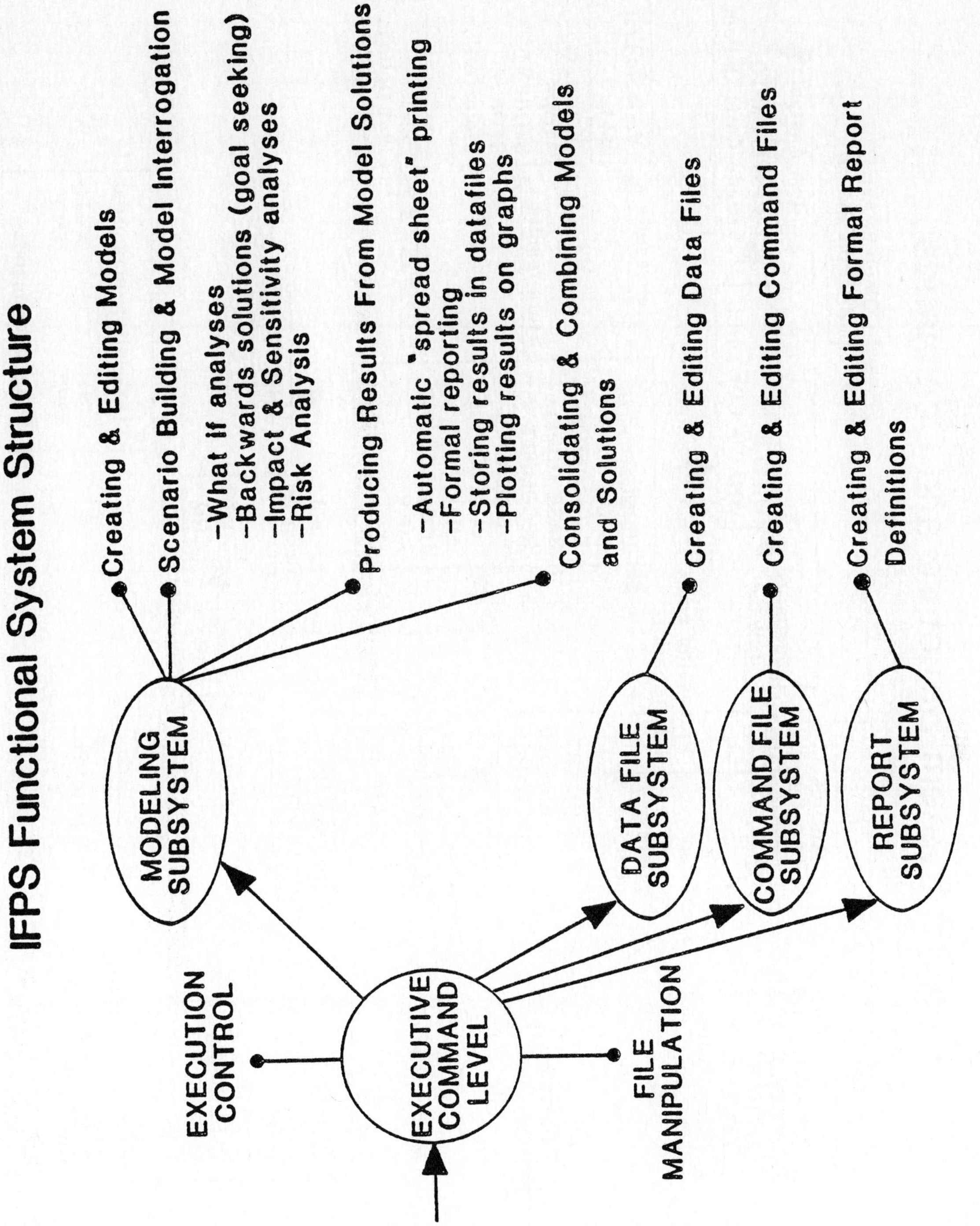

FIGURE 1-9. IFPS FUNCTIONAL SYSTEM STRUCTURE

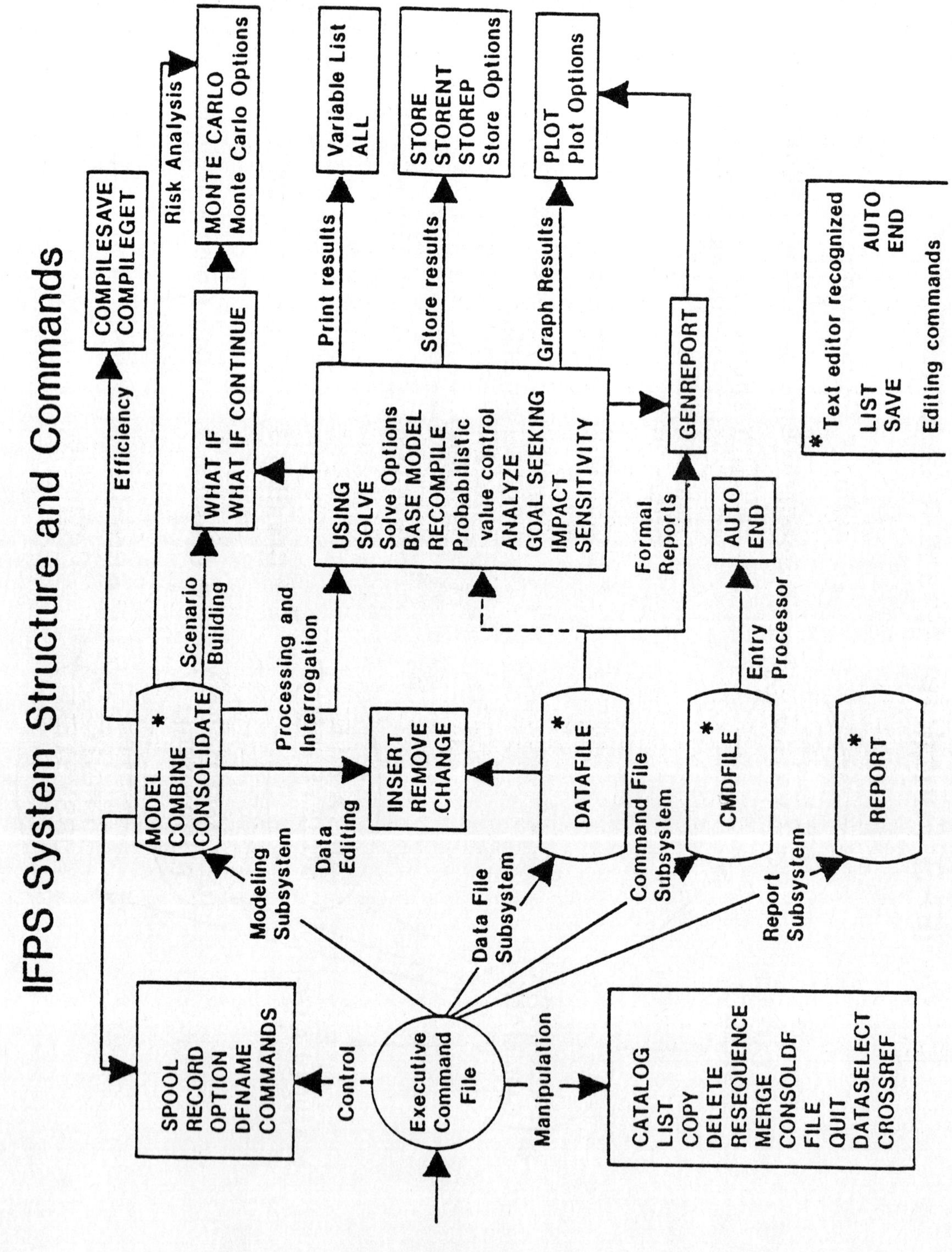

FIGURE 1-10. SYSTEM STRUCTURE AND COMMANDS

MODELING SUBSYSTEM. The modeling subsystem is the core of IFPS. In this subsystem you create new models and edit existing models. You can examine alternative assumptions and build scenarios of what would happen if these assumptions are true. That is, you perform "what if" and various other forms of sensitivity analyses. You can introduce uncertainty to evaluate the effects of risk. This subsystem also produces the results of solving the model. You can choose automatic spread sheet output, a formal report based on formats set up in the report subsystem, graphical output, or output to a data file for future use. Unless otherwise specified, IFPS provides you with spread sheet output. Finally, this subsystem allows you to consolidate and combine models and their solutions so that you can integrate information from various sources.

DATA FILE SUBSYSTEM. The data file subsystem is used to create, edit, and maintain data files for use in the model subsystem. By separating data files from models, you gain flexibility. You can, if you so choose, use one data file with several models or use the same model with several data files. You do not have to have a separate data file to create and solve a model. However, as your IFPS skills increase, you may begin creating more complex models that use large amounts of data. Here the data file subsystem will become of use to you.

REPORT SUBSYSTEM. The report subsystem is used to create and edit report formats. These formats are used in conjunction with models when you want output in other than the automatic spread sheet output. A report format can be saved and used over and over to provide reports in a desired form, for example, in balance sheets or income statements.

COMMAND SUBSYSTEM. This subsystem allows you to create sequences of commands that can be called with a single command.

UNIVERSAL CONSOLIDATION SUBSYSTEM. This subsystem allows you to determine a hierarchial or network structure for an organization and to produce consolidated results at any point in the structure.

This book focuses primarily on the modeling subsystem. The data file and report subsystems are discussed in Sections 4.6 and 4.7. We do not discuss the command or universal consolidation subsystems which are intended primarily for the advanced user.

NOTES

[1]Keen, Peter G. W. and Michael S. Scott-Morton, *Decision Support Systems, An Organizational Perspective.* Addison-Wesley Publishing Company (Reading,MA) 1978.

[2]Keen, Peter G. W. and G. R. Wagner, "DSS: An Executive Mind Suppport System", *DATAMATION* (November 1979), pp. 117-122.

CHAPTER II
BASIC ELEMENTS OF IFPS

2.1 How to Obtain IFPS at Your Terminal and Begin Work

2.1.1 Logging On
2.1.2 Making IFPS Available To You
2.1.3 Entering into IFPS For The First Time
2.1.4 Entering IFPS When You Already Have A File

2.2 Creating and Solving A Simple IFPS Model

2.2.1 A Simple IFPS Model
2.2.2 What You Type At The Terminal (Use of AUTO For Line Numbers)
2.2.3 Listing Your Program (The LIST Command)
2.2.4 The SAVE Command
2.2.5 Obtaining Answers (The Use of SOLVE)

2.3 Multiple Models (The MODEL,FILE, and CATALOG Commands)

2.4 How To Get Out Of IFPS (The QUIT Command)

2.5 Correcting Mistakes (The Edit Commands)

2.5.1 Misspellings While Typing
2.5.2 Error in a Completed Line
2.5.3 Using the C Edit Command
2.5.4 Retyping a Line
2.5.5 Deleting a Line
2.5.6 Inserting a Line
2.5.7 Obtaining a Listing of a Single Line
2.5.8 Obtaining a Listing of a Portion of a Model

2.6 Obtaining a Listing at the Line Printer (The RECORD Command)

2.7 The New Product Model -- An Example

2.8 Some Principles and Rules in Writing Your Model

2.8.1 Columns Statement
2.8.2 Headings and Blank Lines
2.8.3 The = Sign and Defining Variables
2.8.4 Arithmetic Operations

2.8.5 PREVIOUS and FUTURE
2.8.6 FOR
2.8.7 PERIODS
2.8.8 MATRIX

2.9 Example -- A Pro Forma Profit and Loss Statement

2.10 What To Do If You Need Help (The IFPS HELP Commands)

CHAPTER II
BASIC ELEMENTS OF IFPS

This chapter provides the basic information you will need to get started in using IFPS. We will show you how to obtain IFPS at your terminal, enter a model, and leave IFPS. It also shows you how to make corrections in the model and how to obtain a listing on the line printer.

This chapter contains three example models of increasing complexity. Be sure to read and follow these models line by line. They will be referred to frequently throughout the book and will be modified from time to time to illustrate additional concepts.

Finally, the chapter contains two sections you will want to come back to from time to time:

- Some principles and rules in writing your model (Section 2.8).
- What to do if all else fails (the HELP command) (Section 2.10).

2.1 HOW TO OBTAIN IFPS AT YOUR TERMINAL AND BEGIN WORK

Once you have obtained a user number and password for the computer on which you will use IFPS, you can sit down at a terminal and begin work. As its name implies, IFPS is an interactive system. You can use either a video screen terminal (also called a CRT or cathode ray tube), or a printing terminal such as a DECWRITER or a Texas Instruments Silent 700. You will find CRTs generally respond more quickly whereas printing terminals give you the advantage of providing paper copy that serves as a permanent record. If you are working on a video screen, you can also obtain a permanent copy by using the RECORD command (see Section 2.6).

2.1.1 Logging On

The first step in approaching the computer is to log on. You begin by turning the power on and then following the log-on procedures that apply to your computer. Typically these procedures involve the following steps:

1. You tell the computer you want service. This may involve hitting the carriage return or new line key on your terminal.

2. The computer responds by prompting you and asking you for your user number and password.

3. The computer will tell you it is ready for you to begin work.

The foregoing is a very general statement of what happens at most facilities. If you are used to logging on, use the procedure you always use. There is nothing special associated with IFPS. If you have never logged on before or don't recall the details, ask someone to help you -- your instructor if you are a student or someone who works with the computer at your firm. We have left the next few lines blank so that you can write down the log-on procedure here in this guide for easy reference. An easy way of remembering this information is to paste a copy of a log-on sequence that worked in the space below.

LOG ON PROCEDURES FOR MY COMPUTER

2.1.2 Making IFPS Available To You

Once you have logged on, you ask the computer to make IFPS available to you. This is usually a very simple step. In most cases it only involves typing the letters IFPS. As with logging on, the specific things you have to do depend on the computer installation you use. Use the space on the opposite page to note down what you need to do when you ask the computer to make IFPS available to you.

STEPS NEEDED TO MAKE IFPS AVAILABLE ON MY COMPUTER

2.1.3 Entering Into IFPS For The First Time

In this section we describe what happens the first time you create an IFPS file. The next section describes the sequence of steps to follow if you have already saved an IFPS file and want to work on it again.

Figure 2-1 shows the typical sequence of steps that you follow to begin creating an IFPS model in a new file. You type the words that appear in lower case; the computer gives you the rest. You must press the Return key (called New Line on some terminals) after you reach the end of your input. The computer will not respond until after you press the Return key because it does not know that you are finished giving it an instruction.

```
/ifps
INTERACTIVE FINANCIAL PLANNING SYSTEM - 8.0
ENTER MODELS AND REPORTS FILE NAME
? sample
FILE SAMPLE NOT FOUND - NEW FILE WILL BE CREATED
READY FOR EXECUTIVE COMMAND
? model gray
BEGIN ENTERING NEW MODEL
```

FIGURE 2-1. SEQUENCE OF STEPS TO OBTAIN IFPS FOR THE FIRST TIME

1. When you ask for IFPS, the computer types two lines. The first line tells you that you have obtained IFPS and gives you the version number (in this case, 8.0). The second line asks you to enter a file name. Your IFPS models will be kept in a permanent file in your private library. Since you may have many

files each with a different name, IFPS needs to know which file to use.

> *IMPORTANT NOTE:* From here on, whenever the computer types a "?" it is asking you to type something in response. Press the return key "CR" after you type your response. Do NOT start typing until the "?" appears because the computer may not understand you.

2. After the question mark, pick a name for your file. Type the name and *remember* it if you want to use the file again. Choose a name that is different from all existing ones in your private library. The file name should be no longer than the maximum allowed by your computer (e.g.,seven letters on some computers and eight letters on others) and have the appropriate format (e.g., usually the first character must be a letter of the alphabet). In Figure 2-1, we have assigned the name SAMPLE to the file.

3. Since you are creating a new file, the computer tells you that it can't find the name you just typed and that it will create a new file for you. It then tells you that it is ready for an executive command. Executive commands are instructions to IFPS to do something right now rather than adding to or changing the model you are creating.

4. The *first* executive command that you give the computer is that you want to create a model. To do so, type the word MODEL followed by a space and the name of your choice. In Figure 2-1, GRAY is the model name. Like the file name, you must follow the rules that apply to your computer. For most computers, names up to eight characters long with the first character a letter of the alphabet and with no blanks inside the name are acceptable. (These restrictions may be different on your computer.) The model name can be the same or different from the file name. You can keep several models in a file. If you do, each model in the file must have a unique name.

You are now ready to create your IFPS model. Section 2.2 illustrates a simple IFPS model.

2.1.4 Entering IFPS When You Already Have A File

The previous section described the steps to follow when you want to create your first file (or any new file). In this section we describe what you do if you already have a file and want to work on it. For example, you may want to change one of the models, or run a model with different input values, or add new models to the file. Figure 2-2 illustrates the typical sequence followed.

```
/ifps
INTERACTIVE FINANCIAL PLANNING SYSTEM - 8.0
ENTER MODELS AND REPORTS FILE NAME
? sample
FILE SAMPLE PROCESSED
READY FOR EXECUTIVE COMMAND
? model gray
READY FOR EDIT, LAST LINE IS 90
```

FIGURE 2-2. OBTAINING AN EXISTING IFPS MODEL

1. After the first question mark, type the name of the file you want to work on. If you ask for an existing file, for example SAMPLE which you created earlier, the computer will tell you that the file has been processed and that the computer is ready to receive an executive command.

If you can't remember the file name you have used, you can have the computer help jog your memory by asking it to list a catalog or directory of your private library. You must ask for this catalog *before* you ask for IFPS. To obtain a catalog you typically ask for CATALOG, or a CATLIST, or a DIRECTORY. Again, this is a system-dependent feature and what you have to do depends on the computer. Jot down here the way in which you obtain a catalog of file names on your machine.

PROCEDURE FOR OBTAINING A CATALOG OF MY FILES

If seeing the catalog of your files does not jog your memory sufficiently for you to know which file you want, you will have to retrieve each of your files and list them until you find the one you want.

2. Once you have obtained a file, you can find out what is in it. Just as you can obtain a catalog of the names of the files in your private library, you can obtain a catalog of the names of the models in your IFPS file. To do so type CATALOG after you are in IFPS. CATALOG gives you the names of all models and reports stored within an IFPS file. (Once you have created a few models, try CATALOG and see what it does.) The IFPS CATALOG command is discussed further in Section 2.3.

3. If you want to retrieve an existing model or create a new model within the file, type the word MODEL followed by the model's name. For an existing model, IFPS responds by giving you the last line number in the model and telling you that the model is ready to be edited.

2.2 CREATING AND SOLVING A SIMPLE IFPS MODEL

Once you have logged on, obtained IFPS, and told the computer you want to create a model, you are ready to begin work. In this section we present a simple problem, its corresponding IFPS model, and the procedure followed to create and solve the model.

2.2.1 A Simple IFPS Model

THE PROBLEM. A new product is to be introduced. Assuming all dollar values in units of thousands, sales are expected to be 100 during the first year and to grow at a 25% annual rate, compounded. Expenses will start at 75 in the first year and will increase by 25 in each succeeding year up to Year 5, after which they will remain fixed.

Management is interested in determining the net income (that is, sales minus expenses) and will use two ratios:

- expenses/sales
- net income/sales

as measures of effectiveness to decide whether to undertake production. The product is expected to be obsolete after six years with no salvage value.

THE IFPS MODEL. The IFPS model that represents the problem is shown in Figure 2-3.

```
MODEL GRAY  VERSION OF  02/06/82  16:01
10 COLUMNS 1-6
20 SALES = 100,PREVIOUS SALES *1.25
30 EXPENSES = 75,100,125,150,175
40 NET INCOME = SALES -EXPENSES
50 *
60 *                                     RATIO ANALYSIS
70 *PERCENT OF SALES
80 EXPENSE RATIO = EXPENSES/SALES
90 NET INCOME RATIO = NET INCOME/SALES
END OF MODEL
```

FIGURE 2-3. THE SIMPLE NEW PRODUCT MODEL

DETAILED EXPLANATION OF THE IFPS MODEL SHOWN IN FIGURE 2-3.

line 10 The first instruction tells IFPS how many periods are of interest. The word COLUMNS followed by a definition of the column names is typed. Note that 1-6 implies headings 1, 2, 3, 4, 5, 6. If you had wanted to use years, you would have typed 1981-1986. Unless told otherwise, the computer assumes each period is a year when computing net present value or using other routines involving discounting.

line 20 This line specifies the sales in each period. The first number indicates the initial sales of 100. Sales in subsequent periods are obtained by multiplying the sales in the previous period by 1.25 to reflect the 25% growth. The reserved word PREVIOUS is used.

line 30 This line demonstrates how data can be entered directly as input. Note that only five values are shown. The computer will use the last value (175) for each period beyond the last one.

line 40 This line computes net income as the difference between sales and expenses.

lines 50-70 The * at the beginning of each line tells the computer that what follows is a comment and should be printed verbatim. A line with only an * on it results in a blank line, a convenient way of creating white space in your output to make the output more readable. If information is included after the *, the information will be printed in the same location on the printout. Here the heading RATIO ANALYSIS is neatly centered on the printout.

lines 80-90 These lines compute the ratios requested by management.

Several important points are worth noting about this model.

1. Each instruction is preceded by a line number. IFPS uses line numbers as a simple way of organizing and keeping track of things. Line numbers also allow you to make changes and corrections in the model if needed. It is usually good practice to write your model initially with large, regular intervals between line numbers so that you can insert material later. IFPS organizes information in line number sequence for you. We will talk more about line numbers in Section 2.2.2

2. The first line of your model must tell IFPS how many columns you want. If you fail to do this, IFPS assumes your model deals with only one period and your output will only show one column.

> *NOTE:* This assertion is not exact. A COLUMNS statement must appear before the first variable is defined or mentioned. It is a wise procedure to put the COLUMNS statement first .

3. All the instructions that follow the COLUMNS line could have been written in any order. For example, it would have been perfectly reasonable to write:

```
20 NET INCOME = SALES - EXPENSES
30 NET INCOME RATIO = NET INCOME/SALES
40 EXPENSE RATIO = EXPENSES/SALES
50 *
60 *INPUT DATA
70 *
80 SALES = 100,PREVIOUS SALES * 1.25
90 EXPENSES = 75,100,125,150,175
```

In this case we put the calculations first and then provide the input data for the calculations. Most other computer languages with which you might be familiar (such as BASIC or FORTRAN) are "procedural". That is, they require the value of every quantity or variable to be defined before it is used in computation. Because IFPS is "non-procedural", you can write relations down in any order, as long as you define each variable once on the left-hand side (i.e., on the left of the equal sign).

An advantage of the non-procedural approach is that it lets you organize information in the way you think about it or in the way the user of the output thinks about it. Thus, you can use the format of IFPS output as a way of communicating ideas to others.

4. IFPS makes its computations one column at a time. Therefore when you write

```
NET INCOME = SALES - EXPENSES
```

IFPS looks up the value of sales in column 1 and the value of expenses in column 1 and takes the difference of these two values. It then repeats this procedure for each subsequent column.

5. In Line 20 we use the reserved word PREVIOUS. IFPS contains a number of reserved words that have special meanings and are used for specific purposes . Reserved words cannot be used as variable names, model names, or file names. (See Appendix III for a list of reserved words.) PREVIOUS is a particularly powerful way of describing relations because it allows you to use information from earlier time periods. When you write PREVIOUS, IFPS uses the value one column to the left, that is, one period ago. As we will discuss later, you can write PREVIOUS 2 for values 2 periods ago, PREVIOUS 3 for values 3 periods ago, and so on. Even more remarkable is the reserved word FUTURE which allows you to use the value of a variable in the next period (one column to the right). PREVIOUS and FUTURE are discussed further in Section 2.8.5.

2.2.2 What You Type At The Terminal (Use of AUTO For Line Numbers)

The neat printout shown in Figure 2-3 was obtained by asking the computer to list the typed input shown in Figure 2-4. We will show you how to obtain a listing in the next subsection.

Note that by typing AUTO 10 10 the computer prompts you with line numbers starting at 10 and increasing by 10. The executive command AUTO is a request for line number prompting. If you type only AUTO, the computer will give you line numbers starting with 1 and increasing by 1. If you type AUTO 10 the computer will give you line numbers starting with 10 and increasing by 1 (i.e., 10,11,12,...). The first number after AUTO tells the computer where to start line numbering and the second number tells it how much to increment line numbers. Thus, AUTO 10 10 starts at line number 10 and increases in steps of 10.

```
? auto 10 10
10 ? columns 1-6
20 ? sales = 100,previous sales *1.25
30 ? expenses = 75,100,125,150,175
40 ? net income = sales - expenses
50 ? *
60 ? *                                   ratio analysis
70 ? *percent of sales
80 ? expense ratio = expenses/sales
90 ? net income ratio = net income/sales
100 ? end
READY FOR EDIT
```

FIGURE 2-4. TYPING THE INPUT FOR THE SIMPLE NEW PRODUCT MODEL

If you do not ask for AUTO, you can either type in your own line numbers or let IFPS do it for you. If you let IFPS assign line numbers, it starts out by assigning line 1 and increasing by 1. In this case, line numbers are not shown when you type your model but do show up whenever you list it. Try this approach and see whether you like it or not.

If you use AUTO, you type END OF MODEL (or simply END) as the last line. Typing END results in IFPS going back to a question mark as a prompt instead of putting line numbers in for you if you are using the AUTO feature. (Alternate ways of stopping the appearance of line numbers are to type LIST or SOLVE. The meaning and use of LIST and SOLVE are described below).

2.2.3 Listing Your Program (The LIST Command)

It is usually good practice to issue the command LIST after you have entered your model. The result will be a neat typing of the form shown in Figure 2-3. At this point, review your model to make sure it is exactly as you intended it to be. If you find mistakes or want to make changes, follow the editing procedures outlined in Section 2.5.

2.2.4 The SAVE Command

When you have completed the model and it is satisfactory to you, you may want to save it. Typing SAVE in response to a question mark replaces the version of the model stored in your file by the current version. For a new model, SAVE adds the model you wrote to your file. Using SAVE periodically guards against losing the work you have done if your computer happens to go down. At the end of an interactive session, if you have created or changed any models and not yet saved them, IFPS will ask you whether or not you want them saved. You should answer YES to that question. Otherwise, you will have to repeat your work.

2.2.5 Obtaining Answers (The use of SOLVE)

Once you are satisfied that your model is correct, you will want to obtain answers. To do so, you type SOLVE in response to a question mark. The computer tells you the name of the model, when you created it, and how many columns and variables it contains.

If you have made any errors, IFPS will tell you which lines need correcting. Follow the procedures outlined in Section 2.5 to make these corrections and then try SOLVE again.

> **WARNING. Be sure to make at least one correction asked for before you try to SOLVE again. Otherwise, IFPS will assume all variables with errors are undefined, will set them to zero, and will give you answers on that basis. This can lead to strange results.**

If your program is correct, as is the case in Figures 2-3 and 2-4, the computer asks you:

```
ENTER SOLVE OPTIONS
```

The simplest answer is to type ALL. (We discuss other solve options in Section 4.1.) The computer will then print out the names and values of all variables for all periods. In other words, it gives you a complete response.

Figure 2-5 shows the results of SOLVE and ALL for our simple new product problem.

```
? solve
MODEL GRAY  VERSION OF  08/05/82  16:01 -- 6 COLUMNS 5 VARIABLES
ENTER SOLVE OPTIONS

? all

                          1       2       3       4       5       6

SALES                   100     125   156.3   195.3   244.1   305.2
EXPENSES                 75     100     125     150     175     175
NET INCOME               25      25   31.25   45.31   69.14   130.2

                              RATIO ANALYSIS
PERCENT OF SALES
EXPENSE RATIO         .7500   .8000   .8000   .7680   .7168   .5734
NET INCOME RATIO      .2500   .2000   .2000   .2320   .2832   .4266
```

FIGURE 2-5. SOLVING THE SIMPLE NEW PRODUCT MODEL

Go over Figures 2-3 and 2-5 together to make sure you understand how each number in Figure 2-5 is generated from the model in Figure 2-3. For example, in column 1, sales and expenses are input values. Net income is computed by subtracting expenses of 75 from sales of 100. The expense ratio of .7500 is obtained by taking the ratio of expenses to sales, that is 75/100. Similarly, net income ratio is the result of dividing net income of 25 by sales of 100. When IFPS moves to column 2, sales are 1.25 times the sales in the previous column (i.e., column 1) or 125. Expenses of 100 are an input value and net income is again the difference between sales in the column (125) and expenses of 100. The ratios in column 2 are computed on the same basis as those in column 1, but using the values in column 2. Thus, IFPS divides 100 by 125 to obtain an expense ratio of .8000 and divides 25 by 125 to obtain a net income ratio of .2000. You should continue this process until you are sure you understand how each number in Figure 2-5 was obtained. This form of hand checking for consistency is a valuable technique for verifying the model to make sure that it computes values in the way that you want them computed.

2.3 MULTIPLE MODELS (The MODEL, FILE, and CATALOG Commands)

When you are finished with creating and solving one model, you may want to start a new problem that requires a new model. To create a new model, you simply type, in response to a question mark:

```
MODEL newname
```

where "newname" refers to the fact that you want to give the new model you create a different name than existing models within that file. The computer responds just as it did when you first started with:

```
BEGIN ENTERING NEW MODEL
```

When you are finished with this model, you will have two models, each with its own unique name in the same IFPS file. You can put as many models in a file as there is space within a file in your computer. For reasons of computer efficiency, it is generally good practice to keep each file small, with only a few models in it. You will find it advantageous to put models that refer to a particular topic (e.g. financial forecasts, market analysis, production analysis, statistical results) in a separate file.

If you want to retrieve a model that is in a file other than the one you are working on, you first have to tell the computer that you need to retrieve that file. You type:

```
FILE
```

The computer first asks you whether you want to save the changes you made in the file you are currently working on. You must respond either YES or NO. The computer then asks you for the name of the file you want. You can give it either the name of an existing file or a new file name. If you give it an existing file name, you can ask for any model in that file; if you give it a new file name it will tell you that a new file has been created.

If you are working with a particular file and do not know what models are contained in it, you can ask for a catalog of that file by typing:

```
CATALOG
```

The computer will come back with a list of the names of the models and reports within your file and will tell you how many lines each contains.

Figure 2-6 shows a simple dialog with the computer that illustrates the MODEL, FILE, and CATALOG commands.

```
? model amort
BEGIN ENTERING NEW MODEL
? file
SAVE UPDATED M&R FILE SAMPLE (YES OR NO)
? yes

MODELS AND REPORTS SAVED ON FILE SAMPLE
ENTER MODELS AND REPORTS FILE NAME
? study
FILE STUDY PROCESSED
? catalog
NAME        TYPE      NUM
SURTN       MODEL     6
SIMPLE      MODEL     9
FORECAST0   REPORT    8
ACRS        MODEL     8
MOVAVG      MODEL     5
SIMPLE1     MODEL     9
```

FIGURE 2-6. RESPONSES TO MODEL,FILE, AND CATALOG COMMAND

2.4 HOW TO GET OUT OF IFPS (The QUIT Command)

After you have completed work on one or more IFPS models, you will usually want to leave IFPS. To do so, in response to a question mark, type:

```
QUIT
```

If you type QUIT, the computer responds by asking you whether you want to save the changes you made in your file during your session at the terminal. Specifically, if your file name happens to be SAMPLE, IFPS will prompt you with:

```
SAVE UPDATED M&R FILE SAMPLE(YES OR NO)
?
```

If you type YES, it updates the IFPS file in your private library (i.e., the permanent file space assigned to you on your computer). Thus, in our example, we had a file SAMPLE. If you type YES, the version of SAMPLE in your private library is changed to reflect the changes you made during your interactive session at the terminal. If you type NO, the original version in your private library is left untouched. Except for any printout you may have obtained, you lose all record of what you did.

Once you have left IFPS, you are still connected to the computer. You can either leave the computer by logging off (using the appropriate logging off word for your machine, such as BYE, LOGOUT, LOGOFF, etc.) or you can go on and do something else at the computer. You could even decide to call IFPS again and begin working on other IFPS models. Figure 2-7 shows a typical dialog for getting out of IFPS and logging out. What happens on your computer may be somewhat different since logging off procedures vary from machine to machine.

```
?QUIT
SAVE UPDATED M&R FILE STUDY (YES OR NO)
?YES

MODELS AND REPORTS SAVED ON FILE STUDY
18 SBUS USED
IFPS.
```

FIGURE 2-7. TYPICAL SEQUENCE FOR GETTING OUT OF IFPS

Use the space below to describe how to log off your computer.

PROCEDURE FOR LOGGING OUT FROM MY COMPUTER

2.5 CORRECTING MISTAKES (The Edit Commands)

Even the best of us make mistakes in writing a model. If you do, all is not lost. IFPS has a few simple editing commands that let you correct your mistakes.

You will find that your mistakes are of two kinds:

1. Mechanical mistakes such as typing errors.

2. Substantive mistakes where you give incorrect instructions.

The mechanical mistakes are easier to find because IFPS tells you about them through messages either at the time you make the mistake or at the time you try to SOLVE. Substantive mistakes typically involve errors in logic. They show up as strange and unusual numbers in the output.

2.5.1 Misspellings While Typing

If you spot a spelling mistake while typing a line (and before pressing the return key), you can correct it right then and there. On simple terminals and on DECWRITERS, press the "CONTROL" key and the letter "H" simultaneously. Each time you do this, the computer backspaces one letter and erases that letter. On more sophisticated terminals you may have a backspace available to you. If so, use the backspace key. In either case, go back to the beginning of the error and then type in the correct spelling.

For example, if you type:

```
20? PRFOIT
```

and suddenly realize you transposed the F and the O. You backspace using "CONTROL" and "H" all the way to the F and type:

```
OFIT
```

and then continue with the rest of your statement.

> *IMPORTANT NOTE:* On most terminals, you must retype everything you backspaced over since it has been *erased* in the computer. It may still show on your paper copy or on your video screen, but it is not there in memory.

2.5.2 Error in a Completed Line

If you find your error after you have typed the line and pressed the carriage return, you have two choices. You can:

1. Correct the part of the line that was wrong using the C edit command (see Section 2.5.3 below), or

2. Retype the entire line.

You may find it easier to make your corrections *after* you have typed in the complete model rather than while you are in the AUTO MODE. However, if you give editing commands while in the AUTO mode, you will stay in the AUTO mode.

2.5.3 Using The C Edit Command

The sequence for the C edit command is:

line numberC/error/correction/

In place of " line number" type the number of the line containing the error. Do *not* put a space between the line number and the C. Use slash marks to indicate the start and end of the error and the end of the correction. (You may use a : or a " instead of a /.)

You *must* repeat the error exactly as it was made, with *no* spaces other than those in the incorrect or corrected text. For example, if you had typed:

```
30 ? COST = B44
```

and wanted to change the B to a 9, you would type:

```
30C/B/9/
```

and the computer would respond:

```
30 COST = 944
```

That is, the computer will show you the effect of making the correction.

The following are some important notes about the C edit command:

1. When you use the C edit command, the computer scans the indicated line number from left to right until it finds the letter combination that you said was in error. It then replaces the erroneous information with the correction. Thus, if the same letter combination appears twice, it will change the first one. For example, if you had typed:

```
40 PROFIT = OFRTUNE
```

and then had instructed the computer:

```
40C/OF/FO/
```

the computer would respond:

```
40 PRFOIT = OFRTUNE
```

To avoid this problem, it usually pays to include a few letters on one side or the other of the error; for example, you would have been safe if you had typed:

```
40C/OFRT/FORT/
```

2. You can have more letters in the error than in the correction and vice versa. For example

```
50C/PROFITT/PROFIT/
```

works fine.

3. If you have several errors in a line, you can either retype the line number and the whole line or use the C edit command for each error. For example:

```
60 PROIFT = OFRTUNE
```

would be corrected either by:

```
60 PROFIT = FORTUNE
```

or by the sequence:

```
60C/OIF/OFI/
60C/OFR/FOR/
```

2.5.4 Retyping A Line

If you have a lot of errors in a line, or the line is short, you may just want to retype the whole line. As we just demonstrated above, you simply type the line number followed by the correct form of the line. This procedure replaces the incorrect version.

2.5.5 Deleting A Line

If you have a line you want to delete, simply type the line number followed by D, with no space in between. For example, if you want to delete the line:

```
40 PROFIT = FORTUNE
```

you type:

```
40D
```

and the line is gone.

2.5.6 Inserting A Line

If you forgot a line you can insert it at the proper place by choosing an unused line number. For example, if you want to insert a line between 30 and 40 in the Simple New Product Model of Figure 2-4, you might type:

```
35 INTEREST EXPENSE = 10,0
```

IFPS will insert the line in its proper place automatically for you. Line numbers can have up to two decimal places. For example, if you want to insert a line between lines 16 and 17, you can choose 16.5.

2.5.7 Obtaining A Listing Of A Single Line

If you want to check out a single line, you can have it listed just by typing the line number. For example, if you are working on the Simple New Product Model (Figure 2-4) and want to see line 40, you type:

```
40
```

and the computer responds:

```
40 NET INCOME = SALES - EXPENSES
```

NOTE: This differs from languages such as BASIC where typing a line number with nothing after it erases the line.

2.5.8 Obtaining a Listing of A Portion of the Model

If you want to list a part of the model you are currently working on (more than a single line but not the whole model), you simply type the first and last line number you want, separated by commas. For example, if you want to see lines 10 through 40, you type

```
10,40
```

IFPS responds by showing lines 10 through 40 inclusive. The comma is required between the two numbers.

2.6 OBTAINING A LISTING AT THE LINE PRINTER (The RECORD Command)

If you are working on a video terminal rather than a terminal which gives you printed output, you may still want a permanent record of what you are doing. If you are a student you need "hard copy" to hand in to your professor; if you are a professional, you will want records for your permanent files and as a way of communicating results to your co-workers or as an audit trail.

You can obtain "hard copy" by using the following three steps:

1. Once you have entered IFPS and given a file name, you use the executive command.

```
?RECORD
```

By typing RECORD, you are telling IFPS that you want the computer to store the complete history of your session at the terminal from this point forward. Such a record will be kept until either you type:

```
?NORECORD
```

which turns the RECORD feature off or until you have completed your session by typing QUIT.

2. Choose a file name. After you have given the QUIT command, IFPS will check whether you created a RECORD file. If you did, IFPS will ask you:

```
ENTER FILE NAME FOR RECORD FILE (OR NO)
```

The dialog is shown in Figure 2-8. You can choose any valid file name and assign it to your RECORD.

```
?QUIT
ENTER FILE NAME FOR  RECORD (OR NO)
?RECORD
1 SBUS USED
IFPS.
```

FIGURE 2-8. TYPICAL SEQUENCE FOR GETTING OUT OF IFPS WHEN USING A RECORD COMMAND

WARNING: The file name for RECORD should be different from any other file name in your private library.

Note that you can reuse a RECORD file already in your library. What you want to avoid doing is destroying material in existing files that is important to you. If you do not heed this warning, you erase the file with the same name and substitute the RECORD file for it.

SUGGESTION: Use the word RECORD for your file name. In this way you will always remember where the file is and not wipe out a file you wanted to keep. It will also help your computer center (and your company's budget) to erase (DELETE, PURGE, or KILL command, depending on the facility) the RECORD file after you have obtained hard copy .

3. Print Your RECORD File. Providing a file name causes the computer to copy your session into your private library. You can print the contents of this file by the standard procedure used at your computer facility to obtain listings of files.

PROCEDURE FOR OBTAINING A LISTING OF MY RECORD FILE

2.7 THE NEW PRODUCT MODEL -- AN EXAMPLE

Throughout this chapter we have used the simple IFPS model of Section 2.2 as an example. We are now ready to formulate a more complex model. In this example, consider the problem faced by a manufacturer trying to decide whether or not to produce or market a new product. The product is a novelty item which is expected to have a market over the next two years, but its future beyond that is uncertain. Management therefore wants to base its decision on the next two years.

The following information has been gathered about this product. (The numbers have been simplified to make them easier to follow.)

1. Anticipated market	8000 units in the first quarter, 3% market growth/quarter thereafter.
2. Market share	15% in first quarter, growing linearly by 1/2% per quarter thereafter.
3. Unit sales price to dealers	$2.50 during Year 1, $2.75 during Year 2.
4. Unit production cost	$1.25 during Year 1, $1.35 during Year 2.
5. Overhead	80% of production cost.
6. Initial investment	$2500.
7. Discount rate	15%.

These conditions imply an optimistic forecast of the company's position in a growing market. Some changes are expected to occur after a year, specifically cost inflation (of material, labor, etc.) will raise expenses; however, it is anticipated that these cost increases can be passed along to the customer because the product will be established.

Management wants to use two measures of effectiveness, the present value of the cash flows and the internal rate of return associated with the venture. Figure 2-9 shows the IFPS model for solving this problem.

> _NOTE:_ READ the model carefully. Then read the explanation of each line. Make sure you understand each line, what it says and what it does. Once you have mastered this model, you will have come a long way toward understanding IFPS.

To help you follow the model we show each line and the rationale behind it.

10 COLUMNS 1-8

> The column headings are defined first. This model contains 8 columns representing the 8 quarters during the two-year time horizon.

20*
30* NEW PRODUCT MODEL
40*

> These lines begin with an asterisk. They are comments and will be reproduced exactly as shown. It is good practice to put a title on a model so that you can identify it later and know what it does.

50 SALES = MARKET * MARKET SHARE

> Defines sales as the product of market and market share. We can write this relation even though we have not yet defined MARKET and MARKET SHARE. This is perfectly all right, as long as we define these quantities later in the model.

```
MODEL PRODUCT  VERSION OF  10/11/82  12:27
10 COLUMNS 1-8
20 *
30 *              NEW PRODUCT MODEL
40 *
50 SALES   =MARKET*MARKET SHARE
60 MARKET=8000,PREVIOUS MARKET*1.03
70 MARKET SHARE =0.15,PREVIOUS MARKET SHARE +0.005
80 GROSS REVENUE = SALES   *  PRICE
90  PRICE=2.50 FOR 4, 2.75
100 OPERATING EXPENSE = (PRODUCTION COST + OVERHEAD) * SALES
110 PRODUCTION COST= 1.25 FOR 4,1.35
120 OVERHEAD=PRODUCTION COST*0.80
130 NET REVENUE = GROSS REVENUE - OPERATING EXPENSE
140 INVESTMENT = 2500, 0
150 *
160 NET PRESENT VALUE = NPVC(NET REVENUE,DISCOUNT RATE,INVESTMENT)
170 INTERNAL RATE OF RETURN = IRR(NET REVENUE,INVESTMENT)
180 *
190 DISCOUNT RATE = 0.15
200 PERIODS 4
END OF MODEL
```

FIGURE 2-9. THE NEW PRODUCT MODEL
(This Figure Continued on Next Page)

```
? solve
MODEL PRODUCT  VERSION OF  10/11/82  12:27 -- 8 COLUMNS 13 VARIABLES
ENTER SOLVE OPTIONS
? all
```

NEW PRODUCT MODEL

	1	2	3	4	5	6
SALES	1200	1277	1358	1442	1531	1623
MARKET	8000	8240	8487	8742	9004	9274
MARKET SHARE	.1500	.1550	.1600	.1650	.1700	.1750
GROSS REVENUE	3000	3193	3395	3606	4209	4463
PRICE	2.500	2.500	2.500	2.500	2.750	2.750
OPERATING EXPENSE	2700	2874	3055	3245	3720	3944
PRODUCTION COST	1.250	1.250	1.250	1.250	1.350	1.350
OVERHEAD	1	1	1	1	1.080	1.080
NET REVENUE	300	319.3	339.5	360.6	389.8	519.4
INVESTMENT	2500	0	0	0	0	0
NET PRESENT VALUE	-2210	-1913	-1607	-1293	-882	-460.8
INTERNAL RATE OF RET						
DISCOUNT RATE	.1500	.1500	.1500	.1500	.1500	.1500

NEW PRODUCT MODEL

	7	8
SALES	1719	1820
MARKET	9552	9839
MARKET SHARE	.1800	.1850
GROSS REVENUE	4728	5006
PRICE	2.750	2.750
OPERATING EXPENSE	4178	4423
PRODUCTION COST	1.350	1.350
OVERHEAD	1.080	1.080
NET REVENUE	550.2	582.5
INVESTMENT	0	0
NET PRESENT VALUE	-30.01	410.4
INTERNAL RATE OF RET	.1372	.3056
DISCOUNT RATE	.1500	.1500

FIGURE 2-9. THE NEW PRODUCT MODEL
(Continued)

60 MARKET = 8000,PREVIOUS MARKET * 1.03

The market is 8000 in the first quarter. In each succeeding quarter it grows by 3% over the previous quarter.

70 MARKET SHARE = 0.15, PREVIOUS MARKET SHARE + 0.005

The market share starts at 15%, and increases by half a percent (to 15.5, 16, 16.5, 17.....) in each succeeding quarter.

80 GROSS REVENUE = SALES * PRICE

Gross revenue is defined in terms of price and sales.

90 PRICE = 2.50 FOR 4, 2.75

Sales were defined in Line 50, but price was not. Here we use the FOR construct. When we write:

2.50 FOR 4

we are telling IFPS to use the value 2.50 for four periods. The value of 2.75 applies to the fifth period and all periods thereafter.

100 OPERATING EXPENSE = (PRODUCTION COST+OVERHEAD)* SALES

Having defined revenues, we next look at operating expenses. These are proportional to sales and depend on the production cost and the associated overhead.

110 PRODUCTION COST = 1.25 FOR 4, 1.35

This line has the same format as line 90.

120 OVERHEAD = PRODUCTION COST *0.80

The overhead is a fixed percentage of the production cost.

130 NET REVENUE = GROSS REVENUE – OPERATING EXPENSE

The net revenue represents cash inflows from the venture.

140 INVESTMENT = 2500,0

The investment is made in period 1. The way IFPS works, if you specify a single number or expression it applies to all periods. If you want a different value in period 2, you type a comma and follow it with the period 2 value. IFPS uses values one at a time until it reaches the last one. It then uses the last value for all subsequent periods. In our example, we invest in period 1 only. Therefore the form 2500,0 *must* be used to make sure that no other investments are assumed.

160 NET PRESENT VALUE = NPVC(NET REVENUE,DISCOUNT RATE, INVESTMENT)

NPVC is one of many built-in functions in IFPS. (These functions are discussed in detail in Sections 3.2.1 and 6.2.) The format requires specifying cash inflows, then the interest rate, and finally the cash outflows. IFPS will compute the net present value each period, based on all cash flows through that period. Thus, in Figure 2-9, we see the net present value increasing as time passes and additional revenue is generated.

170 INTERNAL RATE OF RETURN = IRR(NET REVENUE,INVESTMENT)

IRR, like NPVC, is a built-in function. It prints out results only if the internal rate of return is positive. (See Section 3.2.1 for a more detailed discussion of IRR.)

190 DISCOUNT RATE = 0.15

We record the input data value here. It is usually good practice to put constants and other input data at the end of the model. Many sensitivity analyses involve varying these inputs.

200 PERIODS 4

The PERIODS statement is needed if the model does not represent one-year intervals and when built-in financial functions (such as NPVC and IRR) are being used. The PERIODS statement automatically converts the data from annual to the specified number of periods per year. Note that the word PERIODS is followed by a space and then the number of periods per year.

Figure 2-9 also shows the results of solving the model. You will see that we left lines 150 and 180 blank so that the measures of effectiveness, net present value and internal rate of return, are highlighted. The results show that the net present value is greater than zero and the internal rate of return is greater than the 15% rate used as a hurdle rate by the company.

EXERCISE: Log on to your computer. Create an IFPS file and enter the model shown in Figure 2-9. Solve the model. Make sure you receive the same answers as are shown in Figure 2-9. Use the AUTO command to enter the model and the various editing commands to correct any mistakes you may make. Be sure to LIST the model to obtain neat printout. When you are finished, use the QUIT command to leave the computer. If you use a video screen to do your work, use RECORD and then obtain a hard copy printout when you are done. Save this model in your private library. You will be asked to do additional exercises using this model in later chapters.

2.8 SOME PRINCIPLES AND RULES IN WRITING YOUR MODEL

The Simple IFPS Model of Section 2.2 and the New Product Model of Figure 2-9 illustrate various principles and rules for creating IFPS models. This section summarizes these principles and rules.

2.8.1 COLUMNS Statement

The number of rows (i.e., the vertical dimension) in the IFPS output matrix is defined by the number of equations in your model. The horizontal dimension of the matrix is defined by the COLUMNS statement.

> *NOTE:* The COLUMNS statement *must* appear before any statement with an equal (=) sign in it.

The COLUMNS statement not only defines the number of columns but also the title of each column. If you type COLUMNS 1-8, as in Figure 2-9, you are defining 8 columns starting in column 1. If you had wanted to label the columns in Figure 2-9 QTR1 and so on, you would have typed:

```
10 COLUMNS QTR1,QTR2,QTR3,QTR4,QTR5,QTR6,QTR7,QTR8.
```

You cannot say QTR1-QTR8. On the other hand, you do not have to start at 1; for example, 1983-1988 defines a matrix having 6 columns starting with the heading 1983.

If you do not include a COLUMNS statement, IFPS assumes you want only one column.

2.8.2 Headings And Blank Lines

It is good practice to include a heading or label at the beginning of a model (and often within a model) so that the reader of the output can quickly learn what problem is being solved. In Figure 2-9, lines 20 through 40 create such a heading. Similarly, you can use blank lines to separate different parts of the model, such as calculations, results, and input data. We have done so in Figure 2-9 by including blanks in lines 150 and 180.

2.8.3 The = Sign And Defining Variables

Each line of an IFPS model consists of a single variable name on the left side of the equal sign followed by a definition of the variable to the right of the equal sign. For example,

```
SALES = MARKET * MARKET SHARE
```

The only constraint is that each variable to the right of the equal sign must be defined somewhere in the model (or in an IFPS data file being used with the model.) Based on this definition, IFPS evaluates sales each period by taking the size of the market and the size of the market share in the same period and multiplying them together.

If only a single definition is given, it is assumed to be true for all columns and the value of the variable is computed in the same way. If the variable is defined differently in each column, then commas are used to separate these definitions. For example

```
SALES = 8000,8500,8700,9000
```

results in different values in columns 1, 2, 3, and 4. If the model is defined for more columns than there are data, the last value defined (in our example, 9000) is used for the additional columns. You will have seen by now that you can use numeric values, variable names, built-in functions, and combinations of these on the right side of the equal sign to define the variable.

2.8.4 Arithmetic Operations

IFPS uses +, −, *, and / for addition, subtraction, multiplication, and division. There is a hierarchy of operations. That is, multiplication and division are performed before addition and subtraction. Operations are performed left to right. If there is ambiguity in your mind as to which order will be followed, use parentheses. Operations within parentheses are performed first. For example,

```
X = 3+4/5-2*2
```

results in a value of –0.2 since 4/5 is computed first, 2*2 is computed next and then 3 + 0.8 – 4 lead to the result. If you had intended (3+4) to be divided by (5–2*2) you would have to write:

```
X = (3+4)/(5-2*2)
```

to obtain the value 7.

2.8.5 PREVIOUS and FUTURE

PREVIOUS and FUTURE are "reserved" words with specific meanings. IFPS has a number of such words (listed in APPENDIX III) which you cannot use as the name of a variable.

PREVIOUS and FUTURE are particularly powerful instructions because they allow you to refer to values in other columns of the output matrix. PREVIOUS refers to the column to the left and FUTURE to the right. If you use PREVIOUS in column 1, IFPS takes the PREVIOUS value to be 0; similarly if you use FUTURE in the last column, it takes the FUTURE value to be 0. You can also refer to values more than one column away. For example, PREVIOUS 4 refers to a value four columns ago. For example, the statement

```
SEASONALITY FACTOR = 1.1,1.03,0.96,0.91,PREVIOUS 4
```

allows you to define the seasonality factors for the four quarters of the first year and then to use the same factors for all subsequent years. If you are referring to a previous value in the same row, that is for the same variable, you do not need to specify the variable name (but it does no harm if you do). If you want to refer to a PREVIOUS or FUTURE value of another variable, you must give its name. For example, you might write:

```
CASH RECEIVED = CASH SALES + PREVIOUS CREDIT SALES
```

2.8.6 FOR

If you want to repeat a value for several periods, you use FOR. Thus,

```
PRICE = 2.75 FOR 4, 3.00
```

is the same as using 2.75, 2.75, 2.75, 2.75, 3.00 in defining price.

2.8.7 PERIODS

As explained in the previous section, PERIODS allows you to model situations that are quarterly or monthly and to state interest rate in annual terms. The form used is PERIODS followed by a space and a number, where the number can be any integer from 1 to 13. PERIODS is needed only if built-in financial functions (Section 3.2) are being used.

2.8.8 MATRIX

Although you have not yet seen MATRIX as an example, we will be using it at several points in this book. MATRIX is a way of referring to a specific location in the model. One way of thinking about an IFPS model is that it creates a two-dimensional array of numbers, what mathematicians usually call a matrix. The numbers in the matrix (in our case, the IFPS model) can be referred to by their location in terms of the row and the column in which they appear. You can use row names and column names in the reference. For example,

```
MATRIX(REVENUE,6)
```

2.9 EXAMPLE -- A PRO FORMA PROFIT AND LOSS STATEMENT

Budget planning usually involves creation of a pro forma profit and loss statement for an upcoming period of time. In this example, we consider a manufacturing organization, let's call it ABC Company, that produces a single product. We want to create a profit and loss statement for the next twelve months based on assumptions about the anticipated nature of the business. We will first present the assumptions made by the budget planners and then show the IFPS model of the profit and loss statement for the 12-month period that embodies these assumptions.

For ease of following the IFPS model, these are the assumptions:

1. ABC sells one product at a price of $1000/unit. The price will remain fixed for the next year.

2. Sales will average 2500 units per month. However, past experience indicates that there is a seasonality factor. The historical seasonal indices are as follows:

JAN	FEB	MAR	APR	MAY	JUN
0.43	0.61	0.73	0.85	0.94	1.05

JUL	AUG	SEP	OCT	NOV	DEC
1.74	1.89	1.52	1.09	0.66	0.49

3. Cost of production involves material and labor costs. Material costs are $430/unit and are expected to start increasing at a rate of 0.3% per month starting in June. Direct labor costs are $150/unit. Renegotiation of the union contract is expected to increase direct labor costs by 10%/unit in June and remain constant thereafter.

4. The inventory at the start of the year will be 2300 units. Production will be constant at 2500 units/month.

5. The following operating expenses are anticipated:

- Advertising expenses will be $26,875 in the first month and 2.5% of the previous month's gross sales, in dollars, thereafter.
- Commissions are 5% of gross sales. They are paid in the month in which the sale takes place.
- Salaries for indirect labor are $70,000/month. A raise of 7% is scheduled for July.
- Payroll and social security taxes are 9.5% of indirect labor.
- The company has a lease on its warehouse and factory that runs through the end of next year. The cost of the lease is $65,000/month.
- The company has a $200,000 note that is not due until after the end of next year. The interest on the note is 1.25% /month (i.e., 15%/year) payable each month. It is a balloon-payment note, with no principal due during the year.
- Depreciation on existing equipment and facilities will be $50,000 in January and will decline at 2%/month, compounded, thereafter.

6. The company expects its tax rate to be 46%.

The IFPS model is shown in Figure 2-10. Note that lines 10 through 420 define the profit and loss statement. Additional input data and the calculation of quantities derived from the input data follow at the bottom of the model. In this way, either a conventional profit and loss statement can be obtained by displying only lines 10 through 420 and the assumptions of the model can be shown explicitly by displaying lines 470 through 610. It is possible to print out only a portion of a model by using the SOLVE options. Specifically, rather than specifying ALL when asked the solve option, you enter :

```
? L10 THRU L420
```

This form tells IFPS that you want all lines from 10 through 420 printed out and no others. Section 4.1 contains further discussion of the SOLVE options.

Read over the model shown in Figure 2-10 line by line and go over the corresponding results in the solution. You will see that the model is set up in the general form of a conventional pro forma profit and loss statement. Each quantity is defined in terms of its accounting relations. For example, GROSS SALES in Line 60 is obtained by multiplying

```
MODEL PROFITLOSS  VERSION OF  01/07/83  11:25
10 COLUMNS 1-12
20 *
30 *                          PROFIT AND LOSS STATEMENT FOR ACME COMPANY
40 *                          ------------------------------------------
50 *
60 GROSS SALES = UNIT PRICE * MONTHLY SALES
70 *
80 *COST OF GOODS SOLD
90 *------------------
100 *
110 BEGINNING INVENTORY =1334000,PREVIOUS ENDING INVENTORY VALUE
120 *
130 *COST OF MANUFACTURING
140 *----------------------
150 *
160 MATERIAL COST =UNIT MATERIAL COST *PRODUCTION
170 DIRECT LABOR = UNIT LABOR COST*PRODUCTION
180 COST OF MANUFACTURING = MATERIAL COST + DIRECT LABOR
190 *
200 TOTAL INVENTORY VALUE = BEGINNING INVENTORY'
201 + COST OF MANUFACTURING
210 ENDING INVENTORY VALUE = TOTAL INVENTORY VALUE '
211 - COST OF GOODS SOLD
220 COST OF GOODS SOLD = MONTHLY SALES * AVERAGE INVENTORY COST
230 *
240 GROSS PROFIT ON SALES =GROSS SALES - COST OF GOODS SOLD
250 *
260 *OPERATING EXPENSES
270 *------------------
280 *
290 ADVERTISING=26875, .025*PREVIOUS GROSS SALES
300 COMMISSIONS =.05*GROSS SALES
310 SALARIES =70000 FOR 6, PREVIOUS *1.07,PREVIOUS
320 PAYROLL TAXES =.095*SALARIES
330 LEASES =65000
340 NOTE INTEREST = .0125*200000
350 DEPRECIATION=50000,PREVIOUS*.98
360 *
370 TOTAL OPERATING EXPENSE = SUM(L290 THRU L350)
380 NET PROFIT BEFORE TAX =GROSS PROFIT ON SALES -'
381 TOTAL OPERATING EXPENSE
390 *
400 INCOME TAX = .46*NET PROFIT BEFORE TAX
410 *
420 NET PROFIT =NET PROFIT BEFORE INCOME TAX -INCOME TAX
430 *
```

FIGURE 2-10. PRO FORMA PROFIT AND LOSS STATEMENT
(This Figure is Continued on the Next Page)

```
440 *INPUT DATA
450 *----------
460 *
470 UNIT PRICE=1000
480 AVERAGE SALES = 2500
490 UNIT MATERIAL COST = 430 FOR 5,PREVIOUS*1.003
500 PRODUCTION = 2500
510 MONTHLY SALES = AVERAGE SALES * SEASONAL INDEX
520 UNIT LABOR COST = 150 FOR 5, 150*1.1
530 SEASONAL INDEX = .43,.61,.73,.85,.94,1.05,1.74,1.89,'
531 1.52,1.09,.66,.49
540 *
550 *QUANTITIES DERIVED FROM INPUT DATA
560 *---------------------------------
570 *
580 STARTING INVENTORY=2300,PREVIOUS STARTING INVENTORY+'
590 PREVIOUS PRODUCTION - PREVIOUS MONTHLY SALES
600 AVERAGE INVENTORY COST = (BEGINNING INVENTORY  +'
610 COST OF MANUFACTURING)/(STARTING INVENTORY + PRODUCTION)
END OF MODEL
```

a. Model

FIGURE 2-10. PRO FORMA PROFIT AND LOSS STATEMENT
(This Figure Is Continued on the Next Page)

```
? solve
MODEL PROFITLOSS   VERSION OF   01/07/83   11:25 -- 12 COLUMNS 29
VARIABLES
ENTER SOLVE OPTIONS
? 110 thru 1420

                          1       2       3       4       5       6

                    PROFIT AND LOSS STATEMENT FOR ACME COMPANY
                    ------------------------------------------

GROSS SALES           1075000 1525000 1825000 2125000 2350000 2625000

COST OF GOODS SOLD
------------------

BEGINNING INVENTORY   1334000 2160500 2726000 3117500 3335000 3422000

COST OF MANUFACTURING
---------------------

MATERIAL COST         1075000 1075000 1075000 1075000 1075000 1078225
DIRECT LABOR           375000  375000  375000  375000  375000  412500
COST OF MANUFACTURIN  1450000 1450000 1450000 1450000 1450000 1490725

TOTAL INVENTORY VALU  2784000 3610500 4176000 4567500 4785000 4912725
ENDING INVENTORY VAL  2160500 2726000 3117500 3335000 3422000 3377498
COST OF GOODS SOLD     623500  884500 1058500 1232500 1363000 1535227

GROSS PROFIT ON SALE   451500  640500  766500  892500  987000 1089773

OPERATING EXPENSES
------------------

ADVERTISING             26875   26875   38125   45625   53125   58750
COMMISSIONS             53750   76250   91250  106250  117500  131250
SALARIES                70000   70000   70000   70000   70000   70000
PAYROLL TAXES            6650    6650    6650    6650    6650    6650
LEASES                  65000   65000   65000   65000   65000   65000
NOTE INTEREST            2500    2500    2500    2500    2500    2500
DEPRECIATION            50000   49000   48020   47060   46118   45196

TOTAL OPERATING EXPE   274775  296275  321545  343085  360893  379346
NET PROFIT BEFORE TAX  176725  344225  444955  549415  626107  710427

INCOME TAX              81294  158344  204679  252731  288009  326797

NET PROFIT              95432  185882  240276  296684  338098  383631
```

FIGURE 2-10. PRO FORMA PROFIT AND LOSS STATEMENT
(This Figure is Continued on the Next Page)

	7	8	9	10	11	12
	PROFIT AND LOSS STATEMENT FOR ACME COMPANY					
GROSS SALES	4350000	4725000	3800000	2725000	1650000	1225000
COST OF GOODS SOLD						
BEGINNING INVENTORY	3377498	2310631	1007521	238855	105156	617740
COST OF MANUFACTURING						
MATERIAL COST	1081460	1084704	1087958	1091222	1094496	1097779
DIRECT LABOR	412500	412500	412500	412500	412500	412500
COST OF MANUFACTURIN	1493960	1497204	1500458	1503722	1506996	1510279
TOTAL INVENTORY VALU	4871458	3807835	2507979	1742577	1612151	2128019
ENDING INVENTORY VAL	2310631	1007521	238855	105156	617740	1388495
COST OF GOODS SOLD	2560827	2800315	2269124	1637422	994411	739524
GROSS PROFIT ON SALE	1789173	1924685	1530876	1087578	655589	485476
OPERATING EXPENSES						
ADVERTISING	65625	108750	118125	95000	68125	41250
COMMISSIONS	217500	236250	190000	136250	82500	61250
SALARIES	74900	74900	74900	74900	74900	74900
PAYROLL TAXES	7116	7116	7116	7116	7116	7116
LEASES	65000	65000	65000	65000	65000	65000
NOTE INTEREST	2500	2500	2500	2500	2500	2500
DEPRECIATION	44292	43406	42538	41687	40854	40037
TOTAL OPERATING EXPE	476933	537922	500179	422453	340994	292052
NET PROFIT BEFORE TAX	1312240	1386764	1030698	665125	314595	193423
INCOME TAX	603631	637911	474121	305958	144714	88975
NET PROFIT	708610	748852	556577	359168	169881	104449

b. Results

FIGURE 2-10. PRO FORMA PROFIT AND LOSS STATEMENT
(This Figure is Continued on the Next Page))

```
ENTER SOLVE OPTIONS
? 1420 thru 1610
```

	1	2	3	4	5	6
INPUT DATA						

UNIT PRICE	1000	1000	1000	1000	1000	1000
AVERAGE SALES	2500	2500	2500	2500	2500	2500
UNIT MATERIAL COST	430	430	430	430	430	431.3
PRODUCTION	2500	2500	2500	2500	2500	2500
MONTHLY SALES	1075	1525	1825	2125	2350	2625
UNIT LABOR COST	150	150	150	150	150	165
SEASONAL INDEX	.4300	.6100	.7300	.8500	.9400	1.050
QUANTITIES DERIVED FROM INPUT DATA						

STARTING INVENTORY	2300	3725	4700	5375	5750	5900
AVERAGE INVENTORY CO	580	580	580	580	580	584.8

	7	8	9	10	11	12
INPUT DATA						

UNIT PRICE	1000	1000	1000	1000	1000	1000
AVERAGE SALES	2500	2500	2500	2500	2500	2500
UNIT MATERIAL COST	432.6	433.9	435.2	436.5	437.8	439.1
PRODUCTION	2500	2500	2500	2500	2500	2500
MONTHLY SALES	4350	4725	3800	2725	1650	1225
UNIT LABOR COST	165	165	165	165	165	165
SEASONAL INDEX	1.740	1.890	1.520	1.090	.6600	.4900
QUANTITIES DERIVED FROM INPUT DATA						

STARTING INVENTORY	5775	3925	1700	400	175	1025
AVERAGE INVENTORY CO	588.7	592.7	597.1	600.9	602.7	603.7

c. Input Data

FIGURE 2-10 PRO FORMA PROFIT AND LOSS STATEMENT
(Continued)

unit price and monthly sales. IFPS finds the value of unit price in line 470 where it is given as an input. The monthly sales have been computed in line 510 by multiplying the average sales by the seasonal index.

NOTE: Seasonal index, like all index numbers, refers to the value relative to some standard; in this case, the ratio of sales in a given month to the average sales. For more about index numbers, see Section 7.8.

The rest of the model is straightforward. The only policy question you have to decide is how to compute the cost of goods sold. Since production is the same every month (2500 units) but sales fluctuate, some months you will produce more than you sell and put the extra goods in inventory while in others you will be using up inventory to satisfy demand. If the cost of production were the same from month to month there would be no problem; however, costs are rising. In a typical month, the goods in inventory cost the company less than the goods produced that month. The following are three ways of dealing with this situation:

1. *Current cost.* Assume that all goods sold were produced that month. In the month when you use the inventory, you will be charging yourself more than the actual production cost and your profit will be reduced. (This is a last-in, first-out type of policy.)

2. *Average cost.* Since the items are identical, you can't tell whether you sold an item from inventory or from production. Therefore, average the cost of beginning inventory and the cost of production to determine the average cost per unit sold.

3. *First in, first out.* Sell the oldest units first. Since these units were produced at the lowest cost, cost decreases and profit increases. However, this approach neglects the replacement cost of the units.

We have chosen the average cost approach in Figure 2-10. The average inventory cost is computed in Line 600 from the relation:

$$AVERAGE\ INVENTORY\ COST = \frac{BEGINNING\ INVENTORY + COST\ OF\ MFG}{STARTING\ INVENTORY + PRODUCTION}$$

where the numerator represents the cost of the previous inventory plus the cost of manufacturing, and the denominator adds the number of units produced to the number of units in the starting inventory.

EXERCISE: Put the model in Figure 2-10 on your computer. Modify the calculation of the cost of goods sold so that it assumes current cost rather than average cost and determine the effect on the total profit for the year.

EXERCISE: Print out only lines 10 through 420 to obtain a pro forma profit and loss statement. You will see that the result is almost, but not quite, in the form commonly used for such statements. We will modify Figure 2-10 in Chapter IV (which deals with customizing output) to obtain the commonly accepted format.

2.10 WHAT TO DO IF YOU NEED HELP (The IFPS HELP Commands)

Despite your newly found skill in IFPS and the information available in this book, you may find yourself in a situation in which IFPS does not do what you want it to do or you cannot understand what is happening. Rather than having to give vent to your frustration, you can use the extensive HELP commands available in IFPS.

The simplest way to ask for HELP, is simply type HELP in response to a ? When you do, the following message appears:

```
? help

HELP COMMAND
FORM(S)
 (1)    HELP
 (2)    HELP HELP
 (3)    HELP WHERE
 (4)    HELP CONTENTS
 (5)    HELP *
 (6)    HELP KEYWORD
USAGE
      "HELP" AND "HELP HELP" PROVIDE THIS MESSAGE TELLING HOW TO
      USE THE HELP COMMAND.
      "HELP WHERE" IDENTIFIES WHICH SUBSYSTEM THE USER IS CURRENTLY
      IN, ALONG WITH  THE  CURRENTLY  ACTIVE  FILE,  AND  SPECIFIC
      MODEL, REPORT,  OR STRUCTURE, AS APPROPRIATE.
      "HELP CONTENTS" PRODUCES A TABLE OF CONTENTS OUTLINING MAJOR
      CATEGORIES WITHIN IFPS.  INSTRUCTIONS ARE ALSO GIVEN FOR A
      SUBSEQUENT HELP COMMAND FOR EACH CATEGORY, TO LIST ALL
      CORRESPONDING KEYWORDS FOR WHICH HELP IS AVAILABLE.
      "HELP *" PRINTS A LIST OF ALL KEYWORDS AVAILABLE WITH THE HELP
      COMMAND.
      "HELP KEYWORD" PRINTS THE HELP MESSAGE FOR THE SPECIFIED
      KEYWORD,VALID FROM ANY LEVEL OF IFPS.  CONTROL WILL REMAIN AT
      THE LEVEL WHERE HELP WAS ENTERED.

READY FOR MODELING LANGUAGE COMMAND
```

FIGURE 2-11. RESULT OF HELP and HELP HELP

As you can see, HELP (or HELP HELP) only gives you an index to the HELP commands.

HELP WHERE tells you where you are inside IFPS. For example, if you are in a file named SAMPLE and are working on a model named GRAY you would see the sequence in Figure 2-12.

```
? help where

SUBSYSTEM: MODELING
MODEL NAME: GRAY
MODEL AND REPORTS FILE NAME: SAMPLE
READY FOR MODELING LANGUAGE COMMAND
```

FIGURE 2-12. THE HELP WHERE COMMAND

HELP CONTENTS, shown in Figure 2-13, gives you a list of the major categories within IFPS that are available to you. You can obtain a list of the keywords in each category by typing HELP followed by the name of the category; for example, HELP MODS provides you with a list of all the modeling language commands. One way of thinking about HELP CONTENTS is that it is a cross-index of the keywords by which help is obtained (see below).

```
? help contents

CONTENTS OF HELP FILE
THE IFPS  HELP  FILE  IS  ORGANIZED  INTO  THE  CATEGORIES SHOWN
BELOW. FOR A LISTING OF THE COMMANDS/OPTIONS IN ANY CATEGORY, ENTER
HELP CATEGORY WHERE  "CATEGORY" IS THE KEYWORD IDENTIFIER SHOWN TO
THE LEFT OF  THE  DESIRED CATEGORY (FOR INSTANCE, HELP REL8).

        UC        UNIVERSAL CONSOLIDATION
        REL8      OTHER RELEASE 8.0 COMMANDS/OPTIONS
        SROPTS    SOLVE/REPORT OPTIONS
        EXECS     EXECUTIVE LEVEL COMMANDS
        MODS      MODELING LANGUAGE COMMANDS
        CMDS      COMMAND FILE COMMANDS
        DATA      DATAFILE SUBSYSTEM COMMANDS; STORE/STORENT OPTIONS
        FUNCS     IFPS FUNCTIONS & SUBROUTINES
        STMTS     SPECIAL MODELING STATEMENTS
        SYS       SYSTEM-DEPENDENT CHARACTERISTICS & SPECIAL HELPS
```

FIGURE 2-13. RESULT OF HELP CONTENTS

HELP * provides you with a list of all the keywords available within the HELP command. This is a table of contents and is shown in Appendix I, which presents a more detailed discussion of HELP. To obtain information about any of these keywords simply type the word HELP followed by the keyword.

CHAPTER III
USEFUL FEATURES OF IFPS

3.1 Using IFPS To Ask Questions About the Model

3.1.1 WHAT IF
3.1.2 SENSITIVITY
3.1.3 GOAL SEEKING
3.1.4 ANALYZE
3.1.5 Finding Out Where You Are (CASELIST)

3.2 Built-In Functions (Financial, Forecasting, Mathematical)

3.2.1 Financial Functions
3.2.2 The PERIODS Statement
3.2.3 Statistical and Forecasting Functions
3.2.4 Mathematical Functions

3.3 Built-In Subroutines (Depreciation, Amortization)

CHAPTER III
USEFUL FEATURES OF IFPS

In Chapter II, we described the basic elements of IFPS. We showed you how to obtain IFPS at the terminal and how to construct simple models. At several points in Chapter II we used some of the built-in functions available in IFPS. In this chapter we explore these and various other useful features that are built into the modeling language. These features include the ability to ask questions and make decisions; the built-in functions for finance, forecasting, and mathematical applications; and built-in subroutines for depreciation and amortization.

3.1 USING IFPS TO ASK QUESTIONS ABOUT THE MODEL

In analyzing the results of your models, you will often be interested in finding out what would happen if conditions turn out to be different from what you assumed. You might ask such questions as:

"What if sales are higher than the marketing department forecast?"

"Will small changes in market size affect our profit?"

"How many units will we have to sell to meet our net income goal?"

IFPS contains a number of commands that allow you to explore these questions in detail. We will discuss three of these commands in this section:

- WHAT IF
- SENSITIVITY
- GOAL SEEKING

These commands all help you understand the effects of changes in assumptions on the measures of effectiveness in your model. In addition, we discuss the

- ANALYZE

command, a useful tool that helps you understand the interrelations that exist within your model.

3.1.1 WHAT IF

The WHAT IF command allows you to change the definition of one or more variables temporarily to see what such a change implies. Being an executive command like MODEL and SOLVE, WHAT IF does not require a line number. Suppose, for example, you are working with the Simple IFPS Model of Section 2.2 (Figure 2-3). You have used the LIST command to display it in front of you at your terminal and you want to find out what happens if sales start at 100 but grow at a rate of 15% rather than 25% per period. To investigate this possibility, you type the command:

```
WHAT IF
```

In response, the computer asks you to:

```
ENTER STATEMENTS
```

This is a request to tell the computer which variable definitions (that is, which lines) you want to change.

As you can see from Figure 3-1, you type in a complete IFPS statement, *without line numbers*, to define the temporary change that you want. What IFPS does in response to this WHAT IF is to replace the old definition of SALES with your new definition.

```
? what if
MODEL GRAY  VERSION OF  08/30/82  16:39 -- 6 COLUMNS 5 VARIABLES
WHAT IF CASE 1
ENTER STATEMENTS
? sales = 100,previous sales*1.15
? solve
ENTER SOLVE OPTIONS
? all

***** WHAT IF CASE 1 *****
1 WHAT IF STATEMENT PROCESSED

                         1       2       3       4       5       6

SALES                  100     115   132.3   152.1   174.9   201.1
EXPENSES                75     100     125     150     175     175
NET INCOME              25      15   7.250   2.088  -.0994   26.14

                            RATIO ANALYSIS
PERCENT OF SALES
EXPENSE RATIO        .7500   .8696   .9452   .9863   1.001   .8701
NET INCOME RATIO     .2500   .1304   .0548   .0137  -.0006   .1299
```

FIGURE 3-1. WHAT IF

After you have specified all the WHAT IF changes you want, you type SOLVE as usual. IFPS asks you to enter SOLVE options. You can ask for ALL, in which case you obtain a complete printout as before. However, you may not need or want to print out an entire model for each WHAT IF case. You have the option of specifying which variables you want printed. For example, in Figure 3-2, we have asked only for SALES and NET INCOME. The idea is to list the names of the variables you want, in sequence, with commas between them.

```
? what if
WHAT IF CASE 2
ENTER STATEMENTS
? sales = 100,previous sales*1.15
? solve
ENTER SOLVE OPTIONS
? sales,net income


***** WHAT IF CASE 2 *****
2 WHAT IF STATEMENTS PROCESSED
                          1       2       3       4       5       6

SALES                   100     115   132.3   152.1   174.9   201.1
NET INCOME               25      15   7.250   2.088  -.0994   26.14
```

FIGURE 3-2. SELECTING OUTPUT IN WHAT IF

You should know the following important things about the WHAT IF option:

1. Do not use line numbers. If you type a line number, IFPS assumes you are making a permanent rather than a temporary change in your model. This is not a fatal mistake, since your IFPS model now contains your WHAT IF condition. However, the line number has taken you out of the WHAT IF mode and has modified the original model. If you want your original model back, you have to retype the original line with its line number.

2. You can change several statements, not just one, in a particular WHAT IF case. For example, you might want to determine the effect of simultaneous changes into both sales and expenses. In this case you would type:

```
? WHAT IF
? SALES = 100, PREVIOUS * 1.15
? EXPENSES = 70, PREVIOUS + 20
? SOLVE
? ALL
```

3. Each WHAT IF case is evaluated with respect to the original model, referred to as the "base model". That is, if you run several WHAT IF cases in a row, the original model is restored each time.

4. If you want to see what happens if every value is changed by a constant

amount, you can write, for example,

```
SALES = SALES * 1.1
```

The result of this statement is to raise every SALES value in the base case by 10%. This form of "circular" definition (where the equal sign stands for "replace") is allowed in WHAT IF statements but is not allowed in the base model.

5. If you want to accumulate changes from one case to the next, you can do so by typing:

```
WHAT IF CONTINUE
```

Figure 3-3 adds a change in EXPENSES to the change in SALES of Figure 3-1 by use of WHAT IF CONTINUE.

```
? what if continue
WHAT IF CASE 3
ENTER STATEMENTS
? expenses = 70,previous + 20
? solve
ENTER SOLVE OPTIONS
? all


***** WHAT IF CASE 3 *****
3 WHAT IF STATEMENTS PROCESSED

                        1       2       3       4       5       6

SALES                 100     115   132.3   152.1   174.9   201.1
EXPENSES               70      90     110     130     150     170
NET INCOME             30      25   22.25   22.09   24.90   31.14

                               RATIO ANALYSIS
PERCENT OF SALES
EXPENSE RATIO       .7000   .7826   .8318   .8548   .8576   .8452
NET INCOME RATIO    .3000   .2174   .1682   .1452   .1424   .1548
```

FIGURE 3-3. WHAT IF CONTINUE

6. If you make WHAT IF changes and then run sensitivity analyses (see Section 3.1.2), the sensitivity analysis will be with respect to the WHAT IF conditions, not the base model. That is, you can combine WHAT IF and sensitivity analysis. Similarly, the GOAL SEEKING (Section 3.1.3) and the ANALYZE (Sec. 3.1.4) commands are combined with the previous WHAT IF command.

7. If you want to return to the original version of your model, just type BASE MODEL in response to a ?.

Figure 3-4 shows you how IFPS organizes storage and manages files. For now, we will concentrate only on the edit area and the WHAT IF area. We will discuss other portions of Figure 3-4 later. For the present what you need to understand is that your base model is located in the edit area. When you specify WHAT IF, in effect, a copy is made of your model, and placed in the WHAT IF area. The WHAT IF changes you specify are made on this copy on a line-for-line replacement basis. When you ask for SOLVE, the SOLVE command checks to see if you are in WHAT IF mode and runs the WHAT IF case rather than the base model. If you ask for another WHAT IF case, IFPS first makes a new copy of the base case (which is still in your edit area) and puts it in the WHAT IF area. It then makes the changes you specify in your new WHAT IF case. However, if you ask for WHAT IF CONTINUE, the previous WHAT IF case is left intact in the WHAT IF area and is modified. Thus, with WHAT IF CONTINUE you can either make aditional changes or you can modify some of your previous changes.

The WHAT IF area is also referred to in SENSITIVITY, GOAL SEEKING, and ANALYZE. In effect, these commands operate in a WHAT IF CONTINUE mode; that is, if you invoke them right after a WHAT IF case, they work on the WHAT IF case rather than on the base model.

3.1.2 SENSITIVITY

Sensitivity analysis is a special form of WHAT IF analysis. It is typically used when you are uncertain about the assumptions you made about a particular variable. What you want to find out is whether changes from the assumed values have major or minor impact on the results, and hence on your decision. In IFPS, sensitivity analysis allows you to step a variable through a number of values and print out the effects of these changes. Figure 3-5 shows you an example of a typical sensititivity analysis. When you type :

```
SENSITIVITY ANALYSIS
```

IFPS first asks you the name of the variable to be stepped and then asks you to enter the START, STOP, STEP PERCENTAGES. Note that IFPS does sensitivity analysis only in percentage terms. The START and STOP percentages refer to the range of sensitivity to be explored. Typically you would pick a negative value such as –10 or –20 as the start value and a positive value such 10 or 20 as the stop value. The step refers to the increment to be used in exploring between the start and stop values. In Figure 3-5, the start value is –10 per cent, the stop value is 10 percent, and the incremental step is 10 percent.

As you can see from the Figure, IFPS gives you a lot of output in sensitivity analysis. You receive three sets of data:

1. the new values of the variables
2. the absolute change from the base value
3. the percentage change from the base value

Because of the large amount of information given to you, it is wise to ask only for the values of the variables you need in decision making when IFPS asks you which variables are to be printed. Otherwise, you will drown in output and will find it difficult to interpret the results. You will also notice that the 0% change case is not given. IFPS assumes you know the values of the base case from solving the problem.

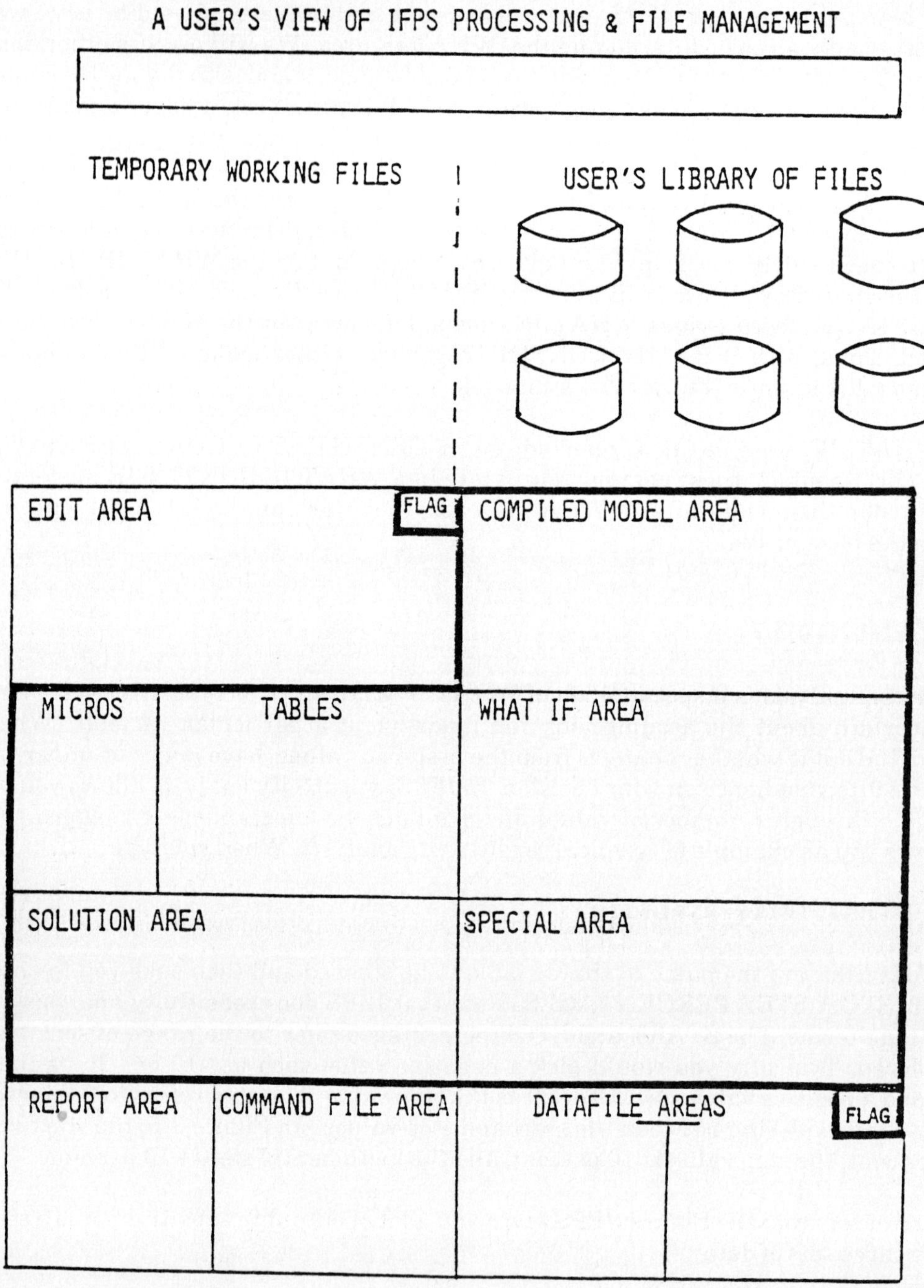

FIGURE 3-4. A USER'S VIEW OF IFPS PROCESSING AND FILE MANAGEMENT

```
? sensitivity analysis
ENTER VARIABLE TO BE STEPPED
? sales
ENTER START,STOP,STEP PERCENTAGES
?-10,10,10
ENTER VARIABLES TO BE PRINTED
? sales,net income,expenses


***** WHAT IF CASE 3 *****
2 WHAT IF STATEMENTS PROCESSED

SENSITIVITY ANALYSIS FOR   -10 PER CENT CHANGE IN SALES

     NEW VALUES

                                1       2       3       4       5       6

SALES                          90   103.5   119.0  .136.9   157.4   181.0
NET INCOME                     20   13.50   9.025   6.879   7.411   11.02
EXPENSES                       70      90     110     130     150     170

     CHANGE FROM BASE

                                1       2       3       4       5       6

SALES                         -10  -11.50  -13.23  -15.21  -17.49  -20.11
NET INCOME                    -10  -11.50  -13.23  -15.21  -17.49  -20.11
EXPENSES                        0       0       0       0       0       0

     PERCENT CHANGE FROM BASE

                                1       2       3       4       5       6

SALES                         -10     -10     -10     -10     -10     -10
NET INCOME                 -33.33     -46  -59.44  -68.86  -70.24  -64.60
EXPENSES                        0       0       0       0       0       0
```

FIGURE 3-5. SENSITIVITY ANALYSIS
(This Figure Continued on the Next Page)

SENSITIVITY ANALYSIS FOR 10 PER CENT CHANGE IN SALES

NEW VALUES

	1	2	3	4	5	6
SALES	110	126.5	145.5	167.3	192.4	221.2
NET INCOME	40	36.50	35.48	37.30	42.39	51.25
EXPENSES	70	90	110	130	150	170

CHANGE FROM BASE

	1	2	3	4	5	6
SALES	10	11.50	13.23	15.21	17.49	20.11
NET INCOME	10	11.50	13.23	15.21	17.49	20.11
EXPENSES	0	0	0	0	0	0

PERCENT CHANGE FROM BASE

	1	2	3	4	5	6
SALES	10	10	10	10	10	10
NET INCOME	33.33	46	59.44	68.86	70.24	64.60
EXPENSES	0	0	0	0	0	0

FIGURE 3-5. SENSITIVITY ANALYSIS
(Continued)

3.1.3 GOAL SEEKING

Through GOAL SEEKING, you can find out the value a particular variable has to have in order to achieve a desired level of performance. You can specify your goal either as:

- performance at a single point in time
- performance over the entire time horizon.

Thus, you might want a net income of $150 in Period 6 or you might require that the initial income is $25 and doubles every period. IFPS asks you which variable you want to adjust to reach your goal. If you have a point goal, then you have to specify a point adjustment (e.g., sales in Period 6); if you have a goal over the time horizon, you specify the variable to be adjusted in each period.

> NOTE: IFPS asks you first for the variable to be adjusted and second for the relation defining the goal.

Figure 3-6 illustrates the two GOAL SEEKING cases. Since you specify the goal, IFPS only prints out the values of the variable to be adjusted to reach the goal. If you want more detail than the values of the variable to be adjusted, you can follow your GOAL SEEKING command immediately with a SOLVE command.

```
? goal seeking
GOAL SEEKING CASE 1
ENTER NAME OF VARIABLE TO BE ADJUSTED TO ACHIEVE PERFORMANCE
? sales
ENTER COMPUTATIONAL STATEMENT FOR PERFORMANCE
? net income = 25, previous net income*2

***** GOAL SEEKING CASE 1 *****

                              1       2       3       4       5       6

SALES                       100     150     225     350     575     975

ENTER SOLVE OPTIONS
? goal seeking
GOAL SEEKING CASE 2
ENTER NAME OF VARIABLE TO BE ADJUSTED TO ACHIEVE PERFORMANCE
? sales(6)
ENTER COMPUTATIONAL STATEMENT FOR PERFORMANCE
? net income(6) = 150

***** GOAL SEEKING CASE 2 *****

                              1       2       3       4       5       6

SALES                       100     125   156.3   195.3   244.1     325

ENTER SOLVE OPTIONS
? all

                              1       2       3       4       5       6

SALES                       100     125   156.3   195.3   244.1     325
EXPENSES                     75     100     125     150     175     175
NET INCOME                   25      25   31.25   45.31   69.14     150

                              RATIO ANALYSIS
PERCENT OF SALES
EXPENSE RATIO             .7500   .8000   .8000   .7680   .7168   .5385
NET INCOME RATIO          .2500   .2000   .2000   .2320   .2832   .4615
```

FIGURE 3-6. GOAL SEEKING

You will find that IFPS has adjusted the values of all variables so that they are consistent with the goal you specified. The way that IFPS does goal seeking is by solving the problem "backwards". That is, it fixes your goal and then uses the relations in the model between your goal and the variable to be adjusted to give that variable the correct value. It also changes the values of all variables that depend on your goal. It does not, however, worry about consistency with respect to the variable being adjusted. You can see this by performing the following exercise.

EXERCISE: Consider the simple model:

```
5  COLUMNS 1
10 NET REVENUE = SALES -EXPENSES
20 SALES = 4.8* ADVERTISING
30 EXPENSES = 200 + ADVERTISING
40 ADVERTISING = 100
50 INVESTMENT = 170
60 INTERNAL RATE OF RETURN =IRR(NET REVENUE,INVESTMENT)
```

SOLVE this model. Then use GOAL SEEKING to determine the value of SALES if your goal is net revenue of 250. If you respond to ENTER SOLVE OPTIONS with ALL you will see that advertising expenditures have not changed even though sales have!

Also observe that the value of internal rate of return has changed to be consistent with the new net revenue.

> *MORAL:* Be careful in interpreting the results of a GOAL SEEKING run! The answers you receive may not be possible in the real world!

Operationally, GOAL SEEKING is treated by IFPS as an addition to any WHAT IF (and WHAT IF CONTINUE) statements. It is carried out in the area of storage labeled *special* in Figure 3-4.

3.1.4 ANALYZE

When developing a new model or trying to understand the relations that led to a complex or strange result, the ANALYZE command is a useful tool. As shown in Figure 3-7, when you ask IFPS to analyze a variable, you obtain a printout of:

- The line of the model defining the variable.
- The values of the variable for each period.
- The values of every variable whose name appears on the right hand side of the definition.

It is the last output that is the power of the ANALYZE command to help you in debugging. You can check each of the components that make up your definition of the variable to make sure that they make sense, and you can begin the process of tracing to find the source of errors.

ANALYZE also helps you see which terms in your definition contribute most the to value of a variable. For example, if you analyze SUBSCRIPTION SALES and find that MAIL

SALES = 100000 while NEWSSTAND SALES = 5000 you might want to take action.

```
?analyze net income ratio

90 NET INCOME RATIO = NET INCOME/SALES

***** GOAL SEEKING CASE 2 *****
```

	1	2	3	4	5	6
NET INCOME RATIO	.2500	.2000	.2000	.2320	.2832	.4615
NET INCOME	25	25	31.25	45.31	69.14	150
SALES	100	125	156.3	195.3	244.1	325

FIGURE 3-7. ANALYZE

Although you can usually find the same information by poring over the detailed printout from the model, the ANALYZE command highlights information and therefore can lead you quickly to defining issues for decision making.

EXERCISE: Enter the New Product Model shown in Figure 2-9 on your computer. Then perform the following steps:

1. Solve the model.

2. Use WHAT IF to determine the effect of using a 20% discount rate.

3. Use WHAT IF to determine the net present value if, in addition to requiring a 20% discount rate, you expect your share to be only 13% increasing by 0.3% per quarter. Would you still undertake the project under these conditions?

4. Make a SENSITIVITY run on market share, in which the market share ranges from –20% to +20% of the base model value in steps of 20%. Print out the effect on net income, rate of return, net present value, and market share.

5. Supposing your supervisor sets a goal of $600 net income in the first quarter, increasing by $100 per quarter thereafter. Determine the market share required to achieve this goal. In addition, use SOLVE to determine the rate of return and net present value implied by this goal.

6. Repeat the previous goal seeking exercise for a net income of $1000 increasing by $500 per quarter.

7. ANALYZE the operating expense and the net revenue in the base model.

3.1.5 Finding Out Where You Are (CASELIST)

Every so often, when you have been working with a large number of WHAT IF, WHAT IF

CONTINUE, and GOAL SEEKING statements, you may find yourself in the position of not knowing exactly which conditions are currently in force. To find out where you are, you ask for SOLVE and then, in response to ENTER SOLVE OPTION, you type:

```
CASELIST
```

CASELIST tells you in detail what the WHAT IF and GOAL SEEKING conditions are. For example, you might see the following as output:

```
ENTER SOLVE OPTIONS
? CASELIST

WHAT IF CASE 2
WHAT IF STATEMENTS
   EXPENSES = 70,PREVIOUS +20
GOAL SEEKING CASE 3
GOAL SEEKING VARIABLE BEING ADJUSTED SALES
GOAL SEEKING PERFORMANCE STATEMENT
   NET INCOME = 130,PREVIOUS +30
```

3.2 BUILT-IN FUNCTIONS (FINANCIAL, FORECASTING, MATHEMATICAL)

IFPS contains three types of built-in functions that make life easier for you:

1. Financial functions

2. Statistical functions including forecasting functions

3. Mathematical functions

We will describe each of these in turn.

To use a particular function, you must refer to it by its name and then specify the values to be used in computing its value. For example, to compute the net present value for each period, you have to specify the anticipated returns (that is, cash inflows), the discount rate, and the investment (that is, cash outflows) in the form:

```
NPVC(RETURN, DISCOUNT RATE,INVESTMENT).
```

NOTE. For all functions you have to provide the values in the exact sequence shown. You cannot be creative about it. If you put the value of the discount rate first in the NPVC function, for example, you will get the wrong answer. Although functions do a lot of computing work for you, you have to know the rules and follow them if they are to do you any good.

3.2.1 Financial Functions

The choice of appropriate financial effectiveness measures is, as you know, often a matter of corporate policy. Different measures can lead you to different conclusions about whether to accept or reject a particular investment. IFPS allows you to compute the measures of your choice including net present value, net terminal value, internal rate of return, and benefit/cost ratio. Figure 3-8 shows the result of using these functions for a project requiring an initial investment of $1000 at the beginning of Year 1 and having returns of $400, $500, $500, and $600 at the end of Years 1, 2, 3, and 4. A discount rate of 15% is assumed.

```
MODEL FUNCT   VERSION OF   11/22/82   15:12
10 COLUMNS 1-4
20 INVESTMENT=1000,0
30 RETURNS =400,500,500,600
40 DISCOUNT RATE=.15
50 NET PRESENT VALUE =NPVC(RETURNS,DISCOUNT RATE,INVESTMENT)
60 NET TERMINAL VALUE = NTV(RETURNS,DISCOUNT RATE,INVESTMENT)
70 INTERNAL RATE OF RETURN =IRR(RETURNS,INVESTMENT)
80 BENEFIT COST RATIO=BCRATIO(RETURNS,DISCOUNT RATE,INVESTMENT)

END OF MODEL
?solve
MODEL FUNCT   VERSION OF   11/22/82   15:12 -- 4 COLUMNS 7 VARIABLES
ENTER SOLVE OPTIONS
?all

                            1        2        3        4

INVESTMENT               1000        0        0        0
RETURNS                   400      500      500      600
DISCOUNT RATE           .1500    .1500    .1500    .1500
NET PRESENT VALUE      -652.2   -274.1    54.66    397.7
NET TERMINAL VALUE       -750   -362.5    83.13    695.6
INTERNAL RATE OF RET                      .1814    .3229
BENEFIT COST RATIO      .3478    .7259    1.055    1.398
```

FIGURE 3-8. FINANCIAL FUNCTIONS (NPVC,NTV,IRR,BCRATIO)

In reviewing Figure 3-8, the following considerations apply to all four measures of effectiveness:

Consideration 1. The functions are defined in the following format:

NET PRESENT VALUE: NPVC(RETURN,DISCOUNT RATE, INVESTMENT)

NET TERMINAL VALUE: NTV(RETURN,DISCOUNT RATE, INVESTMENT)

INTERNAL RATE OF RETURN: IRR(RETURN,INVESTMENT)

BENEFIT/COST RATIO: BCRATIO(RETURN,DISCOUNT RATE, INVESTMENT)

Consideration 2. The return, discount rate, and investment can be defined elsewhere in the model (e.g., in lines 20, 30, and 40 in Figure 3-8) or numerically in the function itself.

For example, we could have written:

```
40 NET PRESENT VALUE = NPVC(RETURN,.15,INVESTMENT)
```

or

```
40 NET PRESENT VALUE = NPVC(PROFIT,RATE,INVESTMENT)
```

On most computers (but not on some Control Data Computers operating under NOS or KRONOS), discount rate can be expressed as either a decimal (e.g., .15) or as a percentage (e.g., 15%). Control Data accepts only the decimal form.

Consideration 3. You do not have to use the word RETURN or the word INVESTMENT in Line 40. You can refer to any variable in your model (that is, the left hand side of an equal sign) or use any arithmetic expression. For example, if you have several sources of income (e.g., DIRECT SALES, SALES THROUGH JOBBERS, MAIL SALES, EXPORT SALES), you can accumulate these sources into a single variable (e.g., NET SALES=DIRECT SALES + SALES THROUGH JOBBERS + MAIL SALES + EXPORT SALES) and call for NPVC(NET SALES,DISCOUNT RATE,INVESTMENT) or you could put all the information into the function by writing NPVC(DIRECT SALES+SALES THROUGH JOBBERS+MAIL SALES + EXPORT SALES, DISCOUNT RATE,INVESTMENT). Similarly, if you had several investments, you could accumulate them into a single variable.

Consideration 4. Investments (cash outflows) are assumed to take place at the beginning of a period and returns (cash inflows) are assumed to take place at the end of the period. These conventions are discussed further in Section 6.16.

Each of the financial functions is described briefly below. Additional descriptions with examples are given in Chapter VI.

NET PRESENT VALUE. The NPVC function determines the value of *all* investments and *all* income over the time of the calculations. The function is quite general. It allows investments to be made at the beginning of any period (not just the first period) and returns (not necessarily equal to one another) to occur at the end of any period. For each period, the function computes the present value of all cash flows up to that time. For example, in Figure 3-8, the present value of −274.1 in Period 2 is the result of the investment of $1000 and the returns of $400 and $500. In Period 3, the discounted return from the $500 received in that period is added to raise the net present value to 54.66.

The NPVC function is discussed in more detail in Section 6.2.1 in the Chapter on Financial Applications. In that section, we also discuss a more specialized function, NPV. The NPV function is used to find the present worth of an annuity which requires an initial investment at the beginning of Year 1 and has fixed annual payments thereafter for a specified lifetime.

NET TERMINAL VALUE. The NTV function computes the compounded cash value up to the end of the current period of all investments and returns. It is computed in the same way as the NPVC function, but both investments and returns are compounded rather than discounted back to the present. The NTV function is described further in Section 6.2.3

INTERNAL RATE OF RETURN. THE IRR function prints out only *positive* values of the internal rate of return except in the last column. When multiple rates of return can be ascribed to a particular set of cash flows, IFPS prints out the smallest positive value. See Section 6.4.3 for a further discussion of IRR.

BENEFIT / COST RATIO. The BCRATIO function is based on the ratio of the net present value of the cash inflows divided by the net present value of the investments. It is really an alternative way of expressing the NPVC function. BCRATIO has a value smaller than 1.0 when the NPVC function is negative and a value greater than 1.0 when the NPVC function is positive. BCRATIO is discussed further in Section 6.4.4.

3.2.2 The PERIODS Statement

Unless told otherwise, the built-in financial functions assume that the discount rates and cash flows are annual values. If the cash flows are more frequent than annual (for example, monthly or quarterly) you have to tell IFPS about it by using the PERIODS statement. We saw an example of the PERIODS statement in the new product model shown in Figure 2-9, where the quarterly nature of the cash flows was indicated in line 200 by:

```
200 PERIODS 4
```

In general, the PERIODS statement requires a line number, the word PERIODS followed by a space, and the number of periods per year. The statement can be put any place in your model; the end of the model is a good place.

The periods statement converts the annual rate into a period rate by the formula:

$$\text{PERIOD RATE} = (1 + \text{ANNUAL RATE})^{1/\text{PERIODS}} - 1 \tag{3-1}$$

The statement also results in giving the correct annualized rate for internal rate of return.

The PERIODS statement is needed only if you use the built-in financial functions (Section 3.2) or the built-in financial subroutines (Section 3.3) in your model. Its only role is to convert interest rates from and to annualized values.

3.2.3 Statistical And Forecasting Functions

IFPS provides both elementary statistical and elementary forecasting functions. The statistical functions, illustrated in Figure 3-9, are:

- MEAN
- MEDIAN
- STDDEV (for standard deviation)

The forecasting functions, which will be illustrated in Figures 3-10, 3-11, and 3-12, respectively, are:

- MOVAVG (for moving average)
- TREND (for trend extrapolation)
- POLYFIT(for fitting linear and quadratic functions to data).

```
MODEL STATFNCT   VERSION OF   08/30/82   16:38
10 COLUMNS 1-6
20   X=25,27,33,26,44,30
30 MEAN VALUE= MEAN(MATRIX(X,1),MATRIX(X,6))
40 MEDIAN VALUE= MEDIAN(MATRIX(X,1),MATRIX(X,6))
50 STANDARD DEVIATION = STDDEV(MATRIX(X,1),MATRIX(X,6))
END OF MODEL
?solve
MODEL STATFNCT   VERSION OF   08/30/82   16:38 -- 6 COLUMNS 4 VARIABLES
ENTER SOLVE OPTIONS
? all

                          1        2        3        4        5        6

X                        25       27       33       26       44       30
MEAN VALUE            30.83    30.83    30.83    30.83    30.83    30.83
MEDIAN VALUE             30       30       30       30       30       30
STANDARD DEVIATION    7.083    7.083    7.083    7.083    7.083    7.083
```

FIGURE 3-9. STATISTICAL FUNCTIONS (MEAN,MEDIAN,STDDEV)

MEAN. The mean function (Figure 3-9) allows you to find the average of the values of a particular variable across a set of columns. A typical reference to the MEAN function is:

AVERAGE COST = MEAN(MATRIX(COST,1),MATRIX(COST,6)) (3-2)

As described in Sections 2.8.8 and 4.4.2, MATRIX is used to refer to a location in the model. MATRIX(COST,1) in Equation (3-2) refers to the row labeled COST and to column 1, while MATRIX(COST,6) refers to the row labeled COST and to column 6. In using the MEAN function, then, you have to specify both a particular row and the number (or names) of the starting column and the ending column. One way of doing this is to use MATRIX twice with the same row reference. Thus, if Equation (3-2) appears in an IFPS model (as it does in Line 30), it results in finding the average of the 6 values in columns 1 through 6.

MEDIAN. The MEDIAN function works in exactly the same way as the mean function, requiring matrix references to the starting and ending columns of a particular row. Instead of finding the average value of these numbers, IFPS selects the value such that half the numbers are smaller than the median and half the numbers are larger than the median. For example, if there are 7 numbers, it choses the 4th largest number, since there are three numbers which are smaller and three numbers which are larger. If there are six numbers, however, IFPS also chooses the 4th largest (as shown in Figure 3-9). (The usual approach in statistics texts is to take the average of the 3rd and 4th values if there are 6 values; be sure to remember that IFPS does not do it this way!).

STDDEV. The STDDEV function finds the standard deviation of the sample defined by the MATRIX references. A typical STDDEV function is:

STD DEVIATION = STDDEV(MATRIX(COST,1),MATRIX(COST,6)) (3-3)

The STDDEV function is discussed in more detail in Section 7.1.5 where the relations among the standard deviation of the sample, the variance of the sample, the standard deviation of the population, and the variance of the population are shown.

MOVAVG. One simple forecast of what will happen is to assume that future values will be equal to the average of past values. A slightly more sophisticated forecast is to use only recent values. This can be done through the use of the MOVAVG function illustrated in Figure 3-10.

```
MODEL MOVAVG   VERSION OF  08/30/82  16:38
10 COLUMNS 1-6
20 X=25,27,33,26,44,30
30 Y=MOVAVG(X,.5,.5)
40 Z=MOVAVG(FUTURE X,.33,.33,.33)
50 W=MOVAVG(X,.5,.3,.2)
END OF MODEL
? solve
MODEL MOVAVG   VERSION OF  08/30/82  16:38 -- 6 COLUMNS 4 VARIABLES
ENTER SOLVE OPTIONS
?all
                    1       2       3       4       5       6

X                  25      27      33      26      44      30
Y                  25      26      30   29.50      35      37
Z                  26   28.33   28.67   34.33   33.33      37
W                  25   25.80   27.20   28.60   33.10   32.20
```

FIGURE 3-10. MOVING AVERAGE

To use the MOVAVG function, you specify the variable to be averaged and the relative weight to be given to each period, starting with the variable and working backwards in that row. In general form:

MOVAVG(variable, weight1,weight2,....weightn).

The last weight (weightn) refers to the current period and each preceding weight to a preceding period. For example:

MOVAVG(variable, weight1,weight2)

assigns weight2 to the current period and weight1 to the previous period. The weights allow you to give different importance to different past periods. The weights should add up to 1; however, if they do not, IFPS scales them for you automatically during the calculation so that they do add to 1.

Note that in Line 40 of Figure 3-10, the starting point for the variable is FUTURE X. FUTURE refers to one period from now (i.e. from the current column) just as PREVIOUS refers to one period ago. In Period 3, for example,

Z = MOVAVG(FUTURE X,.333,.333,.333) (3-4)

finds the average of the value of X in periods 4, 3, and 2.

You must be careful in interpreting the the values computed for MOVAVG for the starting and ending columns in a particular row. If MOVAVG refers to a value that is undefined because it is outside the model, two things happen:

1. the values outside the model are discarded.
2. the weights are rescaled based on the remaining points.

For example, the value given in column 1 for Z is 26, which is the average of the X values in columns 1 and 2 since MOVAVG(FUTURE X,.33,.33,.33) in column 1 calls for the values in columns 2, 1, and 0.

Line 50 in Figure 3-10 shows an example of unequal weights. Here we take MOVAVG(X,.5,.3,.2), which implies the current value contributes less to the forecast than the previous value and the previous value contributing less than the value two periods ago. The value of 27.2 in column 3 for W is obtained by taking 20% of 33, 30% of 27 and 50% of 25. (Check this!)

TREND. The TREND function performs simple linear regression. In Figure 3-11, sales are forecast from the trend line fitted to the relation between advertising and sales. To use TREND, you provide the model with historical values for two or more periods so that a regression line can be determined. In Figure 3-11, five periods of sales and advertising history are given and the sales anticipated in period 6 for the proposed advertising budget of $35,000 is forecast.

```
MODEL TREND  VERSION OF  08/30/82  16:38
10 COLUMNS 1-6
20 ADVERTISING EXPENDITURE =50000,30000,45000,40000,30000,35000
30 SALES=1500000,1400000,1420000,1550000,1600000,'
31 TREND(ADVERTISING EXPENDITURE)
END OF MODEL
?solve
MODEL TREND  VERSION OF  08/30/82  16:38 -- 6 COLUMNS 2 VARIABLES
ENTER SOLVE OPTIONS
?all

                              1       2       3       4       5       6

ADVERTISING EXPENDIT      50000   30000   45000   40000   30000   35000
SALES                   1500000 1400000 1420000 1550000 1600000 1499375
```

FIGURE 3-11. TREND

In computing the TREND function, IFPS generates a linear regression function of the form:

$$a + bX$$

where a and b are the coefficients of the regression line. Normally, these coefficients are not displayed. However, if, at any time before you SOLVE for the trend line you enter OPTION H2 on a separate line, these coefficients are printed out for you from then until you QUIT.

Linear regression models (including the TREND function) are discussed further in Section 7.5.

POLYFIT. Whereas the TREND function deals with the effects of one variable (e.g., advertising) in your model on another (e.g., sales), POLYFIT extrapolates a single variable forward in time. As shown in Figure 3-12, the extrapolation can have three forms, denoted by POLYFIT(0), POLYFIT(1), or POLYFIT(2).

```
MODEL POLY   VERSION OF   08/30/82   16:37
10 COLUMNS 1-6
20  SALES0=125,138,142,159,POLYFIT(0)
30  SALES1=125,138,142,159,POLYFIT(1)
40  SALES2=125,138,142,159,POLYFIT(2)
END OF MODEL
? solve
MODEL POLY   VERSION OF   08/30/82   16:37 -- 6 COLUMNS 3 VARIABLES
ENTER SOLVE OPTIONS
? all

                        1        2        3        4        5        6

SALES0                125      138      142      159      141      141
SALES1                125      138      142      159    167.5    178.1
SALES2                125      138      142      159    172.5    189.1
```

FIGURE 3-12. POLYFIT

If POLYFIT(0) is used, all future values are assumed to be the same and equal to the average of the past values. For POLYFIT(1), a regression line is fitted to the data and is used to extrapolate to the next period. In POLYFIT(2), the extrapolation is based on fitting a quadratic equation to the data and then extrapolating.

In Figure 3-12, the same four data points are used as inputs. The values in columns 5 and 6 are extrapolation values that result from the three forms of the POLYFIT function.

3.2.4 Mathematical Functions

Like BASIC and other computer programming languages, IFPS contains a number of built-in mathematical functions. These functions fall into three groups:

1. Functions of a single variable (natural logarithm, exponential, truncate,

roundup, round, and absolute value).

2. Functions of two or more variables (raising to a power, maximum, and minimum).

3. Table look-up functions (step function, interpolation).

These functions are illustrated in Figure 3-13.

```
MODEL MATH   VERSION OF   11/22/82   15:14
10 COLUMNS 1-6
20 X=1,5,10,12.3,12.7,-5
30 NATURAL LOG=NATLOG(X)
40 E TO THE POWER X=NATEXP(X)
50 TRUNCATE =TRUNCATE(X)
60 ROUNDUP=ROUNDUP(X)
70 ROUND =ROUND(X)
80 ABSOLUTE VALUE=ABS(X)
90 *
100 *FUNCTIONS OF TWO AND MORE VARIABLES
110 *
120 Y= .5,2,3,3.5,4,5
130 X TO THE POWER Y =XPOWERY(X,Y)
140 Z=10
150 MAXIMUM OF X Y AND Z=MAXIMUM(X,Y,Z)
160 MINIMUM OF X Y AND Z=MINIMUM(X,Y,Z)
END OF MODEL
? solve
MODEL MATH   VERSION OF   11/22/82   15:14 -- 6 COLUMNS 12 VARIABLES
ENTER SOLVE OPTIONS
? all
                              1        2        3        4        5        6

X                             1        5       10    12.30    12.70       -5
NATURAL LOG                   0    1.609    2.303    2.510    2.542    1.609
E TO THE POWER X          2.718    148.4    22026   219696   327748    .0067
TRUNCATE                      1        5       10       12       12       -5
ROUNDUP                       1        5       10       13       13       -5
ROUND                         1        5       10       12       13       -5
ABSOLUTE VALUE                1        5       10    12.30    12.70        5

FUNCTIONS OF TWO AND MORE VARIABLES

Y                         .5000        2        3    3.500        4        5
X TO THE POWER Y              1       25     1000     6526    26014    -3125
Z                            10       10       10       10       10       10
MAXIMUM OF X Y AND Z         10       10       10    12.30    12.70       10
MINIMUM OF X Y AND Z      .5000        2        3    3.500        4       -5
```

FIGURE 3-13. MATHEMATICAL FUNCTIONS

FUNCTIONS OF A SINGLE VARIABLE. The NATLOG and NATEXP functions compute natural logarithms (i.e., logarithms to the base e, not the base 10) and e to the power x. These functions occasionally show up in financial models. (The exponential function is also useful for obtaining exponentially distributed random variables in simulations; see Chapter V.)

The TRUNCATE, ROUNDUP, ROUND, and ABS functions are used to present numbers in uniform format. Suppose X = 12.30. TRUNCATE removes all fractional parts; therefore, TRUNCATE(X) = 12. ROUNDUP increases numbers with fractional parts to the next highest integer; therefore ROUNDUP(X) = 13. ROUND, on the other hand, finds the closest integer; therefore, ROUND(X) = 12.

> *IMPORTANT NOTE:* TRUNCATE, ROUNDUP, and ROUND work on the absolute values of numbers. Thus, if X = –4.3, TRUNCATE (X) = –4, ROUNDUP(X) = –5, and ROUND(X) = –4.

ABS finds the absolute value of numbers; that is, it removes the minus sign from negative numbers but leaves positive numbers as they are.

FUNCTIONS OF TWO OR MORE VARIABLES. Of all the mathematical functions, the one you are most likely to use frequently is XPOWERY. This function allows you to raise any positive number X to any power Y and to raise any negative number to an integer power. It is also the function you use to obtain square roots, since IFPS does not have a built-in square root function. For example, to find the square root of 9, you would write:

```
XPOWERY(9,0.5)                                          (3-5)
```

where, of course, the 0.5 represents the one-half power for the square root. You can also do arithmetic inside a mathematical function. For example, you could have written XPOWERY(9,1/2) in Equation (3-5) to obtain the square root.

In the case of maximum and minimum functions, you have to specify the list whose maximum or minimum you want. In lines 150 and 160 of Figure 3-13, three variables are used; you could just as easily have found the maximum or minimum of two or four or as many as nine variables.

INTERPOLATION ON. If you need a function that is not built-in to IFPS, you can represent it in your model by using INTERPOLATION ON. For example, suppose your market forecasts indicate the following relation between PRICE and SALES VOLUME:

PRICE	SALES VOLUME
1.50	10000
1.70	9000
1.85	8000
2.00	6500
2.10	5000

In graphical form:

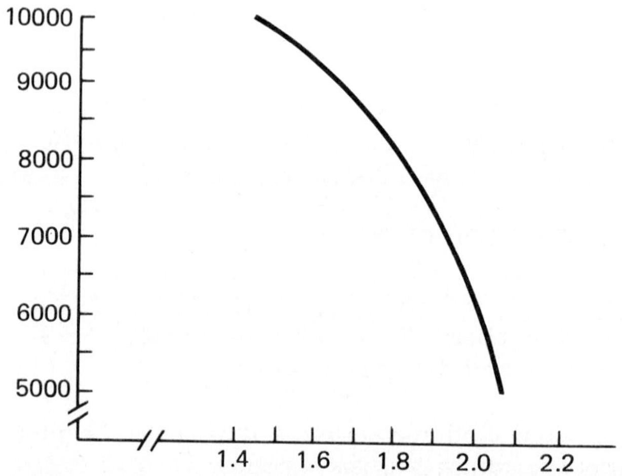

If you ask IFPS to find the SALES VOLUME at a price of 1.75, you are, in effect, asking it to read the graph for you. This is done with the INTERPOLATION ON function. For the forecast data, you would write:

```
10 PRICE = 1.75
20 SALES VOLUME=INTERPOLATION ON(PRICE,1.50,10000, 1.70, 9000,
        1.85, 8000, 2.00,6500,2.10,5000)
```

The INTERPOLATION ON function specifies the variable to be interpolated on (in our case, price) followed successively by the coordinates of points on the graph (in our case, prices and sales volumes). For example, the first pair of values corresponds to a price of 1.50 and a sales volume of 10000. When you specify a price for which the value is not given (e.g., 1.75), IFPS searches until it finds a value of price just greater than the one you asked for. It then assumes that the graph consists of a set of straight lines and computes an approximate value for your price by using "linear interpolation". Although the result is only approximate, it is perfectly adequate for most calculations. Figure 3-14 illustrates the INTERPOLATION ON function.

```
MODEL LISTFNCT   VERSION OF   11/22/82   15:18
10 COLUMNS  1
20 *
30 * INTERPOLATION ON FUNCTION
40 *
50 PRICE = 1.75
60 SALES VOLUME=INTERPOLATION ON(PRICE,1.50,10000,1.70,9000,1.85,'
70 8000,2.00,6500,2.10,5000)
80 *
90 * STEP FUNCTION
100 *
110 NO OF UNITS = 17
120 SALES PRICE=STEP(NO OF UNITS,1,1200,6,1000,11,900,21,800,51,700)
END OF MODEL
```

Figure 3-14. INTERPOLATION ON AND STEP FUNCTION
(This Figure is Continued on the Next Page)

```
? solve
MODEL LISTFNCT  VERSION OF  11/22/82  15:18 -- 1 COLUMNS 4 VARIABLES
ENTER SOLVE OPTIONS
? all
                                    1


 INTERPOLATION ON FUNCTION

PRICE                          1.750
SALES VOLUME                    8667

 STEP FUNCTION

NO OF UNITS                       17
SALES PRICE                      900

ENTER SOLVE OPTIONS
? what if
WHAT IF CASE 1
ENTER STATEMENTS
? price=1.35
?solve
ENTER SOLVE OPTIONS
? sales volume


***** WHAT IF CASE 1 *****
1 WHAT IF STATEMENT PROCESSED
INTERPOLATION VALUE OUT OF RANGE=                1.350
IN COMPUTATION OF VARIABLE SALES VOLUME

                                    1


SALES VOLUME                        0
```

FIGURE 3-14 . INTERPOLATION ON AND STEP FUNCTION
(Continued)

NOTE: In technical terms, given two pairs of values, X1,Y1 and X2,Y2, to find the value of Y corresponding to an X value between X1 and X2, apply the formula:

$$Y = Y1 + (Y2 - Y1)^* \frac{(X - X1)}{(X2 - X1)} \tag{3-6}$$

For example, given the X,Y pairs (10,25) and (20,48), then if X = 13, application of Equation 3-6 results in:

$$Y = 25+(48\text{-}25)*(13\text{-}10)/(20\text{-}10) = 31.9$$

The rules for the INTERPOLATION ON function include:

1. Pairs of values must be presented in increasing order of the first variable. In our example, the prices increased from 1.50 to 2.10. If you specify, for example, 1.85,8000, 1.50,10000, 2.00,6500 you will get incorrect answers.

2. There is a trade-off between accuracy and speed of computation. The more pairs of values you provide, the more accurate the result. However the more values you provide, the slower the search process required to find the answer. The minimum number of data pairs is two, and the maximum is 49.

3. If you ask for a value that is outside the range included in your data, you will receive an error message. For example, in our example above, if you ask for PRICE of 2.20, IFPS would tell you:

```
INTERPOLATION VALUE OUT OF RANGE    2.20
IN COMPUTATION OF VARIABLE SALES VOLUME
```

There is one exception, which occurs if you only specify two data pairs (that is, two points on the graph). Since two points define a straight line, IFPS is smart enough to extrapolate your straight line graph in both directions.

STEP FUNCTION. The STEP function can be used to represent data that are discontinuous such as prices with volume discounts. For example, if a manufacturer prices computer terminals as follows:

No. of Units	Price
1 - 5	1200
6 - 10	1000
11 - 20	900
21 - 50	800
>50	700

the graph would look as follows:

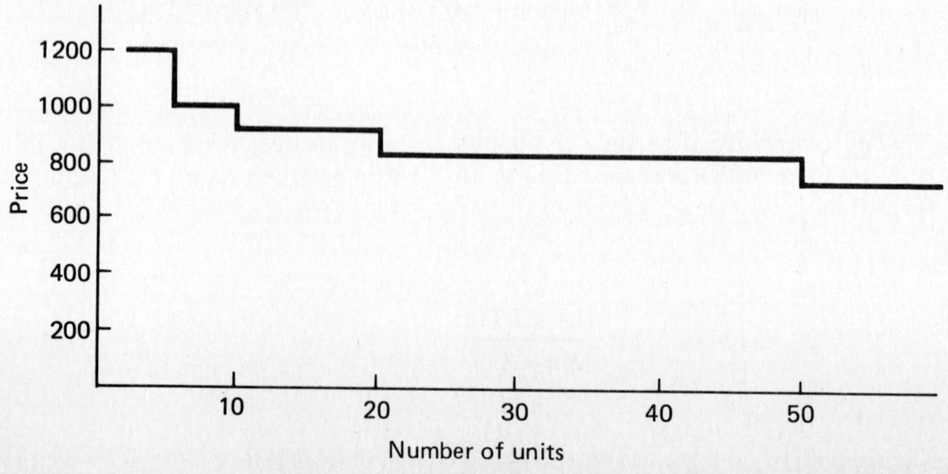

and the corresponding STEP function in IFPS would be:

```
PRICE= STEP(NO OF UNITS, 1,1200,6,1000,11,900,21,800,51,700)
```

As in the case of INTERPOLATION ON, you specify pairs of numbers, the first representing the minimum number of units to achieve that price and the second the corresponding price.

The STEP function can be extended to cover the case when each step has a functional form. To do so, you write expressions rather than constants for the second value of the pair. The STEP function is illustrated in lines 90 through 120 of Figure 3-14.

EXERCISE: Consider the IFPS equation:

```
PRICE = STEP(NO OF UNITS, 1,1200,6,1000 - 5*NO OF UNITS,11,900 -
4*NO OF UNITS,21,800 - 3*NO OF UNITS,51,750 - NO OF UNITS)
```

Plot the resulting price structure. (If you want the computer to do this exercise for you, have IFPS PLOT this function. PLOT is described in Section 4.3)

3.3 BUILT-IN SUBROUTINES (DEPRECIATION, AMORTIZATION)

Depreciation and amortization calculations are performed using subroutines. Subroutines are similar to functions, but differ in two respects:

1. They do not have a left-hand side and equal sign. They occupy one line in a model.

2. They can produce three or more lines of output, rather than a single line which is the case for an ordinary variable.

The straight-line depreciation subroutine shown in Figure 3-15 is typical. The subroutine is called STLINE DEPR and the parentheses are followed by the names of three inputs and three outputs. The inputs represent the investment, the salvage value as a percent of investment, and the lifetime (in years). The outputs are the depreciation during the period, the current book value, and the cumulative depreciation to date.

If you do not want all the output printed, just leave a blank when you specify the subroutine; for example, STLINE DEPR(COST,0.10,10,,BOOK) will print only the book value of the investment depreciated over 10 years to 10% of its initial value. The "blank" is created when you put two commas next to each other with no information between them.

```
MODEL SURTN  VERSION OF  11/22/82  15:19
10 COLUMNS 1-6
20STLINE DEPR(INVESTMENT,SALVAGE,LIFE,PERIODDEPRECIATION,BOOKVALUE,'
30      CUMULATIVE DEPRECIATION)
40 INVESTMENT=150000,0
50 SALVAGE=0.05
60 LIFE=6
END OF MODEL
? solve
MODEL SURTN  VERSION OF  11/22/82  15:19 -- 6 COLUMNS 6 VARIABLES
ENTER SOLVE OPTIONS
? all

                             1        2        3        4        5        6

PERIODDEPRECIATION       23750    23750    23750    23750    23750    23750
BOOKVALUE               126250   102500    78750    55000    31250     7500
CUMULATIVE DEPRECIAT     23750    47500    71250    95000   118750   142500
INVESTMENT              150000        0        0        0        0        0
SALVAGE                  .0500    .0500    .0500    .0500    .0500    .0500
LIFE                         6        6        6        6        6        6
```

FIGURE 3-15. STRAIGHT-LINE DEPRECIATION SUBROUTINE

If you use the same name for an output variable in different depreciation calculations, the individual values will be added up and only the total will be printed out. For example,

```
STLINE DEPR(WIDGETS,0.10,5,DEPRECIATION)
DECBAL DEPR(TRUCKS,0.05,7,DEPRECIATION)
```

will add up the contributions of WIDGETS and TRUCKS to the DEPRECIATION account.

Depreciation subroutines other than straight line depreciation are set up as follows:

SUM OF THE YEAR DIGITS:

SUM DEPR(INVESTMENT, SALVAGE VALUE FRACTION, ASSET LIFE, PERIOD DEPRECIATION,BOOK VALUE,CUMULATIVE DEPRECIATION)

DECLINING BALANCE DEPRECIATION:

DECBAL DEPR(INVESTMENT,SALVAGE VALUE FRACTION,ASSET LIFE, ACCELERATION CONSTANT,SWITCHOVER, PERIOD DEPRECIATION, BOOK VALUE, CUMULATIVE DEPRECIATION)

In declining balance depreciation, the acceleration constant determines the percentage of book value used to calculate the depreciation expense. A 200% constant is represented by a 2.0, a 150% constant by 1.5. The subroutine also allows for a SWITCHOVER of depreciation methods as soon as the alternative method allows for greater depreciation expense. SWITCHOVER can have three values:

0 = no switchover

1 = switchover to straight line

2 = switchover to sum-of-the-years digits.

GENERAL DECLINING BALANCE DEPRECIATION:

GENDECBAL DEPR(INVESTMENT, SALVAGE VALUE FRACTION, ASSET LIFE, ACCELERATION CONSTANT, SWITCHOVER, ALLOCATION, PERIOD DEPRECIATION, BOOK VALUE, CUMULATIVE DEPRECIATION)

This form of declining balance permits allocating a portion of the first year's accelerated depreciation in the first year of service. This is done by specifying the ALLOCATION fraction:

0	makes the routine defer the depreciation for a full year;
0.5	is the half-year convention, and
2	is the same as double declining balance.

ACRS DEPRECIATION:

Under the Economic Recovery Act of 1981, an Accelerated Cost Recovery System (ACRS) was authorized. Under the ACRS method, asset cost is recovered in a shorter time than previously allowed for acquisitions in 1981 or later. The ACRS subroutine,

ACRS DEPR(CATEGORY, PURCHASE YEAR, COST,ANNUAL DEPRECIATION, BOOK VALUE, CUMULATIVE DEPRECIATION)

implements this method. Eligible property is divided in class-life categories of 3, 5, 10, and 15 years. Real estate must be classified as either regular or low-income. The value of CATEGORY must be one of the following numbers, corresponding to the desired category of property:

Category	Category of Property
3	3-year property class
5	5-year property class
10	10-year property class
15	15-year property class
1	Regular real estate
2	Low-income real estate

Due to changes in the law in September 1982, the purchase years should always be entered as 1982.

Figure 3-16 illustrates the ACRS depreciation subroutine.

```
MODEL ACRS   VERSION OF   11/22/82   15:30
10 COLUMNS 1-6
20 ACRS DEPR(CATEGORY,PURCHASE YEAR,INVESTMENT,PERIODDEPRECIATION,'
30 BOOKVALUE,CUMULATIVE DEPRECIATION)
40 *
50 CATEGORY = 5
60 *
70 INVESTMENT = 150000,0
80 PURCHASE YEAR = 1983, PREVIOUS + 1
END OF MODEL
? solve
MODEL ACRS   VERSION OF   11/22/82   15:30 -- 6 COLUMNS 6 VARIABLES
ENTER SOLVE OPTIONS
? all
```

	1	2	3	4	5	6
PERIODDEPRECIATION	22500	33000	31500	31500	31500	0
BOOKVALUE	127500	94500	63000	31500	0	0
CUMULATIVE DEPRECIAT	22500	55500	87000	118500	150000	150000
CATEGORY	5	5	5	5	5	5
INVESTMENT	150000	0	0	0	0	0
PURCHASE YEAR	1983	1984	1985	1986	1987	1988

FIGURE 3-16. ACRS DEPRECIATION

AMORTIZATION SUBROUTINE:

The amortization subroutine is defined by:

AMORT(AMORTIZED LOAN, UNAMORTIZED LOAN, ANNUAL INTEREST RATE, ASSET LIFE, START COLUMN, PAYMENTS PER COLUMN, PAYMENT AMOUNT, PAYMENT TO INTEREST,PAYMENT TO PRINCIPAL, OUTSTANDING PRINCIPAL)

The first six quantities in the amortization subroutine are inputs. The amortized loan is reduced to zero over the life of the loan. The unamortized portion represents the balloon payment at the end (which may be zero). The nominal annual interest rate, the life of the loan in years, the time the loan is made (START COLUMN) and the number of payments per column are the other inputs. If the format is annual, the payments are the number of payments per year; if the PERIODS statement is used, the payments per column is the number of payments per period. As shown in Figure 3-17 on the next page, the amortization subroutine provides output information on the payment, the interest, total payment made to principal, and the current outstanding balance.

```
MODEL AMORT  VERSION OF  08/30/82  16:35
10 COLUMNS 1-6
20 AMORT(100000,0,INTEREST RATE,6,1,1,PAYMENT,INTEREST,PRINCIPAL,'
21 BALANCE)
30 INTEREST RATE=.14
END OF MODEL
? solve
MODEL AMORT  VERSION OF  08/30/82  16:35 -- 6 COLUMNS 5 VARIABLES
ENTER SOLVE OPTIONS
? all

                       1       2       3       4       5       6

PAYMENT            25716   25716   25716   25716   25716   25716
INTEREST           14000   12360   10490    8358    5928    3158
PRINCIPAL          11716   13356   15226   17357   19787   22558
BALANCE            88284   74928   59703   42345   22558       0
INTEREST RATE      .1400   .1400   .1400   .1400   .1400   .1400
```

FIGURE 3-17. AMORTIZATION SUBROUTINE

CHAPTER IV
ADVANCED CAPABILITIES OF IFPS

4.1 Solve Options

4.1.1 Choosing Variables to be Displayed
4.1.2 Choosing Columns to be Displayed
4.1.3 Inverting Rows and Columns
4.1.4 Miscellaneous Solve Options

4.2 WIDTH and OPT

4.3 Plotting Results Graphically

4.3.1 Basics of Plotting
4.3.2 Drawing More Sophisticated Graphs

4.4 Useful Calculational Features (L, MATRIX, SUM, IF, COLUMN)

4.4.1 Using Line Numbers Rather than Variable Names
4.4.2 Referring to a Single Number (MATRIX)
4.4.3 IF Statements in IFPS
4.4.4 SUM Function
4.4.5 Working Across Rather than Down (COLUMN)
4.4.6 Rules for COLUMN Computational Statements

4.5 Useful Command Features (', !, RESEQUENCE, COPY, COMPILESAVE, CROSSREF, EXPAND)

4.5.1 What to Do if Your Expression Does Not Fit on One Line (')
4.5.2 What to Do if You Want to Use a Special Character in its Ordinary Meaning (!)
4.5.3 Cleaning up Line Numbers (RESEQUENCE)
4.5.4 Making a Duplicate Copy of a Model or Report (COPY)
4.5.5 Saving Time in Executing the Model (COMPILESAVE)
4.5.6 Finding All References to a Variable (CROSSREF)
4.5.7 Printing Out Variable Names Rather than Line Numbers (EXPAND)

4.6 Data Files

4.6.1 The Dummy Model
4.6.2 The Data File
4.6.3 Obtaining Answers with a Data File (MODEL ...USING)
4.6.4 Creating and Saving a New Data File (DATAFILE)
4.6.5 Finding Out What Is in a Data File
4.6.6 Changing a Data File
4.6.7 Storing the Output of a Model for Future Use as Data (STORENT)
4.6.8 Combining Data from Several Files into a New File (DATASELECT)

4.7 Generating Formatted Reports (GENREPORT)

4.7.1 Creating a New Report
4.7.2 First Report Example
4.7.3 The WIDTH Command
4.7.4 The COLUMN TITLES Command
4.7.5 The FORMAT Command
4.7.6 The SPACE Command
4.7.7 A Report Format for the Pro Forma Profit and Loss Statement

4.8 Consolidation

4.8.1 Simple, Additive Consolidation
4.8.2 Weighted Consolidation
4.8.3 Variance Analysis
4.8.4 Using the Consolidated Model in Computations
4.8.5 Using Multiple Data Files with a Model
4.8.6 Creating Consolidated Data Files (CONSOLDF)
4.8.7 Modeling Hierarchical Situations

4.9 An Example Involving Data Files, Reports, and Consolidation

4.10 Additional Editing Commands

4.10.1 Using " Rather Than / For Editing
4.10.2 Finding All Occurrences of a Specific Phrase
4.10.3 Changing All Occurrences of a Specific Phrase
4.10.4 Additional Editing Commands for Data Files and Data in Models

CHAPTER IV
ADVANCED CAPABILITIES OF IFPS

The first three chapters are a primer on creating IFPS models. If you know and understand the concepts and ideas in these chapters you can use IFPS as a personal tool to assist you in solving a wide variety of problems and to support you in many decision situations. You have learned how to set up a model, how to perform sensitivity analysis, how to use built-in functions, and how to approach problems involving uncertainty.

IFPS, of course, is more than a personal tool for solving small to medium scale problems. It also provides the capability for dealing with large scale problems and for communicating results within the organization. In this chapter we present additional capabilities of IFPS that are useful particularly for:

- plotting results
- creating reports in a format that improves communication between the creator and the users of models
- handling large volumes of data
- consolidating multiple models into a single report.

Finally, there are a number of convenience features in IFPS that allow you to deal with specific situations or to simplify the mechanics of IFPS. These features are discussed in Sections 4.4 and 4.5.

In the first reading of this Chapter, particularly if you are new to IFPS, you may want to skip Sections 4.6 (Data Files), 4.7 (Generating Formatted Reports) and 4.8 (Consolidation). As you gain skill and tackle larger problems, you will find these sections important for your work.

4.1 SOLVE OPTIONS

When IFPS asks you to ENTER SOLVE OPTIONS it is offering you choices on what information you want displayed on your video screen or hard copy terminal and on how you want the output to appear. That is, solve options are really display control options. No matter which solve options you specify, IFPS will perform the same calculations. The following sections outline some of the options available to you. Figure 4-1 shows examples of some of the solve options for the simple IFPS model shown in Figure 2-9 of Section 2.2.

4.1.1 Choosing Variables To Be Displayed

In most of the examples thus far, we asked IFPS to display the values of all the variables for each time period. Specifically, we replied ALL when IFPS asked us to enter solve options.

```
? solve
MODEL GRAY  VERSION OF  01/07/83  11:46 -- 6 COLUMNS 5 VARIABLES
ENTER SOLVE OPTIONS
? columns 1,4,6
? sales thru net income

                                  1        4        6

SALES                           100    195.3    305.2
EXPENSES                         75      150      175
NET INCOME                       25    45.31    130.2

ENTER SOLVE OPTIONS
? invert
? sales thru net income

                              SALES EXPENSES NET INCO
       1                        100       75       25
       4                      195.3      150    45.31
       6                      305.2      175    130.2

ENTER SOLVE OPTIONS
? columns 6,3,2,1
? normal
? sales,net income

                                  6        3        2        1

SALES                         305.2    156.3      125      100
NET INCOME                    130.2    31.25       25       25
```

FIGURE 4-1. EXAMPLE OF SOLVE OPTIONS

In some examples, such as those dealing with WHAT IF and SENSITIVITY in Chapter III, you may have noticed that we specified the names of only some variables and, when we did, obtained output only of the variables named. This capability for being selective in which rows are displayed is a general capability. The following are typical examples of this solve option.

ENTRY	RESULT
ALL	All variables shown
NET INCOME	Only the line containing NET INCOME diplayed
SALES THRU NET INCOME	All lines starting from SALES and including NET INCOME
SALES,NET INCOME	Only two lines are shown.

Important points you should know:

- Even though you ask for only a partial display of results, IFPS solves the entire model internally. The results are the same no matter which variables you specify in the solve options.

- IFPS accepts only one line of variable names in response to ENTER SOLVE OPTIONS. If you have a long list of names, just keep typing the list without hitting the carriage return key. The terminal will automatically return for you. If you hit a carriage return, IFPS assumes you are through with your list and the remaining variable names you type are ignored. Thus, the variable list is always assumed to be the last line of the solve options and all other solve options must appear ahead of this line.

- THRU is a reserved word. You must use THRU rather than the more normal English speeling of "through". In a list of variables, you can mix single variables and groups of variables. For example, SALES THRU NET INCOME, NET INCOME RATIO is an acceptable specification of the solve option.

4.1.2 Choosing Columns to Be Displayed

In addition to being able to select which rows (i.e., variables) you want displayed, you can also select which columns should appear. This capability is useful, for example, if you have more than six columns and you do not need details for each period. To select columns, you specify the word COLUMNS followed by their values or names. For example,

```
COLUMNS 1-3,6,10
```

will print columns 1 through 3, column 6, and column 10. If you ask for COLUMNS 1983-1985, 1990, 1995 you will get those years.

Important points you should know:

- Columns MUST be specified before variables in the solve option. (The reason is that IFPS begins generating output immediately after you specify one line of variable names.)

- Once you specify a columns option for a model, it remains in force for all subsequence SOLVE commands for that model unless you change it by specifying a different columns option. If you move from one model to another, the columns option is deleted.

- If you do not specify a columns option initially, you get all columns. If you have been using a columns option to restrict output and want to see all the columns, you must repeat the information in the COLUMNS line in your MODEL.

- Columns are always displayed in the order you specify. For example, COLUMNS 10, 1-3 will display column 10 before columns 1 through 3. That is, you can display columns in any order you want.

- A hyphen between two numbers (e.g., 1-3) implies all columns inclusively.

- If you have used names for column headings (e.g., QRT1, QRT2,....) you can specify either the name of the column or its numeric position. You can also use a hyphen to specify a set of columns. For example, if your headings are QRT1 through QRT9, it is perfectly legitimate for you to use COLUMNS 1-3, QRT7-QRT9 to display the first three and last three columns.

4.1.3. Inverting Rows and Columns

In working with some models you may be interested in the values in a large number of columns but only for a few variables. In this case you will find it handy to be able to interchange rows and columns by using the INVERT solve option. As shown in Figure 4-1, you can combine the INVERT option with the columns option and the selection of variables. Like the COLUMNS option, the INVERT option remains in force until changed. If you want to go back to the normal format, type NORMAL as a solve option.

4.1.4 Miscellaneous Solve Options

Other solve options available in IFPS are listed in Table 4-1. Options that are described as being able to restore features are the default options; that is, they are used automatically by IFPS if you do not specify another solve option first. For more detail on how they work, try them out on a simple model of your own.

TABLE 4-1.

ADDITIONAL SOLVE OPTIONS

NOCOMMENTS	Does not display comment lines (i.e.lines beginning with a *). You can improve efficiency by using NOCOMMENTS
COMMENTS	Restores comments for display
NOINDENT	Eliminates all indentation of variable names. NOINDENT can improve efficiency
INDENT	Restores indentation
DOUBLE	Causes output to be printed out double space
SINGLE	Restores single spacing

SPACE n	When included in the variable list, leaves n blank lines in the output, where n is a number such as 1, 2, or 3
ZEROSUP	Suppresses printing a variable (that is, an entire row) if all the values of the variable are zero in the columns selected for printout by the columns option
ZEROPRINT	Restores printing of zero variables
POSOPT+	Prefaces all positive numbers with a + sign
POSOPTCR	Adds CR to all positive numbers
POSOPT	Restores printing of positive numbers without + or CR
NEGOPT	NEGOPT provides optional ways of printing negative numbers. Forms available include NEGOPT PAREN which puts negative numbers in parenthesis, NEGOPT -A which puts the minus sign after the number, NEGOPTDB which adds DB to the number, and NEGOPTCR which adds CR to the number. The default option is NEGOPT, which prefaces numbers with a - sign.

The solve options listed in Table 4-1, as well as options involving COLUMNS, remain in effect as long as you do not change them, but only as long as you work with the current model. If you issue a MODEL command you must ask for these solve options again if you want them to apply.

4.2 WIDTH AND OPT

WIDTH and OPT are really two special solve options and they must be preceded by a SOLVE command. They are sufficiently important that they warrant separate discussion.

WIDTH allows you to specify:

- the overall width of the display (that is, the number of characters on a line)
- the maximum number of characters to be shown for variable names
- the number of characters in each column
- the number of decimal places for each value.

Thus, WIDTH is a simple, yet powerful way of controlling how much information you display in a row and how you space information within a row.

The following is a typical example of the WIDTH command:

```
WIDTH  120 30 10 3
```

The word WIDTH is followed, in order, by the number of characters on the line (in our example, 120), the number of characters for variable names (30), the number of spaces in each column (10), and the number of decimal places in each value (3). If you do not specify WIDTH, IFPS uses the default values listed in Table 4-2. The allowed limits on the value of each parameter are also shown in the table.

TABLE 4-2

DEFAULT VALUES AND PARAMETERS OF THE WIDTH COMMAND

Parameter	Default Value	Allowable Range
Total number of characters	78	20-132
Variable name length	24	1-100
Column width	9	1-32
Number of decimal places	–1	(–1)-9

If you use –1 for the number of decimal places, the location of the decimal point and the number of decimal places will vary. IFPS makes the choice based on the value to be displayed and the number of spaces available in a column. Another restriction on the number of decimal places is that it must be two less than the column width. Thus, for example, you cannot specify 78 20 3 2 but you can specify 78 20 4 2.

If you look at the default values, you see that there are 78 spaces available (typical of the number of columns on a CRT or a portable terminal), 24 of which are reserved for variable names. Hence 54 spaces are available for data. Since the column width is 9, the 54 spaces provide 6 columns. If you have 8 columns (as in the New Product Model of Section 2.7), you can put them all on one line by reducing the column width to 6 or by reducing the variable name space to 22 and the column width to 7. In the case of this book, we have 68 spaces on a line. Therefore, in Figure 4-2, we show you how to put 8 columns on a line by using 68 20 6. Here we use 20 spaces for the variable name and use 6 spaces for each column to present 8 columns of information on a line.

You can, if you so choose, specify only the first, first two, or first three parameters of the WIDTH command. For example,

WIDTH 132 30

requests 132 characters and 30 spaces for names but leaves column width and decimal places at their default value.

Like other SOLVE options, once you specify a WIDTH command, it remains in force until you give another WIDTH command. However, the first parameter of the WIDTH command (total number of characters per line) is more powerful than a SOLVE option; it remains in force throughout an entire terminal session, even when you move from one MODEL to another. (You will find that all other specifications in SOLVE will return to their default values when you move from one MODEL to another.)

The OPT command is a subset of the WIDTH command. It allows you to specify the last three parameters of the WIDTH command and this command applies only while working

```
MODEL PRODUCT  VERSION OF  08/30/82  18:21 -- 8 COLUMNS 13 VARIABLES
ENTER SOLVE OPTIONS
? width 68 20 6
? all

                          1     2     3     4     5     6     7     8


          NEW PRODUCT MODEL
SALES VOLUME           1200  1277  1358  1442  1531  1623  1719  1820
MARKET                 8000  8240  8487  8742  9004  9274  9552  9839
MARKET SHARE          .1500 .1550 .1600 .1650 .1700 .1750 .1800 .1850
GROSS SALES            3000  3193  3395  3606  4209  4463  4728  5006
UNIT PRICE            2.500 2.500 2.500 2.500 2.750 2.750 2.750 2.750
OPERATING COST         2700  2874  3055  3245  3720  3944  4178  4423
PRODUCTION COST       1.250 1.250 1.250 1.250 1.350 1.350 1.350 1.350
OVERHEAD                  1     1     1     1 1.080 1.080 1.080 1.080
NET INCOME              300 319.3 339.5 360.6 489.8 519.4 550.2 582.5
INVESTMENT             2500     0     0     0     0     0     0     0

NET PRESENT VALUE     -2208 -1907 -1595 -1273-847.8-409.6 41.64 506.0
INTERNAL RATE OF RET                                    .1372 .3056

DISCOUNT RATE         .1200 .1200 .1200 .1200 .1200 .1200 .1200 .1200
```

FIGURE 4-2. USING WIDTH TO SHOW EIGHT COLUMNS

on your current model. For example,

```
OPT  14,8,2
```

indicates that you want 14 spaces for the variable name, eight spaces for each column and two decimal places. The OPT command allows you to change the appearance of your printout without having to repeat how many characters wide you want the printout.

4.3 PLOTTING RESULTS GRAPHICALLY

If you have results that you want to present in graphic form, you can ask IFPS to draw you a graph. Like WIDTH, PLOT is a SOLVE option that is so important it deserves a separate section of its own. In Section 4.3.1 we discuss the basic elements of obtaining a plot. If you are only interested in obtaining a quick plot of results for your own use, read Section 4.3.1 and skip Section 4.3.2. If, however, you want to label the graphs and/or use other specialized features, you should read Section 4.3.2, which discusses these features.

4.3.1 Basics of Plotting

To obtain graphic output, you type PLOT. IFPS solves your model and then enters a plotting subsystem. IFPS responds by asking you to ENTER PLOT OPTIONS. You need to:

1. Tell IFPS how you want to graph the data.

2. Tell IFPS what quantities you want plotted.

You do this by first asking for:

```
GRID 36,64,8
```

This is the largest graph you can obtain. It has 36 vertical lines, 64 horizontal spaces, and sets up both a horizontal and a vertical scale for you. The value 8 is a grid option that is explained in Sec. 4.3.2. IFPS uses periods for the horizontal axis. If you forget to specify the GRID, IFPS will use the 36,64,8 format by default.

You then tell IFPS which variables to PLOT , using the format PLOT variable1, variable2,... Note that the word PLOT followed by the names of variables, separated from one another by commas is required. In Figure 4-3 you see plots of three variables: sales, expenses, and net profit. IFPS uses numbers corresponding to the sequence in which you asked for the variables to draw the plots. For example, in Figure 4-3, sales are plotted using the symbol 1. IFPS automatically provides you with a legend indicating the meaning of each symbol.

If you want to draw several graphs, you can issue a series of PLOT commands without repeating the GRID command. If, however, you want to change the GRID specifications, you can do so by issuing another GRID command. A word of advice: Although IFPS lets you plot up to 9 variables on a single graph, don't ask for more than three or four variables on a single plot. Graphs become difficult to interpret if you try to present too much information.

If you are satisfied with the default (or with the current) GRID, you can use a single instruction to obtain your plot. For example, if you simply write:

```
PLOT SALES, EXPENSES,NET PROFIT
```

and nothing else, you will get the same result as Figure 4-3. Try it!

4.3.2 Drawing More Sophisticated Graphs

We will now briefly discuss the various PLOT options available to you. These options must be specified before you give the list of variables to be plotted. Once specified, they remain in force until countermanded by you. This section has been written as a catalog explaining the various options, so you can come back to it when you need specific features. The best way to see the results of using these options is to sit down at a terminal and do each of the EXERCISES.

GRID. If you want fewer than 36 vertical lines or fewer than 64 columns, you simply specify the appropriate number in the GRID command. For example, GRID 12, 24, 8 gives you 12 vertical lines and 24 rows.

You have probably wondered by now why you need the 8 in the GRID specification. Actually, you can use any value from 1 to 9 for this "grid option" position, but the appearance of the graph will change. Table 4-3 list the effects of the grid options.

```
? solve
MODEL GRAY  VERSION OF  01/07/83  11:46 -- 6 COLUMNS 5 VARIABLES
? plot
ENTER PLOT OPTIONS
? grid 36,64,8
? plot sales,expenses,net income


   350


                                                                    1
   300




   250
                                                        1



   200                                      1

                                                        2           2

                                1
   150                                      2

                    1           2                                   3


   100  1           2

        2
                                                        3

    50                                      3

        3           3           3


      0 +-----------+-----------+-----------+-----------+-----------+

        1           2           3           4           5           6


         1 - SALES
         2 - EXPENSES
         3 - NET INCOME
```

FIGURE 4-3. IFPS PLOT EXAMPLE

TABLE 4-3

GRID OPTIONS

Grid Option	Result
1	Horizontal and vertical grid line
2	Horizontal grid lines, vertical axis
3	Vertical grid lines, horizonal axis
4	Horizontal and vertical axes, + sign at grid
5	Horizontal grid lines only
6	Vertical grid lines only
7	No axes or grid lines
8	Horizontal and vertical axes only
9	Closest grid line to zero used for horizontal and vertical axes.

EXERCISE: Plot the data shown in Figure 4-3 for each of the grid options listed in Table 4-3. Use only 20 vertical lines and 40 horizontal spaces.

TITLE. You can put titles on your graphs by specifying both the position of the title and its text. For example, if you specify:

```
TITLE 1 TOP CENTER/RESULTS OF SIMPLE IFPS MODEL
TITLE 2 LEFT CENTER/DOLLARS
```

the result is that shown in Figure 4-4. In general, you specify:

TITLE number location position/text

That is, begin with the word TITLE followed with a sequence number between 1 and 10. The sequence number determines the order of printing and allows you to select which lines you want to change as you move from one plot to the next. The location can contain any of the reserved words:

TOP above the plot
LEFT to the left of the vertical axis
BOTTOM below the plot

Position can refer either to:

CENTER which centers the text on the top, left, or bottom
MARGIN which left justifies the text

Having positioned a line of the title, IFPS prints exactly what you put down after the /.

If you want to remove the entire title, you write:

```
TITLE CLEAR .
```

```
? plot
ENTER PLOT OPTIONS
? grid 36,64,8
? title 1 top center/results of simple ifps model
? title 2 left center/dollars
? plot sales,expenses,net income

                         RESULTS OF SIMPLE IFPS MODEL

   350




                                                                   1
   300




   250
                                                       1



D
O  200                                     1
L
L                                                      2           2
A
R                              1
S  150                                     2

                   1           2                                   3


   100 1           2

       2
                                                       3

    50                                     3

       3            3           3



     0 +-----------+-----------+-----------+-----------+-----------+

       1           2           3           4           5           6

        1 - SALES
        2 - EXPENSES
        3 - NET INCOME
```

FIGURE 4-4. CREATING TITLES AND LABELS ON A PLOT

EXERCISE: Expand the title of Figure 4-4 so that it lists the variables plotted and labels the time axis.

PLOTTING VARIABLES OTHER THAN COLUMN. If you want the horizontal axis to be a variable rather than a column heading, you use the VS option. For example,

```
VS COST
PLOT SALES, PROFIT
```

results in a plot of sales and profit against cost rather than time.

CHOOSING THE RANGE OF VALUES TO BE PLOTTED. You can select the minimum and maximum values of the vertical and horizontal axes by using the RANGE command. For example,

```
RANGE 0,250
```

plots only vertical axis values between 0 and 250. Similarly, RANGE 0,250,2,5 plots only values between 0 and 250 for periods 2 through 5. You must specify the vertical minimum and maximum. If you do not specify the horizontal maximum and minimum, the entire axis is plotted.

EXERCISE: Modify Figure 4-3 so that it shows only values between 0 and 200 and periods 2 through 4.

SCALE. The SCALE option allows you to divide all values by a constant factor before plotting the results. The general form is:

SCALE vertical constant, horizontal constant

For example,

```
SCALE 1000
TITLE 2 LEFT CENTER/THOUSANDS OF DOLLARS
```

results in plotting values in thousands of dollars and labeling the vertical axis accordingly. Scaling of the horizontal axis can be used only in conjunction with the VS option.

USING CHARACTERS OTHER THAN NUMBERS. If you don't like to see numbers on your plot, you can use any typewriter symbol by following the plot specification with a symbol specification. For example:

```
PLOT SALES/$/,EXPENSES/-/,PROFIT/#/
```

results in $ signs appearing for sales, – appearing for expenses, and # appearing for profit. The characters you can use depend on what is available on your terminal.

EXERCISE: Modify Figure 4-3 so that it shows sales in units of 100's of dollars and uses the symbols $, –, and #. Title the axes appropriately.

PUTTING TIME ON THE VERTICAL AXIS. If you want to turn your graph around so that the time period appears on the vertical rather than the horizontal axis, you can do so by specifying INVERT as a plot option. INVERT will remain in force until you specify NORMAL to return time to the horizontal axis.

EXERCISE: Invert Figure 4-3.

WHAT YOU CAN DO WHEN VALUES OVERLAP. Every so often you will find that two or more variables take on the same value. The result is that you observe an * on the printout. The * calls attention to the fact that two or more variables are trying to occupy the same space and that, in fact, two or more curves cross at that point. If you want a character other than an *, you can use the SOVER option. For example SOVER $ puts a $ sign at these values. If you want to use the last character plotted, use SOVER LAST.

4.4 USEFUL CALCULATIONAL FEATURES (L, MATRIX, SUM, IF, COLUMN)

4.4.1 Using Line Numbers Rather than Variable Names

If you choose, you can substitute the line number on which a variable is defined for the name of the variable. For example,

```
10 SALES = L20*L30
20 MARKET = 8000, PREVIOUS MARKET *1.05
30 MARKET SHARE = 0.15, PREVIOUS MARKET SHARE + 0.005
```

is just as valid as writing for Line 10

```
10 SALES = MARKET * MARKET SHARE
```

As shown above, line number references involve the letter L followed by a number. As you become more experienced with IFPS you will find the use of line number references particularly handy. You do have to be careful, however. If you ask IFPS to change line numbers with a RESEQUENCE command (see Section 4.5.3), line number references are corrected for you automatically. However, if for some reason you move the line on which a particular variable is defined, you have to change the references to that variable which are by line number and change them manually. If you are faced with this problem, the CROSSREF command explained in Section 4.5.6 will be of help in finding all references to the variable.

One of the risks of using line number references is that if you do it too often, the model loses its readability and hence loses one of the important advantages of IFPS as a communications tool. Fortunately, you can use the computer to interpret the line number references for you. As described in Section 4.5.7, IFPS has an EXPAND option on the LIST command that results in substituting names for line numbers.

4.4.2 Referring to a Single Number (MATRIX)

If you want to refer to a single number in the model (e.g., the revenue for the year), you use MATRIX. The term comes from the idea that the output of an IFPS model is a two-dimensional matrix whose rows are the variables and whose columns are defined by the COLUMNS statement. For example, if the revenue for the year is given in Column 4 of CUMULATIVE REVENUE, you can refer to it by:

```
MATRIX(CUMULATIVE REVENUE,4)
```

In general, the first term in parenthesis refers to the row (i.e., the variable) and the second term to the column. Figure 4-5 illustrates the use of MATRIX.

```
MODEL SIMPLE1  VERSION OF  08/30/82  18:04
10 COLUMNS 1-4
20 SALES = 100,PREVIOUS SALES *1.25
30 EXPENSES =75,100,125,150
40 NET REVENUE = SALES -EXPENSES
50 CUMULATIVE REVENUE = PREVIOUS + NET REVENUE
60*
70*NET REVENUE THIS QUARTER AS PERCENTAGE OF ANNUAL REVENUE
80*
90 PERCENT OF TOTAL REVENUE=NET REVENUE/MATRIX(CUMULATIVE REVENUE,4)
END OF MODEL
? solve
MODEL SIMPLE1  VERSION OF  08/30/82  18:04 -- 4 COLUMNS 5 VARIABLES
ENTER SOLVE OPTIONS
? all

                          1       2       3       4

SALES                   100     125   156.3   195.3
EXPENSES                 75     100     125     150
NET REVENUE              25      25   31.25   45.31
CUMULATIVE REVENUE       25      50   81.25   126.6

NET REVENUE THIS QUARTER AS PERCENTAGE OF ANNUAL REVENUE

PERCENT OF TOTAL REV  .1975   .1975   .2469   .3580
```

FIGURE 4-5. USE OF MATRIX TO REFER TO A SINGLE VALUE

4.4.3 IF Statements in IFPS

Just as in BASIC or FORTRAN, you can make your results depend on which conditions are true. For example, as shown in Figure 4-6, your tax rate may depend on the size of the year's profit.

The format for an IF statement, which always appears on the right of an = sign, is:

> IF the test is true, THEN assign the value shown, ELSE assign an alternative value.

The alternative value can be a number or an expression.

The test conditions are always expressed with a period before them and after them. They are:

.LT. less than	.LE. less than or equal to
.GT. greater than	.GE. greater than or equal to
.EQ. equal to	.NE. not equal to

```
MODEL IF   VERSION OF  08/30/82  18:03
10 COLUMNS 1-6
20 PROFIT BEFORE TAX=25000,PREVIOUS PROFIT BEFORE TAX*1.2
30 TAX RATE=IF PROFIT BEFORE TAX.LE.30000 THEN .35 ELSE .48
40 TAX=TAX RATE*PROFIT BEFORE TAX
50 NET PROFIT = PROFIT BEFORE TAX - TAX
END OF MODEL
? solve
MODEL IF   VERSION OF  08/30/82  18:03 -- 6 COLUMNS 4 VARIABLES
ENTER SOLVE OPTIONS
? all
```

	1	2	3	4	5	6
PROFIT BEFORE TAX	25000	30000	36000	43200	51840	62208
TAX RATE	.3500	.3500	.4800	.4800	.4800	.4800
TAX	8750	10500	17280	20736	24883	29860
NET PROFIT	16250	19500	18720	22464	26957	32348

FIGURE 4-6. IF STATEMENT

4.4.4 SUM Function

In many models you will calculate the components of a quantity individually (e.g., the components of operating cost) and then add them up. That is, you will want to take totals or subtotals within a column. Rather than having to write out the names of all the variables or put down all the line numbers, you can simply use the SUM function.

The SUM function adds up all the variables specified and records the total. You can either list two variables (e.g., SUM(L20,L35) adds up the values of lines 20 and 35) or you can use THRU to obtain all variables from the beginning to the end of a sequence (e.g., SUM(DOMESTIC SALES THRU INVESTMENT INCOME)). Unfortunately, putting more than two variable names in the list won't work. For example, trying to add lines 20, 35, and 50 together by writing SUM(L20,L35,L50) won't work. You have to write L20 + L35 + L50.

An example of the usefulness of the SUM function can be seen in Figure 2-10 in Section 2.9. There, we wrote

```
370 TOTAL OPERATING EXPENSE = SUM(L290 THRU L350)
```

rather than the more cumbersome:

```
370 TOTAL OPERATING EXPENSE = ADVERTISING + COMMISSIONS +
SALARIES +PAYROLL TAXES + LEASES + NOTE INTEREST +
DEPRECIATION
```

You will generally find it advisable to use the SUM function in a line close to the variables being summed. The reason is that you can easily find the quantities being added and can check the model for correctness. When using THRU references in SUM commands you have to be careful not to include extraneous quantities. Although typically not a problem when setting up your model originally, extraneous quantities can appear if you insert a line that is in the middle of a THRU.

4.4.5 Working Across Rather than Down (COLUMN)

Almost all computational work in IFPS is done row by row, where each row represents a different variable. However, there are occassions when you want to put results in a column rather than a row. For example, you may want to have columns representing quarterly and annual results, where the column headings would be:

```
QUARTER1      QUARTER2      QUARTER3      QUARTER4      ANNUAL
```

where the first four columns represent the quarters and the last column represents the yearly total. One way of achieving this result, based on what we have discussed thus far, is to compute the annual value as:

```
PREVIOUS + PREVIOUS 2 + PREVIOUS 3 + PREVIOUS 4
```

This form is cumbersome to implement, and becomes much worse if you are, for example, trying to add monthly results into annual values. One alternative is to follow the approach used in the consolidation example, Model COMPANY, in Section 4.8.4. There we created a separate line to give cumulative totals. A second alternative, one we believe you will find easier and more natural to implement, is to use the COLUMN computational statement.

> *NOTE:* The COLUMN computational statement is different from the definitions of COLUMNS at the beginning of a model.

The objective in using COLUMN is to define directly the values of an entire column of a model or of specific lines within a column. The following are typical examples of the COLUMN statement:

```
COLUMN 5 = 100*COLUMN 3/COLUMN 4
COLUMN 8 FOR SALES = COLUMN 7/.8
COLUMN 6 FOR L10 THRU L50 = C 4/C 3
COLUMN ANNUAL = SUM(C QUARTER 1 THRU C QUARTER 4)
```

The first example states that each element in column 5 is obtained by taking the ratio of column 3 to column 4 and multiplying by a hundred. That is, COLUMN 5 gives the percentage that column 3 is of column 4.

The second example defines only the value of sales in column 8. That is, FOR defines the row for which the expression on the right hand side is true. You can have a single variable (e.g. SALES), a list of variables (e.g., SALES,COST,PROFIT), or a THRU statement to define a set of variables. The latter is the case in the third example.

In the third example, we define COLUMN 6 for all lines from 10 through 50 in terms of the ratio of columns 4 and 3. Note that we use the abbreviation C for column.

NOTE: You must write out the word COLUMN on the left hand side. However, it is not necessary to write out COLUMN on the right hand side. C can be used as an abbreviation. You can use either C3 or C 3 to refer to column 3.

The last example returns to the problem we posed at the beginning of this section, namely adding columns to obtain totals. This example could also have been written:

```
COLUMN 5 = SUM(C 1 THRU C 5)
```

That is, you can refer to columns either by their name or by their position.

4.4.6 Rules for COLUMN Computational Statements

COLUMN computational statements have several rules and limitations associated with them. You should go over the following list before you start using COLUMN statements.

LOCATION IN MODEL. Like variables, COLUMN statements can be in any order and are written as separate lines in the model.

EXCEPTION: If you use FOR in a COLUMN statement, all the variables referenced after the FOR must have been defined previously, that is, they must have lower line numbers.

ORDER OF COMPUTATION. If any COLUMN statements are used in the model, IFPS partitions the model into two sections, the regular column section and the special column section. The location of the partition, let's call it k, is the first (lowest number) column referred to on the left-hand side of a COLUMN statement. For all columns before k, the usual row logic of IFPS applies; for column k and beyond you must use COLUMN computational statements to obtain answers.

NOTE: The partition between row and column logic acts like a wall. You *cannot* use results from a COLUMN calculation in a row calculation. For example, the following sequence will not work:

```
10 COLUMN 4 = SUM (C1 THRU C3)
20 X = 10,20,30
30 Y = X + MATRIX(X,4)
```

Try it and see what happens!

FORMAT. In general, the left-hand side has the word COLUMN and the name or number of the column to be computed. This column definition can be for the entire column or for part of a column, the latter if FOR is used. The right hand side can be any valid IFPS right hand side, including references to columns, with some specific exceptions.

EXCEPTIONS for RIGHT HAND SIDE:

1. You cannot reference the functions NPVC, MOVAVG, TREND, OR POLYFIT.

2. You cannot reference subroutines such as those for amortization and depreciation

ORDER OF SOLVING. IFPS performs COLUMN computations in column order, no matter what order the columns are referred to. For example,

```
70 COLUMN 4 FOR A,B = C 1 + C 3
80 COLUMN 5 FOR A,B, X THRU Z = C 1 + C 2
90 COLUMN 4 FOR X THRU Z = C 1/TOTAL SALES
```

results in IFPS evaluating all of the column 4 references before column 5.

RESOLUTION OF AMBIGUITY. If you seemingly define column entries twice, IFPS uses the first definition you give. For example,

```
10 COLUMN 4 FOR SALES = C 3
20 COLUMN 4 = SUM(C 1 THRU C3)
```

results in adding the values of columns 1 through 3 for all values in column 4 except the value of sales.

NOT DEFINING A VALUE. If you fail to define a value in a special COLUMN it will be left blank.

4.5 USEFUL COMMAND FEATURES (', !, RESEQUENCE, COPY, COMPILESAVE, CROSSREF, EXPAND)

4.5.1 What to Do If Your Expression Does Not Fit on One Line (')

If there is not enough space on one line for what you want to say, you have two options. If you restrain yourself and do not hit the RETURN or ENTER key when you reach the end of the line, IFPS will automatically continue the line for you. This feature is referred to as wrapping. However, there is a limit of how many characters you can put on a line whether or not it is wrapped. The limit depends on the computer you are using.

An alternative is for you to use the apostrophe (') as a special character. For example,

```
60 TOTAL EXPENSES=MATERIALS + LABOR +'
61 PREVIOUS ADVERTISING +  OVERHEAD
```

When you use the apostrophe at the end of a line, IFPS assumes that the next line in sequence will be a continuation of the current line. It does not expect an equal sign. If you are in AUTO mode, IFPS will automatically assign the continuation a line number for you.

IMPORTANT RULES:

1. You cannot split a variable name with an apostrophe. For example, you cannot split ANNUAL SALES between lines.

2. You cannot split a FOR, PREVIOUS, or FUTURE with an apostrophe.

4.5.2 What to Do if You Want to Use a Special Character in its Ordinary Meaning (!)

IFPS has a number of characters with special meaning. For example, in editing text you might write 10C/A/B/ to tell IFPS that you want to change A to B in Line 10. The / also has the ordinary meaning of division. What do you do if you want to change A/B to C/D? Writing C/A/B/C/D/ won't work. (Try it and see what happens.) The answer is to put an exclamation point in front of the division signs. That is, write:

```
C/A!/B/C!/D/
```

In general, if you want to use a form that is not normally allowed or understood by IFPS, you use an exclamation point to tell IFPS to follow you literally. Another example is:

```
X!-Y = X - Y
```

Here you want to tell IFPS that the variable name is X-Y; if you do not use the exclamation point, IFPS gives you an error message since arithmetic is not allowed in variable names. Try it and see.

The use of exclamation points does not work in certain instances. Specifically, you cannot use the exclamation point in model, report, or file names and you cannot use it in front of an apostrophe if the apostrophe is the last character in the line. The exclamation point will be shown when you list a model or a report but will not be shown when you SOLVE or create a report with GENREPORT.

4.5.3 Cleaning Up Line Numbers (RESEQUENCE)

If you have made many insertions in creating a model, report, or data file, you may feel that the line number system has become cumbersome. You can ask IFPS to renumber lines for you by using RESEQUENCE. Typical examples are:

```
RESEQUENCE MODEL PROFORMA 10 10
RESEQUENCE REPORT OUTPUT 1 3
```

In both cases you first tell IFPS to resequence, then you tell it whether it is a model or a report and give the corresponding name. The two numbers refer to, respectively, the number to be assigned to the first line and the increment to be used for successive lines. Thus, 10 10 tells IFPS to use 10,20,30,....for line numbers whereas 1 3 tells IFPS to use 1,4,7,.... In performing the resequencing, IFPS will automatically change line number references within a model (or a report) so that they are consistent.

If you ask for resequencing of a model, IFPS will ask you whether you have any reports or data files that relate to this model. The reason is that you may have line number references in the report that refer to the model. If you do not have a report or a data file, type NONE in response to the inquiry. Also type NONE as the last entry in the list of reports and the list of data files.

For example, if your model PROFORMA has REPORT STATMNT and DATAFILE RESULTS associated with it, the sequence might look as follows:

```
RESEQUENCE MODEL PROFORMA
ENTER NAME OF RELATED REPORT OR NONE
STATEMNT
NONE

ENTER NAME OF RELATED DATAFILE OR NONE
RESULTS
NONE
```

You can ask to RESEQUENCE either the model you are working on or any other model. To keep things straight for itself, IFPS removes the model you are working on from the workspace and does not replace it when you are done. (The reason is that if you ask to resequence a different model than the one in your workspace, IFPS does not know whether you will want the one you had or the one you resequenced.) That is, IFPS performs the resequencing and then expects you to tell it what you want to do. Typically, you will want to ask for the MODEL you just resequenced; however, you can ask for anything else if you so choose. You cannot just go on as before with, say, LIST and expect to obtain a listing of the resequenced model. If you forget, IFPS gives you an error message asking you for new instructions.

4.5.4 Making a Duplicate Copy of a Model or Report (COPY)

A typical situation when working with IFPS is that you want to use variations of a particular model or create a new model that uses all or parts of an existing model within it. Rather than typing in a new model you can make a copy of the existing model and give it a new name. Examples of the COPY command are:

```
COPY MODEL ALPHA TO BETA
COPY REPORT  A TO B
COPY FILE DATA TO NEWDATA
```

The first command tells IFPS to make a copy of ALPHA and call it BETA. ALPHA and BETA are identical; they only differ in name. The sequence is the word COPY followed by the appropriate definition of model, report, or data file. TO is optional. Finally, you give the name to be assigned to the copy. This name should be different from an existing name in your file, otherwise you will erase the current version. Like RESEQUENCE, you lose what is in your workspace and have to tell IFPS what you want to do next.

4.5.5 Saving Time in Executing The Model (COMPILESAVE)

Once you have completed a model which you plan to use many times, you may find it advantageous to save it in your files in the computer's own language (called "compiled") rather than in the English-like wording that is IFPS. Typical situations include:

- a dummy model that will be used with many data files. (See Section 4.6 for a discussion of data files).

- debugging a REPORT format (Section 4.7) where you use GENREPORT over and over with a particular mode until you are satisfied with the format.

Using the compiled form of the model saves you computer time (and hence computer costs) in these situations compared to using the MODEL .... SOLVE combination you would use ordinarily.

There are three steps involved in the process.

1. Ask IFPS for the model to be compiled by using the MODEL command.

2. Tell IFPS to create a compiled file and give the file a name. To do so, you issue a COMPILESAVE command where the word COMPILESAVE is followed by a name under which the file is to be saved.

3. When you are ready to retrieve the compiled file, you issue a COMPILEGET command, where the word COMPILEGET is followed by the name of the file that was previously compiled.

Figure 4-7 shows the sequence of steps followed. When you issue the COMPILEGET command, IFPS responds by asking you what SOLVE option you want. You can use any valid IFPS solve option or language command.

```
? model product
READY FOR EDIT, LAST LINE IS 200
? compilesave invest
MODEL PRODUCT  VERSION OF  08/30/82  18:21 -- 8 COLUMNS 13 VARIABLES
? compileget invest
MODEL PRODUCT  VERSION OF  08/30/82  18:21 -- 8 COLUMNS 13 VARIABLES
ENTER SOLVE OPTIONS
```

FIGURE 4-7. COMPILESAVE AND COMPILEGET

4.5.6 Finding All References to a Variable (CROSSREF)

In a complicated model, making changes in one place can affect you in many other places. For example, if you decide you want to remove widgets from your product line, you will want to remove all references to widgets in your IFPS model. The CROSSREF command helps you keep track of what goes on in your model by showing you an alphabetized list of all variables in your model. In addition, for each variable it tells you the line on which it is defined and the lines on which it is referred to on the right hand side. Figure 4-8 illustrates the use of CROSSREF for the Simple IFPS Model of Section 2.2. Note that you have to tell IFPS to CROSSREF a particular model name; CROSSREF by itself is not enough. The rest follows automatically.

```
? crossref
INVALID MODEL NAME AFTER CROSSREF COMMAND
READY FOR EXECUTIVE COMMAND
? crossref simple
VARIABLE NAME              DEFN     REFERENCES
EXPENSES                    30        40   80
EXPENSE RATIO               80
NET INCOME                  40        90
NET INCOME RATIO            90
REVENUE                     20        20   40   80   90
```

FIGURE 4-8. CROSSREF

In using CROSSREF you leave the IFPS model but not the file. You have to re-enter the MODEL command (including the name of the model) to continue.

4.5.7 Printing out Variable Names Rather than Line Numbers (EXPAND)

In Section 4.4.1 you saw how you could refer to variables by using the line number where they were defined (i.e., where they are on the left of the equal sign) rather than by their name. Thus, we wrote:

```
10 SALES = L20*L30
20 MARKET = 8000,PREVIOUS MARKET *1.05
30 MARKET SHARE = 0.15,PREVIOUS MARKET SHARE+0.005
```

If you want to see a listing that substitutes the names for the line numbers, all you have to do is type:

```
LIST EXPAND
```

The result for Line 10 will be:

```
10 SALES = MARKET * MARKET SHARE
```

The EXPAND feature is temporary. If you ask for list again, the original (unexpanded) version will be displayed. Similarly, if you ask for a printout of one or more lines, you will get the unexpanded version.

4.6 DATA FILES

If you want to solve the same model for a variety of conditions (e.g., for different departments or divisions) or if you have a large amount of data (e.g., 30 historical periods), you may find it easier to place the input data into a DATAFILE. In this section, we describe a few of the elementary features of data files. IFPS has extensive data handling capabilities. For complex situations, you will find it helpful to obtain the *IFPS USER'S MANUAL* and make use of these capabilities.

4.6.1 The Dummy Model

If you are going to use data files, there is no need for you to include the data in the model. Therefore, what you do is define the variable on the left-hand side of the equal sign and set it equal to 0. That is, you create a dummy model. The dummy model for the Simple IFPS Model of Section 2.7 is shown in Figure 4-9.

```
MODEL DUMMY  VERSION OF  11/22/82  15:38
10 COLUMNS 1-6
20 SALES=0
30 EXPENSES=0
40 NET INCOME=SALES-EXPENSES
50 EXPENSE RATIO=EXPENSES/SALES
60 NET INCOME RATIO=NET INCOME/SALES
END OF MODEL
```

FIGURE 4-9. DUMMY MODEL

4.6.2 The Data File

The data file contains the information to be substituted in the dummy model. Since you will provide data only for some lines of the model, not the entire model, you have to tell IFPS where you want the information to go. Therefore, you have to store both the identity of the line and the data in the data file. Information can be stored either by referring to the variable name or the line number. The data file associated with the dummy model of Figure 4-9 is shown in Figure 4-10. In this figure, SALES is referred to by line number (20) and EXPENSES is used directly. Note that you can put the number of the line on the left hand side and follow it with an equal sign. You can also refer to Line 20 by using L20 (see Section 4.4.1).

```
? list
1 20=100,125,160,195,245,330
2 EXPENSES=75,100,125,150,,175
```

FIGURE 4-10. DATA FILE FOR DUMMY MODEL

4.6.3 Obtaining Answers with a Data File (MODEL ... USING)

The dummy model and the data file have to be brought together before you can solve the model. To do so, you change the way you retrieve the model from the file. Specifically, you ask for:

MODEL modelname USING datafile

where you substitute the appropriate model and data file names. For example, if your model is DUMMY and your data file is GDATA, you type:

```
MODEL DUMMY USING GDATA
```

You then tell IFPS to SOLVE in the usual way. The MODEL ...USING combination does not change the model; rather, it allows the model to use the data file values as it needs them.

A few words of caution. Because of the substitution process involved, if your data file does not contain information about a variable, IFPS simply uses the values in the model. This can result in 0's being used if you forget a line of data. On the other hand, if you have defined a variable in both the model and the data file, the data file normally takes precedence. (Refer to the *IFPS USER'S MANUAL* for information on PROTECT DATA.)

In our example, the growth in sales is replaced by the data file values. If the data file does not provide enough values for all columns, IFPS simply assumes the last value you gave it. On the other hand, if a line of your data file contains more values than there are columns in your model, you will receive an error message. You should make the necessary corrections before proceeding. The important point is that it is up to you to make sure you have the data values you need available to you in your data file.

4.6.4 Creating and Saving a New Data File (DATAFILE)

Creating a new data file involves the same sequence of steps as creating a new model. In response to a ? you type DATAFILE and IFPS asks you for a name. You are then told to BEGIN ENTERING NEW DATAFILE. Figure 4-11 shows you how the data file GDATA was created.

```
? datafile gdata
BEGIN ENTERING NEW DATA FILE
? 20=100,125,160,195,245,330
? expenses=75,100,125,150,,175
? save
DATAFILE SAVED
```

FIGURE 4-11. CREATING AND SAVING A DATA FILE

Once a file is created, you must SAVE it. This is done by typing SAVE.

IFPS will help you remember by asking you whether you want to save the updated file or not. Type YES if you do.

WARNING: If you fail to SAVE a data file you lose it!!

4.6.5 Finding Out What Is in a Data File

If you have a data file, you can find out what is in it by using either LIST or SOLVE. In response to a question mark you first tell IFPS you want the data file in your personal workspace. For example, you might ask for:

```
? DATAFILE BUDGET
```

You can then LIST it and obtain output such as was shown in Figure 4-10. If you want more easily readable ouput in column format, you can ask for SOLVE. This is done in Figure 4-12.

```
? solve
ENTER SOLVE OPTIONS
? all

                     1      2      3      4      5      6

L20                100    125    160    195    245    330
EXPENSES            75    100    125    150      0      0
```

FIGURE 4-12. USING SOLVE TO EXAMINE THE CONTENTS OF A DATA FILE

EXERCISE: Create the dummy model and data file shown in this section and then SOLVE. Convince yourself that you obtain the same results as in Figure 2-5 in Section 2.2.

4.6.6 Changing a Data File

A data file is edited in exactly the same way as a model. You use the editing commands given in Sections 2.5 and Section 4.10 which explain how to correct mistakes. Be sure to SAVE the changed data file. IFPS will prompt you and ask you whether you want to SAVE. If you don't SAVE the changes, the old, unedited data file will remain in your permanent storage.

4.6.7 Storing the Output of a Model for Future Use as Data (STORENT)

If you want to use the results of one model as the inputs to a subsequent model, you can do so with the STORENT command (i.e., Store,No Tag). This command has the form

STORENT datafile

When you give the STORENT command, IFPS immediately solves your model and then asks you which variables you want stored in the data file whose name you have given. If you respond ALL, it will put all output values in the file; if you give it a list of variable names, it will store only those variables. If you used a data file in the model, IFPS will also store all variables that appear in the model.

Figure 4-13 shows you the result of solving MODEL DUMMY (Section 4.6.1) using the GDATA data file in combination with the STORENT command. We chose to call the new data file GDATA, thereby replacing the original with the newly created data file. In this example we are replacing an existing data file. Therefore, since Line 20 was referred to by line number in the original version, it is also referred to as Line 20 in the new version.

4.6.8 Combining Data from Several Files into a New File (DATASELECT)

A situation often encountered in practice is that data for a particular model or for a summary report are scattered among several data files. For example, you may have budget data in one file, actual data in another, and variance data in a third. Furthermore, each data set has quarterly and annual data and you need to create a single annual variance report that combines data from all three files. A simple approach to solving this problem is to use the DATASELECT command. With this command, you can select columns of data from one or more existing data files and combine them into a new data file that can then be used with any model.

Specifically, the DATASELECT command allows you to:

- Select data from an existing data file and put it in a new data file.
- Combine data from two or more data files into a new data file.
- Add (that is, consolidate) or subtract data from two or more files or multiply data by a factor when creating the new data file.

The DATASELECT command works on columns in the existing data files and creates columns in the new data file.

```
? solve
MODEL DUMMY  VERSION OF  11/22/82  15:38 -- 6 COLUMNS 5 VARIABLES
ENTER SOLVE OPTIONS
? all

                            1       2       3       4       5       6

SALES                     100     125     160     195     245     330
EXPENSES                   75     100     125     150     175     175
NET INCOME                 25      25      35      45      70     155
EXPENSE RATIO           .7500   .8000   .7813   .7692   .7143   .5303
NET INCOME RATIO        .2500   .2000   .2188   .2308   .2857   .4697

ENTER SOLVE OPTIONS
? storent gdata
ENTER STORE OPTIONS
? all

STORE UPDATE COMPLETE
ENTER SOLVE OPTIONS
? datafile gdata
READY FOR EDIT, LAST LINE IS 5
? list
1 20=100,125,160,195,245,330
2 EXPENSES =75,100,125,150,175 FOR 2
3 NET INCOME=25 FOR 2,35,45,70,155
4 EXPENSE RATIO=.75,.8,.78125,.769231,.714286,.530303
5 NET INCOME RATIO=.25,.2,.21875,.230769,.285714,.469697
```

FIGURE 4-13. STORING MODEL OUTPUT AS A DATA FILE AND LISTING OF THE RESULTING DATA FILE

Combining these capabilities provides you with powerful data manipulation capability. For example, you can select columns from an existing data file and rearrange them. You can take a column and compute its ratio or percentage with respect to another column (e.g., percent profit or benefit/cost ratio). You can pick summary columns from several files and combine them into a master summary report for top management.

The DATASELECT command is particularly user friendly in that it prompts you through the sequence of steps required to create the new file. For convenience, we will refer to the new file as the "output" file and the files from which we obtain information as the "input" files.

Figure 4-14 leads you through a typical sequence. We will use this sequence again in our example in Section 4.9. What we are trying to do here is combine the annual data for budget, actual, and variance available in column 4 in each of three data files into a single data file. We also want to compute the percent variance of the actual from the budget.

```
?dataselect
ENTER NUMBER OF COLUMNS IN OUTPUT MATRIX
? 4
ENTER DATAFILE NAME OR NONE
? cactual
ENTER DIRECTIVE OR END
? 4 into 1
ENTER DIRECTIVE OR END
? end
ENTER DATAFILE NAME OR NONE
? cbudget
ENTER DIRECTIVE OR END
? 4 into 2
ENTER DIRECTIVE OR END
? end
ENTER DATAFILE NAME OR NONE
? cvar
ENTER DIRECTIVE OR END
? 4 into 4
ENTER DIRECTIVE OR END
? end
ENTER DATAFILE NAME OR NONE
?cavr
ENTER DIRECTIVE OR END
?4 into 4
ENTER DIRECTIVE OR END
?end
ENTER DATAFILE NAME OR NONE
? cbudget
ENTER DIRECTIVE OR END
? divide
ENTER DIRECTIVE OR END
? 4(.01) into 4
ENTER DIRECTIVE OR END
? end
ENTER DATAFILE NAME OR NONE
? none
ENTER OUTPUT FILENAME (STOREOPT OR NAOUTPUT)
? varann
DATA FILES SELECTED AND SAVED ON FILE VARANN
READY FOR EXECUTIVE COMMAND
? datafile varann
READY FOR EDIT, LAST LINE IS 4
? list
1 TOTAL UNITS=460 FOR 2,0 FOR 2
2 TOTAL REVENUE=1212.5,1181.25,-31.25,-2.57732
3 TOTAL COSTS=660,652,-8,-1.21212
4 NET PROFIT=552.5,529.25,-23.25,-4.20814
```

FIGURE 4-14. DATASELECT

The sequence of steps is as follows:

1. Type in the DATASELECT command. At this point IFPS drops its previous work and is ready to create a new data file.

2. IFPS asks you to tell it the number of columns in the output file you are creating (in our case four). The number of columns in the output file need have no relation to the number of columns in any of the input files.

3. IFPS keeps asking you for the name of the file from which to copy data and what you want to do with the data until you type in the word NONE to signify you have finished creating the new file. ENTER DATAFILE NAME OR NONE in our case requires telling IFPS about the input files CBUDGET, CACTUAL, and CVAR.

4. For each input file you are asked to give a DIRECTIVE (or END if you are finished with that file). A DIRECTIVE can copy from any column in the input file to any column in the output file. You can also multiply the input column by any factor by putting the multiplier in parentheses. The format is:

Input column number(factor) INTO ouput column number

The factor is assumed to be equal to 1 unless you specify otherwise. INTO is a keyword to separate input from output column numbers.

You can list several directives on one line by separating them with commas and you can do multiple column transfers using a format that is similar to the FOR-NEXT format used in BASIC for performing looping. For example,

```
?ENTER DIRECTIVE OR END
1-7 STEP 2 INTO 1-4, 9-11 INTO 5-9 STEP 2
```

copies columns 1, 3, 5, and 7 from the input file into the first four columns of the output file and then copies copies columns 9, 10, and 11 from the input file into columns 5, 7, and 9 of the output file.

5. We use the command DIVIDE to create percentage values in column 4 of the output file. We first copied column 4 of the file CVAR into both columns 3 and 4 of the output file. We then told IFPS to consider file CBUDGET again and gave the directive DIVIDE. When prompted again we said to divide column 4 of the input file CBUDGET (multiplied by the factor .01 to create percentages) into column 4 of the output file. Note that the input file is BUDGET and that we had previous copied data from the CVAR file into column 4 of the output file. For example, if the input file value is 70 and the output file value is 35 then this set of instructions results in 35/(70*.01) =50.

In addition to the DIVIDE directive, the DATASELECT command provides a MULTIPLY directive. A typical sequence is:

```
MULTIPLY
1 INTO 3
```

In this sequence, column 1 of the data file multiplies column 3 of the output matrix and puts the result in column 3 of the output matrix.

6. Once you have created the new file, you respond to ENTER DATAFILE NAME OR NONE by typing NONE. IFPS asks you for a name for the output file. This name should be unique. You must be careful not to choose an existing file name, because if you do you will erase that file. In Figure 4-14 we use the name VARANN for annual variance.

7. Figure 4-14 also shows a listing of the data file VARANN to check the success of the DATASELECT process.

4.7 GENERATING FORMATTED REPORTS (GENREPORT)

In presenting results to management, you will usually want to show your output in a neat format, one that is standard for your company. To obtain formatted reports in IFPS, you ask for GENREPORT rather than SOLVE. The format is:

GENREPORT reportname

where reportname refers to a separately defined (and saved) report format. The steps you follow are:

1. Create a MODEL.

2. Either create a REPORT format or use an existing one.

3. Call for GENREPORT rather than SOLVE.

Because GENREPORT creates a report according to the format that you have specified, you cannot choose options (such as printing out different variables each time you run the model) as you can when using SOLVE. However, you can include any SOLVE option within the report format.

Not being able to change the SOLVE options from run to run is not necessarily a disadvantage. In fact, if you are developing a particular model or running a long series of WHAT IF cases in which you use the same SOLVE options over and over, you will find it easier to create a REPORT that contains this repetitive information than to type the same information repeatedly.

Remember that the MODEL and the REPORT are separate. Therefore you can:

- Create different reports for the same model.

- Use a report with a number of models.

Furthermore, not every quantity computed in a model needs to be printed in a report.

4.7.1 Creating a New Report

When you are creating a new report format, you simply tell IFPS:

REPORT reportname

and IFPS will respond with BEGIN ENTERING NEW REPORT. If the report name has been used previously, IFPS will respond with READY FOR EDIT, LAST LINE IS __ . As in the case of MODEL and DATAFILE, you can LIST a report, SAVE it, or use the standard editing commands listed in Section 2.5 and Section 4.10 to modify it.

We will now describe some of the formatting features available. There are many more than we have room for here; the *IFPS USER'S MANUAL* contains a complete description of the many options available. Rather than overloading you with detail, we will concentrate on:

- how to create a heading, blank lines, and underscores
- how to specify column headings
- how to specify variables to be displayed
- how to specify format within a line.

4.7.2 First Report Example

Figure 4-15 is a sample report for the Simple IFPS Model of Section 2.2. We will go over this sample report line by line. The results of generating output by using this report format are also shown in Figure 4-15.

Line 10 This line tells IFPS that only columns 1,4, and 6 are to be displayed. This is done in the same way as the SOLVE option. If you want all columns, line 10 is unnecessary.

Lines 20 through 40 These lines define the report title. Headings can be entered in two ways:

```
*text
CENTER text
```

The * acts like a comment and results in displaying whatever is specified in exactly the spacing shown. If you type only a * on a line, the line is left blank. This is a convenient way of spacing. CENTER takes the text and puts it in the center of the line.

Line 50 COLUMN TITLES, results in headings of the colums being displayed. If this line is left out, headings are omitted. We will discuss column titles shortly.

Line 60 The names of the variables to be displayed must be given explicitly. Only the variables whose names are given appear. You will note, for example, that the expense ratio computed in the original program in Section 2.2 is not called for and hence does not appear. Several variables can be specified on one line, if they are separated by commas. If you want all lines in a model, specify ALL. If you want all lines between two points in the model use L20 THRU L95 or SALES

```
REPORT PRODUCT  VERSION OF  08/30/82  18:20
10 COLUMNS 1,4,6
20 *
30 CENTER NEW PRODUCT FORECAST
40*
50 COLUMN TITLES
60 SALES,EXPENSES
70 UNDERLINE -
80 /PROFIT/NET INCOME
90*
100 NET INCOME RATIO
110 UNDERLINE=
END OF REPORT
? model gray
READY FOR EDIT, LAST LINE IS 90
? genreport product
MODEL GRAY  VERSION OF  01/07/83  11:46 -- 6 COLUMNS 5 VARIABLES


                            NEW PRODUCT FORECAST

                                   1        4        6
SALES                            100    195.3    305.2
EXPENSES                          75      150      175
                             -------  -------  -------
PROFIT                            25    45.31    130.2

NET INCOME RATIO               .2500    .2320    .4266
                             =======  =======  =======
```

FIGURE 4-15. FIRST REPORT EXAMPLE

THRU PROFITS. (See Section 4.4.1 for further discussion of the use of L to refer to line numbers.)

Line 70 UNDERLINE- creates a single underscore. See the description of line 110 below.

Line 80 /PROFIT/NET INCOME. The / format causes a variable name to be replaced by the name you want to use in the output. Here NET INCOME in the model is to be replaced by PROFIT. The general format is to put / / around the name to be printed and follow it by the original name used in the model. Note that while this approach seems similar to that used for editing mistakes, it handles things in reverse order. In the case of reports you define the new name first and then give the original name found in the model.

Line 110 UNDERLINE= causes a double line to be displayed. If you do not specify either -- or = after UNDERLINE, you will get a single underscore.

4.7.3 The WIDTH Command

As explained in Section 4.2, the WIDTH command allows you to specify:

- the total length of the line in number of spaces
- the number of spaces to be used for the variable name
- the number of spaces to be used for each column
- the number of decimal places for each number.

In Figure 4-16, you will see the use of WIDTH 68,20,8,2 to indicate that you want 68 columns with 20 spaces for the variable name, 8 spaces for each column, and two decimal spaces for each number. Table 4-2 showed the default values and ranges allowed for each option.

```
REPORT FORECASTO   VERSION OF   01/07/83   12:08
10 WIDTH 68,20,8,2
20 *
30 CENTER NEW PRODUCT FORECAST
40 *
50 COLUMN TITLES 1ST,2ND,3RD,4TH,5TH,6TH
60 COLUMN TITLES QTR,QTR,QTR,QTR,QTR,QTR
70 *
80 ALL
END OF REPORT
? model gray
READY FOR EDIT, LAST LINE IS 90
? genreport forecast0
MODEL GRAY   VERSION OF   01/07/83   11:46 -- 6 COLUMNS 5 VARIABLES


                          NEW PRODUCT FORECAST

                        1ST      2ND      3RD      4TH      5TH      6TH
                        QTR      QTR      QTR      QTR      QTR      QTR

SALES                100.00   125.00   156.25   195.31   244.14   305.18
EXPENSES              75.00   100.00   125.00   150.00   175.00   175.00
NET INCOME            25.00    25.00    31.25    45.31    69.14   130.18

                               RATIO ANALYSIS
PERCENT OF SALES
EXPENSE RATIO           .75      .80      .80      .77      .72      .57
NET INCOME RATIO        .25      .20      .20      .23      .28      .43
```

FIGURE 4-16. WIDTH AND COLUMN TITLES

The WIDTH command is the simplest formatting device. It provides the same format for all lines following the command. You can use multiple WIDTH commands within a report format; every time a new WIDTH is encountered, it governs everything that follows until the next WIDTH.

If you do not want to change the total length of the line, but do want to change other parameters, you can use the OPT statement instead of WIDTH. OPT was described in Section 4.2.

4.7.4 The COLUMN TITLES Command

You can have IFPS print the column titles you want by specifying the exact heading right after COLUMN TITLES. In the example in Figure 4-16, lines 50 and 60 result in specifying the columns in terms of quarters rather than 1 through 6 as in the model. Multiple COLUMN TITLES lines can be used to produce more than one heading per column.

If you just specify COLUMN TITLES you obtain the headings given in the columns specification at the beginning of the model.

4.7.5 The FORMAT Command

If you want more control over format than is given by the WIDTH command, you can create a format for a line by using the FORMAT command. You may *not*, however, use WIDTH and FORMAT for the same line.

What you type in the FORMAT command is interpreted literally by IFPS, space by space.

The following are special editing symbols:

- A blank space will be displayed as a blank space.
- A 9 indicates any number.
- A single . indicates a decimal point.
- A , indicates a comma.

Examples of the FORMAT command are shown in Figure 4-17. Examine line 10 of this figure and the resulting display. You will see that a string of periods indicates where text is to be shown. If ...... immediately follows the word FORMAT, the amount of space allocated to the variable name is the number of periods plus 6. If, as in line 10, the ...... appear in the middle of the line, the number of spaces is equal to the number of periods.

Using FORMAT requires meticulous attention to detail in planning. You literally have to count spaces to know where things will appear. Planning is particularly important if you use several format statements in a single report. It is easy to create columns that do not line up and it is easy to specify the wrong number of spaces. If you allocate too much space to a variable name, blank spaces will remain at the right end. If you allocate too little space, the name will be truncated.

The FORMAT command is quite rich. Figure 4-18 illustrates other features of the command. In Figure 4-18, two format statements are used, one to obtain numbers with

```
REPORT FORECAST  VERSION OF  08/30/82  18:08
10 FORMAT 9999.99 9999.99 9999.99  ...............  9999.99 '
11 9999.99 99999.99
20*
30 CENTER NEW PRODUCT FORECAST
35 UNDERLINE=
40*
50 COLUMN TITLES 1ST,2ND,3RD,4TH,5TH,6TH
60 COLUMN TITLES QTR,QTR,QTR,QTR,QTR,QTR
70 *
80 SALES,EXPENSES,NET INCOME
85 UNDERLINE-
90*
100 EXPENSE RATIO,NET INCOME RATIO
END OF REPORT
? model gray
READY FOR EDIT, LAST LINE IS 90
? genreport forecast
MODEL GRAY  VERSION OF  08/30/82  18:20 -- 6 COLUMNS 5 VARIABLES


                         NEW PRODUCT FORECAST
                         ====================

  1ST      2ND      3RD                          4TH      5TH      6TH
  QTR      QTR      QTR                          QTR      QTR      QTR

100.00   125.00   156.25   SALES              195.31   244.14   305.18
 75.00   100.00   125.00   EXPENSES           150.00   175.00   175.00
 25.00    25.00    31.25   NET INCOME          45.31    69.14   130.18
------  -------  -------                     -------  -------  -------

   .75      .80      .80   EXPENSE RATIO         .77      .72      .57
   .25      .20      .20   NET INCOME RATIO      .23      .28      .43
```

FIGURE 4-17. PUTTING NAMES IN THE MIDDLE

two decimal places and one to obtain numbers with four decimal places. You will also observe in Figure 4-18, that:

- If you want to use a format several times, you can use the square bracket option; for example, 3[9999.99]. In this case, the first symbol after the [should be a blank so that numbers do not run into one another.

- B and D will also print numbers. However, B will leave any entries that are zero blank, while D replaces a zero value with a single –. If you use () around a number, the result is to show negative numbers with a () around them rather than with a minus sign. (NOTE: the () use up two spaces in the format.)

- Like WIDTH, a FORMAT is followed until a new format is encountered.

```
REPORT NEWPROD  VERSION OF  08/30/82  18:07
10 FORMAT .................. 3[ 9999.99] BBBB.BB (DDDD.DD) 9999.99
20*
30 CENTER NEW PRODUCT FORECAST
40 UNDERLINE=
50 SPACE 2
60 COLUMN TITLES 1981,1982,1983,1984,1985,1986
70 SALES,EXPENSES,NET INCOME
80 SPACE 3
90 FORMAT .................. 6[ 999.999]
100 EXPENSE RATIO,NET INCOME RATIO
END OF REPORT
? model gray
READY FOR EDIT, LAST LINE IS 90
? genreport newprod
MODEL GRAY  VERSION OF  08/30/82  18:20 -- 6 COLUMNS 5 VARIABLES
```

NEW PRODUCT FORECAST
====================

	1981	1982	1983	1984	1985	1986
SALES	100.00	125.00	156.25	195.31	244.14	305.18
EXPENSES	75.00	100.00	125.00	150.00	175.00	175.00
NET INCOME	25.00	25.00	31.25	45.31	69.14	130.18
EXPENSE RATIO	.750	.800	.800	.768	.717	.573
NET INCOME RATIO	.250	.200	.200	.232	.283	.427

FIGURE 4-18. LINE FORMATS

4.7.6 The SPACE Command

If you want to leave several lines blank it is easier to use the SPACE command followed by a blank and the number of lines to be left blank than to use the * method described in Section 4.7.2. Lines 50 and 80 in Figure 4-18 show the use of SPACE 2 and SPACE 3.

4.7.7 A Report Format for the Pro Forma Profit and Loss Statement

In Section 2.9, we presented a pro forma profit and loss statement associated with a particular inventory policy. Figure 4-19a and 4-19b show a formatted version of the pro forma statement shown unformatted in Figure 2-10. For simplicity we have modified the model so that it shows only four months not 12 months. This report contains applications of many of the report features we have discussed here. Study Figure 4-19 and make sure you understand the relation between what is in the REPORT format and the result of using the GENREPORT command. You will see, for example, that the section providing input data and the quantities derived from input data are not included in the report. As implied earlier, not every line in the model has to be printed in the report.

```
REPORT PANDL   VERSION OF   01/07/83   13:15
10 WIDTH 68,30,8,0
20 CENTER 1983 BUDGET
30 CENTER FOR
40 CENTER ABC COMPANY
50 UNDERLINE-
60*
70 COLUMN TITLES JAN,FEB,MARCH,APR
80 UNDERLINE-
90 SPACE 1
100 GROSS SALES
110*COST OF GOODS SOLD
120/ BEGINNING FG INVENTORY/BEGINNING INVENTORY
130* COST OF GOODS MANUFACTURING
140/    DIRECT MATERIAL/MATERIAL COST
150/    DIRECT LABOR/DIRECT LABOR
160 UNDERLINE-
170/ TOTAL/COST OF MANUFACTURING
180*
190/ TOTAL CGM AND FG INV/TOTAL INVENTORY VALUE
200/ ENDING FG INVENTORY/ENDING INVENTORY VALUE
210 UNDERLINE-
220 COST OF GOODS SOLD
230*
240 GROSS PROFIT ON SALES
250*
260*OPERATING EXPENSES
270/ ADVERTISING/ADVERTISING
280/ COMMISSIONS/COMMISSIONS
290/ LEASES/LEASES
300/ NOTE INTEREST/NOTE INTEREST
310/ DEPRECIATION/DEPRECIATION
320UNDERLINE-
330/ TOTAL EXPENSES/TOTAL OPERATING EXPENSE
340*
350NET PROFIT BEFORE INCOME TAX
360*
370NET PROFIT$
380UNDERLINE=
END OF REPORT
```

a. Model

FIGURE 4-19. FORMATTED VERSION OF THE PRO FORMA BALANCE SHEET
(This Figure Continued on the Next Page)

```
? model profitloss
READY FOR EDIT, LAST LINE IS 610
?solve
ENTER SOLVE OPTIONS
? columns 1-4
? genreport pandl
MODEL PROFITLOSS   VERSION OF   08/30/82   18:07 -- 12 COLUMNS 29
VARIABLES
```

1983 BUDGET
FOR
ABC COMPANY

	JAN	FEB	MARCH	APR
GROSS SALES	1075000	1525000	1825000	2125000
COST OF GOODS SOLD				
BEGINNING FG INVENTORY	1334000	2160500	2726000	3117500
COST OF GOODS MANUFACTURING				
DIRECT MATERIAL	1075000	1075000	1075000	1075000
DIRECT LABOR	375000	375000	375000	375000
TOTAL	1450000	1450000	1450000	1450000
TOTAL CGM AND FG INV	2784000	3610500	4176000	4567500
ENDING FG INVENTORY	2160500	2726000	3117500	3335000
COST OF GOODS SOLD	623500	884500	1058500	1232500
GROSS PROFIT ON SALES	451500	640500	766500	892500
OPERATING EXPENSES				
ADVERTISING	26875	26875	38125	45625
COMMISSIONS	53750	76250	91250	106250
LEASES	65000	65000	65000	65000
NOTE INTEREST	2500	2500	2500	2500
DEPRECIATION	50000	49000	48020	47060
TOTAL EXPENSES	274775	296275	321545	343085
NET PROFIT BEFORE INCOME TAX	176725	344225	444955	549415
NET PROFIT	$95432	$185882	$240276	$296684

b. Output of GENREPORT

FIGURE 4-19. FORMATTED VERSION OF THE PRO FORMA BALANCE SHEET (Continued)

The following comments about specific lines will help you follow the REPORT.

Line 10 uses WIDTH to define a 68-character line with 30 spaces used for the name of the variable and 8 spaces for each of the 4 columns. Numbers are to be printed as dollars since we provide 0 decimal places.

Lines 20 through 40 create a centered heading for the budget.

Line 50 provides the single underscore and Line 60 leaves a line blank.

Line 70 substitutes abbreviations for the names of the month for the column headings 1 through 6 in the original.

Line 90 is an alternate way of leaving a line blank.

Line 100 tells IFPS to print the gross sales line as is.

Line 110 uses the comment format to print a heading.

Line 120 uses the substitution feature. Note that the new name, given within the / / is substituted for exactly; therefore, when we leave the first space after the / blank we obtain a name that is indented.

Line 130 by leaving a space after the * indents the heading by one space.

Lines 140 through 200 substitute names to obtain output in the format desired. Note that in line 150 we have to use the substitution format, even though the variable names are the same, in order to achieve the desired indenting.

Lines 220 through 330 use the same ideas as previous lines. It is a general characteristic of reports that you use the same formats repeatedly to achieve a uniform look.

Line 370 NET PROFIT$ indicates that a $ sign should be put in front of every number.

Line 380 creates a final double underline.

Figure 4-19b shows the resulting output. Check the commands in Figure 4-19a against the output in Figure 4-19b and make sure you understand how each line of the output was specified.

4.8 CONSOLIDATION

In many modeling situations you reach a point where you want to combine the solutions of previous models. For example, you may have a model of your own firm and a potential acquisition and want to find out what the combined balance sheet would look like. You may have a forecast done at the beginning of the month and actual figures from the end of the month and want to find out about the variances in performance. You may have monthly results that you want to combine into quarterly results or quarterly results you want to combine into an annual report. CONSOLIDATE is a powerful command that allows you to produce composite reports from two or more models.

4.8.1 Simple, Additive Consolidation

It is important to recognize that CONSOLIDATE is a command in IFPS, just as MODEL or SOLVE are commands. CONSOLIDATE is closer in form to MODEL than to SOLVE which asks you to enter solve options. Just as in MODEL where you have to specify the name of the model, in CONSOLIDATE you have to specify the names of all the models to be consolidated. For example, if you want to consolidate the income statements from two divisions, you would type:

```
CONSOLIDATE DIVISION1 DIVISION2
```

where DIVISION1 and DIVISION2 are existing models. Note that you do NOT use a comma between the model names. The CONSOLIDATE command for two models is the simplest form of this command. The sequence of steps that occurs when you give this command is:

- The DIVISION1 model is solved.
- The DIVISION2 model is solved.
- The output from the two models is combined into a final solution matrix.

In the combination, if a variable has the same name in both models, its values are added up, period by period. If a variable appears in only one of the models, the values from that model will be included in the combination.

Once the combination is complete, you can ask IFPS to print out the results by either using SOLVE or, if you want to format your output, by GENREPORT.

> *NOTE.* You will not get any printout from CONSOLIDATE unless you ask for SOLVE or GENREPORT

The CONSOLIDATE command is not limited to two models. You can specify a long list of models if you so choose.

The following is a typical sequence of steps you might see when you ask for CONSOLIDATE.

```
?CONSOLIDATE MODEL1 MODEL2 MODEL3
ENTER MORE MODEL OR DATA FILE NAMES OR NONE
?MODEL4 MODEL5
ENTER MORE MODEL OR DATA FILE NAMES OR NONE
NONE
```

The above prompting sequence results in consolidating 5 models. When the consolidation is complete, IFPS tells you:

```
CONSOLIDATION COMPLETE, 5 MODELS
```

and you are ready to use SOLVE or GENREPORT to obtain output.

Figure 4-20 illustrates this simple form of consolidation. In this figure we consider our Simple IFPS model from Chapter II and a similar model based on another product. The consolidation shows the results of consolidating these two models to assess their combined impact.

```
MODEL SIMPLE  VERSION OF  08/30/82  18:06
10 COLUMNS 1-6
20 REVENUE = 100,PREVIOUS REVENUE *1.25
30 EXPENSES =75,100,125,150,175
40 NET INCOME = REVENUE -EXPENSES
50*
60 *                               RATIO ANALYSIS
70 *PERCENT OF REVENUE
80 EXPENSE RATIO = EXPENSES/REVENUE
90 NET INCOME RATIO = NET INCOME/REVENUE
END OF MODEL
? model simple2
READY FOR EDIT, LAST LINE IS 90
? list

MODEL SIMPLE2  VERSION OF  08/30/82  18:06
10 COLUMNS 1-6
20 SALES = 150,PREVIOUS SALES * 1.15
30 EXPENSES = 90,120,150,180
40 NET INCOME = SALES -EXPENSES
50 *
60 *                               RATIO ANALYSIS
70 *PERCENT OF SALES
80 EXPENSE RATIO = EXPENSES/SALES
90 NET INCOME RATIO = NET INCOME/SALES
END OF MODEL
? consolidate simple simple 2
ENTER MORE MODEL NAMES OR NONE
? none
CONSOLIDATION COMPLETED 2 MODELS
? solve
ENTER SOLVE OPTIONS
? all
                                1       2       3       4       5       6

SALES                         150   172.5   198.4   228.1   262.4   301.7
EXPENSES                      165     220     275     330     355     355
NET INCOME                     85   77.50   79.63   93.44   151.5   251.9

                                    RATIO ANALYSIS
PERCENT OF SALES
EXPENSE RATIO               1.350   1.496   1.556   1.557   1.403   1.170
NET INCOME RATIO            .6500   .5043   .4439   .4430   .5971   .8299
```

FIGURE 4-20. CONSOLIDATION OF TWO MODELS

4.8.2 Weighted Consolidation

If you own only part of an organization (e.g., a 60% owned joint venture) you can weight the effect of the partial ownership by putting the weighting in parentheses after the model name. For example,

```
CONSOLIDATE CORPORATE SUBA(.60)
```

results in multiplying every value in the output of SUBA by .6 before it is consolidated with CORPORATE.

4.8.3 Variance Analysis

Variance analysis is made simple by using weighted consolidation. You take the budget and multiply it by –1. Thus,

```
CONSOLIDATE ACTUAL BUDGET(-1)
```

results in a variance report. That is, multiplying the budget by –1 and consolidating results in obtaining the difference between actual and budget. Figure 4-21 illustrates this use of consolidation for variance analysis.

In this figure, a company has budgeted and actual data for the number of units to be sold, the price charged, and the costs incurred during each quarter during the past year. The consolidated report shows the variances between the actual and budgeted values.

```
MODEL ACTUAL  VERSION OF  08/30/82  18:06
1 COLUMNS 1-4
10 UNITS =97,112,126,125
20 PRICE =2.5 FOR 3,2.75
30 REVENUE = UNITS*PRICE
40 COSTS = 142,155,172,183
END OF MODEL
?solve
MODEL ACTUAL  VERSION OF  08/30/82  18:06 -- 4 COLUMNS 4 VARIABLES
ENTER SOLVE OPTIONS
? all

                          1        2        3        4

UNITS                    97      112      126      125
PRICE                 2.500    2.500    2.500    2.750
REVENUE               242.5      280      315    343.8
COSTS                   142      155      172      183
```

a. Model ACTUAL

FIGURE 4-21. USING CONSOLIDATION FOR VARIANCE ANALYSIS
(This Figure Continued on the Next Page)

```
ENTER SOLVE OPTIONS
? model budget
READY FOR EDIT, LAST LINE IS 40
? list

MODEL BUDGET  VERSION OF  08/30/82  18:05
1 COLUMNS 1-4
10 UNITS =100,110,120,130
20 PRICE =2.5,2.5,2.75
30 REVENUE =UNITS*PRICE
40 COSTS = 150,170
END OF MODEL
? solve
MODEL BUDGET  VERSION OF  08/30/82  18:05 -- 4 COLUMNS 4 VARIABLES
ENTER SOLVE OPTIONS
? all
```

	1	2	3	4
UNITS	100	110	120	130
PRICE	2.500	2.500	2.750	2.750
REVENUE	250	275	330	357.5
COSTS	150	170	170	170

b. Model Budget

```
ENTER SOLVE OPTIONS
? consolidate actual budget(-1)
ENTER MORE MODEL NAMES OR NONE
? none
CONSOLIDATION COMPLETED 2 MODELS
? solve
ENTER SOLVE OPTIONS
? width 68 20 8
? all
```

	1	2	3	4
UNITS	-3	2	6	-5
PRICE	0	0	-.2500	0
REVENUE	-7.500	5	-15	-13.75
COSTS	-8	-15	2	13

c. Consolidation

FIGURE 4-21. USING CONSOLIDATION FOR VARIANCE ANALYSIS (Continued)

4.8.4 Using the Consolidated Model in Computations

Consolidating several models into a single model can, as indicated above, give you a broader picture of the organization as a whole than observing models individually. The next step is to perform calculations based on the consolidated data. For example, you might want to sum several categories of expenses or you might want to add the anticipated corporate overhead and determine the rate that will have to be charged back to the divisions. IFPS allows you to create such a postprocessing model and apply it as part of the consolidation process. To tell IFPS you are adding a postprocessing model you use the reserved word WITH in the format

```
CONSOLIDATE DIVISION1 DIVISION2 WITH CORPORATE
```

where CORPORATE contains the postprocessing model. In response to this form of the CONSOLIDATE command, IFPS first solves DIVISION1 and DIVISION2 and consolidates the result and then solves the postprocessing model. After IFPS tells you CONSOLIDATION COMPLETED 2 MODELS, you give the command SOLVE (or GENREPORT if you want a REPORT). The model solved consists of both the consolidation and the postprocessing model CONSOLIDATE. The line numbers associated with the variables in the last model consolidated are still available to be referenced by the postprocessing model.

Several restrictions and rules apply when using postprocessing. They are:

- The postprocessing model should have different line numbers from those of the last model consolidated. In this way, you avoid overwriting lines from the consolidation with the postprocessing model.
- The variable names in the postprocessing model should be different from those in the last model consolidated. If the names are the same, the rule is that the values of the most recent occurrence of the name are to be used when variable names are referenced in a report or as a solve option.
- The postprocessing model must have at least as many columns defined as the consolidated model. If more columns are specified, the additional columns are computed by statements in the postprocessing model.

Figure 4-22 shows how postprocessing can be done on consolidated models. In this Figure, BUDGET and ACTUAL are the same as in Figure 4-21. Model COMPANY uses the results of each model to compute the quarterly profits and then to accumulate the values for the year. Thus, the values of total units through net profit represent the values for the entire year.

4.8.5 Using Multiple Data Files with a Model

If you have a large model that requires several data files, you can combine CONSOLIDATE and USING to obtain both data files for solving the model. For example, you might ask for:

```
CONSOLIDATE PRODUCT USING DATA1 DATA2
```

where PRODUCT is a model name and DATA1 and DATA2 are data files. This approach leaves the individual data files intact for future use.

```
MODEL COMPANY  VERSION OF  08/30/82  18:05
1 COLUMNS 1-4
50 PROFIT = REVENUE - COSTS
60*
70 TOTAL UNITS = PREVIOUS + UNITS
80 TOTAL REVENUE =PREVIOUS + REVENUE
90 TOTAL COSTS=PREVIOUS +COSTS
100 NET PROFIT = PREVIOUS + PROFIT
END OF MODEL
? consolidate budget with company
CONSOLIDATION COMPLETED 1 MODELS
? consolidate actual budget(-1) with company
CONSOLIDATION COMPLETED 2 MODELS
? solve
ENTER SOLVE OPTIONS
? all

                             1          2          3          4

UNITS                       -3          2          6         -5
PRICE                        0          0     -.2500          0
REVENUE                 -7.500          5        -15     -13.75
COSTS                       -8        -15          2         13
PROFIT                   .5000         20        -17     -26.75

TOTAL UNITS                 -3         -1          5          0
TOTAL REVENUE           -7.500     -2.500     -17.50     -31.25
TOTAL COSTS                 -8        -23        -21         -8
NET PROFIT               .5000      20.50      3.500     -23.25
```

FIGURE 4-22. USING THE CONSOLIDATED MODEL IN COMPUTATIONS

4.8.6 Creating Consolidated Data Files (CONSOLDF)

If you want to combine two or more data files into a single data file that you can store for use in future computations, you invoke the CONSOLDF command. The form of the CONSOLDF command is indicated by the example:

```
CONSOLDF DATA1 DATA2 NONE
```

The NONE is needed to tell IFPS that you have given it the names of all the files to be consolidated. IFPS responds with:

```
ENTER OUTPUT FILE NAME
```

and you type in a name for the consolidated data file. This name should differ from the names of existing data files; if it does not, you erase the existing data file.

4.8.7 Modeling Hierarchical Situations

In this section on consolidation we have considered situations in which the organizations involved (e.g., divisions) are all on the same level in the organization. However, many situations exist in which there are hierarchical structures; for example, DIVISION1 may have three groups each of which is a cost center of its own. These three groups have to be consolidated into DIVISION1 and then the divisions must be consolidated into a corporate report. IFPS has the capability for dealing with such hierarchies. The details are a bit more involved than what we have discussed here because you have to define the hierarchical structure first before you can undertake the consolidation. The details are given in the Supplement for Release 8.0 of the *IFPS USER'S MANUAL*.

4.9 AN EXAMPLE INVOLVING DATA FILES, REPORTS, AND CONSOLIDATION

In this example we consider the company whose budget and actual quarter-by-quarter results were illustrated in Figures 4-21 and 4-22. What we want to do is create a simple, easy-to-read report for management that shows:

- the budget
- the actual
- the variance
- the percent variance

at the end of the year.

Given the data in quarterly form as in models ACTUAL and BUDGET shown in Figure 4-21, the following steps show one way of achieving this goal. This sequence of steps is illustrated in Figures 4-23 through 4-27.

1. Use model COMPANY and CONSOLIDATE to perform postprocessing and obtain annual data on the actual, budget, and variance. (Figure 4-23.)

2. Create data files by using the STORENT command on each of these three cases.

3. Use the DATASELECT feature of data files to create a new file that consists of the year-end figures and the percent variance, where the percent variance is computed by using divide and factor features available in DATASELECT. (Figure 4-24.)

4. Having put the required data into a data file, create a dummy model that can use the data file. (Figure 4-25.)

5. Write a REPORT that generates the desired format. (Figure 4-26.)

6. Use GENREPORT to obtain the output in the form needed by management. (Figure 4-27.)

```
? consolidate budget with company
CONSOLIDATION COMPLETED 1 MODELS
? solve
ENTER SOLVE OPTIONS
? all

                                1         2         3         4

UNITS                         100       110       120       130
PRICE                       2.500     2.500     2.750     2.750
REVENUE                       250       275       330     357.5
COSTS                         150       170       170       170
PROFIT                        100       105       160     187.5

TOTAL UNITS                   100       210       330       460
TOTAL REVENUE                 250       525       855      1213
TOTAL COSTS                   150       320       490       660
NET PROFIT                    100       205       365     552.5

ENTER SOLVE OPTIONS
? storent cbudget

ENTER STORE OPTIONS
? total units thru net profit

ENTER MORE VARIABLES FOR STORE PROCESSING (OR NONE)
? none
STORE UPDATE COMPLETE
ENTER SOLVE OPTIONS
? consolidate actual with company
CONSOLIDATION COMPLETED 1 MODELS
? solve
ENTER SOLVE OPTIONS
? total units thru net profit

                                1         2         3         4

TOTAL UNITS                    97       209       335       460
TOTAL REVENUE               242.5     522.5     837.5      1181
TOTAL COSTS                   142       297       469       652
NET PROFIT                  100.5     225.5     368.5     529.3
```

FIGURE 4-23. CONSOLIDATE...WITH AND STORENT TO OBTAIN DATA FILES
(This Figure Continued on the Next Page)

```
ENTER SOLVE OPTIONS
? storent cactual
ENTER STORE OPTIONS
total units thru net profit
ENTER MORE VARIABLES FOR STORE PROCESSING (OR NONE)
? none
STORE UPDATE COMPLETE
ENTER SOLVE OPTIONS
? consolidate actual with company
CONSOLIDATION COMPLETED 1 MODELS
? solve
ENTER SOLVE OPTIONS
? total units thru net profit

                           1        2        3        4

TOTAL UNITS               97      209      335      460
TOTAL REVENUE          242.5    522.5    837.5     1181
TOTAL COSTS              142      297      469      652
NET PROFIT             100.5    225.5    368.5    529.3

ENTER SOLVE OPTIONS
? storent cactual
ENTER STORE OPTIONS
? total units thru net profit
ENTER MORE VARIABLES FOR STORE PROCESSING (OR NONE)
? none
STORE UPDATE COMPLETE
ENTER SOLVE OPTIONS
? consolidate actual budget(-1) with company
CONSOLIDATION COMPLETED 2 MODELS
? solve
ENTER SOLVE OPTIONS
? total units thru net profit

                           1        2        3        4

TOTAL UNITS               -3       -1        5        0
TOTAL REVENUE         -7.500   -2.500   -17.50   -31.25
TOTAL COSTS               -8      -23      -21       -8
NET PROFIT             .5000    20.50    3.500   -23.25

ENTER SOLVE OPTIONS
? storent cvar
NEW DATA FILE WILL BE CREATED
ENTER STORE OPTIONS
? total units thru net profit
ENTER MORE VARIABLES FOR STORE PROCESSING (OR NONE)
? none
STORE UPDATE COMPLETE
```

FIGURE 4-23. CONSOLIDATE...WITH AND STORENT TO OBTAIN DATA FILES

```
?DATASELECT
ENTER NUMBER OF COLUMNS  IN OUTPUT MATRIX
? 4
ENTER DATAFILE NAME OR NONE
? cbudget
ENTER DIRECTIVE OR END
? 4 into 1
ENTER DIRECTIVE OR END
? end
ENTER DATAFILE NAME OR NONE
? cactual
ENTER DIRECTIVE OR END
? 4 into 2
ENTER DIRECTIVE OR END
? end
ENTER DATAFILE NAME OR NONE
? cvar
ENTER DIRECTIVE OR END
? 4 into 3, 4 into 4
ENTER DIRECTIVE OR END
? end
ENTER DATAFILE NAME OR NONE
? cbudget
ENTER DIRECTIVE OR END
? divide
ENTER DIRECTIVE OR END
? 4(.01) into 4
ENTER DIRECTIVE OR END
? end
ENTER DATAFILE NAME OR NONE
? none
ENTER OUTPUT FILENAME (STOREOPT OR NAOUTPUT)
? varyear
DATA FILES SELECTED AND SAVED ON FILE VARYEAR
READY FOR EXECUTIVE COMMAND
? datafile varyear
READY FOR EDIT, LAST LINE IS 4
? solve
ENTER SOLVE OPTIONS
? all
```

	1	2	3	4
TOTAL UNITS	460	460	0	0
TOTAL REVENUE	1213	1181	-31.25	-2.577
TOTAL COSTS	660	652	-8	-1.212
NET PROFIT	552.5	529.3	-23.25	-4.208

FIGURE 4-24. USING DATASELECT TO CREATE THE ANNUAL VARIANCE FILE

```
MODEL X  VERSION OF  08/30/82  18:05
1 COLUMNS BUDGET,ACTUAL,VARIANCE,PERCENT
2 TOTAL UNITS =0
3 TOTAL REVENUE =0
4 TOTAL COSTS =0
5 NET PROFIT =0
END OF MODEL
? solve
MODEL X  VERSION OF  08/30/82  18:05 -- 4 COLUMNS 4 VARIABLES
ENTER SOLVE OPTIONS

? all

                         BUDGET  ACTUALVARIANCE PERCENT

TOTAL UNITS                 460     460       0       0
TOTAL REVENUE              1213    1181  -31.25  -2.577
TOTAL COSTS                 660     652      -8  -1.212
NET PROFIT                552.5   529.3  -23.25  -4.208
```

FIGURE 4-25. DUMMY MODEL AND ITS SOLUTION

```
? report variance
READY FOR EDIT, LAST LINE IS 11
? list

REPORT VARIANCE  VERSION OF  08/30/82  18:04
1 FORMAT..........4[     99999.9  ]
2 CENTER COMPANY VARIANCE REPORT
3 CENTER (ANNUAL)
4 SPACE 2
5 COLUMNS 2,1,3,4
6 INVERT NOVAR
7 COLUMN TITLES SALES   ,REVENUE ,,NET     ,
8 COLUMN TITLES  UNITS   ,$     ,COSTS   ,PROFITS,
9 UNDERLINE-
10 DOUBLE
11 TOTAL UNITS THRU NET PROFIT
END OF REPORT
```

FIGURE 4-26. REPORT USED TO GENERATE FIGURE 4-27

```
? genreport variance
```

COMPANY VARIANCE REPORT
(ANNUAL)

	SALES UNITS	REVENUE $	COSTS	NET PROFITS
	-------	-------	-------	-------
ACTUAL	460.0	1181.3	652.0	529.3
BUDGET	460.0	1212.5	660.0	552.5
VARIANCE	.0	-31.3	-8.0	-23.3
PERCENT	.0	-2.6	-1.2	-4.2

FIGURE 4-27. VARIANCE REPORT FOR MANAGEMENT

Immediately after each CONSOLIDATE ... WITH is solved in Step 1, a data file (CACTUAL, CBUDGET, and CVAR) is created with STORENT in Step 2. Note that since we will need only the accumulated data for the year, we only save the total units, total revenue, total costs, and the net profit in these new files.

In Figure 4-24, the DATASELECT feature picks annual data (located in column 4) out of the CACTUAL, CBUDGET, and CVAR data files and puts them into a new file which we have called VARYEAR. This is Step 3. We then compute the percent variance by using the simple computational features available with DATASELECT. (Be sure to go over this figure line by line so that you understand what is being done. Go back to Section 4.6.8 which describes DATASELECT if you don't.) Figure 4-24 also shows you the contents of the newly created file VARYEAR.

Having VARYEAR as a data file, we next create the needed dummy model, which we call MODEL X, and which is shown in Figure 4-25 together with its output when using VARYEAR. This is Step 4.

The transformation of this output into the form desired by management is shown in Figures 4-26 and 4-27. We simply call for GENREPORT VARIANCE to obtain the answer desired. Of course, to do so, we previously had to create the report named VARIANCE. In studying Figure 4-26, note the following points:

- Line 5 reorders the columns from the way that they are stored in the data file.

- Line 6 interchanges the rows and columns in the data file so that management can see actual, budget, and variance as rows rather than as columns. ②

- The column titles differ from the names under which the data are stored. This is perfectly all right.

EXERCISE: Figure 4-28 shows an alternate form of the variance report for management. Write a REPORT which will generate Figure 4-28.

```
? genreport b
```

```
                     COMPANY VARIANCE REPORT
                            (ANNUAL)

                   BUDGET      ACTUAL    VARIANCE     PERCENT
                                                     VARIANCE
                  -------     -------     -------     -------

SALES UNITS         460.0       460.0          .0          .0

REVENUE $          1212.5      1181.3       -31.3        -2.6

COSTS               660.0       652.0        -8.0        -1.2

                  -------     -------     -------     -------

NET PROFIT          552.5       529.3       -23.3        -4.2
```

FIGURE 4-28. ALTERNATE FORM OF THE VARIANCE REPORT

In this section we have taken you, step by step, through the use of CONSOLIDATE, DATAFILE, DATASELECT, and REPORT to create neatly formatted output for management. If you were using the information for your own purposes you might well have stopped after CONSOLIDATE...WITH since the answers you need can be obtained by looking at that output. However, the extra steps are often worthwhile if you need to present information to managers who are used to basing their decisions on information presented in a particular way.

4.10 Additional Editing Commands

In Section 2.5 we presented a series of useful editing commands including:

- C for changing a portion of a line
- D for delete

- Listing a single line by typing its line number.
- Listing a group of lines by typing the first and last line numbers, separated by a comma.
- Replacing a line by retyping it with its line number.

You will find that these edit commands will be sufficient for most editing tasks. In this section we present some additional editing commands that will be helpful in specific situations.

4.10.1 Using " Rather Than / for Editing

IFPS will accept either a quotation mark (") or a slash mark (/) in editing commands. Thus, it is equally valid to write:

```
20C"ORF"ROF"
```

as it is to write:

```
20C/ORF/ROF/
```

4.10.2 Finding All Occurrences of a Specific Phrase

If you want to find all references to a particular variable or phrase or combination of letters, you can use the quote form of the editing command. For example,

```
"SALES"
```

The quote command searches the text of your model until it finds the first time that the combination of letters SALES is used and prints out the entire line. To find the second and later occurrences, you keep repeating the quote editing command.

Figure 4-29 shows you a search for all occurrences of the word SALES in the Simple IFPS Model.

```
? model simple
READY FOR EDIT, LAST LINE IS 90
? "sales"
20 SALES = 100,PREVIOUS SALES *1.25
? "sales"
40 NET INCOME = SALES -EXPENSES
? "sales"
70 *PERCENT OF SALES
? "sales"
80 EXPENSE RATIO = EXPENSES/SALES
? "sales"
90 NET INCOME RATIO = NET INCOME/SALES
? "sales"
20 SALES = 100,PREVIOUS SALES *1.25
```

FIGURE 4-29. FINDING ALL OCCURRENCES OF "SALES" IN THE SIMPLE IFPS MODEL

If you only want to find all references to a particular variable, then the CROSSREF command descibed in Section 4.5.6 is an easier method.

4.10.3 Changing All Occurrences of a Specific Phrase

The C edit command allows you to change a single occurrence of a specific phrase. For example, if you want to change SLAES to SALES in Line 20, you type

```
20C/SLAES/SALES/
```

If, however, you want to make the same change for every time a particular combination of letters or a particular phrase occurs, you can save yourself the tedium of finding and changing each occurrence by using the global change command. For example, if you want to change SALES to REVENUE throughout the Simple IFPS Model, you would type:

```
10,90G"SALES"REVENUE"
```

where the sequence is as follows:

- starting line number followed by a comma (10,)
- ending line number followed by no blank spaces (90)
- G
- quotation mark (or /)
- old text to be replaced (SALES)
- quotation mark (or /)
- new text to be inserted (REVENUE)
- quotation mark (or /).

If you forget the last quotation mark (or last /) IFPS assumes that the new text ends with the last letter that is not a blank space.

Figure 4-30 shows several examples of the global replace command.

```
10,90g"sales"revenue"
20 REVENUE = 100,PREVIOUS REVENUE *1.25
40 NET INCOME = REVENUE -EXPENSES
70 *PERCENT OF REVENUE
80 EXPENSE RATIO = EXPENSES/REVENUE
90 NET INCOME RATIO = NET INCOME/REVENUE
```

a. Use of "SALES"REVENUE"

FIGURE 4-30. ALTERNATE FORMS OF GLOBAL SEARCH
(This Figure Continued on the Next Page)

```
? 10,90g/sales/revenue/
20 REVENUE = 100,PREVIOUS REVENUE *1.25
40 NET INCOME = REVENUE -EXPENSES
70 *PERCENT OF REVENUE
80 EXPENSE RATIO = EXPENSES/REVENUE
90 NET INCOME RATIO = NET INCOME/REVENUE
```

b. Use of /SALES/REVENUE/

```
? 10,90g"sales"revenue
20 REVENUE = 100,PREVIOUS REVENUE *1.25
40 NET INCOME = REVENUE -EXPENSES
70 *PERCENT OF REVENUE
80 EXPENSE RATIO = EXPENSES/REVENUE
90 NET INCOME RATIO = NET INCOME/REVENUE
```

C. Use of "SALES"REVENUE

FIGURE 4-30. ALTERNATE FORMS OF GLOBAL SEARCH (Continued)

4.10.4 Additional Editing Commands for Data Files and Data in Models.

IFPS provides four additional editing commands that can be used with data. The data can be either in a data file or within a model. These commands are:

REMOVE column
INSERT column
CHANGE column
CHANGE variable

If you want only specific elements of a column or a variable, you add the word FOR. For example, to remove the values of sales and expenses in column 4, you would write

REMOVE 4 FOR SALES,EXPENSES

If you want to insert or change, you have to specify not only the column but also the new values. The following are typical examples:

INSERT 4 FOR X = 7
CHANGE 3RD QTR FOR SALES,EXPENSES=250,212
CHANGE SALES FOR 1983 THRU 1986 = 420,435,460,490

The first of these adds the value 7 to column 4 of the variable X. The second changes the current values of sales and expenses in the column labeled 3RD QTR to the values 250 and 212 respectively. The last example changes the variable sales in the columns named 1983, 1984, 1985, and 1986 to the new values indicated.

Figure 4-31 shows examples of three of these editing commands. The following paragraphs describe these commands in more detail.

```
? model product
READY FOR EDIT, LAST LINE IS 200
? insert 5 for unit price = 2.65
NUMBER OF CHANGES PERFORMED WAS 1
? change 1 for market = 7000
NUMBER OF CHANGES PERFORMED WAS 1
? change 1140=3000,0
NUMBER OF CHANGES PERFORMED WAS 2
? 50,140p
50 SALES VOLUME =MARKET*MARKET SHARE
60 MARKET=7000,PREVIOUS MARKET*1.03
70 MARKET SHARE =0.15,PREVIOUS MARKET SHARE +0.005
80 GROSS SALES = SALES VOLUME * UNIT PRICE
90 UNIT PRICE=2.5 FOR 4,2.65,2.75
100 OPERATING COST=(PRODUCTION COST +OVERHEAD)*SALES VOLUME
110 PRODUCTION COST= 1.25 FOR 4,1.35
120 OVERHEAD=PRODUCTION COST*0.80
130 NET INCOME=GROSS SALES -OPERATING COST
140 INVESTMENT =3000,0
```

FIGURE 4-31. INSERT AND CHANGE EDITING COMMANDS

REMOVE: The REMOVE command deletes the data values indicated. It is the simplest of the data file editing commands.

INSERT: The INSERT command adds information which did not exist before. The insert command can always be used to insert data in the first column. However, it can be used for any subsequent column only if the previous column exists in the definition of the model and constant data are given for that column. Thus, if:

```
30 Z = 1,2,3
```

you cannot ask for

```
INSERT 5 FOR Z = 5
```

Similarly, if:

```
30 Z = 1, PREVIOUS +1
```

you cannot ask for:

```
INSERT 3 FOR Z = 4
```

CHANGE: You can change a data value only if that value already exists in the model. Variable names can be referenced by name or line number and columns can be referenced by name or number.

CHAPTER V
MONTE CARLO SIMULATION (RISK ANALYSIS)

5.1 The Rationale and Use of Simulation

5.1.1 The Difference Between Modeling and Simulation
5.1.2 Modeling Uncertainty
5.1.3 Using Random Variables
5.1.4 The Simulation Procedure
5.1.5 Example: A Simple Simulation Experiment
5.1.6 Example: A Second Simple Simulation

5.2 IFPS Approach to Simulation

5.3 Built-In Probability Distributions

5.3.1 Uniform Probability Distribution (UNIRAND)
5.3.2 Triangular Probability Distribution (TRIRAND and T1090RAND)
5.3.3 Normal Probability Distribution (NORRAND)

5.4 Defining Your Own Probability Distribution

5.5 Choosing the Same Random Number for All Periods or a New Value for Each Period

5.6 Example: The Simple IFPS Model with Uncertainty

5.7 Generating Scenarios (HIGH, LOW, MEAN, MOSTP)

5.8 Running A MONTE CARLO Simulation

5.9 The STOP Command (What to Do If you Make an Options Mistake)

5.10 Interpreting MONTE CARLO Results

5.10.1 Frequency Table
5.10.2 Normal Approximation Table
5.10.3 Sample Statistics
5.10.4 Histogram

5.11 The POOL Command

5.12 Example: The New Product Model With Uncertainty

5.13 Example: A Risk Analysis Model

5.14 Example: Testing the IFPS Random Number Generator

CHAPTER V
MONTE CARLO SIMULATION (RISK ANALYSIS)

5.1 THE RATIONALE AND USE OF SIMULATION

In the models discussed in the first four chapters of this book, all input data and all relationships were assumed to be known precisely. Such models are called deterministic. Although this is often (but not always) the case when dealing with historical information (as in bookkeeping), it is rarely the case when making estimates about the future. The future is uncertain and hence, from a business point of view, risky. In making business decisions, these risks must be evaluated.

Consider the New Product Model of Section 2.7. In creating this model, we assumed that we knew precisely what costs and revenues would be each quarter over the next two years. That is, we used single point estimates for all quantities. Although we would know about some changes (e.g., increases in wages resulting from existing labor contracts) and could build them into the model (e.g., production cost increases from $1.25 to $1.35), other changes from the situation modeled would be much less certain. For example, we assumed that market share would start at 15 percent and grow by 1/2 percent per quarter. Such single point estimates typically reflect the average of the values anticipated. The real situation might be market shares of:

.15,.149,.155,.163,.173,.179,.185,.182.

over the eight-quarter time horizon. If this sequence occurs, is the venture still profitable? Supposing there is a different pattern of growth. What then?

One way of exploring the implications of uncertainty is to use the WHAT IF, SENSITIVITY, and GOAL SEEKING features of IFPS. These features allow you to explore alternative situations by modifying the model and determining the effects of changes. Although excellent for exploring the effects of changes in one or two variables or answering specific concerns about the assumptions by senior management, these features are not the most effective way of analyzing risk. A second approach is to make best case and worst case estimates. In this approach, estimates are made of the most favorable and most unfavorable value that each input variable could have. To obtain the best case, the most favorable values are assumed and to obtain the worst case, the most unfavorable values are used. Unfortunately, in the real world all variables do not take on their best values simultaneously nor do they all take on their worst values. Although very useful for examing the most extreme situations, the best case/worst case approach does not give insight into the range of situations which can realistically be expected. The alternative approach is to use simulation, the subject of this chapter.

Simulation is based on the concepts of probability and statistics. We will assume that you have an elementary knowledge of both. If you know nothing about these subjects, then you should first read and understand Sections 7.1 through 7.4. Better still, if you are a student, skip this chapter until you are well into a beginning course in statistics. If you are a professional, work with someone in your organization who is knowledgeable and can help you.

5.1.1 The Difference Between Modeling and Simulation

Until now, we have been concerned with building models. Modeling and simulation differ in that:

- **MODELING involves building a representation of a situation.**
- **SIMULATION involves performing sampling experiments on the model of the situation**

We have emphasized this distinction so that you will engrave it in your memory.

The key words in this definition of simulation are "sampling experiments".

In a sampling experiment, a large number of trials are made. Because of the presence of uncertainty, the outcome of each trial may be different from that of other trials. However, the commonly used concepts of statistics, such as mean and standard deviation, allow inferences to be made about the anticipated outcomes of the situation. In simulation, the sampling experiments are performed on the computer model, thereby allowing many trials to be made at little expense.

5.1.2 Modeling Uncertainty

If you are uncertain about a variable such as market share, you have two choices:

1. Ignore uncertainty by assuming that average or most likely values will occur or
2. Attempt to model the uncertainty.

In most modeling situations you have some idea as to the nature and extent of the uncertainties being faced. In the new product example, market share could theoretically range from 0 to 100 percent; however, based on market survey, historical experience, and analysis of the competition, you can estimate that market share will remain relatively stable from quarter to quarter and have long term growth. You might in fact be willing to state that market share would never increase by more than, say, 2 percent in a quarter nor that it would shrink by more than, say, one percent in a quarter. Furthermore, you may be willing to estimate that 1/2 percent linear growth is most likely. Such beliefs can be converted into the form of probability distributions and these probability distributions can be included explicitly in the IFPS model. We will discuss methods for modeling probability distributions in Sections 5.2 and 5.3. In technical terms, we have introduced a random variable (in our example, growth in market share) with a given probability distribution.

5.1.3 Using Random Variables

Although we cannot predict which value a random variable will take, we know that it will take on some value; the chances of a particular value are defined by the probability distribution. For example, if we roll a pair of dice, we cannot tell what the result will be until the roll ends. However, before the roll we know that there is a 1/36 chance of a 2 and a 1/6 chance of a 7.

In solving a model containing one or more random variables, we have to have a rule for deciding what value that random variable takes on. One way of making this decision is simply to assign a value from the probability distribution and proceed as if this is the value that had occurred. Doing this once leads to a particular outcome, a "scenario". Since in simulation we perform a sampling experiment, we repeat this process many times. Each time we come to a random variable, we choose a value from the probability distribution and use that value in determining the outcome. That is, we choose the value of the random variable so that the frequency of occurrence of particular values is related to the probability distribution. For example, in simulating dice, your experiment might involve generating 36,000 different rolls of the dice on the computer. However, you must arrange things in such a way that approximately 1000 times (that is, 1/36th of the time) the outcome is a 2 and approximately 6000 times the outcome is a seven. (Because of the nature of randomness you should not expect to observe exactly 1000 2's or exactly 6000 7's.)

5.1.4 The Simulation Procedure

In summary, the steps in running a simulation are:

1. Build a model that defines uncertainties and risks in terms of probability.

2. Perform a sampling experiment on the computer in which you run the model a large number of times. Each outcome gives you one possible scenario.

3. Perform statistical analyses on the outcome of the experiment.

4. Use the statistical results obtained for decision making.

You, as modeler, must introduce the uncertainty into your IFPS model. Having done so, you can instruct IFPS how many times you want the model to be run. IFPS makes these runs and presents you with a statistical analysis of the results. After examining the results, you can then ask for additional runs to gain better precision or you can make a decision based on the results presented.

5.1.5 Example: A Simple Simulation Experiment

Before proceeding with the details of how simulation is performed in IFPS, we present two simple examples of simulation which you can perform by hand. If you are an old hand in simulation, you can skip directly to Section 5.2. If you are new to it, read and understand these examples before proceeding.

Your friend Terri offers you $7 to play the following game with her. A coin will be flipped as many times as needed until four tails have appeared. For each flip of the coin, you pay Terri $1. For example, if the first four flips are tails, you receive $7, pay $4 and make a net profit of $3. The chances of this happening are only 1 in 16. However, if it takes 12 flips until the 4th tail occurs, you lose $5. Should you play? If not, can you make Terri a fair counterproposal as to how much she should pay you to play?

Although you can compute your expected winnings (or losses) by probability theory, the calculations are a bit messy. An alternative is to ask for a few minutes to think the proposition over and head for a nearby computer terminal. You remember how to generate random numbers and obtain the following sequence:

1,0,4,8,0,1,5,0,1,1,5,3,6,0,2,0,1,1,8,1,6,4,7,9,1,3,4,6,6,
9,1,4,1,9,4,6,2,5,9,0,3,6,2,0,7,2,0,9,6,9,9,9,5,7,0,9,9,0,
7,0,0,2,3,6,4,1,7,3,3

If you interpret 0 through 4 as tails and 5 through 9 as heads, you see that the first "play" of the game requires 5 flips (a profit of $2). That is, 1,0,4,8,0 corresponds to the sequence T,T,T,H,T (T=tail, H=head). Using this rule, succeeding plays of the game require 5,6,6,9,6,7,14,5, and 6 flips respectively. If you base your decision on the average number of flips observed in these 10 "plays" of the game you would decide to play since the average cost is $6.90 and you will receive $7.00 for playing. However, should you?

EXERCISE. Suppose you interpret 0 through 4 as heads and 5 through 9 as tails. Show that the average cost under this rule for the data given is $9.14 based on a sample of 7 plays requiring 64 flips.

This simple example points out an important characteristic and a problem of simulations. First, the computer can be used to generate random numbers that can be interpreted as the outcome of random events. Second, data interpretation from simulations requires care. If you terminated after the first simulated play of the game, you would expect a profit of $2. If you had used a sample of eight plays, your average cost would have been $7.13 and you would not play. The point is that the "results" of the simulation depend on the size of the sample used in the experiment. Sample size must be chosen with care based on statistical considerations. Although the mean is $6.90, the standard deviation of the sample is $2.76. It also turns out that the true average cost is $8 and that there is approximately a 36% chance of losing $2 or more. Is this risk acceptable to you?

5.1.6 Example: A Second Simple Simulation

The TAG Donut Shoppe buys fresh doughnuts each morning to serve to that day's customers. Doughnuts not sold that day are thrown away. Unfortunately, demand fluctuates. Based on past experience, demand has ranged from 24 to 28 dozen with the probabilities shown in Table 5-1.

TABLE 5-1

DEMAND FOR TAG DOUGHNUTS

Demand (Dozen)	Probability of Demand	Probability of This Demand or Less
23	0.0	0.0
24	0.2	0.2
25	0.1	0.3
26	0.3	0.6
27	0.3	0.9
28	0.1	1.0

TAG pays $2.00 per dozen and sells at $3.00 per dozen. How many dozen should TAG order each day?

It is not difficult to show that the optimal policy, if demand one day does not depend on any other day, is to buy 26 dozen. This policy results in an average daily profit of $24.50. The actual profit (P) on a given day is given by:

$$P = 3.00*D - 2.00*S \quad \text{if } D < S, \text{ and}$$
$$P = 1.00*S \quad \text{if } D >= S \qquad (5\text{-}1)$$

In the second case, demand (D) equals or exceeds supply (S) and all doughnuts are sold at a profit of a dollar a dozen.

To simulate this situation, the procedure is similar to that used in the coin flipping example.

1. Decide on a daily supply, S

2. Determine demand

3. Compute profit from Equation 5-1

4. Repeat steps 2 and 3 a sufficient number of times to estimate the mean and variance of the profit associated with a supply policy, S.

Since the objective is to find that supply policy which yields a maximum profit, the procedure has to be repeated systematically for different levels of supply (i.e., for 24,25,26,...dozen) until a maximum is found. Note that in specifying the simulation procedure we tacitly assumed that the same size order should be placed each day. (Do you see why it should be the same?)

Three problems manifest themselves here.

1. How is demand to be determined?

2. How is supply to be selected?

3. How often do you repeat to be able to make a decision?

To determine demand, we use the column in Table 5-1 labeled "Probability of This Demand or Less". These values are the cumulative probability. First choose a random number between 0 and 1. Suppose it is .532. Then determine the interval in Table 5-1 in which this random number falls (.532 is between 0.3 and 0.6). Select as the demand the value corresponding to the upper end of the interval (26 dozen corresponds to 0.6). Thus, for the data in Table 5-1, if a random number is between 0 and .2, we assume 24 dozen; from .2 to .3 we assume 25 dozen, etc.

The use of random numbers between 0 and 1 to represent cumulative probabilities is one of the fundamental ideas in simulation. That is, you use the fact that the cumulative probability distribution for any random variable is uniformly distributed between 0 and 1. When you pick a random number between 0 and 1, therefore, you are picking a point on the cumulative probability distribution. By finding the corresponding value of the random variable, you have made the decision as to which value it takes on.

The second problem involves the choice of supply, S. Whereas in the coin flipping example, the profit depended only on the number of flips, here the profit depends on two variables, supply and demand. Supply is the decision variable, the one over which you have control, whereas demand is a random variable determined by "nature" or chance. One simple approach, then, is to try different values of S (by WHAT IF) until the one yielding the highest profit is found.

The third problem is a statistical one. Suppose you obtain the following data after 10 replications at each supply:

Supply,S	Average Profit	Std. Deviation of Average Profit
25	24.45	0.20
26	24.47	0.25
27	23.97	0.30

At first glance, the average profits indicate that you could narrow your choice of maximum down to S=25 or S=26 dozen and that the answer most likely is S=26. But can you? If you draw a 90% confidence interval around the average profits, you obtain the region inside which there is a 90% chance that the true mean lies. For our results, you obtain:

Supply,S	Lower Limit on Profit	Upper Limit on Profit
25	24.35	24.55
26	24.34	24.60
27	23.83	24.13

90% confidence intervals are computed from the fomulas:

UPPER LIMIT = AVERAGE + 1.65* STANDARD DEVIATION / √ n
LOWER LIMIT = AVERAGE - 1.65*STANDARD DEVIATION / √ n

where n is the number of replications.

The sketch below plots the confidence intervals for the three daily supplies:

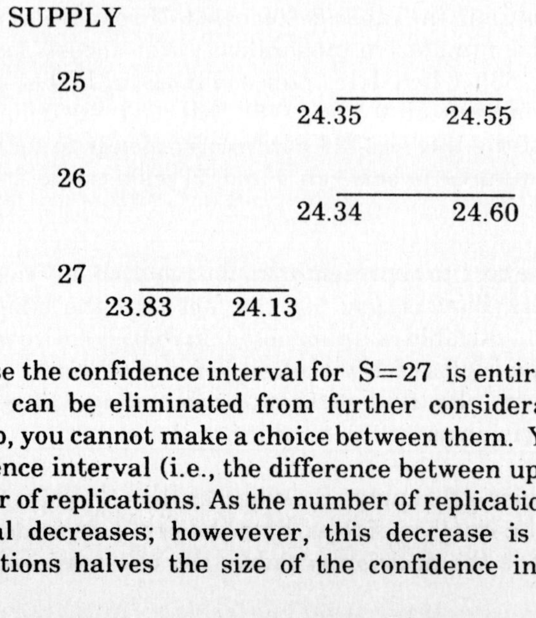

Because the confidence interval for S=27 is entirely below that of the other two choices, S =27 can be eliminated from further consideration. Since the limits for 25 and 26 overlap, you cannot make a choice between them. You can, however, reduce the size of the confidence interval (i.e., the difference between upper and lower limit) by increasing the number of replications. As the number of replications increases, the size of the confidence interval decreases; howevever, this decrease is slow. For example, quadrupling the replications halves the size of the confidence interval. Because of the importance of confidence intervals in making decisions, IFPS calculates confidence intervals for you. You will also see that IFPS allows you to increase the sample size through the use of the POOL command discussed in Section 5.11.

5.2 IFPS APPROACH TO SIMULATION

IFPS provides you with the capability for performing Monte Carlo Simulations. The term Monte Carlo goes back to World War II when the major development of simulation took place. Analysts using the method on a classified project wanted a code word to describe it. Since chance events were being modeled it appeared appropriate to give the method a code name based on the biggest gambling casino which was then located in Monte Carlo.

The procedure you follow is to describe each quantity about which you are uncertain in terms of a probability distribution. The values of these distributions are random variables. When you ask for MONTE CARLO, IFPS solves the model a number of times with different combinations of values picked each time from the distributions you specified. The results of these replications are analyzed statistically by IFPS and you are given the statistical results. These statistical results can be interpreted in terms of the risks involved in the decision. For example, you may find out there is a 10% chance the internal rate of return will exceed 25% and a 90% chance that it will exceed 14%.

If you have a deterministic model, you will find that it is not necessary to change the basic structure of the model to incorporate risk into the analysis. All you have to do is express quantities in terms of probabilities rather than in terms of single point estimates. IFPS contains four built-in distributions (discussed in Section 5.3) and you also have the ability to model any arbitrary cumulative probability distribution of your choice (Section 5.4). Furthermore, as we discuss in Section 5.7, IFPS provides you with the ability to generate scenarios based on assigning high, low, mean, and median values to individual random variables.

5.3 BUILT-IN PROBABILITY DISTRIBUTIONS

Four built-in probability distributions are provided by IFPS:

UNIRAND	uniform distribution
TRIRAND	triangular distribution
T1090RAND	an alternate form of the triangular distribution
NORRAND	normal distribution

In addition, IFPS allows you to model any distribution of your choice through GENRAND and CUMRAND. We will discuss GENRAND and CUMRAND in Section 5.4.

For each of these probability distributions, you must specify the name of the distribution and two or more of its parameters. A typical specification is UNIRAND(10,30) which defines a probability distribution that is uniformly distributed between limits of 10 and 30. We now proceed to discuss each of the built-in distributions.

5.3.1 Uniform Probability Distribution (UNIRAND)

If all values in an interval are equally likely, then we have a uniform probability distribution. For example, in the following uniform distribution

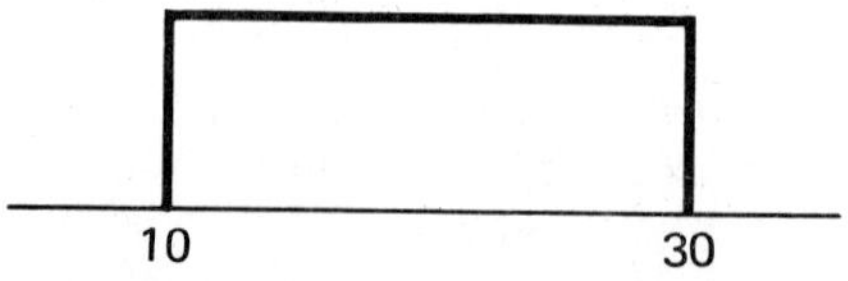

all values between 10 and 30 are equally likely. To generate random values from this distribution, you would write, for example,

```
COST = UNIRAND(10,30)                                        (5-2)
```

In a simulation with many replications, each time IFPS reaches a statement containing UNIRAND(10,30), it selects a value at random between 10 and 30.

In general, UNIRAND(LOWER,UPPER) specifies a uniform distribution between the upper and lower limit. The LOWER limit must be less than the UPPER limit.

5.3.2 Triangular Distribution (TRIRAND and T1090RAND)

The triangular distribution has been found to be particularly useful in modeling risk situations. Three arguments have to be supplied by you:

- the lower limit
- the most probable (maximum) value
- the upper limit

For example,

```
TRIRAND(0.96, 1.05,1.07)
```

tells IFPS to generate values from a triangular distribution of the form

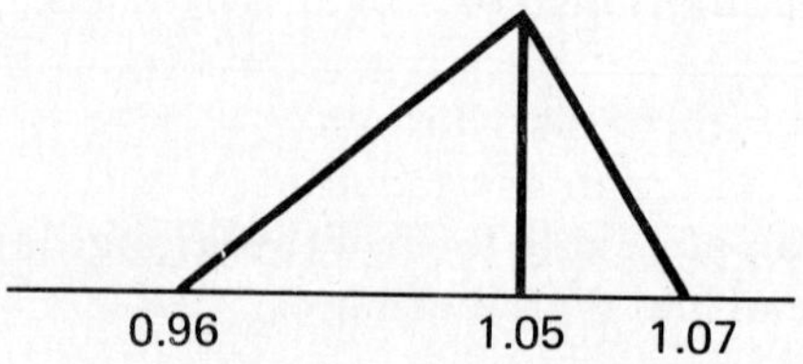

The triangular distribution is a convenient approximation when the range of possible values (i.e., upper and lower limits) is known and the distribution has a single peak. It also provides the capability for expressing the idea that risk is not symmetrically distributed around the most likely value.

The following statement is a typical IFPS application of TRIRAND:

```
MARKET = PREVIOUS MARKET*TRIRAND(0.96,1.05,1.07)
```

It models the idea that the market growth is uncertain, ranging from a 4% decrease (i.e., 0.96*PREVIOUS) to a 7% increase with the most likely value being a 5% increase (i.e., 1.05*PREVIOUS).

If the most probable value is equal to the upper (or lower) limit, a right-angled triangular distribution is generated. For example, TRIRAND (10,10,30) generates the following distribution:

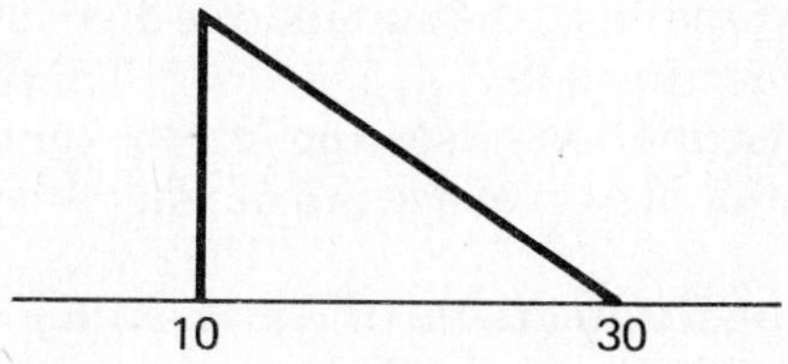

An alternative way of specifying a triangular distribution is to use the T1090RAND function. If you do not know precisely the smallest and largest value that a particular variable can take on, you may be able to estimate the 10th and 90th percentage points on the distribution. In this case, you would write

```
T1090RAND(0.97,1.05,1.065)
```

where .97 and 1.065 represent the 10th and 90th percentiles and 1.05 is the most likely value.

The most likely value of a triangular distribution is the mode, not the average. If the triangular distribution is symmetric (e.g., TRIRAND(10,20,30)) then the average value and the mode are the same. However, if the triangular distribution is skewed left as it is in TRIRAND(0.93,1.00,1.05) then the mean is less than the mode. If it is skewed right, the mean is larger than the mode. Incidentally, the mean of TRIRAND(a,b,c) is equal to (a+b+c)/3.

5.3.3 Normal Probability Distribution (NORRAND)

To generate a normally distributed random variable, you have to specify the mean and the standard deviation. For example,

```
NORRAND(100,10)
```

creates a normal distribution with a mean of 100 and a standard deviation of 10. This distribution is shown below.

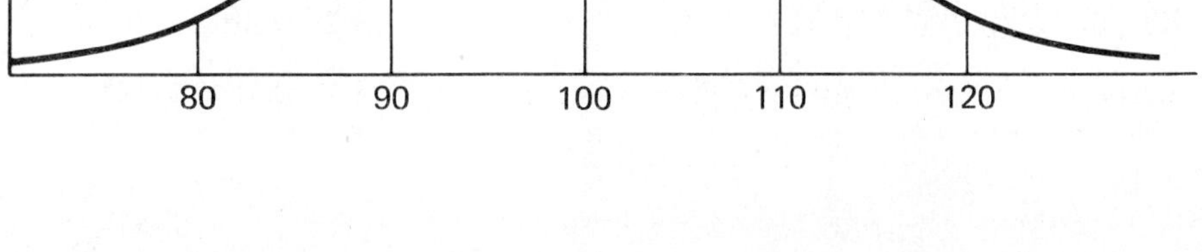

5.4 DEFINING YOUR OWN PROBABILITY DISTRIBUTIONS

Although many business situations can be described in terms of the built-in distributions, occasions where you need some other distribution do arise. In these cases, you can define either a generalized density function (GENRAND) or a generalized cumulative distribution (CUMRAND) to meet your requirements. As you recall, the density function represents the probability of a particular outcome (e.g., throwing a 2 with a pair of dice) whereas the cumulative distribution represents the probability of obtaining all values less than or equal to a given value (e.g., the cumulative distribution for 7 in throwing dice adds up the probabilities of throwing a 2, 3, 4, 5, 6, or 7.) This distinction between density function and cumulative distribution also applies to continuous distributions. For example, the normal distribution shown above is a density function.

In the GENRAND form you approximate the the probability density function with a series of straight lines as shown in Figure 5-1 below.

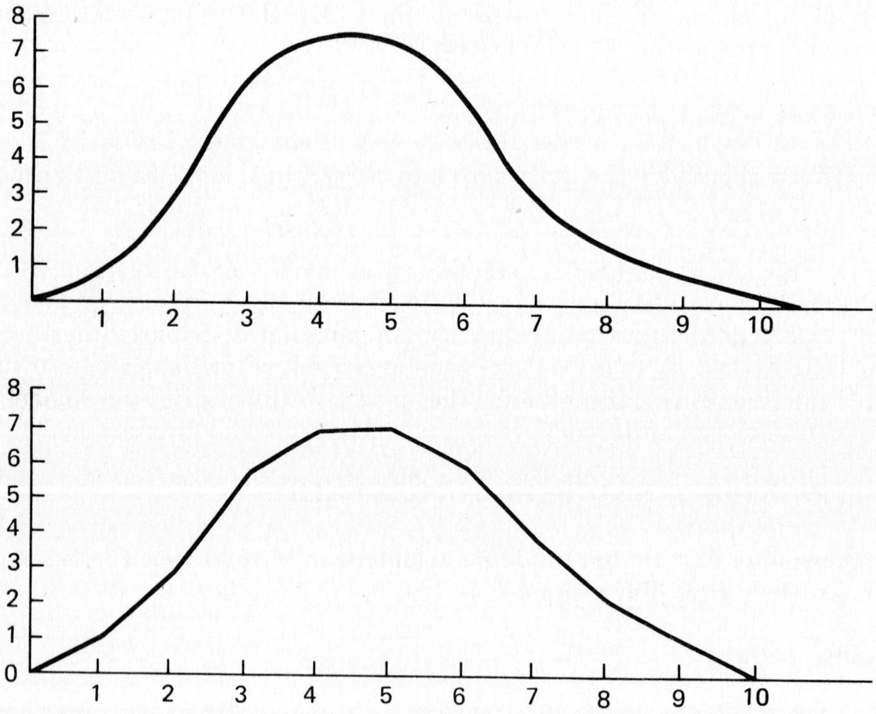

FIGURE 5-1. APPROXIMATING A PROBABILITY DENSITY FUNCTION WITH STRAIGHT LINES

To use the density function, you specify the coordinates in increasing order of X and include the coordinates in the GENRAND function. For example,

```
GENRAND(0,0,1,1,2,3,3,6,4,7,5,7,6,6,8,2,10,0)
```

specifies the points (0,0),(1,1),(2,3), (3,6),(4,7),(5,7), (6,6),(8,2), and (10,0) where the first number in each pair is the X value and the second number is the value of the random variable , given X.

EXERCISE: Use GENRAND to specify a triangular distribution with endpoints 0 and 5 and mode 4. Note that you will have to determine the height of the distribution at the mode.

If you know the cumulative probability distribution rather than the probability density function, you should use CUMRAND rather than GENRAND. In CUMRAND you specify the X value in equal increments of 10% of the cumulative distribution. For example, the figure shows

```
CUMRAND(0,3,5,6,7,7.5,8,8.5,9,10,12)
```

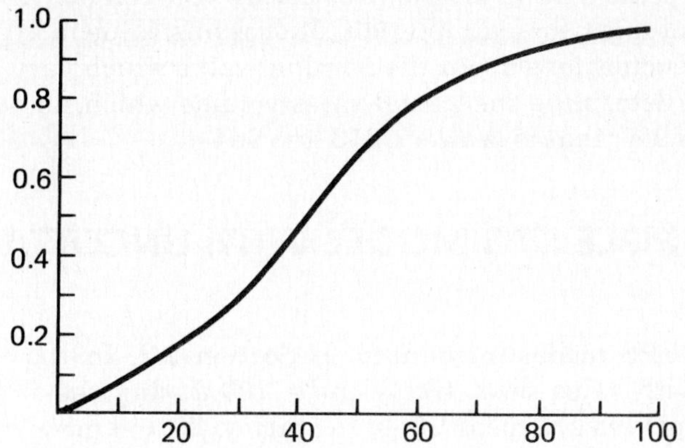

Here, 1/10 of the probability value is between 0 and 3, 1/10th between 3 and 5, etc. There is a 30 percent probability that the value will be less than or equal to 6.

Since IFPS fixes the Y values at 0, 10%, 20%,..., you need to specify only the 11 corresponding X values. A total of 11 values, MUST be included between the parentheses in CUMRAND.

5.5 CHOOSING THE SAME RANDOM NUMBER FOR ALL PERIODS OR A NEW VALUE FOR EACH PERIOD

A particular quantity (such as rental cost) may be uncertain initially but once determined stays fixed, whereas another quantity (such as sales volume) may fluctuate from period to period. IFPS allows you to model both kinds of situations. If you use:

```
UNIRAND,TRIRAND,T1090RAND,NORRAND,GENRAND,or CUMRAND
```

you will make the choice of value once and keep that same value in all following periods. However, if you add an R to any of these definitions of probability distributions, that is, if you use:

```
UNIRANDR,TRIRANDR,T1090RANDR,NORRANDR,GENRANDR,or
CUMRANDR
```

you will obtain a different value each period.

You can combine the two forms. For example:

```
UNIT COST=TRIRAND(10,12,13),PREVIOUS UNIT COST*1.08*
                   UNIRANDR( 0.95,1.06)
```

or:

```
SALES VOLUME=TRIRAND(800,1000,1100)*TRIRANDR(0.97,1.0,1.06)
```

In the first example, IFPS picks a unit cost in the first period. In subsequent periods the cost grows by 8% times a factor between .95 and 1.06. This factor is chosen afresh each period.

In the second example, IFPS picks a value in the first period between 800 and 1100 that represents the nominal level of sales; for example, 900. It uses this value in all subsequent periods. However, there are fluctuations about the nominal value which vary from period to period. These fluctuations determine the actual sales volume which, in our example, are between 97% and 106% of 900, that is between 873 and 954.

5.6 EXAMPLE: THE SIMPLE IFPS MODEL WITH UNCERTAINTY

Consider again the simple IFPS model introduced in Section 2.2. In that example, a product is to be marketed with sales most likely to be 100 during the first year and growing at 25% per year. Expenses are most likely to start at 75 and grow by 25 a year. Although these are the most likely estimates, the outcomes are by no means certain.

Initial sales may be as low as 90 and as high as 120, and sales growth each year may be smaller or larger than 25%. In fact, year-to-year sales growth may vary from being flat to being as high as 50% per year. Similarly, although initial expenses are known to be 75, expense growth is uncertain. Expense growth has a fixed component that will be known by the first year and a variable component that fluctuates from year to year. Figure 5-2 shows the resulting IFPS model.

```
MODEL MONTE  VERSION OF  12/29/80  14:55
10 COLUMNS 1-6
20 SALES=INITIAL SALES,PREVIOUS SALES* SALES GROWTH RATE
30 EXPENSES=75,PREVIOUS EXPENSES + 25 +FIXED EXPENSE GROWTH'
31 +VARIABLE EXPENSE GROWTH
40 NET INCOME=SALES-EXPENSES
50 *
60 *
70*
80 INITIAL SALES=TRIRAND(90,100,120),0
90 SALES GROWTH RATE=1.25*UNIRANDR(0.8,1.2)
100 FIXED EXPENSE GROWTH =UNIRAND(-2,4)
110 VARIABLE EXPENSE GROWTH=UNIRANDR(-3,1)
```

FIGURE 5-2. SIMPLE IFPS MODEL WITH UNCERTAINTY

You can solve this model in two ways:

- by creating scenarios

- by asking IFPS for a MONTE CARLO simulation.

We discuss these two methods in turn.

5.7 GENERATING SCENARIOS (HIGH,LOW, MEAN, MOSTP)

Before undertaking MONTE CARLO simulation runs, it is usually wise to examine the range of answers that can be anticipated. You may want to know what a typical (average or most probable) outcome is and what the best and worst situations would be. This combination of best, worst, and most likely scenarios is an excellent way of beginning to understand a situation and is often a convenient, short-hand way of communicating with management.

To allow the generation of scenarios, IFPS provides you four SOLVE options:

```
HIGH    LOW  MEAN    MOSTP
```

These options set the value of a probability distribution to its maximum, minimum, average, and most likely values. (In the case of NORRAND, the HIGH value is +2.5 standard deviations and the LOW value is –2.5 standard deviations.) The options can be chosen individually for each distribution. Thus, by mixing values, favorable and unfavorable scenarios can be created.

In the Simple IFPS Model with Uncertainty discussed in Section 5.6, the most favorable case occurs if:

- initial sales and sales growth rate are HIGH

- expense growth is LOW

while the most unfavorable case occurs if:

- initial sales and sales growth rate are LOW

- expense growth rate is HIGH

In general, the best case is obtained when all probability distributions are in your favor and the worst case is obtained when all distributions are against you. Figure 5-3 shows the results of running the best and worst cases for the Simple IFPS Model with Uncertainty. Figure 5-3 shows that you use one of the solve option words, such as HIGH, followed by a list of variables separated by commas to tell IFPS what you want. In general, you must first specify the levels you want the variables to have using HIGH, LOW, MEAN, and/or MOSTP and then you must tell IFPS which variables you want printed (for example, ALL in Figure 5-3). Once you specify the variables to be printed, IFPS begins computing.

```
? solve
MODEL MONTE  VERSION OF  12/29/80  14:55 -- 6 COLUMNS 7 VARIABLES
ENTER SOLVE OPTIONS
? high initial sales ,sales growth rate
? low fixed expense growth,variable expense growth
? all

                              1       2       3       4       5       6

SALES                       120     180     270     405   607.5   911.3
EXPENSES                     75      95     115     135     155     175
NET INCOME                   45      85     155     270   452.5   736.3


INITIAL SALES               120       0       0       0       0       0
SALES GROWTH RATE         1.500   1.500   1.500   1.500   1.500   1.500
FIXED EXPENSE GROWTH         -2      -2      -2      -2      -2      -2
VARIABLE EXPENSE GROWTH      -3      -3      -3      -3      -3      -3

ENTER SOLVE OPTIONS
? low initial sales,sales growth rate,
? high fixed expense growth,variable expense growth
? all

                              1       2       3       4       5       6

SALES                        90      90      90      90      90      90
EXPENSES                     75     105     135     165     195     225
NET INCOME                   15     -15     -45     -75    -105    -135


INITIAL SALES                90       0       0       0       0       0
SALES GROWTH RATE             1       1       1       1       1       1
FIXED EXPENSE GROWTH          4       4       4       4       4       4
VARIABLE EXPENSE GROWTH       1       1       1       1       1       1
```

FIGURE 5-3. BEST CASE AND WORST CASE SOLUTIONS OF SIMPLE IFPS MODEL WITH UNCERTAINTY

You can use the modifier ALL with HIGH, LOW, etc. Thus, for example, the combination

```
?HIGH ALL
?ALL
```

sets all probabilistic variables to their high values and then prints out all lines of the solution.

Before proceeding to the most likely case, a word of caution is in order. The absolute best and absolute worst cases are easy to compute but can be dangerous to use for decision making, particularly for models of complex situations. It is rare indeed when all variables take on their absolutely most favorable or most unfavorable values. Therefore absolute best and absolute worst cases are not representative and give a distorted view of the upside and downside risk. A more reasonable approach is to set some variables to HIGH and LOW and leave others at their mean or most probable levels.

The MOSTP and MEAN values are the same for symmetric distributions (such as the uniform and the normal) but differ for non-symmetric triangular distributions. For example, for TRIRAND(90,100,120) the most probable value is 100 but the mean is 103.3. You can set variables to their most probable or their mean values. The results of these two cases will be slightly different. This can be seen from Figure 5-4 which shows what happens when you set all random variables first to their most probable value and then to their mean value.

```
? mostp all
? all

                              1       2       3       4       5       6

SALES                       100     125   156.3   195.3   244.1   305.2
EXPENSES                     75     100     125     150     175     200
NET INCOME                   25      25   31.25   45.31   69.14   105.2


INITIAL SALES               100       0       0       0       0       0
SALES GROWTH RATE         1.250   1.250   1.250   1.250   1.250   1.250
FIXED EXPENSE GROWTH          1       1       1       1       1       1
VARIABLE EXPENSE GROWTH      -1      -1      -1      -1      -1      -1

ENTER SOLVE OPTIONS
? mean all
? all

                              1       2       3       4       5       6

SALES                     103.3   129.2   161.5   201.8   252.3   315.3
EXPENSES                     75     100     125     150     175     200
NET INCOME                28.33   29.17   36.46   51.82   77.28   115.3


INITIAL SALES             103.3       0       0       0       0       0
SALES GROWTH RATE         1.250   1.250   1.250   1.250   1.250   1.250
FIXED EXPENSE GROWTH          1       1       1       1       1       1
VARIABLE EXPENSE GROWTH      -1      -1      -1      -1      -1      -1
```

FIGURE 5-4. MOST PROBABLE AND MEAN CASE SOLUTIONS FOR SIMPLE IFPS MODEL WITH UNCERTAINTY

WARNING: If you set each variable to its most likely value or if you set each variable to its mean value the result is not necessarily the outcome with the highest probability of occurring or the average of all outcomes.

NOTE:

1. If you use SOLVE, your solution is COMPLETELY deterministic.

2. If you do not specify an option, IFPS will assign the MEAN value.

5.8 RUNNING A MONTE CARLO SIMULATION

In MONTE CARLO simulation, the IFPS model is run many times, with each replication using a different combination of randomly drawn values from probability distributions. The objective is to obtain information not only on the average (i.e., expected) outcomes, but also on the distribution of the possible results (i.e., the risk) to be anticipated.

To start the process, you use the MONTE CARLO command in place of the SOLVE command. This command has the form:

MONTE CARLO number

where number refers to the number of iterations to be performed. If you leave out the number, IFPS will perform 100 iterations.

NOTE: MONTE CARLO is an expensive feature. The more iterations you ask for, the longer the computing time. If you double the number of iterations, you nearly double the cost and the waiting time at the terminal. For most problems, 100 iterations is perfectly adequate. However, see the discussion on interpreting MONTE CARLO results in Section 5.10 before deciding on sample size.

Once you have entered, for example, MONTE CARLO 100, IFPS responds with:

```
ENTER MONTE CARLO OPTIONS
```

At this point you have to tell IFPS:

- which variables you want analyzed
- the format to be used for output (e.g., histogram, frequency distribution), and
- the columns (i.e., the time periods) for which you want results printed out.

Two important default values for you to know about are:

- If you do not specify the colums for which you want data, you will automatically receive printout only for the last column of the model. The assumption is that the values at the end of the time period being investigated are the ones being used for decision making.

- For each variable for which you ask for a histogram you will also receive a frequency distribution.

You may choose from the options listed in Table 5-2.

TABLE 5-2

MONTE CARLO OPTIONS

Option	Result
ALL	ALL columns for a variable will be analyzed
COLUMNS	Only those columns specified will be analyzed. For example, COLUMNS 1,5,8,10 would give you those four columns, COLUMNS 4-6 would give you columns 4 through 6 inclusive.
FREQ	Generates a frequency distribution table for the variable. This is a cumulative observed probability distribution.
HIST	Generates a histogram and frequency distribution for the variable.
NORM	Generates a table of normal probability distribution percentile values based on the mean and standard deviation of the variable.
COMB	Generates both FREQ and NORM for the variable.

Once you have listed all the options you want, you MUST use:

NONE	Terminates option entry and starts the MONTE CARLO calculations.

NONE *must* always be the last entry in the options list

For example, the sequence:

```
 ? MONTE CARLO 100
ENTER MONTE CARLO OPTIONS
? COLUMNS 1,4-6
ENTER MONTE CARLO OPTIONS
?HIST SALES, FREQ EXPENSES
ENTER MONTE CARLO OPTIONS
?COMB NET INCOME
ENTER MONTE CARLO OPTIONS
 ?NONE
```

tells IFPS that you want 100 replications in the MONTE CARLO process. Furthermore, you want printout for columns 1, 4, 5, and 6. (Do you see how column 5 is included?) This printout is to consist of a histogram and frequency distribution of sales, a frequency distribution for expenses, and both a frequency distribution and a normal distribution for net income. IFPS keeps prompting you, asking you to enter additional MONTE CARLO options. The only way to stop these requests is by using NONE to tell IFPS you are done.

Figure 5-5 shows the result of using the above sequence on the Simple IFPS Model With Uncertainty of Section 5.6, Figure 5-2. We will discuss the interpretation of this output in Section 5.10.

```
ENTER SOLVE OPTIONS
? monte carlo 100
ENTER MONTE CARLO OPTIONS
? columns 1,4,6
ENTER MONTE CARLO OPTIONS
? hist sales,freq expenses,comb net income,none
```

NORMAL APPROXIMATION TABLE

PROBABILITY OF VALUE BEING GREATER THAN INDICATED

	90	80	70	60	50	40	30	20	10
NET INCOME									
1	21.32	23.96	25.87	27.50	29.02	30.54	32.16	34.07	36.71
4	-5.6	14.9	29.7	42.4	54.2	66.0	78.7	93.5	114.0
6	-3.5	39.6	70.7	97.3	122.2	147.0	173.6	204.7	247.9

FREQUENCY TABLE

PROBABILITY OF VALUE BEING GREATER THAN INDICATED

	90	80	70	60	50	40	30	20	10
SALES									
1	96.0	99.1	100.5	101.9	103.7	105.5	106.8	109.4	113.2
4	154.4	166.8	172.2	184.1	199.2	208.6	225.9	238.8	269.0
6	215	242	259	276	304	334	363	400	464
EXPENSES									
1	75.0	75.0	75.0	75.0	75.0	75.0	75.0	75.0	75.0
4	144.0	145.4	146.9	149.2	150.5	151.6	153.4	155.1	156.4
6	189.3	192.5	195.1	198.0	200.4	203.2	206.2	208.1	210.9
NET INCOME									
1	21.00	24.07	25.55	26.93	28.65	30.49	31.78	34.41	38.17
4	6.8	14.2	23.6	33.2	49.6	60.7	72.8	88.6	117.7
6	12.5	40.5	56.6	81.0	103.8	132.1	156.1	206.7	258.4

FIGURE 5-5. MONTE CARLO SOLUTION OF THE SIMPLE IFPS MODEL WITH UNCERTAINTY
(This Figure Continued on the Next Page)

SAMPLE STATISTICS

	MEAN	STD DEV	SKEWNESS	KURTOSIS	10PC	CONF MEAN	90PC
SALES							
1	104.0	6.003	.1	2.4	103.2		104.8
4	204.4	46.01	.8	3.6	198.5		210.3
6	322.4	96.63	.7	2.9	310.1		334.8
EXPENSES							
1	75	0	.0	.0	75		75
4	150.2	4.962	-.2	2.4	149.6		150.9
6	200.3	8.249	-.2	2.1	199.2		201.3
NET INCOME							
1	29.02	6.003	.1	2.4	28.25		29.78
4	54.19	46.67	.7	3.5	48.22		60.17
6	122.2	98.09	.7	2.9	109.6		134.7

```
     HISTOGRAM FOR COLUMN        1 OF SALES
   17- 18       * * *
   15- 16       * * *
   13- 14       * * *
   11- 12       * * * *
    9- 10     * * * * *
    7-  8   * * * * * *   *
    5-  6   * * * * * * * *
    3-  4   * * * * * * * *
    1-  2 * * * * * * * * * *
          -------------------
                1     1     1
          9     0     0     1
          1     0     8     7
          .     .     .     .
          5     2     9     6
START       90.0  STOP      119.0 SIZE OF INTERVAL        2.90
```

FIGURE 5-5. MONTE CARLO SOULTION OF THE SIMPLE IFPS MODEL WITH UNCERTAINTY

(This Figure Continued on the Next Page)

```
   HISTOGRAM FOR COLUMN        4 OF SALES
 27- 28       *
 25- 26       *
 23- 24       *
 21- 22       * *
 19- 20       * *
 17- 18       * * *
 15- 16       * * *
 13- 14       * * *
 11- 12     * * * *
  9- 10     * * * *   *
  7-  8     * * * * * *   5-  6     * * * * * *
  3-  4     * * * * * * *
  1-  2   * * * * * * * *   *
          -------------------
          1     1     2     3
          2     9     7     4
          3     8     3     8
START     110.0  STOP    360.0 SIZE OF INTERVAL      25.00


   HISTOGRAM FOR COLUMN        6 OF SALES
 19- 20       * *
 17- 18       * *
 15- 16     * * *
 13- 14     * * * *
 11- 12     * * * *
  9- 10     * * * * *
  7-  8   * * * * * * *
  5-  6   * * * * * * *   *
  3-  4   * * * * * * * * *
  1-  2   * * * * * * * * * *
          -------------------
          1     3     4     5
          8     1     4     7
          2     4     6     8
START     160.0  STOP    600.0 SIZE OF INTERVAL      44.00
ENTER POOL OR MODELING LANGUAGE COMMAND
```

FIGURE 5-5. MONTE CARLO SOLUTION OF THE SIMPLE IFPS MODEL WITH UNCERTAINTY (Continued)

You can combine several options on one line as well as listing several variables. For example:

```
?MONTE CARLO 300
ENTER MONTE CARLO OPTIONS
?ALL FREQ HIST EXPENSES,NET INCOME
ENTER MONTE CARLO OPTIONS
?NONE
```

asks IFPS to make 300 iterations and print out both frequency distributions and histograms for all columns for the variable EXPENSES and the frequency distribution for NET INCOME. (IFPS prints out only frequency information unless you specify HIST in front of each variable or you use DEFAULT, which is discussed below.) This simple specification results in a large amount of data if you have, say, eight columns in your model!

If you want the same analysis for all variables, you can use the DEFAULT option. Here you first specify what you want, for example:

```
DEFAULT COLUMNS 1,4-6,COMB, HIST
```

and then specify the list of variables for which DEFAULT applies. For example:

```
?MONTE CARLO 200
ENTER MONTE CARLO OPTIONS
?DEFAULT COLUMNS 1,4-6, COMB, HIST
ENTER MONTE CARLO OPTIONS
?SALES,EXPENSES, NET INCOME,NONE
```

asks for 200 iterations and print outs on the variables SALES, EXPENSES, and NET INCOME. For all three variables information is to be printed out for columns 1, 4, 5 and 6 and a frequency distribution, a normal distribution, and a histogram are to be printed.

A few words about the use of commas in these MONTE CARLO options. If you have a list of variables, such as SALES, EXPENSES, NET INCOME you must separate them with commas. If you ask for different analyses on the same line, such as HIST SALES, FREQUENCY EXPENSES, you must separate the analyses by a comma. The default list must be separated by commas. However, if you want several analyses of the same variable, such as ALL FREQ HIST SALES, you do *not* put commas between the analyses to be performed. ALL FREQ HIST results in creating frequency distributions and histograms for all columns of the variable SALES.

5.9 THE STOP COMMAND (What To Do If You Make An Options Mistake)

When typing in the MONTE CARLO options it is quite easy to make a mistake or to change your mind as to what you want done. You can abort the MONTE CARLO run by typing STOP in response to ENTER MONTE CARLO OPTIONS. However, you must type STOP before your type NONE.

If you use STOP, you cannot restart where you left off. You must start over with MONTE CARLO.

5.10 INTERPRETING MONTE CARLO RESULTS

MONTE CARLO results are printed in a format that differs from the usual IFPS output. A SOLVE command results in a spread sheet that provides a single value for every row and column specified in the SOLVE options. The MONTE CARLO options result in one or more probability distributions being displayed for each variable and column specified. MONTE CARLO ouput is organized in the sequence:

- Normal Approximation Table
- Frequency Table
- Sample Statistics
- Histogram

Within each of these categories, IFPS presents results in the order in which the variables are specified and for each variable in the order in which the columns are specified. The data are given in a fixed format for each category. Before examining each of these outputs, you should be aware of the meaning of the percentile points shown for the Frequency Table and the Normal Approximation Table.

These tables provide the "probability of the value being greater than indicated". For example, a 90 indicates that 90% of the observations will be larger than the number shown; a 50 indicates 50% and a 10 indicates 10%. Thus, in Figure 5-5, 90 of the 100 replications resulted in SALES in time period 1 being above 96.0 and hence, by implication, 10 of the replications resulted in sales less than or equal to 96.0. Similarly, in only 10 of the 100 replications were the SALES in time period 1 above 113.2 and hence by implication in 90 of the 100 replications they were at or below 113.2.

5.10.1 Frequency Table

The Frequency Table shows each time period as a row rather than a column. In Figure 5-5, columns 1, 4, 5, and 6 are shown as rows. For each variable and column, the 90th through 10th percentile points of the observed data are shown in equal increments. The frequency table therefore summarizes the actual experimental data points.

5.10.2 Normal Approximation Table

The Normal Approximation Table is based on the assumption that the variable being displayed comes from a normal probability distribution with mean and variance equal to the mean and variance computed from the data. Except for their mean and variance, the observed data are not used in creating this table! IFPS simply computes the percentile points on a standard normal distribution with that mean and variance. The result is that the 50th percentile point is always equal to the mean and that the distribution shown is symmetric. The 90th and 10th percentile points correspond to -1.28 and $+1.28$ standard deviations from the mean. For example, in Figure 5-5 for NET INCOME in column 1, the mean is 29.02 and the standard deviavion is 6.003 according to the Sample Statistics shown further down in in the printout. Hence the 90th percentile point is $6.003*1.28 =$ 7.68 units below the mean and the 10th percentile point is 7.68 units above the mean. These normal approximation points are different from the observed points, as you can see by looking at the Frequency Table results for NET INCOME in column 1.

When can you use the normal approximation? A simple way of checking is to look at the skewness and kurtosis values in the sample statistics. For a true normal distribution, the skewness is 0 and the kurtosis is 3.0. If the observed values are within 0.3 units of these theoretical values then the hypothesis of normality cannot be rejected. In this case, the normal approximation table can be used to make statements about risk (see the Example in Section 5.12). However, if the data are not normally distributed, this table should not be used for risk statements.

5.10.3 Sample Statistics

A fixed set of statistics is provided about each distribution given in the Frequency Table. Table 5-3 lists and explains the information provided.

TABLE 5-3

DEFINITION OF SAMPLE STATISTICS PROVIDED IN MONTE CARLO

MEAN	Average value of the observation
STD DEV	Standard deviation of the observed sample.
SKEWNESS	Measures the asymmetry of the distribution with respect to the observed mean. A skewness of 0 implies perfect symmetry.
KURTOSIS	Not a dread disease. Kurtosis measures the "peakedness" of the data compared to the peak of a normal distribution. The larger the kurtosis, the more peaked the data. Technically, kurtosis refers to the 4th moment of the observed data. Although a rather obscure measure for most purposes, it proves useful in IFPS because it allows testing if the normal approximation table can be used.
10PC	The 10PC value refers to the 10 percent level of the confidence interval around the mean. As we shall see below, the 10th and 90th percent level create an 80 percent confidence interval that can be used to assess whether additional replications are needed for making decisions.
90PC	The 90 percent level of the confidence interval around the mean.

5.10.4 Histogram

The histogram option, which is shown on a number of figures, is a plot of the observed distribution in simple graphic form. Visually, the histogram shows you the shape of the distribution. Reading the graph numerically, however, may appear tricky until you get the hang of it. The reason is that IFPS always scales the information so that it fits into a fixed format. The height of each column of asterisks tells you the number of data values observed in that interval (read from the vertical scale on the left). The numbers on the X axis (i.e., the horizontal axis) are printed vertically and should be read from top to bottom. These X axis values have to be used in conjunction with the information printed on the bottom of the plot; that is, the start and stop values and the size of the interval. The size of the interval tells you how big each division on the X axis is and saves you the problem of trying to figure out the distance between successive X values. The start and stop values give you the left and right end points on the X axis. The actual numbers printed are located at the midpoints of their particular intervals and are shown only every third column. Because intervals on histograms are determined automatically by the computer in a uniform way and depend so strongly on the data, you should be very careful in making sure that you know what the numbers mean before trying to interpret them.

5.11 THE POOL COMMAND

After the results of a Monte Carlo analysis have been printed out, IFPS will give you the message:

```
ENTER POOL OR MODELING LANGUAGE COMMAND
```

MODELING LANGUAGE COMMAND refers to any command other than POOL. That is, you go on to whatever you need to do next during your session at the terminal. POOL is a specialized command that allows you to continue the present MONTE CARLO run for additional iterations. If you believe you need additional iterations (samples, in statistical terms) to draw conclusions from the output, you type, say:

```
POOL 100
```

IFPS will run 100 additional iterations and then print out the MONTE CARLO output for the combined data from all the iterations performed.

The POOL command should be used if the data indicate large standard deviations or the confidence interval around the mean is large. For example, in Figure 5-5, the observed mean of the Net Income in period 6 is 122.2, based on a sample of 100. The 80% confidence interval around this mean is 109.6 to 134.7. The width of this interval is 134.7 – 109.6 = 35.1. That is, there is an 80% probability that the true mean is between 109.6 and 134.7 and there is a 10% probability that it is below 109.6 or above 134.7. If this level of uncertainty is satisfactory, you can go on and continue your work. However, if it is not, you have the option of asking IFPS to run additional samples and give you a new estimate of the mean and a new confidence interval. Since the width of the confidence interval depends on $1/\sqrt{n}$ (see any statistics text for a discussion and the formula), increasing the sample size reduces the uncertainty; However, because of the square root factor, the rate of decrease is quite slow.

EXERCISE: (a) Enter the IFPS model of Figure 5-2 into your computer and run the model for the conditions shown in Figure 5-5. Use MONTE CARLO 100. You may get different output because of a different choice of random numbers by the computer.
(b) Use the POOL command to obtain a total sample of 200. Examine the output for the net income in period 6. You should observe a different value of the mean and a smaller confidence interval around the mean.

5.12 EXAMPLE: THE NEW PRODUCT MODEL WITH UNCERTAINTY

The New Product Model was introduced in Section 2.7 and was illustrated in Figure 2-9. It is a market planning model that assumes that everything about the market, including its growth and the company's market share, is known. Furthermore, the model assumes that overhead costs would be fixed. These and other assumptions of the New Product Model can be modified to take uncertainty into account. An example of such an analysis is shown in Figure 5-6. In this figure, we use WHAT IF statements to introduce the uncertainty. Specifically, we ask what if:

1. Market growth is triangularly distributed with parameters (0.9, 1.02, 1.08)

2. Market share growth is uniformly distributed between (–0.002, 0.008)

3. Overhead cost relative to production cost is normally distributed with mean 80% and standard deviation of .5%.

The results indicate that under these conditions the expected internal rate of return is reduced from the 30% value in Figure 2-9 to 14.6% (see Column 8 of Figure 5-6) if all variables take on their expected values. When we make a Monte Carlo run with 200 replications, the mean rate of return observed is 14.43%. Furthermore, for the discount rate criterion that we want a 15% rate of return, we see that the investment meets this rate of return criterion slightly more than 50% of the time. On the other hand, the investment will return 11% or more 70 percent of the time. The risks associated with the investment in the new product are now much better defined. The decision can be based on a clearer understanding of the anticipated range of outcomes.

EXERCISE: Solve the New Product Model using the WHAT IF case shown in Figure 5-6 for each of the following conditions:

1. HIGH MARKET, HIGH MARKET SHARE, LOW OVERHEAD.

2. LOW MARKET, LOW MARKET SHARE, LOW OVERHEAD.

3. MOSTP for all variables.

Use IFPS to PLOT the results (see Section 4.3) for net income and net present value.

EXERCISE: Use MONTE CARLO 200 on the NEW PRODUCT MODEL with the WHAT IF conditions shown in Figure 5-6 and with the following additional changes:

1. Initial investment is uncertain. Assume a normal distribution with mean 2500 and standard deviation 500.

2. The initial market share is uncertain. Although its most likely value is 15%, there is a 10% chance it may be as low as 13% and you can be 90% sure that it will not exceed 21%. (HINT: Use T1090RAND).

(This EXERCISE continued following Figure 5-6.)

```
MODEL DECIDE  VERSION OF  06/06/82  13:32
10 COLUMNS 1-8
20 *
30 *
40 *NEW PRODUCT MODEL
50 *
60 SALES VOLUME=MARKET*MARKET SHARE
70 MARKET=8000,PREVIOUS MARKET*1.03
80 MARKET SHARE=0.15,PREVIOUS MARKET SHARE +0.005
90 GROSS SALES =SALES VOLUME *UNIT PRICE
100 UNIT PRICE =2.5 FOR 4,2.75 FOR 4
110 OPERATING COST =SALES VOLUME *(PRODUCTION COST + OVERHEAD)
120 PRODUCTION COST =1.25 FOR 4,1.35
130 OVERHEAD = PRODUCTION COST *0.80
135 NET INCOME =GROSS SALES -OPERATING COST
140 INVESTMENT =2500,0
150 RATE OF RETURN = IRR(NET INCOME,INVESTMENT)
160 NET PRESENT VALUE=NPVC(NET INCOME,DISCOUNT RATE,INVESTMENT)
170 DISCOUNT RATE =.15
180 PERIODS 4
END OF MODEL
? what if
MODEL DECIDE   VERSION OF   06/06/82   13:32  --  8 COLUMNS 13
VARIABLES
WHAT IF CASE 1
ENTER STATEMENTS
? market =8000,previous*trirandr(0.90,1.02,1.08)
? market share = .15,previous + unirandr(-.002,.008)
? overhead = production cost * norrandr(0.80,.005)
? solve
ENTER SOLVE OPTIONS
? all
***** WHAT IF CASE 1 *****
3 WHAT IF STATEMENTS PROCESSED
```

	1	2	3	4	5	6	7	8
NEW PRODUCT MODEL								
SALES VOLUME	1200	1224	1248	1272	1296	1320	1344	1368
MARKET	8000	8000	8000	8000	8000	8000	8000	8000
MARKET SHARE	.1500	.1530	.1560	.1590	.1620	.1650	.1680	.1710
GROSS SALES	3000	3060	3120	3180	3564	3630	3696	3762
UNIT PRICE	2.500	2.500	2.500	2.500	2.750	2.750	2.750	2.750
OPERATING COST	2700	2754	2808	2862	3149	3208	3266	3324
PRODUCTION COST	1.250	1.250	1.250	1.250	1.350	1.350	1.350	1.350
OVERHEAD	1	1	1	1	1.080	1.080	1.080	1.080
NET INCOME	300	306	312	318	414.7	422.4	430.1	437.8
INVESTMENT	2500	0	0	0	0	0	0	0
RATE OF RETURN							.0012	.1465
NET PRESENT VALUE	-2210	-1925	-1644	-1367	-1019	-676.7	-340.0	-8.950
DISCOUNT RATE	.1500	.1500	.1500	.1500	.1500	.1500	.1500	.1500

FIGURE 5-6. NEW PRODUCT MODEL WITH UNCERTAINTY
(Continued)

```
ENTER SOLVE OPTIONS
? monte carlo 200
ENTER MONTE CARLO OPTIONS
? freq rate of return,,net present value,none


***** WHAT IF CASE 1 *****


                    FREQUENCY TABLE

    PROBABILITY OF VALUE BEING GREATER THAN INDICATED

        90      80      70      60      50      40      30      20      10

  RATE OF RETURN
  8   .069    .094    .112    .131    .152    .165    .176    .197    .220

  NET PRESENT VALUE
  8 -201.9  -142.4   -95.7   -49.0     4.3    37.1    66.5   118.2   179.8


                    SAMPLE STATISTICS

           MEAN    STD DEV SKEWNESS KURTOSIS  10PC CONF MEAN  90PC

  RATE OF RETURN
     8    .1443     .0591      -.2       2.7       .1389       .1496

  NET PRESENT VALUE
     8   -12.75     149.2      -.2       2.7      -26.26       .7557
ENTER POOL OR MODELING LANGUAGE COMMAND
```

FIGURE 5-6. NEW PRODUCT MODEL WITH UNCERTAINTY
(Continued)

3. The extent of the price increase after period 4 is uncertain. You have the following three possibilities for prices (HINT: Use GENRAND.)

2.50	20% chance of happening
2.65	30% chance of happening
2.90	50% chance of happening

Obtain histograms of net income and net present value and obtain frequency and normal approximation tables for rate of return.

Based on the data from this MONTE CARLO simulation, should the company invest or not? Explain.

5.13 EXAMPLE: A RISK ANALYSIS MODEL

This model is based on the classic paper by David Bendel Hertz, "Risk Analysis in Capital Investment" *Harvard Business Review*, January-February 1964. Assume that a medium-sized chemical firm is considering a $10 million improvement program for its main plant. The improvement is expected to have a lifetime of 10 years. Management has determined that the key input factors in analyzing the profitability of this proposed capital investment are:

- Market size
- Selling price
- The company's market share
- Total investment
- Salvage value of the investment
- Operating costs
- Fixed costs

Unfortunately, all of these quantities have uncertainties associated with them. Table 5-4 lists these uncertainties.

TABLE 5-4

UNCERTAINTIES IN CAPITAL BUDGET

Quantity	Distribution	Values
Initial Market	Triangular	100000,250000,34000
Market Growth	Triangular	1, 1.03,1.06
Selling Price	Triangular	385,510,575
Market Share	Uniform	12% to 17%
Investment ($ Million)	Triangular	3.5,4.5,5.0
Operating Cost per unit	Triangular	375,435,545
Fixed Cost ($Thousands)	Triangular	250,300,375
Salvage Value	Triangular	3.5,4.5,5

The data in Table 5-4 indicate the great range of uncertainty that can be encountered. In building its forecast, the company knows that it has the option of closing the plant down if the selling price goes below the operating cost. In such a case, it would still have to pay the fixed costs.

Figure 5-7 shows the IFPS model for this situation. The various probability distributions shown in Table 5-4 have been incorporated into the model as well as the condition for shutting down. The shutdown condition is expressed by using the built-in maximum function to determine the revenue. If the selling price is below the operating cost, the revenue is 0; if it is above, there is a contribution from sales.

```
MODEL RISK  VERSION OF  06/06/82  13:41
10 *
20 *
30 *
40*              RISK MODEL FOR CHEMICAL COMPANY
50 *
60 COLUMNS 1-10
70 MARKET=TRIRAND(100000,250000,340000),PREVIOUS*'
71 TRIRAND(1,1.03,1.06)
80 SELLING PRICE = TRIRAND(385,510,575)
90 MARKET SHARE = UNIRAND(.12,.17)
100 SALES VOLUME = MARKET * MARKET SHARE
110 INVESTMENT =TRIRAND(7,9.5,10.5)*1000000,0
120 LIFE = 10
130 OPERATING COST = TRIRAND(370,435,545)
140 FIXED COST = TRIRAND(250,300,375)*1000
150 REVENUE = MAXIMUM(0,(SELLING PRICE - OPERATING COST)*SALES
VOLUME)
160 NET INCOME = REVENUE - FIXED COST
170 SALVAGE VALUE =0 FOR 9,TRIRAND(3.5,4.5,5)*1000000
180 *
190 RATE OF RETURN =IRR(NET INCOME + SALVAGE VALUE,INVESTMENT)
200 *
END OF MODEL
```

FIGURE 5-7. RISK MODEL

Figure 5-8 shows the result of solving this model with all variables set to their expected values (the default option if no other specification is given). The results indicate a 9.92% internal rate of return.

A much richer set of information is obtained when we ask for MONTE CARLO 200 (Figure 5-9). We see that even by year 10, the net income can fluctuate wildly (between a loss of over $300,000 and a profit of over $4 million). Furthermore, the rate of return on this investment ranges from –12.1% to 42.0% with only more than a 40% chance that it will exceed 15%.

The histograms indicate that there is a significant risk of losing money, resulting from shutdowns when the operating cost exceeds the selling price. If you are a manager facing this situation, you have to come to grips with the problems that would arise if the venture fails. If there is a significant chance of failure, you may well not want to take the risk even though the project's expected payout is above 10%

```
? solve
MODEL RISK  VERSION OF  06/06/82  13:41 -- 10 COLUMNS 12 VARIABLES
ENTER SOLVE OPTIONS
? columns 1-3,8-10
? all
```

RISK MODEL FOR CHEMICAL COMPANY

	1	2	3	8	9	10
MARKET	230000	236900	244007	282871	291357	300098
SELLING PRICE	490	490	490	490	490	490
MARKET SHARE	.1450	.1450	.1450	.1450	.1450	.1450
SALES VOLUME	33350	34351	35381	41016	42247	43514
INVESTMENT	9000000	0	0	0	0	0
LIFE	10	10	10	10	10	10
OPERATING COST	450	450	450	450	450	450
FIXED COST	308333	308333	308333	308333	308333	308333
REVENUE	1334000	1374020	1415241	1640652	1689871	1740567
NET INCOME	1025667	1065687	1106907	1332318	1381538	1432234
SALVAGE VALUE	0	0	0	0	0	4333333
RATE OF RETURN				.0093	.0357	.0992

FIGURE 5-8. EXPECTED VALUE SOLUTION OF THE RISK MODEL

EXERCISE: Suppose the firm can tell at the beginning of each year whether it has to shut the plant down because of low operating cost. It has an arrangement with the bank to carry a loan for $100,000 if they are shut down. That is, the company can shut down with only this fixed cost if revenue is less than operating cost. Modify Figure 5-7 to reflect these conditions and repeat the runs shown in Figures 5-8 and 5-9. Are there improvements in net income and internal rate of return? Are these improvement sufficient?

EXERCISE: Suppose the firm's policy is to shut down whenever revenue is less than fixed cost (i.e., the net income is negative). Are there improvements in net income and internal rate of return? How much are they? Are these improvements sufficient?

EXERCISE: Use IFPS to determine the minimum net income required to obtain an expected internal rate of return of 18%. Find this income based on most probable values. Repeat using MONTE CARLO. Use a criterion of exceeding 18% internal rate of return at least 50% of the time.

```
ENTER SOLVE OPTIONS
? monte carlo 200
ENTER MONTE CARLO OPTIONS
? hist net income
ENTER MONTE CARLO OPTIONS
? hist rate of return
ENTER MONTE CARLO OPTIONS
? none
```

FREQUENCY TABLE

PROBABILITY OF VALUE BEING GREATER THAN INDICATED

	90	80	70	60	50	40	30	20	10
NET INCOME									
10	-314	-282	189	794	1449	2222	3056	3659	4624
*1000									
RATE OF RETURN									
10	-.121	-.109	-.050	.030	.107	.174	.252	.329	.420

SAMPLE STATISTICS

	MEAN	STD DEV	SKEWNESS	KURTOSIS	10PC CONF MEAN	90PC
NET INCOME						
10	1884388	2056701	.8	2.9	1698237	2070539
RATE OF RETURN						
10	.1291	.2194	.6	2.6	.1093	.1490

FIGURE 5-9. MONTE CARLO SIMULATION OF RISK MODEL
(This Figure Is Continued on the Next Page)

```
    HISTOGRAM FOR COLUMN       10 OF NET INCOME
  57- 60  *
  53- 56  *
  49- 52  *
  45- 48  *
  41- 44  *
  37- 40  *
  33- 36  *
  29- 32  *
  25- 28  *
  21- 24  *
  17- 20  * * * *     *
  13- 16  * * * *   * *
   9- 12  * * * * * * * * *
   5-  8  * * * * * * * * * * *
   1-  4  * * * * * * * * * * * * *   *
          ----------------------------
                1     3     5     6
          -     6     3     0     7
          8     3     5     7     9
          1     7     7     6     6
          4     9     3     7     1
          3     6     6     6     6
          3     7     7     7     7
START -368000.0  STOP   8229000 SIZE OF INTERVAL  573133.3

    HISTOGRAM FOR COLUMN       10 OF RATE OF RETURN
  49- 52  *
  45- 48  *
  41- 44  *
  37- 40  *
  33- 36  *
  29- 32  *
  25- 28  *
  21- 24  *
  17- 20  * * * * * * *
  13- 16  * * * * * * * *
   9- 12  * * * * * * * * *   *
   5-  8  * * * * * * * * *   *
   1-  4  * * * * * * * * * * * *     *
          ----------------------------
          -
          .     .     .     .     .
          1     0     2     4     6
          2     8     8     8     9
          1     2     5     8     2
START        -.2  STOP         .9 SIZE OF INTERVAL        .07
ENTER POOL OR MODELING LANGUAGE COMMAND
```

FIGURE 5-9. MONTE CARLO SIMULATION OF RISK MODEL
(Continued)

5.14 EXAMPLE: TESTING THE IFPS RANDOM NUMBER GENERATOR

NOTE: The problem discussed in this section is primarily of interest to the professional in simulation. We present it here to illustrate the use of the IFPS MONTE CARLO commands. You can skip this section without losing continuity or missing any new points.

A critical consideration in simulation is the effectiveness of generating random numbers. In this example, we show you how to generate:

- random numbers between 0 and 1
- random integers between 0 and 9
- normally distributed random numbers with mean 0 and standard deviation 1 (or arbitrary mean and standard deviation)
- exponentially distributed random numbers.

We also show you how to test the random numbers generated to determine if they are indeed randomly selected from the desired probability distribution.

Figure 5-10 shows the IFPS model for generating these four kinds of numbers. As shown in Figure 5-10 (and discussed in Section 5.3), UNIRAND (0,1) and UNIRANDR(0,1) generate random numbers uniformly distributed between 0 and 1. These numbers are decimals. Because they are uniformly distributed, we should expect that the first digit of these numbers should also be uniformly distributed. That is, we should expect as many numbers to start with .0 as with .3 as with .6 or with .9. Therefore, a simple way to generate uniformly distributed random integers between 0 and 9 is to use the first digit of the random numbers created by UNIRAND. To do so, we multiply the random number by 10 and then delete the decimal part by using the TRUNCATE function described in Section 3.2.4. For example, if the random number is:

.35721,

multipyling it by 10 results in:

3.5721.

Truncating the decimal part (in this case, truncating .5721) leaves 3.

```
MODEL RANDNOS   VERSION OF   02/06/81   21:13
1 COLUMNS 1-12
2 RANDOM NUMBER=UNIRANDR(0,1)
3 RANDOM INTEGER = TRUNCATE(10*RANDOM NUMBER)
4 SUM=RANDOM NUMBER,PREVIOUS SUM+RANDOM NUMBER
5 Z=SUM-6
6 EXPRANDOM=-NATLOG(RANDOM NUMBER)
END OF MODEL
```

FIGURE 5-10. MODEL FOR TESTING RANDOM NUMBER GENERATION IN IFPS

One approximate way of obtaining normally distributed random numbers is to use the Law of Large Numbers of probability theory. This law states that if you add up a large number of values each of which was drawn independently from any particular probability distribution, the result will be a number drawn from a normal distribution. Specifically, if you use a sample of size n, the normal distribution will have a mean equal to n times the mean of the original distribution and a variance equal to n times the variance of the original distribution. It turns out that in theory a "large number" is really infinite but in practice, it is relatively small. For the uniform distribution a sample of size 12 is more than adequate.

We therefore use the fact that the mean of the uniform distribution is one-half and its variance is 1/12. If we add 12 uniform random numbers, the resulting sum should be a sample drawn from a normal distribution that has a mean of $12*0.5 = 6$ and a variance of $12*(1/12)=1$. To obtain a normal distribution with a mean of 0, we simply subtract 6 from every sum. In IFPS terms, we create 12 columns and:

```
SUM = RANDOM NUMBER, PREVIOUS SUM + RANDOM NUMBER
```

gives us a normally distributed number in Column 12. If we then subtract 6, that is,

```
Z = SUM - 6
```

the result should be a normal random number with mean equal to 0 and variance equal to 1. If you look at tables of the normal distribution in any text, you will find it is the normal with mean 0 and variance 1 (hence standard deviation equal to 1) that is tabulated.

In practical terms, you can obtain random numbers with any mean, M, and any standard deviation, S, by using the standard formula from statistics that:

```
X = Z*S + M
```

The exponential distribution, which shows up in simulating waiting lines and other phenomena where events occur at random, is defined by:

```
EXPRANDOM = - NATLOG(RANDOM NUMBER)
```

In this form, you generate an exponential distribution with mean 1. If you want a mean M, you take:

```
EXPRANDOM = - M*NATLOG(RANDOM NUMBER)
```

To illustrate what happens when you ask IFPS to generate random numbers from these four distributions, Figure 5-11 shows the results for samples of 1000 random numbers. (To keep memory space requirements and costs reasonable, IFPS has a built-in limit of 1000 replications.) This sample size is usually considered small for testing random numbers; however, the observed means and standard deviations are quite close to the theoretical means and standard deviations, and the histograms show that the observed distributions have the shapes anticipated for these distributions. There is, of course, some fluctuation but that is to be anticipated by the nature of randomness. Do you agree?

```
? monte carlo 200
MODEL RANDNOS  VERSION OF  02/06/81  21:13 -- 12 COLUMNS 5 VARIABLES
ENTER MONTE CARLO OPTIONS
? hist random number,none


                   FREQUENCY TABLE

     PROBABILITY OF VALUE BEING GREATER THAN INDICATED

          90      80      70      60      50      40      30      20      10

 RANDOM NUMBER
   12   .124    .245    .340    .444    .505    .579    .674    .780    .910

                   SAMPLE STATISTICS

              MEAN    STD DEV SKEWNESS KURTOSIS  10PC CONF MEAN   90PC

    RANDOM NUMBER
      12    .5114     .2748      .0       2.0       .4865       .5363


    HISTOGRAM FOR COLUMN        12 OF RANDOM NUMBER
  21- 22                  *
  19- 20                * *
  17- 18                * *           *
  15- 16        *   * * *     *     *
  13- 14  *       *   * * *     *   * *
  11- 12  * * *   * * * * * * * *   * *
   9- 10  * * *   * * * * * * * *   * *
   7-  8  * * * * * * * * * * * *   * *
   5-  6  * * * * * * * * * * * *   * *
   3-  4  * * * * * * * * * * * * * * *
   1-  2  * * * * * * * * * * * * * * *
          -----------------------------
          .     .     .     .     .
          0     2     4     6     8
          4     4     3     3     3
          4     0     7     4     0
START        .0  STOP       1.0 SIZE OF INTERVAL        .07
ENTER POOL OR MODELING LANGUAGE COMMAND
```

a. Uniform Random Numbers

FIGURE 5-11. RESULTS OF TESTING RANDOM NUMBER GENERATOR IN IFPS
(This Figure Continued on the Next Page)

```
? monte carlo 200
ENTER MONTE CARLO OPTIONS
? hist random integer,none


                          FREQUENCY TABLE

      PROBABILITY OF VALUE BEING GREATER THAN INDICATED

            90      80      70      60      50      40      30      20      10

 RANDOM INTEGER
   12     1.00    2.00    3.00    4.00    5.00    5.00    6.00    7.00    8.50


                          SAMPLE STATISTICS

                 MEAN    STD DEV SKEWNESS KURTOSIS  10PC CONF MEAN  90PC

    RANDOM INTEGER
      12        4.500      2.778        .0      1.9      4.249       4.751


    HISTOGRAM FOR COLUMN        12 OF RANDOM INTEGER
  27- 28                    *
  25- 26                *   *
  23- 24          *     *   *
  21- 22          *     *   * *
  19- 20   *      *     *   * *       *
  17- 18   * *    *     *   * *   *   *
  15- 16   * *    *     *   * *   *   * *
  13- 14   * *    * *   *   * *   *   * *
  11- 12   * *    * *   *   * *   *   * *
   9- 10   * *    * *   *   * *   *   * *
   7-  8   * *    * *   *   * *   *   * *
   5-  6   * *    * *   *   * *   *   * *
   3-  4   * *    * *   *   * *   *   * *
   1-  2   * *    * *   *   * *   *   * *
          -----------------------------
                  2     3     5     7
           .      .     .     .     .
           3      1     9     7     5
           0      2     4     6     8
START          .0  STOP        9.1 SIZE OF INTERVAL        .61
ENTER POOL OR MODELING LANGUAGE COMMAND
```

b. Uniform Random Integers

FIGURE 5-11. RESULTS OF TESNTING RANDOM NUMBER GENERATOR IN IFPS
(This Figure Continued on the Next Page)

```
? monte carlo 200
ENTER MONTE CARLO OPTIONS
? comb hist z,none


                   NORMAL APPROXIMATION TABLE

     PROBABILITY OF VALUE BEING GREATER THAN INDICATED

          90     80     70     60     50     40     30     20     10

 Z
  12 -1.267  -.843  -.537  -.276  -.032   .213   .474   .780  1.204

                   FREQUENCY TABLE

     PROBABILITY OF VALUE BEING GREATER THAN INDICATED

          90     80     70     60     50     40     30     20     10

Z
  12 -1.365  -.835  -.515  -.206  -.026   .199   .407   .797  1.153

                   SAMPLE STATISTICS

            MEAN    STD DEV SKEWNESS KURTOSIS  10PC CONF MEAN  90PC

Z
     12    -.0316     .9639        .0       2.7      -.1189       .0556

    HISTOGRAM FOR COLUMN        12 OF Z
  34- 36                *
  31- 33                *
  28- 30                *
  25- 27                * *
  22- 24              * * *
  19- 21            * * * *   *
  16- 18            * * * * * *
  13- 15        * * * * * * * *
  10- 12        * * * * * * * *
   7-  9      * * * * * * * * * * *
   4-  6    * * * * * * * * * * * *   *
   1-  3  * * * * * * * * * * * * *   *
          -----------------------------
          -     -
          2     1     -                 1
          .     .     .     .     .
          3     3     3     6     6
          3     3     3     7     7
START      -2.5  STOP        2.5 SIZE OF  INTERVAL        .33
```

c. Normally Distributed Random Numbers

FIGURE 5-11. RESULTS OF TESTING RANDOM NUMBER GENERATOR IN IFPS
(This Figure Continued on the Next Page)

```
? monte carlo 200
ENTER MONTE CARLO OPTIONS
? hist exprandom,none


                    FREQUENCY TABLE

      PROBABILITY OF VALUE BEING GREATER THAN INDICATED

         90     80     70     60     50     40     30     20     10

 EXPRANDOM
   12  .120   .193   .318   .468   .629   .895  1.176  1.549  2.143


                    SAMPLE STATISTICS

               MEAN   STD DEV SKEWNESS KURTOSIS  10PC CONF MEAN  90PC

 EXPRANDOM
      12     .9254      .8638      1.4      4.9      .8472      1.004


     HISTOGRAM FOR COLUMN      12 OF EXPRANDOM
  53- 56  *
  49- 52  *
  45- 48  *
  41- 44  * *
  37- 40  * *
  33- 36  * *
  29- 32  * *
  25- 28  * *
  21- 24  * * * *
  17- 20  * * * *
  13- 16  * * * * *
   9- 12  * * * * * *   *
   5-  8  * * * * * * * *
   1-  4  * * * * * * * * * * * * *   *
          ----------------------------
                1     1     2     3
          .     .     .     .     .
          1     0     9     8     7
          5     5     5     5     5
START           .0  STOP        4.5 SIZE OF INTERVAL          .30
ENTER POOL OR MODELING LANGUAGE COMMAND
```

FIGURE 5-11. RESULTS OF TESTING RANDOM NUMBER GENERATION IN IFPS (Continued)

EXERCISE: Write an IFPS model that creates

1. Uniformly distributed numbers between 0 and 10
2. Uniformly distributed integers between 0 and 99
3. Normally distributed numbers with mean 20 and standard deviation 5
4. Exponentially distributed numbers with mean 6

Obtain a frequency distribution and histogram for each distribution based on a sample of 1000.

EXERCISE: Our argument that IFPS generates adequate random numbers was based on the "reasonable" agreement of the means, variances, frequency distributions, and histograms produced. Such an argument is not mathematically adequate. What you have to do is test the observed distribution against the theoretical distribution. The simplest such test, given cumulative probability distributions as is the case here, is the Kolmogorov-Smirnov (usually abbreviated K-S) test. If you know something about statistics, go back to one of the standard statistics textbooks and perform a K-S test on the data shown in Figure 5-11.

CHAPTER VI

APPLICATIONS IN FINANCE

6.1 INTRODUCTION

This chapter shows you how to use IFPS in problems of corporate finance. Financial problems, particularly financial forecasts, were the inspiration for IFPS. Thus, as you saw in Section 3.2, IFPS has many built-in features that make financial calculations simple, including built-in capabilities for net present value, internal rate of return, and depreciation calculations.

In writing this chapter, we have followed the sequence of presentation and used many of the examples in the book *PRINCIPLES OF CORPORATE FINANCE* by Richard Brealy and Stewart Myers (McGraw-Hill, 1981). If you need more information about a particular method or topic, you can refer to the Brealey and Myers book or to any similar introductory finance text. We have tried to present the following material in such a way that if you have a working understanding of finance concepts you can use this chapter to solve finance problems without having to refer to outside sources.

6.2 NET PRESENT VALUE

The concept of present value is fundamental to finance. It is assumed that an individual or a firm values a dollar today more than a dollar tomorrow. Furthermore, the amount of the decrease in value between today and tomorrow is expressed in terms of a "discount factor". The discount factor is given as:

$$\text{DISCOUNT FACTOR} = 1/(1+r)$$

where r is the rate of return; that is, the reward that investors demand for accepting delayed payment.

In general, in financial calculations we are interested in a series of investments by us and returns to us over time. Typically, these occur at one year intervals, with the assumption made that investments occur at the beginning of the year and returns occur at the end of the year. The general formula for finding NET PRESENT VALUE is:

$$\text{NPV} = \Sigma\, C(t) / (1+r)^t \qquad (6\text{-}1)$$

where: NPV is net present value,
C(t) is the cash flow at time t,
r is the rate or return or "discount rate" at time t.

Note that in this formula, a plus sign is assumed for returns and a minus sign for investments requiring cash outlays.

As shown in Section 3.2, IFPS contains built-in net present value functions. The three functions available are:

```
NPVC(RETURN,DISCOUNT RATE,INVESTMENT)

NPV(YEARLY RETURN,DISCOUNT RATE,LIFE,INVESTMENT)

NTV(RETURN,DISCOUNT RATE,INVESTMENT)
```

6.2.1 NPVC

The NPVC function computes the net present value each year for all investments and returns made up to that point. Figure 6-1 shows the net present value for an investment of $150,000 at the beginning of Year 1 followed by an investment of $100,000 at the beginning of Year 2 and leading to a return of $300,000 at the end of Year 2. Such a stream of cash flows might occur, for example, in a commercial construction venture.

```
MODEL NPV   VERSION OF   08/24/81   20:53
10 COLUMNS 1-2
20 * THIS MODEL ILLUSTRATES THE NPVC FUNCTION
30 *
40 NET PRESENT VALUE=NPVC(RETURN,DISCOUNT RATE,INVESTMENT)
50 INVESTMENT=150000,100000
60 RETURN=0,300000
70 DISCOUNT RATE=0.07
END OF MODEL
? solve
MODEL NPV   VERSION OF   08/24/81   20:53 -- 2 COLUMNS 4 VARIABLES
ENTER SOLVE OPTIONS
?all

                                  1          2

 THIS MODEL ILLUSTRATES THE NPVC FUNCTION

NET PRESENT VALUE           -150000      18574
INVESTMENT                   150000     100000
RETURN                            0     300000
DISCOUNT RATE                 .0700      .0700
```

FIGURE 6-1. NPVC FUNCTION

Note the following points about this IFPS model:

1. Investment and returns are shown year-by-year on separate lines. RETURN in the NPVC function can refer to any variable in the problem or to a combination of variables in an expression. If you have several sources of income (e.g., DIRECT SALES, SALES THROUGH JOBBERS, EXPORT SALES) you can accumulate these sources into a single variable (e.g., NET

SALES = DIRECT SALES + SALES THROUGH JOBBERS + EXPORT SALES). Alternatively, you could write NPVC(DIRECT SALES + SALES THROUGH JOBBERS + EXPORT SALES, DISCOUNT RATE, INVESTMENT). The same considerations apply to investments.

If in doubt as to what the conventions are, do a little testing. Take an example worked out in detail in your reference text and write an IFPS model that replicates it. Make sure you get the two to match and that you understand why they match.

If this particular convention troubles you, turn to Section 6.16 at the end of this chapter and you will find an additional discussion of the great Year 0 vs. Year 1 controversy.

2. Whereas the formula treats investments as negative numbers, IFPS shows investments as positive numbers. IFPS can do this because it asks you to specify investments and returns separately in the built-in financial functions.

3. The discount rate used is a constant. However, we could just as easily have specified a variable or any IFPS expression and thereby used a different discount rate for each period.

WARNING. Some texts, including Brealey and Myers, define the initial investment as occurring at the end of Year 0 rather than at the start of Year 1. This difference does not change the numerical answers; however, it does cause the data presentation formats to differ from those of IFPS. Be sure to understand the conventions followed in any reference text that you may use. Watch out for the difference!

EXERCISE: Write an IFPS program using data from Figure 6-1 that computes net present value directly from the formula.

6.2.2 NPV

The NPV function is used for the special case of an annuity, that is, a single initial investment made now that pays a fixed return for a fixed number of years (called the life of the annuity). Figure 6-2 shows an example of the NPV function. In this example, the present value of an annuity paying $5000 per year for 20 years is computed on the assumption of no investment (e.g., an inheritance) and a 10% discount rate.

EXERCISE: Use the model given in Figure 6-2 to determine the present value of an annuity that requires a $20000 investment and which pays $4000 a year for 15 years. Assume a 20% discount rate.

6.2.3 NTV

The NTV function determines the net terminal value. It is computed the same way as the NPVC function except that values are compounded rather than discounted. Equation (6-1) is modified such that

$$NTV = \Sigma C(t) * (1 + r) \qquad (6\text{-}2)$$

```
MODEL NPV2  VERSION OF  12/28/82  11:45
10 *THIS MODEL ILLUSTRATES THE NPV FUNCTION
20 COLUMNS 1
30 YEARLY RETURN=50000
40 DISCOUNT RATE=.10
50 LIFE =20
60 INVESTMENT=0
70 *
80 PRESENT VALUE = NPV(YEARLY RETURN,DISCOUNT RATE,LIFE,INVESTMENT)
END OF MODEL
? solve
MODEL NPV2  VERSION OF  12/28/82  11:45 -- 1 COLUMNS 5 VARIABLES
ENTER SOLVE OPTIONS
? aLL
                                     1

THIS MODEL ILLUSTRATES THE NPV FUNCTION
YEARLY RETURN                    50000
DISCOUNT RATE                    .1000
LIFE                                20
INVESTMENT                           0

PRESENT VALUE                   425678
```

FIGURE 6-2. NPV FUNCTION FOR FINDING NET PRESENT VALUE OF AN ANNUITY

Thus, NTV can be used to find the balance in a savings account if money is deposited today and left there for a period of time. Figure 6-3 illustrates NTV for the same stream of investments as Figure 6-1.

```
MODEL NTV  VERSION OF  08/24/81  20:57
10 COLUMNS 1-2
20 *THIS MODEL ILLUSTRATES THE NTV FUNCTION
30 *
40 NET TERMINAL VALUE = NTV(RETURN,DISCOUNT RATE,INVESTMENT)
50 INVESTMENT=150000,100000
60 RETURN = 0,300000
70 DISCOUNT RATE=.07
END OF MODEL
? solve
MODEL NTV  VERSION OF  08/24/81  20:57 -- 2 COLUMNS 4 VARIABLES
ENTER SOLVE OPTIONS
? all
                                     1          2

THIS MODEL ILLUSTRATES THE NTV FUNCTION

NET TERMINAL VALUE             -160500      21265
INVESTMENT                      150000     100000
RETURN                               0     300000
DISCOUNT RATE                    .0700      .0700
```

FIGURE 6-3. NTV FUNCTION FOR FINDING NET TERMINAL VALUE

6.2.4 Non-Annual Payments

Thus far in this section we have assumed that all transactions are yearly. If they are periodic (e.g., monthly, quarterly), then the PERIODS statement described in Section 3.2 must be used. PERIODS can be put anywhere in the model, although putting it right after the COLUMNS statement or as the last statement in the model is good practice. When PERIODS is specified, IFPS assumes all rates are given as annual rates and automatically converts them to periodic rates. Compounding is performed correctly in all built-in financial functions. With the PERIODS statement, IFPS regards each column as being one period rather than one year.

6.3 PRESENT VALUE OF BONDS AND STOCKS

6.3.1 A Bond's Yield to Maturity

When you buy a bond and hold it to maturity, you receive periodic interest payments and you receive the face value of the bond at maturity. If the interest offered is less than the current market interest rate, the bond is sold for less than its face value. That is, it is discounted. The investor wants to determine the present value of the bond since that is the amount the investor should pay for it.

For example if a bond yields:

1979	1980	1981	1982	1983
70	70	70	70	1070

and the market interest rate is 9.2%, then the model shown in Figure 6-4 can be used to determine its value. This is a simple present value calculation with 0 investment. The present value of the bond is shown in the 1983 column of Figure 6-4 to be $914.90.

EXERCISE: Assume that you buy a bond for $914.90 with the cash flows shown above. Determine the rate of return.

EXERCISE: Suppose the bond pays $35 every six months. Modify Figure 6-4 to determine the present value of the bond with semi-annual payments. *Hint:* Double the number of columns, change the payments, and use the PERIODS statement.

6.3.2 Value of a Common Stock

Finding the value of a common stock is slightly more complicated than finding the value of a bond because a stock has two forms of return, dividends and price appreciation. Furthermore, both the dividends and the appreciation can vary over time, and the stock has an infinite life. Consider the simple case in which both the current dividend and the current stock price are expected to have the same growth rate. Then, we can make the following statments:

1. We make an initial investment at the beginning of Year 1.

2. At the end of Year 1 we receive a dividend and the (future) price of the stock increases by the growth rate.

```
MODEL BONDYIELD  VERSION OF  12/28/82  11:49
10 * BOND VALUE EXAMPLE
20 *
30 COLUMNS 1979-1983
40 CASH FLOWS = 70 FOR 4,1070
50 PAYMENTS=0
60 MARKET INTEREST RATE=.092
70 PRESENT VALUE= NPVC(CASH FLOWS,MARKET INTEREST RATE,PAYMENTS)
END OF MODEL
? solve
MODEL  BONDYIELD   VERSION  OF   12/28/82   11:49  --  5  COLUMNS  4
VARIABLES
ENTER SOLVE OPTIONS
? all

                              1979      1980      1981      1982      1983

 BOND VALUE EXAMPLE

CASH FLOWS                      70        70        70        70      1070
PAYMENTS                         0         0         0         0         0
MARKET INTEREST RATE         .0920     .0920     .0920     .0920     .0920
PRESENT VALUE                64.10     122.8     176.6     225.8     914.9
```

FIGURE 6-4. FINDING THE PRESENT VALUE OF A BOND GIVEN THE MARKET INTEREST RATE

3. At the end of each subsequent year, the dividend and the future price of the stock (= FUT PRICE) increases by the growth rate.

4. The net present value of the stream of annual dividends can be obtained by using the NPVC function.

5. The present value of the future price of the stock requires more care in computation. Unlike dividends, which we receive annually, we can sell the stock only once. Therefore, we must compute the present value of a single payment received in the future. The NPVC function cannot be used for this purpose because if would compute the present value of all the possible sales combined. Rather, we must use some other approach. In Figure 6-5 we have chosen to compute the net present value of the payment directly. It is obtained from the formula:

NPV OF FUTURE PRICE = FUT PRICE / (1 + DISCOUNT RATE) (6-3)

where FUT PRICE refers to the future price.

An alternative approach is to use two statements and compute the difference between the current period's and the previous period's NPVC values. In Figure 6-5, we would replace lines 60 and 61with:

```
60 CUMULATIVE NPV = NPVC(FUT PRICE,DISCOUNT RATE,0)
62 PREVIOUS NPV =PREVIOUS CUMULATIVE NPV
64 NPV OF FUTURE PRICE = CUMULATIVE NPV  PREVIOUS NPV
```

6. The total present value is obtained by adding the results of steps 4 and 5.

Figure 6-5 illustrates the computation of common stock value under the assumption that a growth stock selling for $100 will have a 10% annual increase in dividends and, as a result, a 10% annual increase in price. The discount rate (=capitalization rate) is assumed to be 15%.

```
MODEL STOCKVALUE   VERSION OF   12/28/82   11:53
10 COLUMNS 1-20
20 DIVIDEND =INITIAL DIVIDEND,PREVIOUS DIVIDEND * GROWTH RATE
30 FUT PRICE=INVESTMENT *GROWTH RATE,PREVIOUS*GROWTH RATE
40 NPV OF DIVIDENDS = NPVC(DIVIDEND,DISCOUNT RATE,PAYMENT)
50 NPV OF FUT PRICE =INVESTMENT*GROWTH RATE/(1+DISCOUNT RATE),'
60 PREVIOUS*GROWTH RATE/(1+DISCOUNT RATE)
70 TOTAL PRESENT VALUE=NPV OF DIVIDENDS + NPV OF FUT PRICE
80 *
90 *
100 INVESTMENT=100,0
110 INITIAL DIVIDEND=5,0
120 PAYMENT=0
130 DISCOUNT RATE=.15
140 GROWTH RATE =1.1
END OF MODEL
? solve
MODEL STOCKVALUE   VERSION OF   12/28/82   11:53  --  20 COLUMNS 10
VARIABLES
ENTER SOLVE OPTIONS
? all
```

	1	2	5	10	15	20
DIVIDEND	5	5.500	7.321	11.79	18.99	30.58
FUT PRICE	110	121	161.1	259.4	417.7	672.7
NPV OF DIVIDENDS	4.348	8.507	19.93	35.89	48.66	58.89
NPV OF FUT PRICE	95.65	91.49	80.07	64.11	51.34	41.11
TOTAL PRESENT VALUE	100	100	100	100	100	100
INVESTMENT	100	0	0	0	0	0
INITIAL DIVIDEND	5	0	0	0	0	0
PAYMENT	0	0	0	0	0	0
DISCOUNT RATE	.1500	.1500	.1500	.1500	.1500	.1500
GROWTH RATE	1.100	1.100	1.100	1.100	1.100	1.100

FIGURE 6-5. VALUE OF A COMMON STOCK
(This Figure Continued on the Next Page)

```
ENTER SOLVE OPTIONS
? what if
WHAT IF CASE 1
ENTER STATEMENTS
? npv of fut price = fut price/xpowery(1+discount rate,n)
WARNING - NEW VARIABLE WAS CREATED
? n=1,previous +1
? solve
ENTER SOLVE OPTIONS
? pv of fut price


***** WHAT IF CASE 1 *****
2 WHAT IF STATEMENTS PROCESSED

                          1       2       5      10      15      20

NPV OF FUT PRICE      95.65   91.49   80.07   64.11   51.34   41.11
```

FIGURE 6-5. VALUE OF A COMMON STOCK
(Continued)

In Figure 6-5 the net present value of the future price is computed in two ways. In the model, the investment increases by the growth rate and is reduced by the discount rate each year, with the values each year being computed from the values in the previous year. In the alternative form, shown in the WHAT IF case, the net present value is computed directly by applying Equation (6-3). The results are identical; however, the direct computation from Equation (6-3) is less efficient computationally. Note that in the direct computation we have to use a separate line to establish the year number, N.

If we assume a constant growth rate, g, for dividends from now into perpetuity, then we can estimate the discount rate (or capitalization rate for a stock), r, from the formula:

$$r = (\text{DIVIDEND/PRESENT VALUE OF STOCK}) + g \qquad (6\text{-}4)$$

That is, the capitalization rate of a stock is the sum of the dividend yield and the dividend growth rate,g. The dividend and the current stock price are known. If growth is financed internally, the growth rate is estimated by multiplying the "plowback ratio" by the "return on equity". The plowback ratio refers to the fraction of the year's earnings reinvested in the firm and can be found by taking (1 – DIVIDEND/EARNINGS PER SHARE). The return on equity is the ratio EARNINGS PER SHARE/BOOK EQUITY PER SHARE. Earnings per Share and Book Equity per Share are known quantities that can be obtained from published data.

Figure 6-6 shows the IFPS model for determining capitalization rate. Like many IFPS models you will see in this book, it is quite straightforward once you have gone through the series of steps needed to understand the process being modeled. The input values of dividend rate, selling price, earnings per share, and book value per share shown are based on American Telephone and Telegraph performance in 1977/1978.

```
MODEL CAPRATE  VERSION OF  12/28/82  12:03
10 * CAPITALIZATION  RATE  -- CURRENT DATA ONLY
20 *
30 COLUMNS 1
40 DIVIDEND YIELD=DIVIDEND RATE/SELLING PRICE
50 PLOWBACK RATIO =1-DIVIDEND RATE/EARNINGS PER SHARE
60 RETURN ON EQUITY = EARNINGS PER SHARE/BOOK EQUITY PER SHARE
70 DIVIDEND GROWTH RATE=PLOWBACK RATIO*RETURN ON EQUITY
80 CAPITALIZATION RATE= DIVIDEND YIELD +DIVIDEND GROWTH RATE
90 *
100 *     INPUT DATA
110 DIVIDEND RATE =4.60
120 SELLING PRICE = 60.00
130 EARNINGS PER SHARE =7.66
140 BOOK EQUITY PER SHARE =69.63
END OF MODEL
? solve
MODEL CAPRATE  VERSION OF  12/28/82  12:03 -- 1 COLUMNS 9 VARIABLES
ENTER SOLVE OPTIONS
? all
                                          1

 CAPITALIZATION  RATE  -- CURRENT DATA ONLY

DIVIDEND YIELD                         .0767
PLOWBACK RATIO                         .3995
RETURN ON EQUITY                       .1100
DIVIDEND GROWTH RATE                   .0439
CAPITALIZATION RATE                    .1206

     INPUT DATA
DIVIDEND RATE                          4.600
SELLING PRICE                             60
EARNINGS PER SHARE                     7.660
BOOK EQUITY PER SHARE                  69.63
```

FIGURE 6-6. ESTIMATING CAPITALIZATION RATE BASED ON CURRENT DATA ONLY

6.3.3 Capitalization Rate Taking Future Estimated Changes Into Account

The previous model of capitalization rate assumed that growth could be maintained at current levels forever. This is an optimistic assumption, particularly for high growth firms that exceed the growth in Gross National Product by considerable amounts. An alternative model assumes that the current growth will continue for a fixed time and growth will then drop to a lower rate.

In the previous model, we could solve Equation (6-4) for the present value of the stock:

$$\text{PRESENT VALUE OF STOCK} = \text{DIVIDEND} / (r-g) \tag{6-5}$$

In this case, it turns out that the appropriate model is to take the present value of the stream of earnings for the number of years that the current growth rate is expected to continue, and then to apply Equation (6-5). In formula terms,

$$PRESENT\ VALUE\ OF\ STOCK = \sum_{I=1}^{K-1} \frac{DIV(I)}{(1+r)^I} + \frac{P(K)}{r-g} \tag{6-6}$$

where: DIV(I) is the dividend in Year I.
P(K) us the stock price in Year K when the growth rate changes
g is the growth rate
r is the discount rate.

Figure 6-7 implements this model. In the example shown, the current dividend of 50 cents on a \$50 stock price grows by 20% annually for *three* years and then grows by only 8% per year. It can then be shown that the capitalization rate must be greater than 8% (the eventual growth rate) but less than the capitalization rate obtained from Equation (6-4) for the initial growth rate.

```
MODEL CAPRTE2  VERSION OF  12/28/82  12:07
10 *CAPITALIZATION RATE-TAKING FUTURE ESTIMATED CHANGES INTO ACCOUNT
20 *
30 COLUMNS 1-4
40 DIVIDEND =INITIAL DIVIDEND, PREVIOUS *DIVIDEND GROWTH RATE
50 DENOMINATOR=1+CAPITALIZATIONRATE,PREVIOUS*'
51 (1+CAPITALIZATION RATE) FOR 2,'
60 PREVIOUS *(CAPITALIZATION RATE -G)
70 PRESENT VALUE OF STOCK =DIVIDEND/DENOMINATOR,
71 PREVIOUS+DIVIDEND/DENOMINATOR
80 *
90 *INPUT DATA
100 *
110 INITIAL DIVIDEND =.50,0
120 DIVIDEND GROWTH RATE=1.2 FOR 3,1.08
130 G=0 FOR 3,.08
140 CAPITALIZATION RATE = .21,PREVIOUS
END OF MODEL
```

a. Model

FIGURE 6-7. ESTIMATING THE CAPITALIZATION RATE TAKING FUTURE ESTIMATED CHANGES INTO ACCOUNT
(This Figure Continued on Next Page)

```
? solve
MODEL CAPRTE2  VERSION OF  12/28/82  12:07 -- 4 COLUMNS 7 VARIABLES
ENTER SOLVE OPTIONS
? all

                                 1        2        3        4

CAPITALIZATION RATE-TAKING FUTURE ESTIMATED CHANGES INTO ACCOUNT

DIVIDEND                       .5000    .6000    .7200    .7776
DENOMINATOR                    1.210    1.464    1.772    .2303
PRESENT VALUE OF STOCK         .4132    .8230    1.229    4.606

INPUT DATA

INITIAL DIVIDEND               .5000        0        0        0
DIVIDEND GROWTH RATE           1.200    1.200    1.200    1.080
G                                  0        0        0    .0800
CAPITALIZATION RATE            .2100    .2100    .2100    .2100
```

b. Results Based on 21% Capitalization Rate

FIGURE 6-7. ESTIMATING THE CAPITALIZATION RATE TAKING FUTURE ESTIMATED CHANGES INTO ACCOUNT

(This Figure Continued on Next Page)

EXERCISE. Show that if the current dividend is 50 cents, the current stock price is $50 and the growth rate is 20%, then the maximum capitalization rate is 21%.

The problem the analyst faces is how to determine r. It cannot be done directly; it has to be done by successive approximation. In Figure 6-7b we show one such approximation scheme, called "interval halving". We know initially that the value of the capitalization rate has to be between 8% and 21%; in fact it cannot be equal to 8% since Equation (6-6) would then require division by 0. For simplicity, assume that the capitalization rate is between 8.1% and 21%. You will note in Figure 6-7 that we set the capitalization rate at 21% initially in the model and use a WHAT IF case to compute the present value of the stock for 8.1%. The results indicate that 21% implies a present value of the stock of $4.60 (too low) and 8.1% implies a present value of $617 (too high). We can conclude from these two answers that the capitalization rate that yields the current $50 value of the stock has to be between 8% and 21%. We can depict the situation as follows:

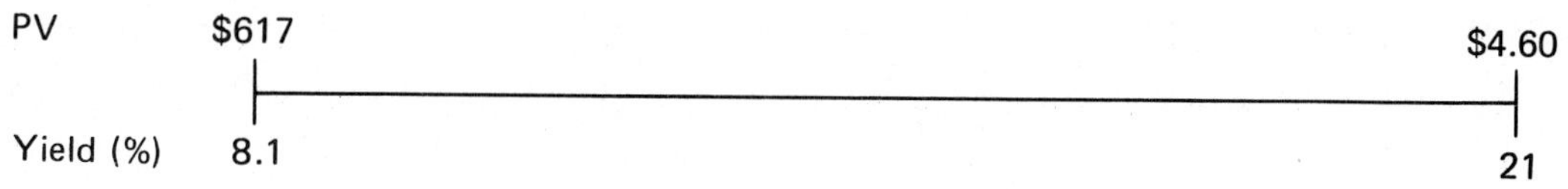

It is clear that we should pick a value in the interval from 8.1% to 21%. The easiest thing to do is to divide the interval in half and pick, say 14% for the next try. (We could have picked the exact half-way point, 14.55%, but precision is not needed in this process until we are close to the answer.) Since 14% yields a value of $10.14, we can conclude that the correct value is between 8.1% and 14% since all values above 14% would lead to even smaller present values. (Do you see why? If not, try it on the computer for a few values

```
ENTER SOLVE OPTIONS
? what if
WHAT IF CASE 1
ENTER STATEMENTS
? capitalization rate =.0810
? solve
ENTER SOLVE OPTIONS
? present value of stock,capitalization rate
 ***** WHAT IF CASE 1 *****
1 WHAT IF STATEMENT PROCESSED

                            1        2        3        4

PRESENT VALUE OF STOCK .4625    .9760    1.546    617.1
CAPITALIZATION RATE    .0810    .0810    .0810    .0810

WHAT IF CASE 2
ENTER STATEMENTS
? capitalization rate =.14
? solve
ENTER SOLVE OPTIONS
? present value of stock,capitalization rate
***** WHAT IF CASE 2 *****
1 WHAT IF STATEMENT PROCESSED

                            1        2        3        4

PRESENT VALUE OF STOCK .4386    .9003    1.386    10.13
CAPITALIZATION RATE    .1400    .1400    .1400    .1400

WHAT IF CASE 3
ENTER STATEMENTS
? capitalization rate = .11
? solve
ENTER SOLVE OPTIONS
? present value of stock, capitalization rate
***** WHAT IF CASE 3 *****
1 WHAT IF STATEMENT PROCESSED

                            1        2        3        4

PRESENT VALUE OF STOCK .4505    .9374    1.464    20.42
CAPITALIZATION RATE    .1100    .1100    .1100    .1100
```

b. Results Based on 8.1%,14%, and 11%

FIGURE 6-7. ESTIMATING THE CAPITALIZATION RATE TAKING FUTURE ESTIMATED CHANGES INTO ACCOUNT

(This Figure Continued on the Next Page)

```
WHAT IF CASE 4
ENTER STATEMENTS
? capitalization rate = .10
? solve
ENTER SOLVE OPTIONS
? present value of stock,capitalization rate
***** WHAT IF CASE 4 *****
1 WHAT IF STATEMENT PROCESSED

                              1        2        3        4

PRESENT VALUE OF STOCK .4545    .9504    1.491    30.70
CAPITALIZATION RATE     .1000    .1000    .1000    .1000

WHAT IF CASE 5
ENTER STATEMENTS
? capitalization rate = 0.09
? solve
ENTER SOLVE OPTIONS
? present value of stock,capitalization rate
***** WHAT IF CASE 5 *****
1 WHAT IF STATEMENT PROCESSED

                              1        2        3        4

PRESENT VALUE OF STOCK .4587    .9637    1.520    61.56
CAPITALIZATION RATE     .0900    .0900    .0900    .0900
```

b. Results Based on 10% and 9%

FIGURE 6-7. ESTIMATING THE CAPITALIZATION RATE TAKING FUTURE ESTIMATED CHANGES INTO ACCOUNT (Continued)

between 14% and 21% and convince yourself.) Dividing the interval in half again and again, each time choosing the capitalization rate integer, we find that the closest answer is 9%. The diagram below shows the sequence of steps followed.

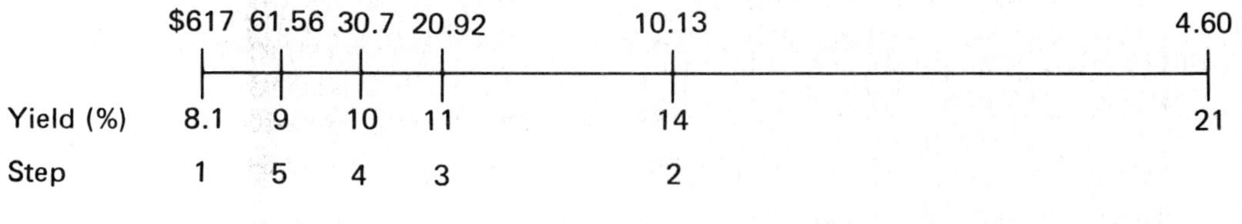

EXERCISE: The data in Figure 6-7 indicate that 9% is too low and 10% is too high a value of capitalization rate. Use interval halving repeatedly to obtain the capitalization rate to the nearest 0.1%.

6.3.4 Present Value of Growth Opportunities

For a growth stock, it is appropriate to consider its value as consisting of two components:

1. the present value of a level stream of earnings, and

2. the present value resulting from growth opportunities.

The present value of the level stream of earnings is simply the earnings per share divided by the capitalization rate (i.e., EPS/R). The present value of growth opportunities (PVGO) is given by:

$$PVGO = NPV(1) / (r\text{-}g) \qquad (6\text{-}7)$$

where NPV(1) is determined by considering the investment (a negative number!) in growth at the beginning in Year 1 (the amount plowed back from earnings) plus the return from this investment assumed to continue into perpetuity. This return is obtained by taking the investment times the return on equity and dividing by the capitalization rate.

Figure 6-8 illustrates the calculation of the present value of growth opportunities for Fledgling Electronics, a firm whose earnings per share are $8.33, dividend growth rate is 10%, and capitalization rate is 15%. Fledgling plows back 40% of its dividend into growth. It is assumed that this growth equity is able to earn 25%. The results show the portion of the stock price due to level earnings and due to growth opportunities.

```
MODEL GROOPP  VERSION OF  12/28/82  12:29
10 *PRESENT VALUE OF GROWTH OPPORTUNITIES
20 *
30 * FLEDGLING ELECTRONICS EXAMPLE
40 *
50 COLUMNS 1
60 PV OF LEVEL EARNINGS =EARNINGS PER SHARE/CAPITALIZATION RATE
70 PV OF GROWTH OPPORTUNITIES =NPV1/(CAPITALIZATION RATE -'
71 DIVIDEND GROWTH RATE)
80 NPV1=-INITIAL INVESTMENT+INITIAL INVESTMENT*RETURN ON EQUITY/'
81 CAPITALIZATION RATE
90 *
100 SHARE PRICE = PV OF LEVEL EARNINGS +PV OF GROWTH OPPORTUNITIES
110 *
120 *INPUT DATA
130 *
140 EARNINGS PER SHARE =8.33
150 CAPITALIZATION RATE =.15
160 DIVIDEND GROWTH RATE =0.10
170 INITIAL INVESTMENT =.4*EARNINGS PER SHARE
180 RETURN ON EQUITY = .25
END OF MODEL
```

FIGURE 6-8. PRESENT VALUE OF GROWTH OPPORTUNITIES FOR A STOCK
(This Figure Continued on the Next Page)

```
? solve
MODEL GROOPP  VERSION OF  12/28/82  12:29 -- 1 COLUMNS 9 VARIABLES
ENTER SOLVE OPTIONS
? all
                                               1

PRESENT VALUE OF GROWTH OPPORTUNITIES

 FLEDGLING ELECTRONICS EXAMPLE

PV OF LEVEL EARNINGS                       55.53
PV OF GROWTH OPPORTUNITIES                 44.43
NPV1                                        2.22

SHARE PRICE                                99.96

INPUT DATA

EARNINGS PER SHARE                          8.33
CAPITALIZATION RATE                          .15
DIVIDEND GROWTH RATE                         .10
INITIAL INVESTMENT                          3.33
RETURN ON EQUITY                             .25
```

FIGURE 6-8. PRESENT VALUE OF GROWTH OPPORTUNITIES FOR A STOCK (Continued)

6.4 ALTERNATIVE CRITERIA FOR INVESTMENT DECISIONS

In this section we consider various alternative criteria for evaluating investment decisions. Each of these criteria can be implemented in a relatively straightforward way in IFPS. We will present these criteria without comment as to their relative virtues and faults; we leave these arguments to the various finance texts. All of these criteria are being used in practice. In many cases the choice of criterion within a particular firm is based on historical rather than technical reasons; that is, it has always been done that way.

The five criteria are:

1. Net Present Value

2. Payback Period

3. Average Return on Book Value

4. Internal Rate of Return

5. Profitability Index.

Net present value was discussed extensively in Sections 6.2 and 6.3. Therefore, in Figure 6-9 which illustrates all five criteria, we simply show the net present value calculation for comparison.

The stream of incomes that we consider is as follows:

- A $2000 investment at the beginning of Year 1.
- A $1000 return at the end of Years 1 and 2, followed by $5000 at the end of Year 3.
- A discount rate of 10%.

```
MODEL CRITERIA  VERSION OF  12/28/82  12:36
10 *THIS MODEL ALLOWS EVALUATING INVESTMENTS BY FIVE DIFFERENT'
11 * CRITERIA:
20 *
30 *1)PRESENT VALUE 2)PAYBACK 3) AVERAGE RETURN ON BOOK 4)IRR'
31 * 5)PROFITABILITY INDEX
40 *
50 COLUMNS 1-3
60 INVESTMENT =2000,0
70 RETURN =1000,1000,5000
80 DISCOUNT RATE =.10
90 NET PRESENT VALUE = NPVC(RETURN,DISCOUNT RATE,INVESTMENT)
100 *
110 PAYBACK AMOUNT =-INVESTMENT + RETURN,PREVIOUS + RETURN
120 DISCOUNTED PAYBACK=IF NPVC(RETURN,DISCOUNT RATE,INVESTMENT).LT.'
121 0 THEN 0 ELSE 1
130 *
140 GROSS BOOK VALUE =2000
150 AVERAGE INVESTMENT=(GROSS BOOK VALUE-SALVAGE VALUE)/2
160 NET INCOME=1000,1000,5000
170 CUMULATIVE INCOME=NET INCOME,PREVIOUS +NET INCOME
180 AVG NET INCOME = CUMULATIVE INCOME/NYEARS
190 SALVAGE VALUE=0
200 NYEARS=1,PREVIOUS +1
210 AVG BOOK RATE OF RETURN = AVG NET INCOME/AVERAGE INVESTMENT
220 *
230 INTERNAL RATE OF RETURN =IRR(RETURN,INVESTMENT)
240 *
250 PRESENT VALUE =NPVC(RETURN,DISCOUNT RATE,0)
260 INITIAL INVESTMENT=INVESTMENT,PREVIOUS
270 PROFITABILITY INDEX = PRESENT VALUE/INITIAL INVESTMENT
280 BENEFIT COST RATIO=BCRATIO(RETURN,DISCOUNT RATE,INVESTMENT)
END OF MODEL
```

a. Model

FIGURE 6-9. ALTERNATIVE INVESTMENT CRITERIA
(This Figure Continued on the Next Page)

```
? solve
MODEL CRITERIA    VERSION OF    12/28/82    12:36 -- 3 COLUMNS 19
VARIABLES
ENTER SOLVE OPTIONS
? all
```

	1	2	3
THIS MODEL ALLOWS EVALUATING INVESTMENTS BY FIVE DIFFERENT CRITERIA:			
1)PRESENT VALUE 2)PAYBACK 3) AVERAGE RETURN ON BOOK 4)IRR 5)PROFITABILITY INDEX			
INVESTMENT	2000	0	0
RETURN	1000	1000	5000
DISCOUNT RATE	.1000	.1000	.1000
NET PRESENT VALUE	-1091	-264.5	3492
PAYBACK AMOUNT	-1000	0	5000
DISCOUNTED PAYBACK	0	0	1
GROSS BOOK VALUE	2000	2000	2000
AVERAGE INVESTMENT	1000	1000	1000
NET INCOME	1000	1000	5000
CUMULATIVE INCOME	1000	2000	7000
AVG NET INCOME	1000	1000	2333
SALVAGE VALUE	0	0	0
NYEARS	1	2	3
AVG BOOK RATE OF RETURN	1	1	2.333
INTERNAL RATE OF RETURN		0	.6815
PRESENT VALUE	909.1	1736	5492
INITIAL INVESTMENT	2000	2000	2000
PROFITABILITY INDEX	.4545	.8678	2.746
BENEFIT COST RATIO	.4545	.8678	2.746

FIGURE 6-9. ALTERNATIVE INVESTMENT CRITERIA
(Continued)

6.4.1 Payback Period

The payback period is determined by finding the time, in years, at which the forecasted cash flow (without discounting!) equals the initial investment. Typically, companies specify a number of years and accept projects for which the payback amount, given by equation (6-8), is positive within that time.

$$\text{PAYBACK AMOUNT} = -\text{INVESTMENT} + \text{SUM OF RETURNS} \qquad (6\text{-}8)$$

Contributions to return that occur beyond the cutoff time are ignored. In Figure 6-9, the payback period is two years, for at that time the payback exactly equals the investment.

A modified form of the payback period considers discounted cash flows. The discounted payback period is the time at which the net present value becomes positive. A quick way of highlighting this time on your output is to use the IF...THEN...ELSE construction in IFPS. Specifically, if the net present value of the cash flow (i.e., NPVC) is negative, show a 0 in your output, whereas if the NPVC value is 0 or positive show a 1. This is what is done in Line 120 of the model and results in showing that the discounted payback becomes positive in the third year under the assumed 10% discount rate.

6.4.2 Average Return on Book Value

This criterion is given by equation (6-9):

AVG. RETURN ON BOOK VALUE = AVG. RETURN/AVERAGE INVESTMENT (6-9)

A project is accepted if this ratio is better than some pre-specified value, such as the average for the company or the industry.

To compute the average return, you divide the cumulative return (undiscounted) by the time since the start of the project. The average investment is, similarly, the initial investment divided by time if straight line depreciation is used.

EXERCISE: Revise the calculation for average book value in Figure 6-9 under the assumption of 3-year life and the declining balance depreciation. *Hint:* Use the built-in depreciation functions available in IFPS (Section 3.3).

6.4.3 Internal Rate of Return

The internal rate of return is defined as that interest rate for which the net present value equals 0 at the end of the time horizon. That is, if we had chosen the internal rate of return as the discount rate, we would have a project which just broke even in net present value terms. Computing the internal rate of return directly is difficult task, requiring a successive approximation technique such as interval halving which we used in Section 6.3.3 for determining capitalization rate. Fortunately, IFPS contains a built-in internal rate of return function, IRR. As explained in Section 3.2, this function prints blanks for negative rates of returns (except in the last column). Typically, an investment is accepted if its internal rate of return is greater than the opportunity cost of obtaining capital on the open market.

The internal rate of return sometimes leads to difficulties. Specifically, if the total cumulative cash flow changes sign more than once, you may find that there are multiple rates of return. If there is only one change of sign from negative to positive, then the internal rate of return is defined uniquely. This is true, for example, in the simple case of of a single investment at the start of Year 1. If there are both negative and positive values of internal rate of return, IFPS will choose the smallest positive one; of there are several values that are all positive, IFPS will choose the smallest positive value. If you suspect multiple rates, you can use the modified internal rate of return function provided in IFPS. This function is defined by:

MIRR(RETURN,DISCOUNT RATE,INVESTMENT) (6-10)

What MIRR does is first compute the difference between the return in one year and the investment at the beginning of the next year. (Remember that the convention in IFPS is that investments are made at the beginning of a year.) If this difference is negative, it treats the amount as an investment and "returns" this investment to the start of the first year, using the discount rate. MIRR then computes an internal rate of return based on an effective initial investment and only positive cash flows thereafter. MIRR, like IRR, is an annual rate.

6.4.4 Profitability Index (or Benefit/Cost Ratio)

The profitability index is the ratio of the present value of returns to the initial investment. The profitability index can be computed directly from this definition by determining the value of the NPVC function with no investment and dividing by the investment. Alternatively, the built-in BCRATIO function can be used since, if you examine the definition of profitability index, you see that it is the ratio of benefits (i.e., returns on investment) divided by costs (investment). The BCRATIO function is given by:

BCRATIO (RETURN,DISCOUNT RATE,INVESTMENT) (6-11)

6.5 OPTIMAL TIMING FOR SELLING AN ASSET OR MAKING AN INVESTMENT

Suppose you have an asset whose current value you know and you can forecast, to some extent, what its value will be in the future. For example, you own a valuable painting. Similarly, suppose you have a choice as to whether to make an investment now or later where the value of the investment may be larger if made later. You face the same problem in either case; namely, what is the best time to act.

Figure 6-10 shows the calculations involved in making such a decision. The example assumes that the current value is $50,000 and that you have determined, by some means, the value of the asset or the investment at the end of each of the next five years. The model computes the present value of the asset at each point in time.

Note that you do not obtain the right answer if you simply compute the NPVC function for this purpose. (Try it and see!) The NPVC function assumes that you receive a payment every period. However, if you own a single asset (or make a single investment) which you hold for a period of time and then sell, you receive only one payment and it occurs when you sell. (For example, you receive no income from owning a painting.) Therefore, you must compute the present value of each of the sales prices. One way of doing so is to take the difference between NPVC and the previous NPVC. If you think about it, you recognize that the NPVC function computes the present worth of all payments from period 1 to the current period (e.g., from period 1 through period 5) whereas the previous NPVC value computes the present worth of all payments up to one period ago (e.g., in period 5, PREVIOUS NPVC covers periods 1 through 4). The difference therefore is just the present value of the current payment (e.g., period 5).

> **WARNING: In some implementations of IFPS, you will obtain the wrong answer if PREVIOUS refers to an NPVC statement on the same line. For example:**
>
> **PRESENT VALUE = NPVC(INCOME,INTEREST,0) – PREVIOUS PRESENT VALUE**

```
MODEL OPTIME  VERSION OF  01/20/82  15:42
10 COLUMNS 1-5
20*
30*OPTIMAL TIMING OF AN INVESTMENT
40*
50 CURRENT VALUE=50,0
60 NET FUT VALUE =64.4,77.5,89.4,100,109.4
70 PCT CHANGE IN VALUE = 100*(NET FUT VALUE -CURRENT VALUE)/'
71 CURRENT VALUE, 100*(NET FUT VALUE-PREVIOUS NET FUT VALUE)'
72 /PREVIOUS NET FUT VALUE
80 CUMULATIVE NPV =NPVC(NET FUT VALUE,DISCOUNT RATE,CURRENT VALUE)
90 NET PRESENT VALUE = CUMULATIVE NPV - PREVIOUS CUMULATIVE NPV
100*
110 DISCOUNT RATE =.1
120*
130* NOTE1: CURRENT VALUE IS AT BEGINNING OF YEAR 1
140* NOTE2: NET FUT VALUE IS NET FUTURE VALUE AT END OF YEAR
END OF MODEL
? solve
MODEL OPTIME  VERSION OF  01/20/82  15:42 -- 5 COLUMNS 6 VARIABLES
ENTER SOLVE OPTIONS
? all
```

	1	2	3	4	5
OPTIMAL TIMING OF AN INVESTMENT					
CURRENT VALUE	50	0	0	0	0
NET FUT VALUE	64.40	77.50	89.40	100	109.4
PCT CHANGE IN VALUE	28.80	20.34	15.35	11.86	9.400
CUMULATIVE NPV	8.545	72.60	139.8	208.1	276.0
NET PRESENT VALUE	8.545	64.05	67.17	68.30	67.93
DISCOUNT RATE	.1000	.1000	.1000	.1000	.1000

```
NOTE1: CURRENT VALUE IS AT BEGINNING OF YEAR 1
NOTE2: NET FUT VALUE IS NET FUTURE VALUE AT END OF YEAR
```

FIGURE 6-10. OPTIMAL TIMING OF AN INVESTMENT

Lines 80 and 90 in Figure 6-10 show the computation of the present value of the single payment. You will note that Line 80 shows the cumulative present value, whereas Line 100 pinpoints the present value from a single sale by taking the difference between the current and previous cumulative values.

EXERCISE: An alternate way of computing the value of a single payment at the end of year N is the relation:

```
NET PRESENT VALUE = PAYMENT*DISCOUNT FACTOR
```

where in Figure 6-10 the payment is the NET FUT VALUE of the asset. The discount factor is 1/(1+DISCOUNT RATE) raised to the nth power (see Section 6.2). Modify Figure 6-10 so that it uses this form.

To determine the optimal timing, examine the net present values computed. The best time to act will be when the present value is largest. In Figure 6-10, this time is at the end of Year 4.

This model, like all the models you see in this chapter, implicitly assumes that the discount rate describes the rate of return you could obtain if you made an alternative investment. In the case of selling an asset, as long as the rate of return from the asset is greater than the discount rate, you hold it. In the case of making an investment, you do not make it until the rate of return from future earnings exceeds the discount rate.

EXERCISE: Run the model of Figure 6-10 for discount rates of 8, 10, and 20% and determine the optimum time for selling the asset.

6.6 A LARGER EXAMPLE -- THE GUANO PROJECT

Until now in this chapter we have considered very specific calculations involving determination of value. At this point we will undertake a more ambitious example in which we put together projections for both profitability and cash flows. It is these larger, integrated models that are the rationale for using financial planning languages. You now know enough, if you have followed the text, to be able to undertake such a larger calculation.

Consider the following situtation. You have the opportunity to invest $10,000 in plant and machinery at the start of a project for producing guano. (Guano is obtained from the droppings of the guano bird and is used as fertilizer.) The project will last six years and, during the seventh year, you expect to be able to sell the machinery for scrap and receive $1000. The IRS will let you depreciate your investment over the six-year life to a $500 book value. Your firm uses straight line depreciation. Your operating groups have made estimates of working capital, sales, operating and other costs. Your tax rate is estimated to be 46%. Finally, if you decide to undertake the project you estimate that you will incur operating costs of $4,000 to start up the project. Being operating costs, these pre-investment costs are tax deductible (we assume you are making a profit and have income to offset these costs) and hence their net cost to you is

$4000*(1–TAX RATE) = $4000*(1–0.46) = $2,160.

Figure 6-11 shows the model for this scenario. You will note that there are really three models shown: (1) projections of after tax-profits without taking inflation into account, (2) projections of after-tax profits with inflation, and (3) a cash flow analysis. The reason for including all three in one IFPS Model is that the data are interconnected and some data are repeated. The initial projections do not take inflation into account. However, some input variables (specifically, working capital, sales, operating costs, other costs) are subject to inflation, which is assumed to be 10% annually. Other variables (e.g., depreciation) are not. The second set of projections, therefore, modifies the first by multiplying the input data by an inflation factor. The inflation factor is simply the value of $1 compounded at a 10% annual rate. The cash flow analysis uses the projections with inflation to derive the net present value of the investment, under the assumption that you have a 20% discount rate.

```
MODEL GUANO  VERSION OF  12/28/82  12:43
10 COLUMNS 1-7
20 *
30 * A GUANO PROJECT -- PROJECTIONS WITHOUT INFLATION
40 *
50 CAPITAL INVESTMENT=10000,0
60 SALVAGE VALUE =0 FOR 6,1000
70 STLINE DEPR(CAPITAL INVESTMENT,.05,6,DEPRCIATION,'
80 YR END BOOK VALUE,ACCUM DEPRECIATION)
90 WORKING CAPITAL = 500,1065,2450,3340,2225,1130,0
100 TOTAL BOOK VALUE = YR END BOOK VALUE + WORKING CAPITAL
110 *
120 PREINVESTMENT COSTS =4000*(1-.46),0
130 *
140 ANNUAL SALES =475,10650,24500,33400,22250,11130,0
150 OPERATING COSTS= 761,6388,14690,20043,13345,6678,0
160 OTHER COSTS=2000,0
170 PRETAX PROFIT = ANNUAL SALES - OPERATING COSTS -OTHER COSTS'
180 -DEPRCIATION FOR 6, SALVAGE VALUE -PREVIOUS YR END BOOK VALUE
190 TAX AT 46 PERCENT=PRETAX PROFIT*.46
200 PROFIT AFTER TAX=PRETAX PROFIT-TAX AT 46 PERCENT
210 *
220 *A GUANO MODEL PROJECTIONS WITH INFLATION
230 *
240 CAPITAL INVESTMENT = L50
250 SALVAGE VALUE = L60*INFLATION FACTOR
260 STLINE DEPR(CAPITAL INVESTMENT,.05,6,DEPRECIATION,'
270 YEAR END BOOK VALUE,ACCUMULATED DEPRECIATION)
280 WORKING CAPITAL =L90*INFLATION FACTOR
290 TOTAL BOOK VALUE = L260 + L280
300 *
310 PREINVESTMENT COSTS = L120
320 *
330 SALES=L140*INFLATION FACTOR
340 OPERATING COSTS =L150 *INFLATION FACTOR
350 OTHER COSTS=L160* INFLATION FACTOR
360 PRETAX PROFIT = L330-L340-L350-DEPRECIATION FOR 6,SALVAGE VALUE'
370 -PREVIOUS YEAR END BOOK VALUE
380 TAX AT 46 PERCENT=PRETAX PROFIT*.46
390 PROFIT AFTER TAX = PRETAX PROFIT -TAX AT 46 PERCENT
400 INFLATION FACTOR = 1.1,PREVIOUS * 1.1
410 *
420 *
```

FIGURE 6-11. THE GUANO PROJECT
(This Figure Continued on the Next Page)

```
430 * CASH FLOW ANALYSIS
440 *
450 INCOME FROM SALES=SALES
460 COSTS FROM OPERATIONS = OPERATING COSTS
470 OTHER COST=OTHER COSTS
480 TAX ON OPERATIONS =TAX AT 46 PERCENT FOR 6,0
490 *
500 CASH FLOW FROM OPERATIONS = L450 -L460-L470-L480
510 *
520 CHANGE IN WORKING CAPITAL=PREVIOUS WORKING CAPITAL-'
530 WORKING CAPITAL FOR 6,0
540 TOTAL INFLOWS=CASH FLOW FROM OPERATIONS+'
550 CHANGE IN WORKING CAPITAL FOR 6,SALVAGE VALUE-TAX AT 46 PERCENT
550
560 *
570 TOTAL OUTFLOWS = CAPITAL INVESTMENT + PREINVESTMENT COSTS,0
580 *
590 NET PRESENT VALUE=NPVC(TOTAL INFLOWS,DISCOUNT RATE,'
600 TOTAL OUTFLOWS)
610 *
620 DISCOUNT RATE=.20
END OF MODEL
? solve
MODEL GUANO  VERSION OF  12/28/82  12:43 -- 7 COLUMNS 39 VARIABLES
ENTER SOLVE OPTIONS
? all
```

A GUANO PROJECT -- PROJECTIONS WITHOUT INFLATION

	1	2	3	4	5	6	7
CAPITAL INVESTMENT	10000	0	0	0	0	0	0
SALVAGE VALUE	0	0	0	0	0	0	1000
DEPRCIATION	1583	1583	1583	1583	1583	1583	0
YR END BOOK VALUE	8417	6833	5250	3667	2083	500	500
ACCUM DEPRECIATION	1583	3167	4750	6333	7917	9500	9500
WORKING CAPITAL	500	1065	2450	3340	2225	1130	0
TOTAL BOOK VALUE	8917	7898	7700	7007	4308	1630	500
PREINVESTMENT COSTS	2160	0	0	0	0	0	0
ANNUAL SALES	475	10650	24500	33400	22250	11130	0
OPERATING COSTS	761	6388	14690	20043	13345	6678	0
OTHER COSTS	2000	0	0	0	0	0	0
PRETAX PROFIT	-3869	2679	8227	11774	7322	2869	500
TAX AT 46 PERCENT	-1780	1232	3784	5416	3368	1320	230
PROFIT AFTER TAX	-2089	1446	4442	6358	3954	1549	270

FIGURE 6-11. THE GUANO PROJECT

(This Figure Continued on the Next Page)

A GUANO MODEL PROJECTIONS WITH INFLATION

CAPITAL INVESTMENT	10000	0	0	0	0	0	0
SALVAGE VALUE	0	0	0	0	0	0	1949
DEPRECIATION	1583	1583	1583	1583	1583	1583	0
YEAR END BOOK VALUE	8417	6833	5250	3667	2083	500	500
ACCUMULATED DEPRECI	1583	3167	4750	6333	7917	9500	9500
WORKING CAPITAL	550	1289	3261	4890	3583	2002	0
TOTAL BOOK VALUE	2133	2872	4844	6473	5167	3585	0
PREINVESTMENT COSTS	2160	0	0	0	0	0	0
SALES	522.5	12887	32610	48901	35834	19717	0
OPERATING COSTS	837.1	7729	19552	29345	21492	11830	0
OTHER COSTS	2200	0	0	0	0	0	0
PRETAX PROFIT	-4098	3574	11474	17973	12758	6304	1449
TAX AT 46 PERCENT	-1885	1644	5278	8267	5869	2900	666.4
PROFIT AFTER TAX	-2213	1930	6196	9705	6889	3404	782.3
INFLATION FACTOR	1.100	1.210	1.331	1.464	1.611	1.772	1.949

CASH FLOW ANALYSIS

INCOME FROM SALES	522.5	12887	32610	48901	35834	19717	0
COSTS FROM OPERATIO	837.1	7729	19552	29345	21492	11830	0
OTHER COST	2200	0	0	0	0	0	0
TAX ON OPERATIONS	-1885	1644	5278	8267	5869	2900	0
CASH FLOW FROM OPER	-629.6	3513	7779	11289	8473	4987	0
CHANGE IN WORKING C	-550	-738.7	-1972	-1629	1307	1582	0
TOTAL INFLOWS	-1180	2774	5807	9659	9780	6569	1282
TOTAL OUTFLOWS	12160	0	0	0	0	0	0
NET PRESENT VALUE	-13143	-11216	-7856	-3197	732.7	2933	3290
DISCOUNT RATE	.2000	.2000	.2000	.2000	.2000	.2000	.2000

FIGURE 6-11. THE GUANO PROJECT
(Continued)

As you go over this model and read the results you should note the following:

- The capital investment occurs at the start of Year 1. The salvage value refers to the anticipated sale for scrap. The difference between book value and what you realize from the sale for scrap is taxable income in Year 7.

- In using the straight line depreciation function, the salvage fraction is 5%, since you will write the investment down from $10,000 to $500. That is, at the end of its life, the investment is worth 5% of what it was at the beginning.

- The depreciation function computes and prints out the annual depreciation, year-end book value, and accumulated depreciation in that order.

- Working capital is an input. Total book value is obtained by adding working capital to year-end book value.

- Pre-investment costs are shown at the beginning of Year 1. These costs are called out separately since, although they form part of the investment costs for determining present value in cash flow analysis, they are not capitalized and hence not depreciated.

- The salvage value in Year 7 results in a profit after taxes which, in turn, contributes to the present value in the cash flow analysis.

- In the cash flow analysis, the cash flow from operations is the difference between sales income and outflows for costs and taxes. To find the total inflows, add in the change in working capital.

- The contribution to cash flow from salvage is obtained by subtracting the taxes paid ($666) from the proceeds realized ($1948).

Figure 6-11 also illustrates several points about IFPS.

- The same variable name is used several times; for example, SALES, WORKING CAPITAL, OTHER COSTS. IFPS can give strange results if you are not careful about such multiple use. The rule followed is that the value used is the most recent previous one for which data is given. When in doubt, use line number references since line numbers are absolute values and do not need to be interpreted. You will see some examples where variables are repeated to improve readability, and the reference on the righthand side is to the previous mention of the same variable.

- In the case of the STLINE DEPR function, different names are used for the output in lines 70 and 80 and 260 and 270 .This use of multiple names is mandatory because IFPS adds up all depreciation values with the same name. In our case, all we want to do is repeat the information.

- Because of the need for repetition and the linkages that exist, we wrote a single model containing all three cases. However, we used the ability in the SOLVE option to print only a portion of the model to create separate printouts of the three cases.

EXERCISE: Rewrite Figure 6-11 with a minimum number of lines; that is, without duplicating any information. Then use the SOLVE option to select lines of printout so as to duplicate the output obtained in Figure 6-11.

6.7 MEAN AND VARIANCE OF THE RETURN FROM A PORTFOLIO OF TWO STOCKS

The simplest portfolio is one consisting of two assets, such as stocks. Figure 6-12 illustrates the computation of the mean and variance of such a portfolio.

In this calculation it is assumed that a different amount is invested in each stock and that each has a different rate of return and different standard deviation of the rate of return associated with it. Furthermore, the formulas allow for the returns from the two investments to be correlated (e.g., if the stocks are in the same industry, their prices may move up and down together). The formulas themselves, WRITTEN IN IFPS style, are the standard formulas for mean and variance (see Section 7.1). Specifically:

$$\text{MEAN} = \text{INVESTMENT1*RETURN1} + \text{INVESTMENT2*RETURN2} \tag{6-12}$$

$$\begin{aligned}\text{VARIANCE} = {} & \text{INVESTMENT1*INVESTMENT1*VARIANCE1} \\ & + \text{INVESTMENT2*INVESTMENT2*VARIANCE2} \\ & + 2\text{*INVESTMENT1*INVESTMENT2} \\ & \quad \text{*CORRELATION COEFFICIENT12*STD.DEVIATION1} \\ & \quad \text{*STANDARD DEVIATION2}\end{aligned} \tag{6-13}$$

In both equations the investment and the return are expressed as percentages. This can also be seen in Figure 6-12 where 25% of the investment is in Stock 1. Note that you need information on both the investments and on the correlation between them to use these formulas.

```
MODEL MEANVAR  VERSION OF  09/15/81  20:54
10 COLUMNS 1
20*
30*MEAN AND VARIANCE OF A PORTFOLIO OF TWO STOCKS
40*
50 INVEST1=.25
60 INVEST2=1-INVEST1
70 RETURN1= .12
80 RETURN2 =.08
90 STD DEVIATION1=.08
100STD DEVIATION2=.05
110 CORRELATION=.2
115*
120 VARIANCE1=STD DEVIATION1*STD DEVIATION1
130 VARIANCE2=STD DEVIATION2*STD DEVIATION2
140*
150 MEAN = INVEST1*RETURN1 + INVEST2*RETURN2
160 VARIANCE=INVEST1*INVEST1*VARIANCE1+INVEST2*INVEST2*VARIANCE2 +'
161 2*INVEST1*INVEST2*CORRELATION*STD DEVIATION1*STD DEVIATION2
170 STANDARD DEVIATION = XPOWERY(VARIANCE,0.5)
END OF MODEL
```

FIGURE 6-12. MEAN AND VARIANCE OF THE RETURN FROM A PORTFOLIO OF TWO STOCKS

(This Figure Continued on the Next Page)

```
? solve
MODEL MEANVAR  VERSION OF  09/15/81  20:54 -- 1 COLUMNS 12 VARIABLES
ENTER SOLVE OPTIONS
? all
                                         1

MEAN AND VARIANCE OF A PORTFOLIO OF TWO STOCKS

INVEST1                                .2500
INVEST2                                .7500
RETURN1                                .1200
RETURN2                                .0800
STD DEVIATION1                         .0800
STD DEVIATION2                         .0500
CORRELATION                            .2000

VARIANCE1                              .0064
VARIANCE2                              .0025

MEAN                                   .0900
VARIANCE                               .0021
STANDARD DEVIATION                     .0459
```

FIGURE 6-12. MEAN AND VARIANCE OF THE RETURN FROM A PORTFOLIO OF TWO STOCKS
(Continued)

EXERCISE: Extend the formula for the average return from a given portfolio (i.e., Equation (6-12)) to a portfolio containing n stocks, where n could be 3, 4, 5, etc. Implement your formula in an IFPS program in which you evaluate the average return of a portfolio consisting of 20% returning 8%, 30% returning 12%, 42% returning 15%, and 8% losing 3%.

EXERCISE: (more difficult) Look up the general formula for finding the variance of a portfolio containing many stocks. Implement this formula in IFPS for the following data:

INVESTMENT No. Amt.	RETURN	STD.DEV.	CORRELATION COEFFICIENTS i-1	i-2	i-3	i-4
1: 20%	8%	4%	-	.34	.78	.95
2: 30%	12%	7%	.34	-	.43	.05
3: 42%	15%	9%	.78	.43	-	.50
4: 8%	–3%	5%	.95	.05	.50	-

The correlation coefficients in column i-1 ,for example, refer to the correlations between 1-1, 2-1, 3-1, and 4-1.

6.8 CAPITAL ASSET PRICING MODEL

The Capital Asset Pricing Model is a simple model that relates the risk and return associated with investments. The key quantity in this model is beta, a measure of how sensitive the return on an investment is to movements in the market. Beta is really the ratio of the standard deviation of a well-diversified portfolio of assets compared to the standard deviation of a market portfolio. The beta of the market is 1.0. The beta of risk-free treasury bonds is 0.0. A beta of, say, 2.0 implies an investment that outperforms the market when the market is going up but goes down much faster than the market when the market return is less than the risk-free rate. A beta of, 0.3 implies the investment is relatively insensitive to market fluctuations.

The concept of beta is related to the concept of risk premium, that is the additional return that must be offered investors to induce them to accept the risk associated with a given investment. Risks are expressed in terms of annual rates of return and three quantities are of interests

1. The risk-free rate, rf, (e.g. Treasury bills)

2. The market risk, rm, (based on a portfolio consisting of all assets; historically, the market risk has averaged about 8.8% above the risk-free rate).

3. The expected rate of return of the investment, r.

These quantities are related to one another and beta by:

$$r = beta*rm + (1-beta)*rf \qquad (6\text{-}14)$$

The expected risk premium is (r – rf) and the expected market risk premium is (rm–rf). Figures 6-13 and 6-14 show small IFPS models for finding r and for finding beta given the other quantities.

```
MODEL BETA   VERSION OF   09/12/81   13:04
10 COLUMNS 1
20*
30*  CAPITAL ASSET PRICING MODEL
40*
50 RISK= BETA *RETURN OF MARKET + (1-BETA)*RISK FREE RATE
60*
70 RISK PREMIUM = RISK - RISK FREE RATE
80 MARKET RISK PREMIUM = RETURN OF MARKET - RISK FREE RATE
90*
100*DATA
110*
120 RISK FREE RATE=.08
130 RETURN OF MARKET =.168
140 BETA =.8
END OF MODEL
```

FIGURE 6-13. SOLVING THE CAPITAL ASSET PRICING MODEL TO DETERMINE RISK
(This Figure Continued on the Next Page)

```
? solve
MODEL BETA  VERSION OF  09/12/81  13:04 -- 1 COLUMNS 6 VARIABLES
ENTER SOLVE OPTIONS
? all
                                     1

  CAPITAL ASSET PRICING MODEL

RISK                               .1504

RISK PREMIUM                       .0704
MARKET RISK PREMIUM                .0880

DATA

RISK FREE RATE                     .0800
RETURN OF MARKET                   .1680
BETA                               .8000
```

FIGURE 6-13. SOLVING THE CAPITAL ASSET PRICING MODEL TO DETERMINE RISK (Continued)

The concept of beta can be extended to leveraged investments; that is, investments in which part of the capital is obtained by borrowing. If you view the interest paid on the borrowing as rf and let rE be the return on equity, then:

$$r^*(DEBT + EQUITY) = rf^*DEBT + rE^*EQUITY \quad (6\text{-}15)$$

Solving for the rate of return:

$$r = rf^*DEBT/(DEBT + EQUITY) + rE^*EQUITY/(DEBT + EQUITY) \quad (6\text{-}16)$$

that is, the expected return on the total investment is a weighted average of the return on the debt, rf, and on the equity investment, rE.

The same approach applies to a firm and its leveraging of capital investment. The beta for an asset which is partly financed by borrowing is similar to Equation (6-16):

$$\begin{aligned} beta(ASSET) = {} & beta(DEBT)^*DEBT/(DEBT + EQUITY) \\ & + beta(EQUITY)^*EQUITY/(DEBT + EQUITY) \end{aligned} \quad (6\text{-}17)$$

If you assume that the debt is risk free, then beta(DEBT) = 0. You can then solve Equation (6-17) for beta(EQUITY):

$$beta(EQUITY) = beta(ASSET)^*(1 + DEBT/EQUITY) \quad (6\text{-}18)$$

Equation (6-18)shows that the risk (i.e., beta) increases with debt. For example, if you borrow an amount equal to your investment, DEBT/EQUITY = 1 and your risk has doubled since then beta(EQUITY) = 2*beta(ASSET).

```
MODEL BETA2  VERSION OF  05/25/82  15:12
10 COLUMNS 1
20 *
30* FINDING BETA
40 BETA=(REQUIRED RATE OF RETURN-RISK FREE RATE)/(RETURN OF MARKET'
41 -RISK FREE RATE)
50*
60*DATA
70*
80 REQUIRED RATE OF RETURN = .12
90 RETURN OF MARKET = .12
100 RISK FREE RATE = .04
END OF MODEL
? solve
MODEL BETA2  VERSION OF  05/25/82  15:12 -- 1 COLUMNS 4 VARIABLES
ENTER SOLVE OPTIONS
? all

                                          1

 FINDING BETA

BETA                                      1

DATA

REQUIRED RATE OF RETURN               .1200
RETURN OF MARKET                      .1200
RISK FREE RATE                        .0400
```

FIGURE 6-14. SOLVING THE CAPITAL ASSET PRICING MODEL TO FIND BETA

Figure 6-15 shows the effect of leverage on return. A total investment of $20,000 based on $10,000 cash and $10,000 debt at 5% interest is assumed. Figure 6-15 shows the percentage return on the cash investment for different percentage returns on the asset. The results are also plotted in Figure 6-15 using the IFPS PLOT routine. (See Sec. 4.3 for the options available to you in PLOT.)

It will help you to interpret the plot by connecting the points with the same numbers to obtain curves for the results. The curve for interest (shown by numeral 1) is horizontal, reflecting the risk-free investment. The curve for percentage return on asset (shown as 2) goes through the origin with a slope of 1. (Do you see why?) The percentage return on investment (shown as 3) has a slope of 2 which reflects the fact that beta (EQUITY)= 2*BETA(ASSET) for this case where equity equals debt.

The PLOT routine, although giving very simple plots, is helpful in visualizing the answers. However, you have to be careful in how you set your plots up. You will notice that in Figure 6-15 we carefully labeled COLUMNS so that (1) the headings would be the same as percent return on asset and (2) so that they would be equally spaced. The reason for this choice was twofold:

- The plot routine uses column headings for labeling the X axis.
- Equal spacing of values assures that the linear relation of Equation (6-18) woulld be reflected in linearity in the output. Non-equal spacing would have resulted in distortion (i.e., non-linearity).

6.9 ANALYZING PROJECT PROPOSALS: Break-Even and Sensitivity Analysis

Managers, when presented with a project proposal, usually try to ascertain the range of conditions they may face because of the risks involved. A variety of analyses help in understanding these risks. The approaches used include:

- break-even analysis
- sensitivity analysis
- scenarios
- simulation

In this and the following two sections we will explore these approaches in terms of a particular example, the Electric Car Project. The situation is relatively straightforward. A manufacturer is considering whether or not to enter the market for electrically powered vehicles. He has the following estimates from his marketing group: For an investment of $150 million, revenues of $375 million will be generated for each of the next 10 years. The annual variable cost is estimated to be $300 million, the annual fixed cost $30 million, and annual straight line depreciation $15 million. The company has a 50% marginal tax rate and a 10% opportunity cost of capital. The resultant IFPS model, shown in Figure 6-16 indicates a net present value of $34.4 million.

```
MODEL LEVERAGE  VERSION OF  09/07/81  15:23
10 COLUMNS -10,0,10,20,30,40
20 *
30 * EXAMPLE OF POSSIBLE OUTCOMES OF LEVERAGED INVESTMENT
40 * $10000 INVESTED AND $10000 BORROWED
45 * VARIOUS RETURNS ON ASSET
50*
60 PCT RETURN ON ASSET = -10,PREVIOUS +10
70 DOLLAR RETURN = TOTAL INVESTMENT * PCT RETURN ON ASSET/100
80 INTEREST = AMT BORROWED * INTEREST RATE
85 PCT INTEREST ON DEBT =100*INTEREST RATE
90 NET DOLLAR RETURN = DOLLAR RETURN - INTEREST
100 PCT RETURN ON INVESTMENT = 100*NET DOLLAR RETURN/INVESTMENT
110*
120* DATA
130*
140 INVESTMENT=10000
150 AMT BORROWED =10000
160 TOTAL INVESTMENT =INVESTMENT + AMT BORROWED
170 INTEREST RATE = .05
END OF MODEL
? solve
MODEL LEVERAGE  VERSION OF  09/07/81  15:23 -- 6 COLUMNS 10
VARIABLES
ENTER SOLVE OPTIONS
? all
                            -10      0     10     20     30     40


 EXAMPLE OF POSSIBLE OUTCOMES OF LEVERAGED INVESTMENT
 $10000 INVESTED AND $10000 BORROWED
 VARIOUS RETURNS ON ASSET

PCT RETURN ON ASSET         -10      0     10     20     30     40
DOLLAR RETURN             -2000      0   2000   4000   6000   8000
INTEREST                    500    500    500    500    500    500
NET DOLLAR RETURN         -2500   -500   1500   3500   5500   7500
PCT INTEREST ON DEBT          5      5      5      5      5      5
PCT RETURN ON INVEST        -25     -5     15     35     55     75

 DATA

INVESTMENT                10000  10000  10000  10000  10000  10000
AMT BORROWED              10000  10000  10000  10000  10000  10000
TOTAL INVESTMENT          20000  20000  20000  20000  20000  20000
INTEREST RATE             .0500  .0500  .0500  .0500  .0500  .0500
```

FIGURE 6-15. FINDING THE POSSIBLE OUTCOMES OF A LEVERAGED INVESTMENT USING THE CAPITAL ASSET PRICING MODEL

(This Figure Continued on the Next Page)

```
ENTER SOLVE OPTIONS
? plot
pct return on asset, pct interest on debt,pct return on investment



 80
                                                                3


 60
                                                    3


 40                                                             1
                                        3
                                                    1


 20                                     1
                            3
                            1

    2           2           2           2           2           2
  0 +-----------1-----------+-----------+-----------+-----------+
                3

    1

-20
    3



   -10          0          10          20          30          40


    1 - PCT RETURN ON ASSET
    2 - PCT INTEREST ON DEBT
    3 - PCT RETURN ON INVESTMENT
```

FIGURE 6-15. FINDING THE POSSIBLE OUTCOMES OF A LEVERAGED INVESTMENT USING THE CAPITAL ASSET PRICING MODEL
(Continued)

```
MODEL CAR  VERSION OF  09/07/81  20:20
1 COLUMNS 1-10
10 * ELECTRIC CAR PROJECT FORECASTS
20 *
30 INVESTMENT=150,0
40 REVENUE =375
50 VARIABLE COST=300
60 FIXED COST =30
70 DEPRECIATION =15
80 PRETAX PROFIT =REVENUE-VARIABLE COST-FIXED COST -DEPRECIATION
90 TAX = .5 *PRETAX PROFIT
100 *
110 NET PROFIT = PRETAX PROFIT -TAX
120*
130 OPERATING CASH FLOW =NET PROFIT + DEPRECIATION
140 DISCOUNT RATE =.1
150*
160 NET PRESENT VALUE = NPVC(OPERATING CASH FLOW,
161 DISCOUNT RATE,INVESTMENT)
END OF MODEL
? solve
MODEL CAR  VERSION OF  09/07/81  20:20 -- 10 COLUMNS 11 VARIABLES
ENTER SOLVE OPTIONS
? all
```

	1	2	5	10
ELECTRIC CAR PROJECT FORECASTS				
INVESTMENT	150	0	0	0
REVENUE	375	375	375	375
VARIABLE COST	300	300	300	300
FIXED COST	30	30	30	30
DEPRECIATION	15	15	15	15
PRETAX PROFIT	30	30	30	30
TAX	15	15	15	15
NET PROFIT	15	15	15	15
OPERATING CASH FLOW	30	30	30	30
DISCOUNT RATE	.1000	.1000	.1000	.1000
NET PRESENT VALUE	-122.7	-97.93	-36.28	34.34

FIGURE 6-16. ELECTRIC CAR MODEL: ASSUMPTIONS NOT SHOWN

So far, so good. However, the model presented as in Figure 6-16 hides the assumptions made. It is essential that the assumptions made be spelled out because you cannot understand the results otherwise. Figure 6-17 is a modification of Figure 6-16 which shows that the following assumptions were made by marketing:

1. The total market for cars will be 10 million units.

2. Your company's share of the market will be 1% of the total car market.

3. You will be able to price individual cars at $3750.

4. You will be able to produce cars at $3000 per unit variable cost.

5. Fixed costs will be $30 million.

The model in Figure 6-17 is more complex because you have to derive some of the quantities (e.g, unit sales) and because you have to be careful about scaling quantities so they are in compatible units. For example, revenue must be divided by 1 million to put it in the same units as the costs so that profit can be computed.

```
MODEL CAR2  VERSION OF  09/10/81  22:19
1 COLUMNS 1-10
10 * ELECTRIC CAR PROJECT FORECASTS INCLUDING ASSUMPTIONS
20*
30 INVESTMENT=150,0
40 REVENUE = UNIT SALES * PRICE PER UNIT/1000000
50 VARIABLE COST = VARIABLE COST PER UNIT * UNIT SALES/1000000
60 FIXED COST = L230
70 DEPRECIATION = 15
80 PRETAX PROFIT= REVENUE-VARIABLE COST-FIXED COST-DEPRECIATION
90 TAX = .5* PRETAX PROFIT
100*
110 NET PROFIT = PRETAX PROFIT - TAX
120 OPERATING CASH FLOW =NET PROFIT + DEPRECIATION
130*
140 NET PRESENT VALUE = NPVC(OPERATING CASH FLOW,'
141 DISCOUNT RATE,INVESTMENT)
150*
160*ASSUMPTIONS
170*
180 TOTAL MARKET =10000000
190 MARKET SHARE = .01
200 UNIT SALES =TOTAL MARKET * MARKET SHARE
210 PRICE PER UNIT = 3750
220 VARIABLE COST PER UNIT =3000
230 FIXED COST =30
240 DISCOUNT RATE =.1
END OF MODEL
```

FIGURE 6-17. ELECTRIC CAR MODEL: ASSUMPTIONS SHOWN
(This Figure Continued on the Next Page)

```
? solve
MODEL CAR2  VERSION OF  09/10/81  22:19 -- 10 COLUMNS 17 VARIABLES
ENTER SOLVE OPTIONS
? all
                                1        2        5       10

 ELECTRIC CAR PROJECT FORECASTS INCLUDING ASSUMPTIONS

INVESTMENT                    150        0        0        0
REVENUE                       375      375      375      375
VARIABLE COST                 300      300      300      300
FIXED COST                     30       30       30       30
DEPRECIATION                   15       15       15       15
PRETAX PROFIT                  30       30       30       30
TAX                            15       15       15       15

NET PROFIT                     15       15       15       15
OPERATING CASH FLOW            30       30       30       30

NET PRESENT VALUE          -122.7   -97.93   -36.28    34.34

ASSUMPTIONS

TOTAL MARKET                  1E7      1E7      1E7      1E7
MARKET SHARE                .0100    .0100    .0100    .0100
UNIT SALES                 100000   100000   100000   100000
PRICE PER UNIT               3750     3750     3750     3750
VARIABLE COST PER UN         3000     3000     3000     3000
FIXED COST                     30       30       30       30
DISCOUNT RATE               .1000    .1000    .1000    .1000
```

FIGURE 6-17. ELECTRIC CAR MODEL: ASSUMPTIONS SHOWN
(Continued)

All four of the above assumptions are subject to challenge. The analysis methods are really designed to determine the risks involved if the assumptions turn out not to be true. The simplest form of analysis of the assumptions is break-even analysis. Break-even analysis is used to determine the conditions under which the net present value of an investment is 0; that is, the point at which you are indifferent between undertaking and not undertaking the investment. Typically, break-even analysis is done on one variable at a time. The variables used most often are sales and cost. Since we are trying to find the point at which net present value is 0, we can again use the interval halving technique first described in Section 6.3.3 and illustrated in Figure 6-7. This is done in Figure 6-18 for a break-even analysis on sales. The result is that the project will break even if unit sales are as low as 85,000, all other things remaining the same. From a finance point of view it is important to recognize that the appopriate criterion for break-even is zero net present value, not an accounting break-even of cash in equals cash out. The latter is the kind of calculation done for payback period (See Section 6.4.1.)

```
? what if
WHAT IF CASE 1
ENTER STATEMENTS
? unit sales = 50000
? solve
ENTER SOLVE OPTIONS
? column 10
? net present value

***** WHAT IF CASE 1 *****
1 WHAT IF STATEMENT PROCESSED

                                10

NET PRESENT VALUE       -80.87

ENTER SOLVE OPTIONS
? wha if
WHAT IF CASE 2
ENTER STATEMENTS
? unit sales = 75000
? solve
ENTER SOLVE OPTIONS
? net present value

***** WHAT IF CASE 2 *****
1 WHAT IF STATEMENT PROCESSED

                                10

NET PRESENT VALUE       -23.27

ENTER SOLVE OPTIONS
? what if
WHAT IF CASE 3
ENTER STATEMENTS
? unit sales = 87500
? solve
ENTER SOLVE OPTIONS
? net presevent value

***** WHAT IF CASE 3 *****
1 WHAT IF STATEMENT PROCESSED

                                10

NET PRESENT VALUE        5.534
```

FIGURE 6-18. BREAK-EVEN ANALYSIS ON ELECTRIC CAR PROJECT
(This Figure Continued on the Next Page)

```
ENTER SOLVE OPTIONS
? what if
WHAT IF CASE 4
ENTER STATEMENTS
? unit sales = 85000
? solve
ENTER SOLVE OPTIONS
? net present value


***** WHAT IF CASE 4 *****
1 WHAT IF STATEMENT PROCESSED

                                     10

NET PRESENT VALUE        -.2262
```

FIGURE 6-18. BREAK-EVEN ANALYSIS ON ELECTRIC CAR PROJECT (Continued)

In running the break-even analysis, it is not necessary to print out all the values calculated. In fact, the decision criterion is the net present worth of the project as a whole. This value is shown in column 10 of Figure 6-17 since the time horizon is 10 years. By using the COLUMNS option in SOLVE to show column 10 only in the outputs of the WHAT IF cases, we speed up the search for break even. Note also that we terminated when we were very close to 0 net present value; in this case, only the order of magnitude (not the exact value) is important for decision making.

EXERCISE: Try using GOAL SEEKING to find the break-even point. You may find that this feature gives you an impossible answer. Explain why.

The next stage of analysis involves sensitivity to changes in one variable at a time. This can be done in two ways. One way is to use the SENSITIVITY analysis feature of IFPS (Section 3.1.2) and have the computer tell you how changes in each assumption affect the measure of effectiveness, in our case net present value. To do so, you specify the largest percentage decrease, the largest percentage increase, and the step size for the variable whose sensitivity is being investigated. This feature is particularly useful if you have only a vague idea of the range of values to be encountered. An alternative approach is to estimate the most pessimistic (worst case) and most optimistic value (best case) that the variable can have and run WHAT IF cases.

EXERCISE: Run a sensitivity analysis on each of the variables indicated below one at a time:

	PESSIMISTIC	NORMAL	OPTIMISTIC
MARKET SIZE(MILLION)	9	10	11
MARKET SHARE(%)	.4	1	1.6
UNIT PRICE($)	3500	3750	3800
UNIT VARIABLE COST($)	3600	3000	2750
FIXED COST($MILLION)	40	30	20

EXERCISE: Use the SENSITIVITY analysis feature of IFPS to find the break-even point for sales. Assume that you do not know the answer given above and find a rational way of applying sensitivity analysis to solve the problem.

The major problem with sensitivity analysis is that it assumes that changes are independent of one another and therefore that changes in one assumption will not affect other assumptions. This is usually not true. For example, if you come in with a high unit variable cost for your car you are likely to have to raise your price which, in turn, may reduce your market share. Scenarios and simulation, discussed in the next two sections, are a way of overcoming these shortcomings.

6.10 USING SCENARIOS TO EVALUATE PROJECT PROPOSALS

A scenario is a set of assumptions made about future outcomes. Typically, a manager will use a number of alternative scenarios as a way of understanding the risks in a project. A scenario usually revolves around one or two ideas or combinations of ideas which are carried through to their logical conclusion. A good scenario must meet three criteria:

1. The conditions assumed must be logically consistent.

2. The conditions must be possible, that is, they could happen.

3. The conditions must be plausible, that is, they must be believable to a decision maker.

The simplest use of scenarios involves assuming that there are three possible outcomes, a worst-worst case in which everything goes wrong (e.g., total market down, costs up), a nominal case in which everything occurs at the expected value (i.e. the initial calculation which serves as a base case), and a best-best case in which everything is favorable (e.g., total market up, costs down). The best-best and worst-worst scenarios rarely happen in the real world; thus, they are not plausible. However, they are often used to bracket the range of outcomes that have to be considered. The easiest way to create a scenario in IFPS is to run a WHAT IF case in which a number of variables are changed simultaneously. For example, to obtain worst-worst and best-best scenarios for the electric car example of Figure 6-17, you could use the set of pessimistic and optimistic values, respectively, given in the EXERCISE above in two WHAT IF cases. Figure 6-19 shows the worst-worst case results. Note that in this case, some value are higher (e.g., unit variable cost and fixed cost) while others are lower (e.g., market size and market share). More important, the worst-worst case is not plausible since a firm faced with a selling price below its variable cost would either go on a cost-reduction program or would withdraw from the market

EXERCISE: Use the set of optimistic values in the previous EXERCISE to obtain a best-best case. You should find a net present value of 240 million.

The net present value results of the worst-worst case (loss of 238 million), the nominal case of Figure 6-17 (gain of 34 million) and of the best-best case (gain of 240 million) are sufficiently broad that they really don't help in decision making. Under these conditions, you may want to examine specific consistent, possible, plausible scenarios. One such scenario would be the possibility of another sharp rise in world oil prices combined with a

```
? what if
WHAT IF CASE 1
ENTER STATEMENTS
? total market = 9000000
? market share =.004
? price per unit = 3500
? variable cost per unit = 3600
? fixed cost = 40
? solve
ENTER SOLVE OPTIONS
? 130 thru 1140


***** WHAT IF CASE 1 *****
5 WHAT IF STATEMENTS PROCESSED
```

	1	2	5	10
INVESTMENT	150	0	0	0
REVENUE	126	126	126	126
VARIABLE COST	129.6	129.6	129.6	129.6
FIXED COST	40	40	40	40
DEPRECIATION	15	15	15	15
PRETAX PROFIT	-58.60	-58.60	-58.60	-58.60
TAX	-29.30	-29.30	-29.30	-29.30
NET PROFIT	-29.30	-29.30	-29.30	-29.30
OPERATING CASH FLOW	-14.30	-14.30	-14.30	-14.30
NET PRESENT VALUE	-163	-174.8	-204.2	-237.9

FIGURE 6-19. WORST-WORST CASE FOR ELECTRIC CAR PROJECT

recession and inflation. In such a case, the total market might go down precipitously, even below the pessimistic estimate (say, to 8 million units) but the market share for electric cars might go up (say, to 1.3%). Because unit variable cost and fixed costs would go up under inflation, price would also have to go up. The details of the assumptions and the results of this scenario are shown in Figure 6-20.

EXERCISE: Suppose you learn that a competitor is working on a steam-powered car that would compete with the electric car. If this development is successful, it would hit the market three years from now and would reduce your market share by 0.1% each year (i.e., to 0.9% in Year 4, 0.8% in Year 5, etc.). You also expect that you should be able to achieve production economies by the start of Year 5 that would reduce the unit variable cost to $2800 and would allow you to reduce price. You estimate that each $100 in price reduction allows you to gain 0.1% of the market. Set up and run this scenario. (Hint: You may have to experiment to determine what pricing policy is appropriate under these conditions). What do you conclude from the results? What probability would you assign to the occurrence of this scenario? Justify your estimate. Based on your estimate of probability of occurrence, how seriously would the results affect your decision?

```
WHAT IF CASE 2
ENTER STATEMENTS
? total market = 8000000
? market share = .013
? price per unit = 4313
? variable cost per unit = 3450
? fixed cost =35
? solve
ENTER SOLVE OPTIONS
? 130 thru 1140

***** WHAT IF CASE 2 *****
5 WHAT IF STATEMENTS PROCESSED
```

	1	2	5	10
INVESTMENT	150	0	0	0
REVENUE	448.6	448.6	448.6	448.6
VARIABLE COST	358.8	358.8	358.8	358.8
FIXED COST	35	35	35	35
DEPRECIATION	15	15	15	15
PRETAX PROFIT	39.75	39.75	39.75	39.75
TAX	19.88	19.88	19.88	19.88
NET PROFIT	19.88	19.88	19.88	19.88
OPERATING CASH FLOW	34.88	34.88	34.88	34.88
NET PRESENT VALUE	-118.3	-89.47	-17.79	64.30

FIGURE 6-20. HIGH OIL PRICE AND RECESSION SCENARIO FOR ELECTRIC CAR PROJECT

6.11 USING SIMULATION TO EVALUATE PROJECT PROPOSALS

In this section we discuss the use of simulation to evaluate risky investments. Before reading this section, go back to Chapter V, which describes the use of probability distributions and MONTE CARLO commands in IFPS as a way of running financial simulations. Once you have mastered that Chapter, return to this section.

As a first step consider the case in which the annual total market is expected to range from a pessimistic 9 million to an optimistic 11 million, with an average market of 10 million. If we believe that all values between 9 and 11 million are equally likely, we could represent the probability distribution of sales by a uniform distribution and use the UNIRAND function. If however, we believe that the further away from 10 million the less likely the outcome, we may want to use a triangular distribution of the form TRIRAND(9000000,10000000,11000000). This is done in Figure 6-21. Here we introduce three WHAT IF cases for the Electric Car Model. The total market is represented by a triangular distribution as follows:

WHAT IF CASE	TOTAL MARKET
1	TRIRAND (9000000,10000000,11000000)
2	TRIRANDR(9000000,10000000,11000000)
3	10000000*TRIRAND(.9,1,1.1),PREVIOUS*TRIRAND(.9,1,1.1)

In the first case, in each MONTE CARLO iteration, a market value is picked at the beginning of Year 1 and followed for all 10 years. In the second, the total arket varies from year to year, picking a different value between 9 and 11 million each year. The most interesting case is the last one, in which a value is picked from the distribution in the first year, and the values in each subsequent year depends on the value in the previous year. The results in Figure 6-21 show that on the average the first two cases are little different than the deterministic case; however, if the forecast fluctuations from year to year are tied together, the net present value increases from 34 to approximately 38. (Can you explain why these results should occur?)

```
WHAT IF CASE 3
ENTER STATEMENTS
? total market = trirand(9000000,10000000,11000000)
? monte carlo 200
ENTER MONTE CARLO OPTIONS
? net present value,none

***** WHAT IF CASE 3 *****

                    FREQUENCY TABLE

  PROBABILITY OF VALUE BEING GREATER THAN INDICATED

          90     80     70     60     50     40     30     20     10

 NET PRESENT VALUE
  10    20.1   24.2   26.9   30.0   33.8   36.0   39.5   41.8   46.3

                    SAMPLE STATISTICS

             MEAN    STD DEV SKEWNESS KURTOSIS  10PC CONF MEAN  90PC

    NET PRESENT VALUE
      10     33.21     9.826       .1      2.3        32.32     34.10
```

FIGURE 6-21. UNCERTAINTY IN MARKET FOR ELECTRIC CAR PROJECT;Simulation Results
(This Figure Cntinued on the Next Page)

```
? what if
WHAT IF CASE 4
ENTER STATEMENTS
? total market = trirandr(9000000,10000000,11000000)
? monte carlo 200
ENTER MONTE CARLO OPTIONS
? frequency net present value,none

***** WHAT IF CASE 4 *****

                    FREQUENCY TABLE

  PROBABILITY OF VALUE BEING GREATER THAN INDICATED

          90     80     70     60     50     40     30     20     10

 NET PRESENT VALUE
   10  30.08  31.88  32.72  33.41  34.24  35.05  36.28  37.36  38.14

                    SAMPLE STATISTICS

              MEAN   STD DEV SKEWNESS KURTOSIS  10PC CONF MEAN  90PC

    NET PRESENT VALUE
      10      34.38    3.106       .1       2.5      34.10      34.66

? what if
WHAT IF CASE 5
ENTER STATEMENTS
? total market=10000000*trirand(.9,1,1.1),previous*trirand(.9,1,1.1)
? monte carlo 200
ENTER MONTE CARLO OPTIONS
? frequencey net present value,none

***** WHAT IF CASE 5 *****

                    FREQUENCY TABLE

  PROBABILITY OF VALUE BEING GREATER THAN INDICATED

          90     80     70     60     50     40     30     20     10

 NET PRESENT VALUE
   10   -9.4    3.8   15.1   22.8   32.4   40.9   51.9   68.9   94.2

                    SAMPLE STATISTICS

              MEAN   STD DEV SKEWNESS KURTOSIS  10PC CONF MEAN  90PC

    NET PRESENT VALUE
      10      37.01    37.08       .5       2.6      33.66      40.37
```

FIGURE 6-21. UNCERTAINTY IN MARKET FOR ELECTRIC CAR PROJECT; Simulation Results

A more sophisticated simulation introduces probability distributions for all of the variables. This is done in Figure 6-22 where we show the result of using triangular distributions for each of the input values. The end points of these distributions are the pessimistic and optimistic values used in the exercises above. When all variables are allowed to vary simultaneously, the result is a decrease in the expected net present value! In fact, the net present value becomes negative because the average net profit is reduced to 5 and hence the operating cash flow is reduced from 30 to 20. Here as a user of the model you must be very careful in interpreting results. Why did this happen? Introducing uncertainty into which variables or combination of variables caused the reduction of operating cash flow? Given that the frequency table indicates that the net present value is positive less than 40% of the time, do you still undertake the project? The independent setting of variable cost per unit and price per unit can lead you to combinations in which you sell the car for less than your variable cost. Should you change your model to make price per unit be, say, 1.25*variable cost or perhaps a more sophisticated pricing scheme that takes both variable and fixed costs into account since realistic pricing would do so? The point of the matter is that you have to be very careful in using simulation to make sure that you represent possible cases accurately. In particular, as Figure 6.22 illustrates so vividly, you must look for interactions among variables and must modify your model so that you represent these interactions correctly. They can affect the validity of your results.

One final note. The model used for simulation can also be used to create scenarios. All you have to do is decide which probability distributions should take on their HIGH,MOSTP, MEAN, or LOW values (see Section 5.7 for a discussion of these options).

EXERCISE: Revise the model in Figure 6-22 to reflect the relation between price per unit and variable and fixed costs. State and justify the assumptions that you make about this relation. Run your revised model and analyze the results for reasonableness and accuracy.

EXERCISE: Use the HIGH and LOW options to create the best-best and worst-worst scenarios of Section 6-10.

6.12 THE BLACK-SCHOLES FORMULA FOR CALL OPTIONS

Options allow investors the right to buy or sell stocks at agreed upon prices at some time in the future. The right to buy is a "call option" and the right to sell is a "put option". The problem faced by the investor is whether or not to buy the option at its market price.

The Black-Scholes formula for the appropriate price of a call option is based on the assumption that call options are priced in such a way that the average return on portfolios in which all risk is hedged away equals the risk-free rate of interest. (Recall the Capital Asset Pricing Model which was discussed in Section 6.8). The formula appears at first glance to be quite complex. It is given by:

PV OF CALL OPTION = P*N(d1)-EX*exp(-rf*t)*N(d2) (6-16)

where P is the current price of the stock
N(d) is the cumulative normal probability density function evaluated at d
EX is the exercise price of the option
rf is the risk free rate

```
? what if
WHAT IF CASE 6
ENTER STATEMENTS
? total market = trirandr(9000000,10000000,11000000)
? market share = trirand(.004,.01,.016)
? price per unit = trirand(3500,3750,3800)
? fixed cost = trirand(20,30,40)
? monte carlo 200
ENTER MONTE CARLO OPTIONS
? freq

***** WHAT IF CASE 6 *****


                  FREQUENCY TABLE

  PROBABILITY OF VALUE BEING GREATER THAN INDICATED

        90      80      70      60      50      40      30      20      10

 OPERATING CASH FLOW
   10  13.97  17.01   20.67   22.74   24.77   26.92   28.60   33.02   37.85

 NET PROFIT
   10  -1.03   2.01    5.67    7.74    9.77   11.92   13.60   18.02   22.85

 NET PRESENT VALUE
   10  -67.3  -45.2   -23.6    -9.9     2.6    12.9    28.7    53.9    83.6


                  SAMPLE STATISTICS

             MEAN   STD DEV SKEWNESS KURTOSIS  10PC CONF MEAN  90PC

   OPERATING CASH FLOW
     10      25.26     9.204       .4      2.8       24.43       26.09

   NET PROFIT
     10      10.26     9.204       .4      2.8       9.426       11.09

   NET PRESENT VALUE
     10      5.695     57.40       .4      2.8       .4997       10.89
```

FIGURE 6-22. ELECTRIC AR SIMULATION WITH INPUTS TRIANGULARLY DISTRIBUTED

t is the time to exercise date (in years)
and d1 and d2 are given respectively by:

$$d1 = (\log(P/EX) + rf^{*}t + \text{VARIANCE}^{*}t/2)/(\text{STD DEVIATION}^{*}\ t)$$

$$d2 = (\log(P/EX) + rf^{*}t + \text{VARIANCE}^{*}t/2)/(\text{STD DEVIATION}^{*}\ t)$$

These formulas are quite formidable when evaluated by hand or with the aid of a hand-calculator. However, IFPS has the needed built-in functions to make this evaluation quite simple. Figure 6-23 shows the implementation of the formula in IFPS, including a sample set of data. The natural log function (NATLOG), the exponential function (NATEXP), and the XPOWERY function (see Section 3.2.4) are used to obtain the needed log, e to the x, and square root. Perhaps most unfamiliar is the use of INTERPOLATION ON to represent the normal distribution.

```
MODEL BLKSCHO  VERSION OF  09/15/81  21:17
10 COLUMNS 1
20* BLACK-SCHOLES FORMULA
30*
40 PRESENT VALUE OF CALL=PRICE*CUMPROB1-EXERCISE PRICE*'
41 CUMPROB2/NATEXP(RFT)
50*
60*
70 D1 =(NATLOG(PRICE/EXERCISE PRICE)+ RFT+PERIOD VARIANCE OF ROR *'
71 TIME TO EXERCISE/2)/DENOMINATOR
80 D2=(NATLOG(PRICE/EXERCISE PRICE)+RFT - PERIOD VARIANCE OF ROR *'
81 TIME TO EXERCISE/2)/DENOMINATOR
90*
100 CUMPROB1=INTERPOLATION ON(D1,-5,0,-2,.023,-1.5,.067,-1.2,.115,'
101 -1,.159 ,-.8,.21,-.6,.274,0,.5,.6,.726,.8,.788,1,.841,1.2,'
102 .884,1.5,.93,2,.997,5,1)
110 CUMPROB2=INTERPOLATION ON(D2,-5,0,-2,.023,-1.5,.067,-1.2,.115,'
111 -1,.159,-.8,.21,-.6,.274,0,.5,.6,.726,.8,.788,1,.84,1.2,.884,'
112 1.5,.93,2,.977,5,1)
120*
130*INPUT DATA
140*
200 PRICE=90
210 EXERCISE PRICE =100
220 RISK FREE RATE =.1
230 TIME TO EXERCISE =.5
240 RFT = RISK FREE RATE *TIME TO EXERCISE
250 STD DEVIATION OF ROR =.42
260 PERIOD VARIANCE OF ROR=STD DEVIATION OF ROR*STD DEVIATION OF ROR
270 DENOMINATOR= STD DEVIATION OF ROR * XPOWERY(TIME TO EXERCISE,.5)
END OF MODEL
```

FIGURE 6-23. BLACK-SCHOLES MODEL
(This Figure Continued on the Next Page)

```
? solve
MODEL BLKSCHO   VERSION OF   09/15/81   21:17 -- 1 COLUMNS 13 VARIABLES
ENTER SOLVE OPTIONS
? all
                                         1

 BLACK-SCHOLES FORMULA

PRESENT VALUE OF CALL               8.153

D1                                 -.0379
D2                                 -.3349

CUMPROB1                            .4857
CUMPROB2                            .3739

INPUT DATA

PRICE                                  90
EXERCISE PRICE                        100
RISK FREE RATE                      .1000
TIME TO EXERCISE                    .5000
RFT                                 .0500
STD DEVIATION OF ROR                .4200
PERIOD VARIANCE OF ROR              .1764
DENOMINATOR                         .2970
```

FIGURE 6-23. BLACK-SCHOLES MODEL
(Continued)

The normal distribution cannot be evaluated directly; however, you can use IFPS to look up the value in a table just as you would do if you were solving the problem by hand. IFPS allows you to specify tables through the INTERPOLATION ON function (see Section 3.2.4). You first give the name of the variable (in our case either d1 or d2) and then the table in which the value of the variable is to be looked up. The table is specified as successive pairs of values. For example, in Figure 6-23, we specify -5 standard deviations as 0, -2 standard deviations as .023, -1.5 standard deviations as .067, etc. What IFPS does is find the interval in which the value of the variable occurs and then performs linear interpolation within the interval to find the answer. Thus, for example, if d1 happened to be 0.4, IFPS would first determine that 0.4 falls between the table values of 0 and 0.6. Next, it would find that since 0.4 is 2/3 of the way between 0 and 0.6, the value of d1 should be 2/3 of the way between 0.5 and 0.72, that is that d1 = 0.6507.

In constructing the INTERPOLATION ON function, you are constrained in three ways:

- **A maximum of 49 pairs of numbers can be used to define the function. The pairs must be in increasing order of the first variable.**

- **If you call for a value outside the region of definition during computation you will receive an error message.**

- Your table cannot exceed the maximum line length of IFPS (155 characters). If you have more data than the maximum line length, use the ' the apostrophe) to indicate that the statement is continued on the next line. The next line must have a line number.

6.13 FINANCIAL RATIO ANALYSIS

Although modern textbooks on finance warn their readers that the use of ratios based on current balance sheets and income statements is simplistic, such ratios are still very popular and useful ways of evaluating company performance. We will not get into the middle of this controversy here; our attitude is that if you want to use these ratios it is your choice and you do so knowing the risks. Figure 6-24 is an IFPS model that includes most of the commonly used ratios. You will find that the model shows three types of indicators:

- Indicators of leverage.
- Indicators of liquidity.
- Indicators of efficiency.

The ratios are quite simple to compute once you have the needed balance sheets and income statements. The data in Figure 6-24 are based on balance sheets for two years and a current income statement. Although the indicators of leverage and liquidity depend only on the current year, most of the efficiency indicators are based on the changes in the balance sheet with respect to the previous year. You should be able to determine the specific indicators both from the names of the variables in the output and from their definition in lines 530 through 761 of the model.

The balance sheet and income statement are input data and are printed out separately from the financial ratios. All three, however, are included in the same IFPS model. We have used the COLUMNS option in SOLVE to print out information in neat, simple form suitable for management use. In the present case with some data involving two years and some one year, the IFPS model creates two full columns; however only some portions of the second column (i.e., in the balance sheet) are needed.

You may also note a seeming contradiction in the program. The columns in the balance sheet are presented in the order 1980 and 1979, that is, most recent year first as is the custom in accounting presentations. As a result, the references to the 1979 column have to be "FUTURE" even though 1979 is a previous year. IFPS requires you to refer to columns to the right of the current column as "FUTURE". If you do not feel comfortable with this form of reference, you can use the MATRIX reference. We have used MATRIX(ACCOUNTS RECEIVABLE,2) in line 761 in place of FUTURE ACCOUNTS RECEIVABLE. The same numeric result is obtained either way.

Finally, a note on format. You will notice that SALES TO NET WORKING CAPITAL RATIO requires over 30 letters. If we had ignored this length, IFPS would have arbitrarily chopped the name to fit the 24 column format available for variable names. To get around this limitation, we used the WIDTH command, described in Section 4.2. The WIDTH statement is shown in Figure 6-24. It is used as a SOLVE option and is included before the specification of COLUMNS. Rather than using the default options on WIDTH (that is, a 78 column wide output, with the first 24 used for the variable name, and 6 columns each 9 spaces wide), we used:

```
WIDTH 68 40 9
```

to indicate that:

1. The results should be displayed over 68 columns (all we have available in this book).

2. Variable names should occupy 40 spaces.

3. Each column should contain 9 digits.

The WIDTH option is a simple way to achieve some of the features that are available through creating a REPORT (Section 4.7)

```
MODEL RATIOS  VERSION OF  12/28/82  14:56
10 COLUMNS 1980,1979
20 *
30 * THIS MODEL SHOWS A BALANCE SHEET AND INCOME STATEMENT
40 * IT USES THIS INFORMATION TO COMPUTE STANDARD FINANCIAL RATIOS
50 *
60 * BALANCE SHEET
70 *
80 *ASSETS
90 CASH&MRKTBLE SECURITIES=50,75
100 ACCOUNTS RECEIVABLE =250,200
110 INVENTORIES =300,250
120 *
130 CURRENT ASSETS = L90+L100+L110
140 GROSS FIXED ASSETS =600,550
150 ACCUMULATED DEPRECIATION = 200,175
160 *
170 NET FIXED ASSETS = GROSS FIXED ASSETS -ACCUMULATED DEPRECIATION
180 *
190 TOTAL ASSETS = CURRENT ASSETS + NET FIXED ASSETS
200 *
210 *LIABILITIES
220 BANK NOTES&LOANS PAYABLE=75,50
230 ACCOUNTS PAYABLE =175,175
240 *
250 CURRENT LIABILITIES = L220 +L230
260 LONG TERM DEBT = 150,150
270 COMMON STOCK = 100
280 SURPLUS = 500,425
290 *
300 TOTAL STOCKHOLDER EQUITY =L270 + L280
310 TOTAL LIABILITIES = L250+L260+L300
320 *
330 *
```

FIGURE 6-24. FINANCIAL RATIOS
(This Figure Continued on the Next Page)

```
340 * INCOME STATEMENT
350 *
360 SALES =1200,0
370 COST OF GOODS SOLD = 900,0
380 SELLING ADM &GEN EXPENSE=175,0
390 DEPRECIATION =50,0
400 *
410 EARNINGS BEFORE INT&TAX=L360-L370-L380-L390
420 INTEREST=10,0
430 *
440 EARNINGS BEFORE TAX=L410-L420
450 INCOME TAXES =30,0
460 *
470 EARNINGS AFTER TAX=EARNINGS BEFORE TAX -INCOME TAXES
480 COMMON DIVIDENDS = 12,0
490 RETAINED EARNINGS =EARNINGS AFTER TAX -COMMON DIVIDENDS
500 *
510 *INDICATORS OF LEVERAGE
520 *---------- -- --------
530 FINANCIAL LEVERAGE=LONG TERM DEBT/(LONG TERM DEBT+'
531 TOTAL STOCKHOLDER EQUITY)
540 TIMES INTEREST EARNED = EARNINGS BEFORE INT&TAX/INTEREST
550 *
560 *INDICATORS OF LIQUIDITY
570 *---------- -- ---------
580 NET WORKING CAPITAL TO NET ASSETS = (CURRENT ASSETS -'
590 CURRENT LIABILITIES)/TOTAL ASSETS
600 CURRENT RATIO = CURRENT ASSETS/CURRENT LIABILITIES
610 QUICK RATIO= (CURRENT ASSETS -INVENTORIES)/CURRENT LIABILITIES
620 CASH RATIO = CASH&MRKTBLE SECURITIES/CURRENT LIABILITIES
630 *
640 *INDICATORS OF EFFICIENCY
650 *---------- -- ----------
660 SALES TO TOTAL ASSETS = SALES/((TOTAL ASSETS +'
661 FUTURE TOTAL ASSETS)/2),0
670 SALES TO NET WORKING CAPITAL=SALES/(( CURRENT ASSETS+'
680 FUTURE CURRENT ASSETS-CURRENT LIABILITIES -'
681 FUTURE CURRENT LIABILITIES)/2),0
690 RETURN ON TOTAL ASSETS IN PCT = 100*(EARNINGS BEFORE INT&TAX - '
700 INCOME TAXES)/((TOTAL ASSETS + FUTURE TOTAL ASSETS)/2),0
710 RETURN ON EQUITY IN PCT=100*EARNINGS AFTER TAX/'
720 ((TOTAL STOCKHOLDER EQUITY+FUTURE TOTAL STOCKHOLDER EQUITY)/2),0
730 NET PROFIT MARGIN IN PCT=100*(EARNINGS BEFORE INT&TAX-'
740 INCOME TAXES)/SALES,0
750 INVENTORY TURNOVER =COST OF GOODS SOLD/'
751 ((INVENTORIES+FUTURE INVENTORIES)/2),0
760 AVERAGE COLLECTION PERIOD IN DAYS=((ACCOUNTS RECEIVABLE +'
761 MATRIX(ACCOUNTS RECEIVABLE,2))/2)/(SALES/365),0
END OF MODEL
```

FIGURE 6-24. FINANCIAL RATIOS

(This Figure Continued on the Next Page)

```
? solve

ENTER SOLVE OPTIONS
? 150 thru 1310
                                  1980     1979


 BALANCE SHEET

ASSETS
CASH&MRKTBLE SECURITIES             50       75
ACCOUNTS RECEIVABLE                250      200
INVENTORIES                        300      250

CURRENT ASSETS                     600      525
GROSS FIXED ASSETS                 600      550
ACCUMULATED DEPRECIATION           200      175

NET FIXED ASSETS                   400      375

TOTAL ASSETS                      1000      900

LIABILITIES
BANK NOTES&LOANS PAYABLE            75       50
ACCOUNTS PAYABLE                   175      175

CURRENT LIABILITIES                250      225
LONG TERM DEBT                     150      150
COMMON STOCK                       100      100
SURPLUS                            500      425

TOTAL STOCKHOLDER EQUITY           600      525
TOTAL LIABILITIES                 1000      900
```

FIGURE 6-24. FINANCIAL RATIOS
(This Figure Continued on the Next Page)

```
ENTER SOLVE OPTIONS
? width 68 40 9
? column 1
? 1340 thru 1760
                                                  1980

 INCOME STATEMENT

SALES                                             1200
COST OF GOODS SOLD                                 900
SELLING ADM &GEN EXPENSE                           175
DEPRECIATION                                        50

EARNINGS BEFORE INT&TAX                             75
INTEREST                                            10

EARNINGS BEFORE TAX                                 65
INCOME TAXES                                        30

EARNINGS AFTER TAX                                  35
COMMON DIVIDENDS                                    12
RETAINED EARNINGS                                   23


INDICATORS OF LEVERAGE
---------- -- --------
FINANCIAL LEVERAGE                               .2000
TIMES INTEREST EARNED                            7.500

INDICATORS OF LIQUIDITY
---------- -- ---------
NET WORKING CAPITAL TO NET ASSETS                .3500
CURRENT RATIO                                    2.400
QUICK RATIO                                      1.200
CASH RATIO                                       .2000

INDICATORS OF EFFICIENCY
---------- -- ----------
SALES TO TOTAL ASSETS                            1.263
SALES TO NET WORKING CAPITAL                     3.692
RETURN ON TOTAL ASSETS IN PCT                    4.737
RETURN ON EQUITY IN PCT                          6.222
NET PROFIT MARGIN IN PCT                         3.750
INVENTORY TURNOVER                               3.273
AVERAGE COLLECTION PERIOD IN DAYS                68.44
```

FIGURE 6-24. FINANCIAL RATIOS
(Continued)

In going through Figure 6-24, note one fine point on the use of parentheses. In lines 660 through 761 some of the ratios involve averages such as average assets. The result is a quantity of the form A/B/C. IFPS can give you wrong answers unless you use parentheses to avoid ambiguity. For example, 3/(4/5) = 3.75 whereas (3/4)/5 = 0.15. In general, extra parentheses don't hurt you but too few parentheses can cause you trouble. Statements starting on lines 660, 670, and 710 are typical examples where the extra parentheses are needed. If you don't believe the need for them, try the model with the parentheses deleted.

6.14 CASH MANAGEMENT MODEL

The management of the cash balance of a firm can be modeled in terms of inventory theory. Although we will discuss inventory ideas in much more detail in Chapter VIII, we can see these ideas intuitively and use them to understand the Miller-Orr model for cash management.

A firm generally has a policy to keep a minimum amount of cash on hand to run its day-to-day affairs. The amount is sometimes determined by requirements imposed by the firm's banks. There is also a maximum desirable amount. This maximum reflects a trade-off between the transaction cost of investing in a liquid investment such as Treasury bills and the cost of lost interest because cash is not invested. Cash can be considered to be like any other good that the company keeps in its inventory. The Miller-Orr model assumes that you know the minimum cash balance required, the variance of daily cash flows, the daily interest rate, and the transaction cost for each sale or purchase of securities.

The Miller-Orr model applies the principles of inventory theory to the foregoing information to compute the spread between the maximum and minimum cash limits. The relation used is:

$$\text{SPREAD} = 3*(.75*\text{TRANSACTION COST}*\text{VARIANCE OF CASH FLOWS}/\text{INTEREST RATE})^{.333} \tag{6-20}$$

Knowing the minimum cash balance and the spread, you can compute the maximum cash balance and the return point:

MAXIMUM CASH BALANCE = MINIMUM CASH BALANCE + SPREAD

RETURN POINT = MINIMUM CASH BALANCE + SPREAD/3

These formulas tell us that whenever the cash balance reaches the maximum, we should invest the difference between the maximum cash balance and the return point; similarly, whenever the minimum cash balance is reached, we should sell sufficient securities to reach the return point. Note that the return point is not midway between maximum and minimum cash balance, but one-third of the distance between them and on the low side.

Figure 6-25 shows the Miller-Orr model in IFPS and applies it to a particular example. As usual, the XPOWERY function is used; in this case to find the cube root needed in determining the spread according to Equation (6-20).

```
MODEL MILLERORR  VERSION OF  09/15/81  21:48
10 COLUMNS 1
20*
30* MILLER-ORR CASH MANAGEMENT MODEL
40*
50 SPREAD = 3*XPOWERY(0.75*TRANSACTION COST *'
51 VARIANCE OF CASH FLOWS/INTEREST RATE,.33333)
60*
70 UPPER LIMIT = MINIMUM CASH BALANCE + SPREAD
80 RETURN POINT = MINIMUM CASH BALANCE + SPREAD/3
90*
100*DECISION RULES
110*
120 INVESTMENT AT UPPER LIMIT = UPPER LIMIT - RETURN POINT
130 SECURITY SALES AT MINIMUM CASH BALANCE = RETURN POINT'
131 - MINIMUM CASH BALANCE
140*
150* DATA
160*
170 MINIMUM CASH BALANCE =10000
180 STD DEVIATION OF CASH FLOWS = 2500
190 VARIANCE OF CASH FLOWS = XPOWERY(STD DEVIATION OF CASH FLOWS,2)
200 INTEREST RATE = .00025
210 TRANSACTION COST = 20
END OF MODEL
? solve
MODEL MILLERORR   VERSION OF   09/15/81   21:48 -- 1 COLUMNS 10
VARIABLES
ENTER SOLVE OPTIONS
? all
                                            1

 MILLER-ORR CASH MANAGEMENT MODEL

SPREAD                        21632

UPPER LIMIT                   31632
RETURN POINT                  17211

DECISION RULES

INVESTMENT AT UPPER LIMIT     14421
SECURITY SALES AT MINIMUM      7211

 DATA

MINIMUM CASH BALANCE          10000
STD DEVIATION OF CASH FLOWS    2500
VARIANCE OF CASH FLOWS      6250000
INTEREST RATE                 .0003
TRANSACTION COST                 20
```

FIGURE 6-25. MILLER-ORR CASH MANAGEMENT MODEL

6.15 PRO FORMA FINANCIAL FORECAST MODELS

We conclude this chapter by presenting a generalized financial forecast model that allows you to create:

- Income statements
- Sources and uses of funds
- Balance sheets

for from one year to as many years as you please. The choice of number of years is incorporated in the COLUMNS statement. In a typical financial planning model you make estimates of the revenues anticipated in future years, external variables over which your firm has little or no control (e.g., interest rates), and policy variables such as dividend payout.

Figure 6-26 shows a generalized five-year pro forma forecast, with 1980 assumed as the current year. As you read through this model you will see that it is really an accounting model that is based on the following assumptions:

- The anticipated growth of the business, i.e., revenues and stock issues.
- Relations between revenues and other quantities. Specifically, the cost of goods sold, the value of fixed assets, and the net working capital are assumed proportional to revenues. These are expressed as ratios in the list of assumptions.
- Dividend payout is proportional to net income.
- Current (i.e., 1980) data on revenues, debt, and equity as well as current and anticipated tax and interest rates.
- Change in working capital and investment in 1980 are arbitrarily set to 0 since data were not given; however, in a real company you would have this information.

In using this model, you should view it as a basis for creating financial forecasts that are tailored to the situation of your own company and its accounting conventions. You will want to add and delete lines. You will also want to modify the assumptions to fit your expectations. In the simple model shown here, for example, growth is at a constant rate, tax and interest rates are fixed, and dividends are proportional to net income rather than being constant. You may believe that more complex situations will prevail and can easily include them in your model. We will ask you to do this in the exercises that follow.

EXERCISE: Modify Figure 6-26 to reflect the following conditions: Interest rates are expected to increase 2% per year for the next three years and then stabilize. The corporate tax rate will go down to 40% in 1982. You anticipate a stock issue of $300,000 in 1982 and of $200,000 in 1984. Revenues will grow 30% for two years but will then grow at only 10%. The company's president has announced that the 1981 dividend will be $60 and that the dividend will stay at that level through the 1980's. To improve productivity, the company plans to become more capital intensive. As a result, fixed assets will grow from 37% in 1980 to 40% in 1983 (1% increase annually) but will be fixed thereafter. Run the model with these changes included.

```
MODEL FORECAST  VERSION OF  12/28/82  15:07
10 COLUMNS 1980-1985
20 *
30 *A GENERALIZED FIVE YEAR PRO FORMA FORECAST
40 *
50 *INCOME STATEMENT
60 *------ ---------
70 *
80 REVENUES = L620
90 COST OF GOODS SOLD = COST OF GOODS SOLD RATIO*REVENUES
100 *
110 EARNINGS BEFORE INTEREST&TAX=REVENUES-COST OF GOODS SOLD
120 INTEREST = INTEREST RATE * DEBT
130 *140 EARNINGS BEFORE TAX=EARNINGS BEFORE INTEREST&TAX-INTEREST
150 TAX = TAX RATE * EARNINGS BEFORE TAX
160 *
170 NET INCOME =EARNINGS BEFORE TAX - TAX
180 *
190 *SOURCES AND USES OF FUNDS
200 *------- --- ---- -- -----
210 *
220 *SOURCES
230    NET INCOME = L170
240    DEPRECIATION = DEPRECIATION PERCENTAGE*FIXED ASSETS
250 *
260    OPERATING CASH FLOW =L170 +DEPRECIATION
270    BORROWING =CHANGE IN NET WRKNG CAPITAL + INVESTMENT +'
280    DIVIDENDS - L170 -DEPRECIATION-STOCK ISSUES
290    STOCK ISSUES = L630
300 *
310    TOTAL SOURCES =OPERATING CASH FLOW+BORROWING+STOCK ISSUES
320 *
330 *
340 *USES
350    CHANGE IN NET WRKNG CAPITAL = 0, NET WORKING CAPITAL'
360    -PREVIOUS NET WORKING CAPITAL
370    INVESTMENT =0,DEPRECIATION+FIXED ASSETS-PREVIOUS FIXED ASSETS
380    DIVIDENDS = DIVIDEND PAYOUT RATIO *L170
390    *
400    TOTAL USES=CHANGE IN NET WRKNG CAPITAL+INVESTMENT+DIVIDENDS
410 *
```

FIGURE 6-26. A GENERALIZED FIVE-YEAR PRO FORMA FORECAST
(This Figure Continued on the Next Page)

```
420 *
430 *BALANCE SHEETS
440 *------- ------
450 *
460 *ASSETS
470    NET WORKING CAPITAL =NET WORKING CAPITAL RATIO *L620
480    FIXED ASSETS =FIXED ASSETS RATIO *REVENUES
490 *
500    TOTAL ASSETS = NET WORKING CAPITAL + FIXED ASSETS
510 *
520 *LIABILITIES
530    DEBT=INITIAL DEBT,BORROWING + PREVIOUS DEBT
540    BOOK EQUITY=INITIAL EQUITY,PREVIOUS BOOK EQUITY+L170-'
550 DIVIDENDS + STOCK ISSUES
560 *
570    TOTAL LIABILITIES = DEBT + BOOK EQUITY
580 *
590 *ASSUMPTIONS
600 *-----------
610 *
620 REVENUES =2160,PREVIOUS * 1.3
630 STOCK ISSUES = 0
640 COST OF GOODS SOLD RATIO = .9
650 INTEREST RATE = .09
660 TAX RATE = .50
670 DEPRECIATION PERCENTAGE = .10
680 DIVIDEND PAYOUT RATIO =.60
690 NET WORKING CAPITAL RATIO =.093
700 FIXED ASSETS RATIO = .37
710 INITIAL DEBT = 400,0
720 INITIAL EQUITY =600,0
END OF MODEL
```

FIGURE 6-26. A GENERALIZED FIVE-YEAR PRO FORMA FORECAST
(This Figure Continued on the Next Page)

```
? solve
SIMULTANEOUS EQUATIONS DETECTED - DO YOU WANT TO PRINT THE VARIABLES
INVOLVED
? no
MODEL  FORECAST   VERSION  OF    12/28/82    15:07  --  6  COLUMNS  34
VARIABLES
ENTER SOLVE OPTIONS
?150  thru 1400
```

	1980	1981	1982	1983	1984	1985
INCOME STATEMENT						
------ ---------						
REVENUES	2160	2808	3650	4746	6169	8020
COST OF GOODS SOLD	1944	2527	3285	4271	5552	7218
EARNINGS BEFORE INTE	216	280.8	365.0	474.6	616.9	802.0
INTEREST	36	59.01	89.15	128.6	180.0	247.1
EARNINGS BEFORE TAX	180	221.8	275.9	346.0	436.9	554.8
TAX	90	110.9	137.9	173.0	218.5	277.4
NET INCOME	90	110.9	137.9	173.0	218.5	277.4
SOURCES AND USES OF FUNDS						
------- --- ---- -- -----						
SOURCES						
NET INCOME	90	110.9	137.9	173.0	218.5	277.4
DEPRECIATION	79.92	103.9	135.1	175.6	228.3	296.7
OPERATING CASH FL	169.9	214.8	273.0	348.6	446.7	574.2
BORROWING	-115.9	255.7	334.9	437.8	571.8	745.9
STOCK ISSUES	0	0	0	0	0	0
TOTAL SOURCES	54	470.5	607.9	786.4	1018	1320
USES						
CHANGE IN NET WRKNG CAP	0	60.26	78.34	101.8	132.4	172.1
INVESTMENT	0	343.7	446.8	580.8	755.0	981.5
DIVIDENDS	54	66.54	82.77	103.8	131.1	166.5
TOTAL USES	54	470.5	607.9	786.4	1018	1320

FIGURE 6-26. A GENERALIZED FIVE-YEAR PRO FORMA FORECAST
(This Figure Continued on the Next Page)

```
ENTER SOLVE OPTIONS
?1430 thru 720
```

	1980	1981	1982	1983	1984	1985
BALANCE SHEETS						
------- ------						
ASSETS						
NET WORKING CAPIT	200.9	261.1	339.5	441.3	573.7	745.9
FIXED ASSETS	799.2	1039	1351	1756	2283	2967
TOTAL ASSETS	1000	1300	1690	2197	2856	3713
LIABILITIES						
DEBT	400	655.7	990.5	1428	2000	2746
BOOK EQUITY	600	644.4	699.5	768.7	856.1	967.1
TOTAL LIABILITIES	1000	1300	1690	2197	2856	3713
ASSUMPTIONS						

REVENUES	2160	2808	3650	4746	6169	8020
STOCK ISSUES	0	0	0	0	0	0
COST OF GOODS SOLD RATI	9000	.9000	.9000	.9000	.9000	.9000
INTEREST RATE	.0900	.0900	.0900	.0900	.0900	.0900
TAX RATE	.5000	.5000	.5000	.5000	.5000	.5000
DEPRECIATION PERCENT	.1000	.1000	.1000	.1000	.1000	.1000
DIVIDEND PAYOUT RATIO	.6000	.6000	.6000	.6000	.6000	.6000
NET WORKING CAPITAL	.0930	.0930	.0930	.0930	.0930	.0930
FIXED ASSETS RATIO	.3700	.3700	.3700	.3700	.3700	.3700
INITIAL DEBT	400	0	0	0	0	0
INITIAL EQUITY	600	0	0	0	0	0

FIGURE 6-26. A GENERALIZED FIVE-YEAR PRO FORMA FORECAST
(Continued)

EXERCISE: Suppose you anticipate inflation in the next five years to be 2% below the interest rate Assume that the data generated in the previous exercise are in absolute, not current, dollars. Modify the model in the previous exercise to create results in current (i.e., 1980) dollars. Discuss how the future looks in current dollar terms.

If you try to solve this model on your computer, you will find that the response to SOLVE will be:

```
SIMULTANEOUS EQUATIONS DETECTED-DO YOU WANT TO PRINT VARIABLES
INVOLVED
```

If you respond YES, IFPS will display a list of variables which form a set of simultaneous equations. In the case of Figure 6-26, these variables are:

```
120 INTEREST
140 EARNINGS BEFORE TAX
150 TAX
170 NET INCOME
380 DIVIDENDS
270 BORROWING
530 DEBT
```

After providing the list, IFPS will ask you:

```
DO YOU WANT TO PROCEED WITH COMPILATION
```

If you respond YES, IFPS will proceed and attempt to solve the simultaneous equations. It uses the "Gauss-Seidel" method (an interative technique) to solve the simultaneous equations in each column independently. Because of this method of solution, you cannot have any FUTURE references in any column for the definitions of the variables involved in the simultaneous equations. Furthermore, under some conditions you may require many iterations. If too many iterations are required, IFPS may tell you:

```
NO CONVERGENCE FOR SIMULTANEOUS EQUATIONS IN COLUMN ...
```

If you know that you have simultaneous equations and want to avoid having to answer questions, you can put the statement SIMULTANEOUS AUTO anywhere in your model and IFPS will find all sets of simultaneous equations and will take perform the necessary calculations.

CAUTION: Simultaneous equations and their solution can be a tricky business. Success is not guaranteed and seemingly simple situations can lead to trouble. Trouble can include the NO CONVERGENCE statement or, worse, incorrect answers without any message telling you that the answers are wrong. Try the exercises below to see what can happen to you.

In general it is good practice, if simultaneous equations exist, to:

- Check that the equations correspond to the situation being modeled.
- Check as many of the numbers produced as possible to make sure that they are correct and consistent with the assumptions of the model.

EXERCISE: Solve the following model:

```
10 COLUMNS 1-3
20 X = 2*Y +1
30 Y = 3*X +2
```

EXERCISE: Solve the following model:

```
10 COLUMNS 1
20 INCOME =1000
30 EXPENSES = 2200
40 BORROW = 1000 + DEFICIT
50 DEFICIT = EXPENSES   - INCOME - BORROW
```

6.16 ADDENDUM: YEAR 0 VS. YEAR 1

As we pointed out in Section 6.1, IFPS uses the convention that all investments occur at the beginning of a year and all returns occur at the end of a year. This differs from the convention followed in some finance texts that places the initial investment at the end of Year 0 and all subsequent investments at the end of subsequent years.The difference in approach reflects different viewpoints on what "present" means in "net present value". It is usually assumed that "present" refers to the time at which the first investment is made. Up to the point of initial commitment of funds, the project could be scrapped at no additional cost (a simplification in that we treat as sunk cost the cost of analyst and managerial time in reaching a decision). Furthermore, if the project is undertaken, returns occur only some time after the initial investment. To make this distinction between initial investment and later returns, many finance texts choose different year numbers for the initial investment and the initial returns.

In a modeling language such as IFPS, investments and returns are both calculated. Each variable must either be specified or computed for every column. It is more convenient to start both sets of calculations in the first column. The alternative would be to create a column to represent Year 0 and to set the value of every return to 0 in this column. In the author's personal view, this creates an artificiality that can easily lead to clerical errors in setting up the model.

You can see the difference between the two approaches in Figure 6-27. This figure shows the same problem modeled with a Year 1 and a Year 0 approach. Note that in the YEAR 0 approach the number of columns is increased by one and that all returns start with 0. You also have to define the NPVC and IRR functions differently. That is, you compute the difference between return and investment (i.e., the net return) and delete explicit reference to investment in these functions. Finally, the present values computed by IFPS are with respect to the BEGINNING of YEAR 0. You are interested in the returns at the end of YEAR 0 (which is equal to the beginning of YEAR 1). To make the results conform to your idea of what "present" represents, you have to multiply by (1+DISCOUNT RATE). (Can you explain why?)

If you feel more comfortable starting with Year 0, by all means do so. However, be careful that your IFPS model correctly reflects your choice.

```
MODEL FIRST  VERSION OF  02/03/82  13:57
10 COLUMNS 1-5
20 INVESTMENT = LAND + BUILDING
30 RETURN = SALES -COSTS
40 PRESENT VALUE = NPVC(RETURN,DISCOUNT RATE,INVESTMENT)
50 IRR = IRR(RETURN,INVESTMENT)
60 *
70 * INPUT DATA
80 *
90 LAND = 200,0
100 BUILDING = 100,150,0
110*
120 SALES =500,600,700
130 COSTS = SUM (MATERIALS THRU LABOR)
140 MATERIALS = 10 + 0.20*SALES
150 OVERHEAD =50,60,70
160 LABOR = 20 + 0.40*SALES
170*
180 DISCOUNT RATE = 0.20
END OF MODEL
? solve
MODEL FIRST  VERSION OF  02/03/82  13:57 -- 5 COLUMNS 12 VARIABLES
ENTER SOLVE OPTIONS
? all
```

	1	2	3	4	5
INVESTMENT	300	150	0	0	0
RETURN	120	150	180	180	180
PRESENT VALUE	-200	-220.8	-116.7	-29.86	42.48
IRR			0	.1604	.2462
INPUT DATA					
LAND	200	0	0	0	0
BUILDING	100	150	0	0	0
SALES	500	600	700	700	700
COSTS	380	450	520	520	520
MATERIALS	110	130	150	150	150
OVERHEAD	50	60	70	70	70
LABOR	220	260	300	300	300
DISCOUNT RATE	.2000	.2000	.2000	.2000	.2000

a. Investments Assumed to Occur at Start of Year 1

FIGURE 6-27. COMPARISON OF YEAR 1 AND YEAR 0 CONVENTIONS FOR INITIAL INVESTMENT

(This Figure Continued on Next Page)

```
MODEL SECOND  VERSION OF  02/03/82  14:00
10 COLUMNS 0-5
20 INVESTMENT = LAND + BUILDING
30 RETURN = SALES -COSTS
40 PRESENT VALUE=NPVC(RETURN-INVESTMENT,DISCOUNT RATE,0)'
41 *(1+DISCOUNT RATE)
50 IRR = IRR(RETURN-INVESTMENT,0)
60 *
70 * INPUT DATA
80 *
90 LAND = 200,0
100 BUILDING = 100,150,0
110*
120 SALES =0,500,600,700
130 COSTS = SUM (MATERIALS THRU LABOR)
140 MATERIALS = 0,10 + 0.20*SALES
150 OVERHEAD =0,50,60,70
160 LABOR = 0,20 + 0.40*SALES
170*
180 DISCOUNT RATE = 0.20
END OF MODEL
? solve
MODEL SECOND  VERSION OF  02/03/82  14:00 -- 6 COLUMNS 12 VARIABLES
ENTER SOLVE OPTIONS
? all
```

	0	1	2	3	4	5
INVESTMENT	300	150	0	0	0	0
RETURN	0	120	150	180	180	180
PRESENT VALUE	-300	-325	-220.8	-116.7	-29.86	42.48
IRR				0	.1604	.2462
INPUT DATA						
LAND	200	0	0	0	0	0
BUILDING	100	150	0	0	0	0
SALES	0	500	600	700	700	700
COSTS	0	380	450	520	520	520
MATERIALS	0	110	130	150	150	150
OVERHEAD	0	50	60	70	70	70
LABOR	0	220	260	300	300	300
DISCOUNT RATE	.2000	.2000	.2000	.2000	.2000	.2000

B. Investments Assumed to Occur at the End of Year 0

FIGURE 6-27. COMPARISON OF YEAR 1 AND YEAR 0 CONVENTIONS FOR INITIAL INVESTMENT
(Continued)

CHAPTER VII
APPLICATIONS IN STATISTICS

7.1 Summary Measures -- Mean, Variance, Standard Deviation

7.1.1 Mean and Moving Average
7.1.2 Mean of Grouped Data
7.1.3 Average of Weighted Data
7.1.4 Median
7.1.5 Measures of Dispersion

7.2 Permutations and Combinations

7.3 Probability Distributions

7.3.1 Binomial Distribution
7.3.2 Poisson Distribution

7.4 Chi-Square Tests of Goodness of Fit and Independence

7.5 Linear Regression

7.5.1 Computing the Regression Coefficients
7.5.2 Correlation Analysis
7.5.3 Statistical Inferences in Regression

7.6 Multiple Regression

7.7 Time Series and Forecasting

7.7.1 Short-Term Forecasting
7.7.2 Long-Term Forecasting

7.8 Index Numbers

CHAPTER VII
APPLICATIONS IN STATISTICS

This chapter shows you how to use IFPS in problems involving statistics. Statistical techniques are needed in solving many problems in finance, marketing, accounting, economics, and other disciplines. As you will see from the examples shown in this chapter, IFPS, because of its ability to lay out information in matrix form and its WHAT IF capabilities, is often an easy way to understand what is going on in a statistical procedure. In other words, it is a way of de-mystifying statistics as well as a way of communicating results to management in a meaningful way.

As in Chapter VI, we have used many of the examples in an existing text. In this case, we used *STATISTICS FOR BUSINESS AND ECONOMICS* by Marion G. Sobol and Martin K. Starr (McGraw-Hill, 1982). If you need more information about a particular method or topic you can refer to the book by Sobol and Starr or to any similar introductory statistics text for business applications. We have tried, however, to present the following material in such a way that if you have a working understanding of statistical concepts you can use this chapter to solve statistical problems without having to refer to outside sources.

This chapter contains a representative sample of IFPS applications in statistics. It is intended to show you what can be done and to encourage you to build your own IFPS models to solve statistical problems you encounter in your work.

7.1 SUMMARY MEASURES -- MEAN, VARIANCE, STANDARD DEVIATION

7.1.1 Mean and Moving Average

If you gather a large amount of data about a particular subject, you usually will find it easier to communicate your results to management by summarizing the information into a few commonly understood numbers. The simplest of these are the mean, the variance, and the standard deviation.

The mean is simply the average value of the numbers. It is obtained by adding all the data values, X, and dividing by n, the number of data points. In formula terms:

$$MEAN = (X1 + X2 + X3 + \ldots Xn) / n \qquad (7\text{-}1)$$

where X1,X2,...are the observations and n is the number of observations.

IFPS has a built-in function for finding the mean. As shown in Figure 7-1, you follow these steps:

1. Specify the number of columns to be equal to the number of observations.

2. Type in your X values.

3. Ask for the average by using the MEAN function.

The MEAN function requires two inputs, the location of the first observation and the last observation (Your X1 and Xn). Since you are referring to two columns in a particular row, you must use MATRIX. For example, to find the mean of 10 numbers, you ask for:

AVERAGE =MEAN(MATRIX(X,1),MATRIX(X,10))

As described in Section 4.4.2, MATRIX refers to a particular column of a variable. In Figure 7-1 we use MATRIX to define the values of a variable X whose values are given in columns 1 and 10.

```
MODEL STAT1   VERSION OF   08/27/82   22:18
5 COLUMNS 1-10
10 X=15,18,25,30,14,42,63,220,49,42
20*
30*         AVERAGE AND MOVING AVERAGE
40*
50 AVERAGE=MEAN(MATRIX(X,1),MATRIX(X,10))
60 MOVINGAVERAGE1=MOVAVG(X,.5,.5)
70 MOVINGAVERAGE2=MOVAVG(FUTURE X,.33,.33,.33)
END OF MODEL
?solve
ENTER SOLVE OPTIONS
? all
```

	1	2	3	4	5	6	7	8	9	10
X	15	18	25	30	14	42	63	220	49	42
AVERAGE AND MOVING AVERAGE										
AVERAGE	51.8	51.8	51.8	51.8	51.8	51.8	51.8	51.8	51.8	51.8
MOVINGAVERAGE1	15	16.5	21.5	27.5	22	28	52.5	142	135	45.5
MOVINGAVERAGE2	16.5	19.3	24.3	23	28.7	39.7	108	111	104	45.5

FIGURE 7-1. AVERAGE AND MOVING AVERAGE

When dealing with data that occur over time (for example, weekly sales or quarterly profits), the average of all the data we have may tell us very little because things change over time. However, we may want to smooth out random fluctuations to be able to observe the changes over time. A simple way to do this is to take a "moving average". Here we average data obtained over a specific time period. As shown in Figure 7-1, IFPS has a built-in moving average function, MOVAVG. To use this moving average function, you specify the variable to be averaged and the relative weight to be given to each period starting from (n-1) columns before the current one and working up to the current column. In general form:

MOVAVG(variable,weight1,weight2,...weightn) (7-2)

The weights do not have to be equal. However, they should add up to 1. If they do not, IFPS adjusts them in proportion so that they do. Note that in the second example of MOVAVG in Figure 7-1 (Line 70) the averaging begins with the next period (i.e., FUTURE). This form is useful in forecasting (see Section 7.7).

If the MOVAVG function specifies a column before the first or after the last, IFPS recognizes that the data points in these columns do not exist and uses only the data available. Thus, for example, MOVINGAVERAGE1 has a value of 15 in column 1 because the average is based on just that data point. Similarly, the value of MOVINGAVERAGE in column 10 is 45.5 because it is the average of just the last two points.

EXERCISE: In each implementation of IFPS there is a limit on the number of columns you can have (e.g., 250 on the CDC-6600 computer). This limits the number of data points that can be averaged using the model of Figure 7-1. Modify Figure 7-1 so that it can average, say 600 data points. Note that with large amounts of information, you will want to use the data features of IFPS described in Section 4.6.

EXERCISE: Write an IFPS model that finds the moving average using the mean function. Assume that the data points are to be equally weighted and are to include the current point and the three previous points. Your model need not match the results obtained by the MOVINGAVERAGE function for columns 1, 2, and 3.

7.1.2 Mean of Grouped Data

When data have been grouped into categories, that is, into a "frequency distribution", computing the mean becomes slightly more complicated. What is conventionally done is to assume that all the observations in the interval lie at the midpoint of the interval. For example, suppose data on weekly earnings of sales people are given by the following table:

SALARIES	65	75	85	95	105	115	125
	75	85	95	105	115	125	135
PEOPLE	5	10	20	36	22	12	5

You treat these data as if there were five people earning \$70, 10 people earning \$80, etc. In terms of a simple formula:

$$\text{Average} = \Sigma f{*}m/n \qquad (7\text{-}3)$$

where f is number in each interval, m is the midpoint of the interval and n is the total number of individuals. Figure 7-2 shows how to implement this procedure in IFPS. The data shown for total earnings, total sales people, and average earnings are cumulative; that is, each column is obtained from all the data from column 1 to the current column. Use the IFPS reserved word MEAN.

EXERCISE: Write an alternative version of Figure 7-2 using the MEAN function to find average earnings. What do you sacrifice by using the MEAN function?

```
MODEL STAT2  VERSION OF  08/23/82  00:08
1 COLUMNS 1-7
10*
20*          MEAN FOR GROUPED DATA
30*
40 BOTTOM OF RANGE = 65,PREVIOUS+10
50 TOP OF RANGE =BOTTOM OF RANGE+10
60 MIDPOINT OF RANGE=BOTTOM OF RANGE+(TOP OF RANGE'
61 - BOTTOM OF RANGE)/2
70 NUMBER OF EMPLOYEES =5,10,20,36,22,12,5
80 TOTAL EARNINGS =PREVIOUS +NUMBER OF EMPLOYEES*MIDPOINT OF RANGE
90 TOTAL EMPLOYEES=PREVIOUS+NUMBER OF EMPLOYEES
100 AVERAGE EARNINGS=TOTAL EARNINGS/TOTAL EMPLOYEES
END OF MODEL
? solve
MODEL STAT2  VERSION OF  08/23/82  00:08 -- 7 COLUMNS 7 VARIABLES
ENTER SOLVE OPTIONS
? all
```

	1	2	3	4	5	6	7
MEAN FOR GROUPED DATA							
BOTTOM OF RANGE	65	75	85	95	105	115	125
TOP OF RANGE	75	85	95	105	115	125	135
MIDPOINT OF RANGE	70	80	90	100	110	120	130
NUMBER OF EMPLOYEES	5	10	20	36	22	12	5
TOTAL EARNINGS	350	1150	2950	6550	8970	10410	11060
TOTAL EMPLOYEES	5	15	35	71	93	105	110
AVERAGE EARNINGS	70	76.67	84.29	92.25	96.45	99.14	100.5

FIGURE 7-2. MEAN FOR GROUPED DATA

7.1.3 Average of Weighted Data

Suppose you want to find the average GPA of students at six universities that play in the same football conference. The data are as follows:

SCHOOL	AU	BU	CU	DU	EU	FU
STUDENTS(1000's)	28.4	17.6	14.4	8.9	11.7	14.3
GPA	2.43	2.37	2.39	2.79	2.56	2.22

Simply averaging the six GPA's given to obtain 2.46 (check this!) does not take into account the different sizes of the schools. The correct way to deal with the problem is to apply the formula:

$$\text{Weighted Average} = \Sigma w^*X/\ w \qquad (7\text{-}4)$$

where w is the weight (in our case the number of students) and X is the observed value (i.e., the grade point average). Equation (7-4) tells you to multiply each observation by the number of students who generated it and to divide by the total number of students in the six schools. This approach is implemented in IFPS in Figure 7-3.

```
MODEL STAT3   VERSION OF   08/27/82   22:49
10 COLUMNS 1-6
20 *
30 *           MEAN FOR WEIGHTED DATA
40 *
50 THOUSANDS OF STUDENTS  = 28.4,17.6,14.4,8.9,11.7,14.3
60 GPA  = 2.43,2.37,2.39,2.79,2.56,2.29
70 TOTAL GRADE POINTS=GPA*THOUSANDS OF STUDENTS
80 *
90 CUMULATIVE GRADEPOINTS  = PREVIOUS + TOTAL GRADEPOINTS
100CUMULATIVE NO OF STUDENTS=PREVIOUS+THOUSANDS OF STUDENTS
110WEIGHTED AVG GPA=CUMULATIVE GRADEPOINTS/CUMULATIVE NO OF STUDENTS
120*
END OF MODEL
? solve
MODEL STAT3   VERSION OF   08/27/82   22:49 -- 6 COLUMNS 6 VARIABLES
ENTER SOLVE OPTIONS
? all

                                      1        2        3        4        5        6


          MEAN FOR WEIGHTED DATA

THOUSANDS OF STUDENTS             28.40    17.60    14.40    8.900    11.70    14.30
GPA                               2.430    2.370    2.390    2.790    2.560    2.290
TOTAL GRADE POINTS                69.01    41.71    34.42    24.83    29.95    32.75

CUMULATIVE GRADEPOINTS            69.01    110.7    145.1    170.0    199.9    232.7
CUMULATIVE NO OF STUDENTS         28.40       46    60.40    69.30       81    95.30
WEIGHTED AVG GPA                  2.430    2.407    2.403    2.453    2.468    2.441
```

FIGURE 7-3. MEAN FOR WEIGHTED DATA

7.1.4 Median

The mean is a good way of describing data when observations are relatively close together or the frequency distribution is nearly symmetric. For the data used in Figure 7-1 this was not the case; the mean was larger than 8 of the 10 numbers because of the very large value of 220. When there are a few observations that are very different from the rest, the median is a better way of describing the data in terms of a single, most typical value. In simple terms, the median is the middle value of a set of observations. An equal number of observed values are above the median and below the median. For example, for observations of 1, 3, 5, 7, and 29, the mean is 15 and the median is 5.

The median is obtained by ordering the values of the observations in increasing (or decreasing) order and taking the middle observed value. This is easy to do if there are an odd number of observations (e.g., take the 3rd value of 5) but slightly more difficult if there is an even number of observations. The convention that is followed for an even number of observations is to take the average of the two middle values. For example, if we observe 1, 3, 5, 7, 9, and 29 we take the average of 5 and 7; that is, the median is 6.

Figure 7-4 uses the same data as Figure 7-1 and shows that all you need to do is replace the reserved word MEAN by the reserved word MEDIAN to use the MEDIAN function.

```
MODEL STAT4   VERSION OF   09/01/82   20:54
10 COLUMNS 1-10
20 DATA = 15,18,25,30,14,42,63,220,49,42
30 AVERAGE=MEAN(MATRIX(DATA,1),MATRIX(DATA,10))
40 MEDIAN=MEDIAN(MATRIX(DATA,1),MATRIX(DATA,10))
50 MOVING MEDIAN=MEDIAN(PREVIOUS 2 DATA,FUTURE DATA)
END OF MODEL
? solve
MODEL STAT4   VERSION OF   09/01/82   20:54 -- 10 COLUMNS 4 VARIABLES
ENTER SOLVE OPTIONS
? all

                    1     2     3     4     5     6     7     8     9    10

DATA               15    18    25    30    14    42    63   220    49    42
AVERAGE          51.8  51.8  51.8  51.8  51.8  51.8  51.8  51.8  51.8  51.8
MEDIAN             42    42    42    42    42    42    42    42    42    42
MOVING MEDIAN      18    18    25    25    30    42    63    63    63    49
```

FIGURE 7-4. MEDIAN

EXERCISE: Write an IFPS model that uses the median function to find a moving median. Assume you want the mean of five points, starting with the next column, with all the points equally weighted.

EXERCISE: Finding the median of a frequency distribution is slightly more complicated. The problem is that you first have to find the group in which the middle observation occurs and then have to estimate the value of that middle observation. Use the data in Section 7.1.2 on the earnings of sales people and write an IFPS model to determine the median. Note that the sample contains 110 observations. Because a frequency distribution for the purpose of finding the median is considered continuous, you have to find the 110/2 or 55th value. To do so, you will first have to find that the 55th observation lies in the 4th interval and then you will have to assume that the observations are uniformly distributed within the fourth interval. You will find the following formula helpful:

$$\text{MEDIAN} = L + ((n/2 - \Sigma f(L-1)) / f(L)) * X(L) \qquad (7\text{-}5)$$

where L is the bottom of the range containing the median,
n is the total sample size,
f(L-1) is the total sample up to the median class,
f(L) is the number in the median class, and
X(L) is the size of the interval containing the median.

In our case, L=95, n=110, f(L-1)=35, f(L)=36, and X(L)=10.

This is not a simple exercise. Don't try to sit at a terminal and write the solution. Think about how to do it first and write it out on scratch paper. You will find it useful to use IF...THEN...ELSE. (see Section 4.4.3).

7.1.5 Measures of Dispersion

In the preceding sections we have discussed various ways of obtaining a single number, either the mean or the median, for summarizing data. Although such a single number is useful, it does not tell the whole story. You can obtain the same median, for example, from 1, 2, 3, 4, 5 and from –10, –5, 3, 11, 27; however, these two sets of data are quite different. The usual approach therefore is to characterize data in terms of two or more numbers, one of which indicates a central location while the others measure the dispersion around this center. This subsection deals with measures of dispersion. It includes discussions of:

- standard deviation and variance of a sample and a population
- skewness
- kurtosis
- average deviation and range
- confidence interval
- coefficient of variation

You have encountered almost all these measures previously when you examined the output from MONTE CARLO calculations in Chapter V. Figure 7-5 shows how to compute each of these measures in IFPS. The data in Figures 7-1 and 7-4 are used. Figure 7-5 repeats the observed data and the mean and median from the previous figures.

STANDARD DEVIATION OF THE SAMPLE. IFPS has a built-in function for computing the standard deviation of a sample, STDDEV. As in the case of the MEAN and MATRIX function you specify the locations of the first and last points by using the MATRIX form. That is, you write

STDDEV(MATRIX(OBSERVED DATA,1),MATRIX(OBSERVED DATA,n)) (7-6)

where OBSERVED DATA contains the values observed and n refers to the number of columns of data.(In Figure 7-5, n=10). What STDDEV computes is:

$$\text{STDDEV} = \sqrt{\Sigma(\text{X - MEAN})^2/(\text{N-1})} \qquad (7\text{-}7)$$

This is known as the standard deviation of the sample since it takes into account that we only estimate the mean from the data, we do not know its underlying (i.e., true) value. In Equation (7-7), X represents observed values and MEAN the average of the observed values computed by using the MEAN function.

VARIANCE OF THE SAMPLE. The variance of the sample is obtained by squaring the standard deviation.

```
MODEL STAT5  VERSION OF  09/01/82  22:37
10 COLUMNS 1-10
20 OBSERVED DATA = 15,18,25,30,14,42,63,220,49,42
25*
30 MEAN=MEAN(MATRIX(OBSERVED DATA,1),MATRIX(OBSERVED DATA,10))
40 MEDIAN=MEDIAN(MATRIX(OBSERVED DATA,1),MATRIX(OBSERVED DATA,10))
45*
50 STD DEV OF SAMPLE=STDDEV(MATRIX(OBSERVED DATA,1),'
51 MATRIX(OBSERVED DATA,10))
60 SAMPLE VARIANCE=XPOWERY(STD DEV OF SAMPLE,2)
70*
80*DIRECT CALCULATION OF VARIANCE OF POPULATION
90*
100 VARIANCE=0 FOR 9,SUM OF SQUARES/NCOL-MEAN*MEAN
110 STD DEVIATION=XPOWERY(VARIANCE,0.5)
120*
130*OTHER MEASURES OF DISPERSION
140*
150 SKEWNESS=3*(MEAN-MEDIAN)/STD DEV OF SAMPLE
160*
170 KURTOSIS = 0 FOR 9,(SUM OF 4TH POWERS/NCOL)/'
180 XPOWERY(SAMPLE VARIANCE,2)
190*
200 AVERAGE DEVIATION=PREVIOUS +ABS(OBSERVED DATA-MEAN)/NCOL
210*
220 RANGE = LARGEST VALUE - SMALLEST VALUE
225*
230 LOWER CONFIDENCE LIMIT = MEAN - 1.65*STD DEV OF SAMPLE
240 UPPER CONFIDENCE LIMIT= MEAN +1.65*STD DEV OF SAMPLE
250*
260 COEFFICIENT OF VARIATION = STD DEV OF SAMPLE*100/MEAN
270*
280*      INTERMEDIATE CALCULATIONS AND VALUES
290*
300 SUM OF SQUARES =PREVIOUS +OBSERVED DATA*OBSERVED DATA
310 NCOL=10
320 SUM OF 4TH POWERS =PREVIOUS +XPOWERY((OBSERVED DATA-MEAN),4)
330 LARGEST VALUE =OBSERVED DATA,MAXIMUM(PREVIOUS,OBSERVED DATA)
340 SMALLEST VALUE =OBSERVED DATA,MINIMUM(OBSERVED DATA,PREVIOUS)
END OF MODEL
```

FIGURE 7-5. MEASURES OF DISPERSION
(This Figure Continued on the Next Page)

```
? solve
MODEL STAT5  VERSION OF  09/01/82  22:37 -- 10 COLUMNS 19 VARIABLES
ENTER SOLVE OPTIONS
? all

                        1    2    3    4    5    6    7    8    9   10

OBSERVED DATA          15   18   25   30   14   42   63  220   49   42

MEAN                 51.8 51.8 51.8 51.8 51.8 51.8 51.8 51.8 51.8 51.8
MEDIAN                 42   42   42   42   42   42   42   42   42   42


STD DEV OF SAMPLE    61.2 61.2 61.2 61.2 61.2 61.2 61.2 61.2 61.2 61.2
SAMPLE VARIANCE      3748 3748 3748 3748 3748 3748 3748 3748 3748 3748

DIRECT CALCULATION OF VARIANCE OF POPULATION

VARIANCE                0    0    0    0    0    0    0    0    0 3374
STD DEVIATION           0    0    0    0    0    0    0    0    0 58.1

OTHER MEASURES OF DISPERSION

SKEWNESS             .480 .480 .480 .480 .480 .480 .480 .480 .480 .480

KURTOSIS                0    0    0    0    0    0    0    0    0 5.74

AVERAGE DEVIATION    3.68 7.06 9.74 11.9 15.7 16.7 17.8 34.6 34.9 35.9

RANGE                   0    3   10   15   16   28   49  206  206  206

LOWER CONFIDENCE L-49.2-49.2-49.2-49.2-49.2-49.2-49.2-49.2-49.2-49.2
UPPER CONFIDENCE L  153  153  153  153  153  153  153  153  153  153

COEFFICIENT OF VAR  118  118  118  118  118  118  118  118  118  118

     INTERMEDIATE CALCULATIONS AND VALUES

SUM OF SQUARES      225  549 1174 2074 2270 4034 8003  6E4  6E4  6E4
NCOL                 10   10   10   10   10   10   10   10   10   10
SUM OF 4TH POWERS   2E6  3E6  4E6  4E6  6E6  6E6  6E6  8E8  8E8  8E8
LARGEST VALUE        15   18   25   30   30   42   63  220  220  220
SMALLEST VALUE       15   15   15   15   14   14   14   14   14   14
```

FIGURE 7-5. MEASURES OF DISPERSION
(Continued)

DIRECT CALCULATION OF VARIANCE AND STANDARD DEVIATION. In Figure 7-5 we also show an alternate way of computing the variance that does not use the STDDEV function. It is based on the computational formula for the variance of the population:

$$\text{VARIANCE} = (\Sigma X^2 /N) - \text{MEAN} \qquad (7\text{-}8)$$

Note that here we assume that the population mean is known and hence we can divide by N rather than N-1. As a result, the variance and standard deviation of the population are smaller than the variance and standard deviation of the sample. In Figure 7-5, the population standard deviation is 58.1 whereas the sample standard deviation is 61.2.

EXERCISE: Modify Line 100 of the alternate calculation of the variance in Figure 7-5 so that it computes the variance of the sample rather than the variance of the population.

The variance is also called the "second moment" around the mean. This terminology comes from physics where the same calculation is performed in mechanics. You can see the origin of the name if you rewrite Equation (7-8) in the form:

$$\text{VARIANCE} = \Sigma\ (\text{OBSERVED DATA -MEAN})^2 /N \qquad (7\text{-}9)$$

That is, you add up the second powers of the differences between the observed data and the average value. We will use the concept of moment again when we discuss kurtosis later in this subsection.

SKEWNESS. Skewness refers to the symmetry or lack of symmetry of a frequency distribution that has a single peak. Skewness is usually measured in terms of the Pearson Coefficient of Skewness which is given by:

$$\text{SKEWNESS} = 3 * (\text{MEAN -MEDIAN})/\text{STANDARD DEVIATION} \qquad (7\text{-}10)$$

where STANDARD DEVIATION is the standard deviation of the sample as is Equation (7-7). If the mean is equal to the median, then the skewness is equal to 0 and the distribution is symmetric. However, the more the the mean and median differ in location, the more asymmetric the distribution and hence the larger the value of skewness. If the Pearson Coefficient of Skewness is positive then the mean is bigger than the median and the distribution typically has a long tail to the right, whereas if it is negative there is a tail to the left. Values of skewness larger than +1 or smaller than –1 indicate significant skewness.

KURTOSIS. The next measure of dispersion, kurtosis (a word that comes from the Greek), measures how big the peak of a distribution is. As shown below, distributions having the same mean can be relatively peaked or flat:

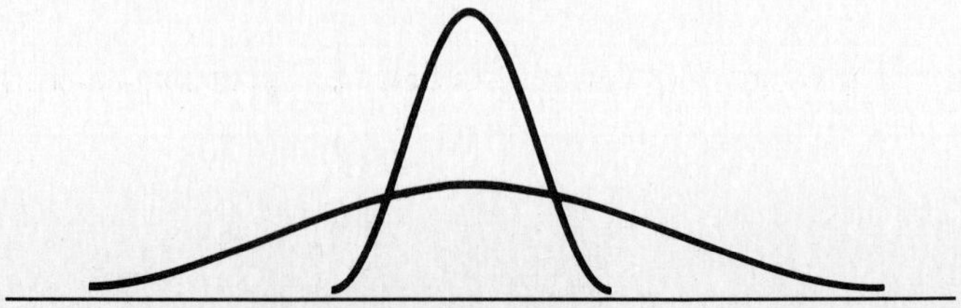

The more peaked the distribution, the greater the kurtosis. As a reference, you will find that the kurtosis of a normal distribution is equal to 3. Kurtosis is computed from the ratio:

$$\text{KURTOSIS} = \text{M4/(VARIANCE)}^2 \qquad (7\text{-}11)$$

where M4 represents what is called the 4th moment about the mean. M4 is computed from the relation:

$$\text{M4} = \Sigma \text{ (OBSERVED DATA - MEAN)}^4 \text{ /N} \qquad (7\text{-}12)$$

As you can see the 4th moment is just like the variance of the population in form except that it adds up the 4th power rather than the square of the deviation from the mean. In Figure 7-5 the cumulative sum of the fourth power of (OBSERVED DATA –MEAN) is computed in Line 320 and used in Line 170 to compute kurtosis. Since the values of the fourth power are over a million and we provide only six spaces for printing out the values, IFPS reports them in the exponential form (e.g.2E6). However, the exact values are kept inside memory and the value of kurtosis shown is based on the exact value, not the approximation printed in exponential form.

The skewness and kurtosis values that you saw in MONTE CARLO simulation (see Section 5.10) help you decide whether the normal distribution is a suitable approximation to a variable or not. If the skewness is close to 0 and the kurtosis is close to 3, then the normal approximation is valid and you can use the results of the NORM option in MONTE CARLO.

AVERAGE DEVIATION. The average deviation measures how close individual values are to the mean. The average deviation is given by:

$$\text{AVERAGE DEVIATION} = \Sigma \text{ (ABSOLUTE VALUE (X - MEAN))/ n} \qquad (7\text{-}13)$$

Unlike the standard deviation which adds up the square of the difference between observed and mean values, the average deviation is a linear measure and hence does not weight outlying points as heavily.

RANGE. The range is simply the difference between the largest and smallest values observed. It is a relatively poor measure of dispersion since a single outlying point can affect the result drastically. For example (1,2,3,4,5) has a range of (5-1)=4 whereas (1,2,3,4,11) has a range of (11-1)=10.

In computing the RANGE you will notice that we used the IFPS MAXIMUM and MINIMUM functions to find the largest and smallest values of the data. Since these functions take the largest (or smallest) value of their arguments, we compare the previous maximum (or minimum) with the current data point. If the current data point is larger (smaller) than any before it, this point becomes the new maximum (minimum).

CONFIDENCE INTERVALS. The mean value computed from a set of data is, of course, only an estimate of the true mean of the total population if the sample represents only a fraction of the total population. The question to be resolved is how good is the estimate of the mean. The usual way to resolve this issue is to define a "confidence interval". This interval is constructed in such a way that a specified percentage of the time (e.g., 90% or 95%) the interval determined by the procedure contains the true mean.

In MONTE CARLO simulation (Section 5.1.6), one of the standard statistics provided is the 90% confidence interval for the mean. It is obtained by computing:

$$\text{LOWER LIMIT (10\%)} = \text{MEAN} - 1.65*\text{STD DEVIATION} / \sqrt{N} \qquad (7\text{-}14)$$

$$\text{UPPER LIMIT (90\%)} = \text{MEAN} + 1.65*\text{STD DEVIATION} / \sqrt{N} \qquad (7\text{-}15)$$

These formulas are standard. If you want to obtain a 95% confidence interval, you replace 1.65 by 1.96. Between them the lower limit and the upper limit define the range of values inside which you expect the true mean to lie. In Figure 7-5, for example, the sample mean is 51.8 and the 90% confidence limits are –49.2 and 153. In this case the limits are quite broad because we have only a few data points and they scatter. As the sample size increases, the confidence limit typically get closer to the estimate of the mean. However, this convergence is slow, decreasing as the square root of the sample size, N. Thus, you typically need four times as many points as you have if you want to cut the width of the confidence interval in half.

COEFFICIENT OF VARIATION. The population coefficient of variation measures the ratio of the standard deviation of the sample to the mean. It is given by:

$$\text{COEFFICIENT OF VARIATION} = \text{STD DEVIATION}*100/\text{MEAN} \qquad (7\text{-}16)$$

This is a percentage measure and can therefore be used to compare the variability of different distributions. The coefficient of variation is particularly useful when you are comparing quantities that are expressed in different units (e.g., family income in dollars and family living space in square feet) or when comparing quantities in the same units but of different orders of magnitude (e.g., Gross National Product in millions and personal income in thousands). In Figure 7-5, the coefficient of variation is 118% since the mean is 51.8 and the standard deviation is 61.2.

7.2 PERMUTATIONS AND COMBINATIONS

In computing probabilities it is often necessary to determine how many different ways particular outcomes can occur. There are two cases to consider:

- The order in which events occur is important (i.e., permutation).
- The order in which events occur is immaterial (i.e., combination).

For example, HT (two coin flips resulting in "heads", H followed by "tails",T) is a different permutation than TH since H and T are in different order, whereas HT and TH are the same combination.

We are usually interested in determining the number of permutations or the number of combinations of n things taken k at a time. For example, how many ways can you pick 3 numbers out of 5? Symbolically, we write, ${}_5P_3$ or ${}_5C_3$ for permutations and combinations, respectively.

To compute permutations we recognize that if we have n objects (e.g., numbers) then we can select the first one n different ways. However, once the first one is selected, there are only (n-1) objects left, so there are only (n-1) ways to pick it. In general, if we want to pick x objects out of n,

$$_nP_x = n*(n-1)*(n-2)*...*(n-x) \tag{7-17}$$

This can be done recursively. That is, the relation:

$$_nP_x = {_nP_{x-1}} *(n-x+1), \qquad x=1,2,...,n \tag{7-18}$$

holds, where $_nP_0 = 1$.

Figure 7-6 shows this form of the computation in IFPS. In using this model you should be careful. Permutations become very large numbers very fast because you are multiplying integers.

```
MODEL PERMUTE   VERSION OF   08/31/82   22:56
10 COLUMNS 0-5
20 * MODEL FOR COMPUTING PERMUTATIONS
30 *
40PERMUTATIONS =1,PREVIOUS*(N-X+1)
50*
55 N=5
60 X=0,PREVIOUS+1
END OF MODEL
? solve
MODEL PERMUTE   VESION OF   08/31/82   22:56 -- 6 COLUMNS 3 VARIABLES
ENTER SOLVE OPTIONS
? all

                                 0     1     2     3     4     5
 MODEL FOR COMPUTING PERMUTATIONS

PERMUTATIONS                     1     5    20    60   120   120

N                                5     5     5     5     5     5
X                                0     1     2     3     4     5
```

FIGURE 7-6. PERMUTATIONS

Combinations are much smaller numbers than permutations since each combination includes many permutations. The formula for combinations is:

$$_nC_x = {_nP_x}/x! \tag{7-19}$$

Like permutations, combinations can be calculated recursively. Specifically,

$$_nC_0 = 1,$$

and

$$_nC_x = {_nC_{x-1}} * (n-x+1)/x \tag{7-20}$$

Equation (7-20) is implemented in IFPS in Figure 7-7 which shows how to compute combinations for n things taken 1, 2, and so on up to n at a time. Note that we provide 20 columns in our COLUMNS definition but use only six in our SOLVE option since we chose n=5. To use this model for other values of n, you need only change n with a WHAT IF statement. If you have values of n greater than 20 you also have to change the COLUMNS definition.

```
MODEL COMBINE  VERSION OF  08/31/82  23:00
10 COLUMNS 0-20
20*
30*MODEL FOR COMPUTING COMBINATORIALS
40*
50 COMBINATORIAL = 1,PREVIOUS*(N-X+1)/X FOR N,0
60 *
80 N=5
90 X= 0,PREVIOUS +1
100*
END OF MODEL
? solve
MODEL COMBINE  VERSION OF  08/31/82  23:00 -- 21 COLUMNS 3 VARIABLES
ENTER SOLVE OPTIONS
? columns 0-5
? all

                                0      1      2      3      4      5

MODEL FOR COMPUTING COMBINATORIALS

COMBINATORIAL                   1      5     10     10      5      1

 DATA
N                               5      5      5      5      5      5
X                               0      1      2      3      4      5
```

FIGURE 7-7. COMBINATIONS

EXERCISE: Suppose you are trying to form a committee of 6, with three representatives from Department A and three 3 from Department B. Department A has 7 people and Department B has 9 people. How many different committees can you form? This is a standard probability problem. Set up the appropriate combinatorials and then use IFPS to obtain your numeric answer.

EXERCISE: Suppose the order in which people are appointed to your committee determines their seniority. How many "different" committees can you form in this case?

7.3 PROBABILITY DISTRIBUTIONS

To understand probability distributions we must begin with random variables. Random variables are numerical descriptions of the outcome of experiments. The specific outcome of a particular situation may be unknown beforehand, but we usually can say something about the possible outcomes and we can say it in numeric terms. For example, if you inspect a shipment of 100 television sets, you may observe anywhere between 0 and 100 defective sets. Furthermore, you may even have prior information as the probability of 0 or 1 or 2 or more than 2 defective sets. The numeric values of these probabilities form a probability distribution. In this section, we describe how to determine the values of two standard probability distributions using IFPS:

- Binomial distribution.
- Poisson distribution.

If you want to find a single value from a particular binomial or Poisson distribution, you will do better by using your hand caclulator; however the power of using IFPS comes in creating a table of values each of which can then be used in larger calculations.

7.3.1 Binomial Distribution

The binomial probability distribution arises in situations in which there are two possible outcomes, such as heads and tails. If there is a probability, p, of one outcome (e.g. heads), then the probability of the other outcome must be (1–p). Usually, we set q = 1–p and talk about a probability p of a favorable outcome and q of an unfavorable outcome. The binomial probability distribution occurs if we perform an experiment (e.g., flipping a coin) a fixed number of times. Each experiment has the same two possible outcomes with probability p and q respectively. The question is what is the probability of 0,1, 2, ..., x, ...n successes (e.g., heads) in n trials. The probability of x successes in n trials with probability p of success on each trial is denoted by P(X). The formula for the binomial probability distribution involves computing:

$$P(X) = {}_{n}C_{x}\, p^{x} q^{n-x} \qquad (7\text{-}21)$$

We showed how to compute the combinatorial x in the previous section. Here we have to multiply the combinatorial by powers of p and q. The IFPS program for accomplishing this is shown in Figure 7-8. You will see in the figure that the easy way to perform this calculation and to obtain the entire distribution for a given probability p and number of trials n is to use the fact that:

$$P(X) = P(X\text{-}1)^{*}\,(n-x+1)^{*}p\,/\,(q^{*}x) \qquad (7\text{-}22)$$

where P(0) is given by q^n. The quantity P(0) represents the case of no successes (e.g., all tails). Equation (7-22) shows that, for given n and p, the probability for x successes is computed by multiplying the probability for (x-1) successes by a constant that depends on the probability of success p, the number of trials, n, and the number of successes x.

If you look at the IFPS program in Figure 7-8, you will see that we have specified columns 0 to 20 simply to allow you to compute binomial probabilities for up to 20 trials; if you have more than that, you will have to change the COLUMNS statement in Line 10. To obtain results for other than the sample values of n and p given (n=5 and p=0.3), use WHAT IF statements to put in your data. Finally, print out only the columns through n by specifying the number of columns you need as a SOLVE option. Note, however, that you must specify column numbers numerically. You can't say COLUMNS 0-N; you must say, for example, COLUMNS 0-5.

```
MODEL BINOMIAL  VERSION OF  08/31/82  23:05
10 COLUMNS 0-20
20*MODEL FOR COMPUTING BINOMIAL PROBABILITIES
25*X SUCCESSES IN N TRIALS WITH PROBABILITY OF SUCCESS P PER TRIAL
30 *
40 BINOMIAL XNP=XPOWERY(Q,N),PREVIOUS*(P*(N-X+1))/(Q*X) FOR N,0
50 CUMULATIVE BINOMIAL XNP=BINOMIAL XNP+'
51 PREVIOUS CUMULATIVE BINOMIAL XNP
55*
60*DATA
80 Q=1-P
90 N=5
100 X=0,PREVIOUS+1
END OF MODEL
? solve
MODEL BINOMIAL  VERSION OF  08/31/82  23:05--21 COLUMNS 6 VARIABLES
ENTER SOLVE OPTIONS
? columns 0-5
? all

                                0       1       2       3       4      5

MODEL FOR COMPUTING BINOMIAL PROBABILITIES
X SUCCESSES IN N TRIALS WITH PROBABILITY OF SUCCESS P PER TRIAL

BINOMIAL XNP                .1681   .3602   .3087   .1323   .0284  .0024
CUMULATIVE BINOMIAL         .1681   .5282   .8369   .9692   .9976      1

DATA
P                           .3000   .3000   .3000   .3000   .3000  .3000
Q                           .7000   .7000   .7000   .7000   .7000  .7000
N                               5       5       5       5       5      5
X                               0       1       2       3       4      5
```

FIGURE 7-8. BINOMIAL DISTRIBUTION

In Figure 7-8 you will find not only the binomial probability distribution for the input data values of n and p, but also the cumulative distribution. The cumulative distribution is found by adding up all the values from $x=0$ through the current value of x. Thus, in the example, if $x=0$, both the binomial probability and the cumulative probability distribution have a value of 0.1681. For $x=1$, the binomial probability is 0.3602 and the the cumulative distribution is equal to 0.1681 + 0.3602 or 0.5283 (Note: IFPS displays rounded answers; hence the cumulative shown on the output may differ slightly from the answer you obtain by adding up the output values of the individual probabilities.)

7.3.2 Poisson Distribution

The Poisson distribution describes the probability of 0, 1, 2, or more events occurring in a fixed time interval where we know that:

- events occur "at random"
- the average number of occurrences in the time interval is m.

This distribution describes, for example, random arrivals at service facilities such as trucks at terminals, phone calls at a switchboard, or customers at a fast food restaurant. The form of the distribution is:

$$P(x) = m^{x} / (NATEXP(m)*x!) \qquad x=0,1,2,\ldots \quad (7\text{-}23)$$

As in the case of the binomial distributions, it is easier to calculate this distribution recursively in IFPS. Equation (7-23) can be rewritten as:

$$P(x) = P(x-1)* m/x \qquad (7\text{-}24)$$

where P(0) = 1/NATEXP(m) as in Equation (7-23). This form of computing the Poisson distribution is illustrated in Figure 7-9. This figure shows both the probability of exactly x arrivals and the probability of up to x arrivals (that is, the cumulative probability distribution).

The Poisson distribution differs from the binomial in that it has, at least in theory, an infinite number of terms; practically, however, the individual probabilities become small as x becomes larger.

EXERCISE: Suppose customers arrive at random at a fast food restaurant at a rate of 20 per hour. Compute the probability of exactly 0, 1, 2, 3, ... arrivals during a 10-minute interval by modifying Figure 7-9. Write a model that combines Figure 7-9 with the models for mean and variance of Section 7.1 to compute the mean and variance of this Poisson distribution. You should find the mean is equal to the input value and, furthermore, that the mean and the variance of the Poisson distribution are equal.

EXERCISE: The Poisson distribution is considered a good approximation to the binomial distribution if the number of binomial trials is 20 or more and the probability of success, p, is 5% or less. Since the mean of the binomial is equal to n*p, you approximate the binomal with a Poisson whose mean is equal to n*p. Write a model that combines Figure 7-8 and Figure 7-9 and computes both the binomial and its Poisson approximation for n=20 and p=.05. Compare the binomial and the Poisson by using the plot feature of IFPS to plot the cumulative distributions.

EXERCISE: Repeat the previous exercise for the case n=5, p=.05 and for the case n=20, p=.60. Again, plot the results to compare the answers.

7.4 CHI-SQUARE TESTS OF GOODNESS OF FIT AND INDEPENDENCE

The chi-square distribution is a tabulated probability distribution that is used in testing two hypotheses:

1. The agreement between an observed distribution and an assumed distribution.

2. The independence of two variables.

These are quite different problems. In the first case, we typically have a notion based on theory or analysis that a phenomenon should follow some specified distribution and we

```
MODEL POISSON  VERSION OF  09/22/81  19:04
10 COLUMNS 0-20
20*POISSON DISTRIBUTION FOR MEAN M
30*
40 X= 0,PREVIOUS+1
50 PROBABILITY OF X=1/NATEXP(MEAN),PREVIOUS*MEAN/X
60 CUMULATIVE PROBABILITY = PREVIOUS + PROBABILITY OF X
70*
80*DATA
90*----
100 MEAN = 5
? solve
MODEL POISSON  VERSION OF  09/22/81  19:04 -- 21 COLUMNS 4 VARIABLES
ENTER SOLVE OPTIONS
? columns 0-17
? all
                               0       1       2       3       4       5

POISSON DISTRIBUTION FOR MEAN M

X                              0       1       2       3       4       5
PROBABILITY OF X           .0067   .0337   .0842   .1404   .1755   .1755
CUMULATIVE PROBABILI       .0067   .0404   .1247   .2650   .4405   .6160

DATA
----
MEAN                           5       5       5       5       5       5

                               6       7       8       9      10      11

POISSON DISTRIBUTION FOR MEAN M

X                              6       7       8       9      10      11
PROBABILITY OF X           .1462   .1044   .0653   .0363   .0181   .0082
CUMULATIVE PROBABILI       .7622   .8666   .9319   .9682   .9863   .9945
DATA
----
MEAN                           5       5       5       5       5       5

                              12      13      14      15      16      17

POISSON DISTRIBUTION FOR MEAN M

X                             12      13      14      15      16      17
PROBABILITY OF X           .0034   .0013   .0005   .0002       0       0
CUMULATIVE PROBABILI       .9980   .9993   .9998   .9999       1       1

DATA
----
MEAN                           5       5       5       5       5       5
```

FIGURE 7-9. POISSON DISTRIBUTION

want to see if that notion is correct. That is we want to see how well the hypothesized distribution fits the data. Such a test is called a "goodness of fit" test. For example, we believe that if we throw an honest pair of dice, a 2 should show up 1/36th of the time, a 7 should show up 6/36th of the time, etc. If we throw a pair of dice 3600 times and observe 105 2's and 585 7's, can we reject the hypothesis that this is a fair pair of dice?

Figure 7-10 shows how such a goodness of fit test is conducted in IFPS. The input data are the observed and expected number of times of each outcome from 2 through 12 in throwing a pair of dice 3600 times. These values are used to compute the value of chi-square from the formula:

$$\chi^2 = \Sigma((\text{OBSERVED} - \text{EXPECTED})^2 / (\text{EXPECTED}) \quad (7\text{-}25)$$

where the observed and expected values are taken column by column. The program computes the individual terms of the sum and cumulates values as it goes along. The result is the chi-square value shown in the last column.

```
MODEL CHISQ1   VERSION OF   07/09/81   22:38
10 COLUMNS 2-12
20*
30*    DETERMINING GOODNESS OF FIT
40*
50 OBSERVED=95,190,315,380,470,640,510,420,280,210,90
60 EXPECTED=100,200,300,400,500,600,500,400,300,200,100
70 CHISQUARE TERMS=(OBSERVED-EXPECTED)*(OBSERVED-EXPECTED)/EXPECTED
80 CHISQUARE= PREVIOUS + CHISQUARE TERMS
? solve
MODEL CHISQ1  VERSION OF   07/09/81   22:38 -- 11 COLUMNS 4 VARIABLES
ENTER SOLVE OPTIONS
? all
```

DETERMINING GOODNESS OF FIT

	2	3	4	5	6	7
OBSERVED	95	190	315	380	470	640
EXPECTED	100	200	300	400	500	600
CHISQUARE TERMS	.2500	.5000	.7500	1	1.800	2.667
CHISQUARE	.2500	.7500	1.500	2.500	4.300	6.967

DETERMINING GOODNESS OF FIT

	8	9	10	11	12
OBSERVED	510	420	280	210	90
EXPECTED	500	400	300	200	100
CHISQUARE TERMS	.2000	1	1.333	.5000	1
CHISQUARE	7.167	8.167	9.500	10	11

FIGURE 7-10. USING CHI-SQUARE TO DETERMINE GOODNESS OF FIT

To use this result we need two additional pieces of data: the degrees of freedom and the desired probability level. For a simple distribution such as this one, the number of degrees of freedom is one less than the number of categories (in our case 11 categories implies 10 degrees of freedom). The usual probability level is 5%. You look up the test value for the degrees of freedom and probability level in a chi-square table in your favorite statistics book. If the chi-square value you observe is greater than the test value from the table, you reject the hypothesis that the observed distribution fits the assumed distribution. In Figure 7-10, the observed chi-square value was 11. The tabulated value for 10 degrees of freedom and 5% is 18.307. Therefore, we cannot reject the hypothesis that the dice are fair.

In the second case, we are interested in whether two characteristics depend on one another or not. For example, supposing we are trying to determine whether support of a particular candidate is independent of the education level of voters. Then the hypothesis to be tested is that the chance of preferring a candidate is independent of educational level. The best evidence of this would be that the chance of supporting a candidate is the same whether the voter had some high school, was a high school graduate, had some college, or was a college graduate.

To determine whether this is so or not we set up a contingency table such as the following for three candidates whom we shall call Jones, Kenner, and Hartz:

	SOME HS	HS GRAD	SOME COL	COLLEGE	TOTAL
JONES	50	80	60	30	220
KENNER	20	60	80	20	180
HARTZ	30	60	60	50	200
TOTAL	100	200	200	100	600

EXPECTED VOTES

JONES EXPECTED	36.67	73.33	73.33	36.67	220
KENNER EXPECTED	30.00	60.00	60.00	30.00	180
HARTZ EXPECTED	33.33	66.67	66.67	33.33	200

The first three lines above represent actual experience. The expected votes for each candidate are computed from the row and column totals. Since 100 out of 600 have some high school, we should expect 1/6 of each candidates' supporters to be in the some high school category; for example, we should expect 30 out of Kenner's 180 supporters to have some high school.

We are now at the point where we can apply Equation (7-25) and determine the value of chi-square. This is done in Figure 7-11. This figure looks like our table above. Adding up the data in each column is done in the usual way in Line 70. Finding the row totals on the right, however, is somewhat more difficult. We could have used the available COLUMNS command and written:

```
COLUMN 5 = SUM(COLUMN 1 THRU COLUMN 4)
```

However, IFPS is basically a row logic not a column logic language. Although you can compute the value in a given column, such as column 5, you cannot use the column command results for computation. For contingency tables we use the row totals in computing the expected values. To get around this difficulty, we show two alternate ways of performing the calculations. The first of these, shown in Figure 7-11a, keeps the same

```
MODEL CHISQ2  VERSION OF  08/22/82  21:08
10 COLUMNS SOME HS,HS,SOME COLLEGE,COLLEGE,TOTAL
20*CHI SQUARE TEST OF INDEPENDENCE
30*
40 JONES=50,80,60,30,PREVIOUS+PREVIOUS 2 + PREVIOUS 3 + PREVIOUS 4
50 KENNER=20,60,80,20,PREVIOUS+PREVIOUS 2 +PREVIOUS 3 + PREVIOUS 4
60 HARTZ = 30,60,60,50,PREVIOUS+PREVIOUS 2 + PREVIOUS 3 + PREVIOUS 4
70 TOTAL =JONES + KENNER + HARTZ
80*
90* EXPECTED VOTES
95*100 JONES EXPECTED= MATRIX(JONES,5)*TOTAL/MATRIX(TOTAL,5)
110 KENNER EXPECTED=MATRIX(KENNER,5)*TOTAL/MATRIX(TOTAL,5)
120 HARTZ EXPECTED = MATRIX(HARTZ,5)*TOTAL/MATRIX(TOTAL,5)
130*
140 CHISQ ROW1 =XPOWERY((JONES-JONES EXPECTED),2)/JONES EXPECTED
150 CHISQ ROW2 =XPOWERY((KENNER-KENNER EXPECTED),2)/KENNER EXPECTED
160 CHISQ ROW3=XPOWERY((HARTZ-HARTZ EXPECTED),2)/HARTZ EXPECTED
170*
180 CHISQUARE = PREVIOUS + CHISQ ROW1 + CHISQ ROW2 +CHISQ ROW3
END OF MODEL
? solve
MODEL CHISQ2  VERSION OF  08/22/82  23:44 -- 5 COLUMNS 11 VARIABLES
ENTER SOLVE OPTIONS
? all
```

	SOME HS	HS	SOME COL	COLLEGE	TOTAL
CHI SQUARE TEST OF INDEPENDENCE					
JONES	50	80	60	30	220
KENNER	20	60	80	20	180
HARTZ	30	60	60	50	200
TOTAL	100	200	200	100	600
EXPECTED VOTES					
JONES EXPECTED	36.67	73.33	73.33	36.67	220
KENNER EXPECTED	30	60	60	30	180
HARTZ EXPECTED	33.33	66.67	66.67	33.33	200
CHISQ ROW1	4.848	.6061	2.424	1.212	0
CHISQ ROW2	3.333	0	6.667	3.333	0
CHISQ ROW3	.3333	.6667	.6667	8.333	0
CHISQUARE	8.515	9.788	19.55	32.42	32.42

a. Standard Form

FIGURE 7-11. CHI-SQUARE TEST OF INDEPENDENCE
(This Figure Continued on the Next Page)

```
MODEL CHISQ3  VERSION OF   09/07/82  22:02
10 COLUMNS JONES,KENNR,HARTZ,TOTAL,EXPJ,EXPK,EXPH,CHIJ,CHIK,CHIH,'
11 TOTCH
20 SOME HS=50,20,30
30 HS GRAD=80,60,60
40 SOME COL = 60,80,60
50 COLLEGE GRAD=30,20,50
60 TOTAL = SUM(SOME HS THRU COLLEGE GRAD)
65*
70 COLUMN TOTAL = C JONES + C KENNER + C HARTZ
80 COLUMN EXPJ =MATRIX(TOTAL,1)*C TOTAL/MATRIX(TOTAL ,4)
90 COLUMN EXPK= MATRIX(TOTAL,2)*C TOTAL/MATRIX(TOTAL,4)
100 COLUMN EXPH= MATRIX(TOTAL,3)*C TOTAL/MATRIX(TOTAL,4)
110 COLUMN CHIJ=XPOWERY(C JONES-C EXPJ,2)/C EXPJ
120 COLUMN CHIK=XPOWERY(C KENNR-C EXPK,2)/C EXPK
130 COLUMN CHIH=XPOWERY(C HARTZ-C EXPH,2)/C EXPH
140 COLUMN TOTCH FOR SOME HS THRU COLLEGE GRAD=C CHIJ'
141 +C CHIK +C CHIH
150 COLUMN TOTCHFOR TOTAL=SUM(SOME HS THRU COLLEGE GRAD)
END OF MODEL
? solve
MODEL CHISQ3  VERSION OF   09/07/82  22:02 -- 11 COLUMNS 5 VARIABLES
ENTER SOLVE OPTIONS
? width 68 13 5
? all

             JONESKENNRHARTZTOTAL EXPJ EXPK EXPH CHIJ CHIK CHIHTOTCH

SOME HS          50   20   30  100 36.7   30 33.3 4.85 3.33 .333 8.52
HS GRAD          80   60   60  200 73.3   60 66.7 .606    0 .667 1.27
SOME COL         60   80   60  200 73.3   60 66.7 2.42 6.67 .667 9.76
COLLEGE GRAD     30   20   50  100 36.7   30 33.3 1.21 3.33 8.33 12.9
TOTAL           220  180  200  600  220  180  200    0    0    0 32.4
```

b. Alternate Form

FIGURE 7-11 CHI-SQUARE TEST OF INDEPENDENCE
(Continued)

output format as above but requires computing the row totals in a rather cumbersome way. The PREVIOUS command is used to refer to each of the earlier numbers in the row. We also had to be very careful and use MATRIX references to retrieve these row totals in computing expected values. This is not entirely satisfactory because it is becomes awkward if there are many observations. The observed and expected values are then used to apply Equation 7-25 and find the contribution of each element of the table to chi-square. The final chi-square value appears in the lower right hand corner and is equal in our example to 32.42.

The alternate form, shown in Figure 7-11b, inverts the rows and the columns, showing the categories as rows and what was previously row information as columns. It is also an example of using the COLUMN commands (Section 4.4.5) in calculations. Go over both forms; you will find that one or the other methods is easier for you to use.

The number of degrees of freedom for a test of independence is determined differently than for a test of goodness of fit. Specifically, if r is the number of rows and c is the number of columns, then the number of degrees of freedom is equal to (r-1)*(c-1). In our case we have 3 rows and 4 columns; therefore we have (3-1)*(4-1) = 6 degrees of freedom. At the 5% level and six degrees of freedom, the chi-square table gives a test value of 12.592. Since the observed value is 32.42, we must reject the hypothesis that the chance of supporting a given candidate does not depend on educational level.

EXERCISE: Rewrite Figure 7-11a so that it has only four columns, SOME HS, HS, SOME COL and COLLEGE. That is, do not show the totals column explicitly. You will have to compute the values in the totals column as separate rows; however, you can suppress these intermediate calculations in your printout. The resulting format is different but the results should be the same. Which do you prefer?

7.5 LINEAR REGRESSION

In this section (and in the next section) we are concerned with using data for prediction. The simplest case is one in which there are two variables, for example, soda consumption and temperature, which we believe related. If we can find the relation between the variables, then given the value of one (e.g., temperature),we can use the relationship to forecast the value of the other (e.g., soda consumption).

In general, if we do not know the relation between the variables we must infer the relationship from a sample of data. Usually, it is possible to plot sample data in the form of "scatter diagrams" such as this one:

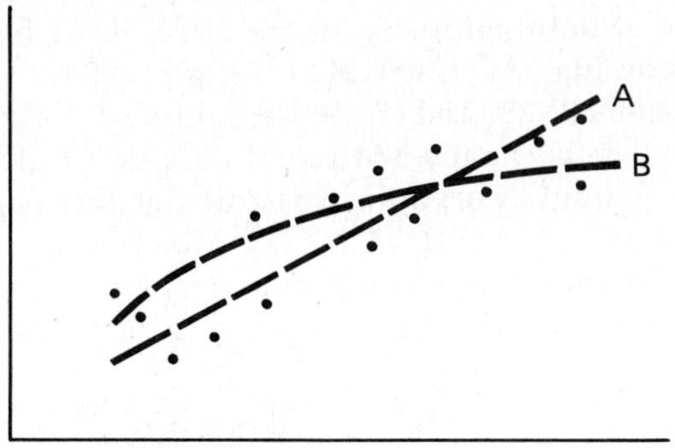

The relation may appear to be linear (Curve A) or curvilinear (Curve B) as shown by the dashed lines. The first decision you have to make is what form of relation is appropriate. (You can, of course, try several forms and pick the one that fits best according to test; we will discuss these tests later.) To illustrate the procedure we will assume a linear relation, that is, a relation of the form:

$$Y = a + bX \tag{7-26}$$

Here Y refers to the value of Y that is computed given a value of X. The problem, thus, is to determine the values of the coefficients *a* and *b* in such a way as to specify the straight line that best fits the sample data that we have.

Although "best fits" is a simple-sounding criteria, we must have some way of operationalizing it. A number of criteria are possible; however, the standard way the problem of obtaining the best fit is solved is to find those values of a and b for which:

$$\Sigma (Y - Y_C)^2 \tag{7-27}$$

is a minimum and for which $\Sigma(Y - Y_C) = 0$. The first criterion makes the total squared deviation of the observed values from the computed values as small as possible. Since this line may not be unique, we impose the additional constraint that the average deviation of the observations from the computed values must be 0; this means that the line goes through the average value of the observed X's and Y's. (Do you see why?)

7.5.1 Computing the Regression Coefficients

The coefficients a and b in Equation(7-26) are computed from the following relations:

$$b = \frac{SUM(X*Y) - n*XBAR*YBAR}{SUM(X*X) - n*XBAR*XBAR} \tag{7-28}$$

$$a = YBAR - b * XBAR \tag{7-29}$$

where SUM refers to adding up all values (e.g., SUM(X*Y) = XY in the conventional notation of mathematics), and XBAR and YBAR are the average values of X and Y, respectively, computed as in Section 7.1.1. These calculations are shown in Figure 7-12. For simplicity of presentation, we have used only six data points; however the relations are valid for any number of data points up to the IFPS limit for your computer on the maximum number of columns. As lines 50 through 190 in Figure 7-12 show, the seemingly complex Equations (7-28) and (7-29) become relatively simple when expressed in IFPS. You can literally see how each additional data point affects the estimate of the coefficients a and b. It is helpful to organize the calculations neatly, first obtaining the needed sums and then the averages XBAR and YBAR (by dividing the sum of the X and Y values by the number of points) before computing b and a. Note that the values of b and a depend on the number of observations and that the values based on all the data appear in the last column.

Once you have obtained the coefficients a and b, you can estimate the value of Y for any value of X. In Figure 7-12, for example, for the 6 data points given, a =-2.545 and b=34.49. You will find these values in column 6 of Figure 7-12. The values of a and b given in columns 2 through 5 represent the values of a using all the data up to that point; for example, the value in column 4 is based on the first four observed values. Based on the six data points available,

$$Y = -2.545 + 34.49X \tag{7-30}$$

Hence, if you want to know the expected value of Y if X=1.8, simply substitute 1.8 for X in Equation (7-30) to obtain Y=59.534. This is also done in Figure 7-12.

Before proceeding further, a few words are in order about the relation between the REGRESS model shown in Figure 7-12 and the TREND and POLYFIT functions described in Section 3.2.3. As you recall, in the TREND function you supply X and Y

```
MODEL REGRESS  VERSION OF  01/12/83  19:36
10 COLUMNS 1-6
30 * SUMS
40 *
50 SUMX=PREVIOUS +X
60 SUMY=PREVIOUS +Y
70 SUMXY=PREVIOUS +X*Y
80 SUMXSQUARE=PREVIOUS+X*X
90 SUMYSQUARE=PREVIOUS+Y*Y
100 *
110 * AVERAGES
120 *
130 XBAR=SUMX/N
140 YBAR=SUMY/N
150 *
160 *A AND B COEFFICIENCTS OF REGRESSION LINE
170 *
180 B=0,(SUMXY -N*XBAR*YBAR)/(SUMXSQUARE-N*XBAR*XBAR)
190 A=0,YBAR-B*XBAR
200 *
210 * ESTIMATION
220 *
230 X TO BE ESTIMATED= 1.8
240 Y TO BE ESTIMATED= A+B*X TO BE ESTIMATED
250 *
260 *COEFFICIENT OF DETERMINATION,RSQUARE, AND CORRELATION'
261 COEFFICIENT,R
270 *
280 RSQUARE=0,0, (A*SUMY +B*SUMXY-N*YBAR*YBAR)/'
281 (SUMYSQUARE-N*YBAR*YBAR)
290 R=XPOWERY(RSQUARE,0.5)*MULTIPLIER
300 MULTIPLIER = IF B.GT.0 THEN 1 ELSE (-1)
310 *
320 *T STATISTIC--TEST FOR POPULATION CORRELATION COEFFICIENT RHO=0
330 *
340 T = 0,0,R/XPOWERY((1-RSQUARE)/(N-2),.5)
350 *
360 *CONFIDENCE INTERVAL FOR REGRESSION COEFFICIENT B
370 *
380 STD ERROR OF ESTIMATE=0,0,XPOWERY((SUMYSQUARE-A*SUMY-B*SUMXY)'
381 /(N-2),.5)
390 DENOMINATOR1 =0,0,SUMXSQUARE-N*XBAR*XBAR
400 STD ERROR OF REGRESSION COEFFICIENT = 0,0,'
410 STD ERROR OF ESTIMATE/XPOWERY(DENOMINATOR1,0.5)
420 UPPER CONFIDENCE LIMIT=B+TCRITICAL*'
421 STD ERROR OF REGRESSION COEFFICIENT
430 LOWER CONFIDENCE LIMIT=B-TCRITICAL*'
431 STD ERROR OF REGRESSION COEFFICIENT
440 *
450 *
490 Y=50,100,75,45,20,50
500 TCRITICAL = 2.776
510 N=1,PREVIOUS +1
```

FIGURE 7-12. LINEAR REGRESSION

```
? solve
MODEL REGRESS  VERSION OF  01/12/83  19:36 -- 6 COLUMNS 24 VARIABLES
ENTER SOLVE OPTIONS
? all
                              1       2       3       4       5       6
 SUMS

SUMX                      1.700   4.700   6.700   8.200   8.800   10.30
SUMY                         50     150     225     270     290     340
SUMXY                        85     385     535   602.5   614.5   689.5
SUMXSQUARE                2.890   11.89   15.89   18.14   18.50   20.75
SUMYSQUARE                 2500   12500   18125   20150   20550   23050

 AVERAGES

XBAR                      1.700   2.350   2.233   2.050   1.760   1.717
YBAR                         50      75      75   67.50      58   56.67

A AND B COEFFICIENCTS OF REGRESSION LINE

B                             0   38.46   35.07   36.84   34.56   34.49
A                             0  -15.38  -3.327  -8.026  -2.829  -2.545

 ESTIMATION

X TO BE ESTIMATED         1.800   1.800   1.800   1.800   1.800   1.800
Y TO BE ESTIMATED             0   53.85   59.80   58.29   59.38   59.54

COEFFICIENT OF DETERMINATION,RSQUARE, AND CORRELATION COEFFICIENT,R

RSQUARE                       0       0   .9119   .9378   .9646   .9649
R                             0       0   .9549   .9684   .9821   .9823
MULTIPLIER                   -1       1       1       1       1       1
 T STATISTIC--TEST FOR POPULATION CORRELATION COEFFICIENT RHO=0

T                             0       0   3.217   5.491   9.039   10.48

CONFIDENCE INTERVAL FOR REGRESSION COEFFICIENT B

STD ERROR OF ESTIMATE         0       0   10.50   7.737   6.636   5.764
DENOMINATOR1                  0       0   .9267   1.330   3.012   3.068
STD ERROR OF REGRESSION CO    0       0   10.90   6.709   3.824   3.291
UPPER CONFIDENCE LIMIT        0   38.46   65.34   55.47   45.18   43.63
LOWER CONFIDENCE LIMIT        0   38.46   4.805   18.22   23.95   25.36

INPUT DATA

X                         1.700       3       2   1.500   .6000   1.500
Y                            50     100      75      45      20      50
TCRITICAL                 2.776   2.776   2.776   2.776   2.776   2.776
N                             1       2       3       4       5       6
```

FIGURE 7-12. LINEAR REGRESSION
(Continued)

values for as many X,Y combinations as you have data. You then give IFPS the X value(s) you want and ask for TREND(X) values to be shown as Y. In this form you do not need the linear regression program since IFPS does linear regression for you; however you do need to run an extra column beyond the data for each X value for which you want an estimate. If, in response to SOLVE OPTIONS you specify

```
OPTION H2
```

IFPS will also print out for you the a and b coefficients of the linear regression equation as well as the coefficient of determination, called R^2 (which is discussed in Section 7.5.2). Figure 7-13 illustrates the TREND function and option H2.

```
MODEL TREND   VERSION OF   09/01/82   19:45
10 COLUMNS 1-7
20*
30*USING TREND FUNCTION AND OPTION H2 FOR FORECASTING
40*
50 X=1.7,3.0,2.0,1.5,.6,1.5,1.8
60 Y=50,100,75,45,20,50,TREND(X)
END OF MODEL
? OPTION H2
READY FOR MODELING LANGUAGE COMMAND
? solve
MODEL TREND   VERSION OF   09/01/82   19:45 -- 7 COLUMNS 2 VARIABLES
ENTER SOLVE OPTIONS
? all
TREND FUNCTION COEFFICIENTS-LINE 60       34.49 * IND VAR +     -2.545
R SQUARED IS      .9649

                             1        2        3        4        5        6        7


USING TREND FUNCTION AND OPTION H2 FOR FORECASTING

X                        1.700        3        2    1.500    .6000    1.500    1.800
Y                           50      100       75       45       20       50    59.54
```

FIGURE 7-13. USING THE TREND FUNCTION AND OPTION H2 FOR REGRESSION ANALYSIS

Since both the linear regression equation and the forecast points are available much more simply with the use of TREND than by creating the REGRESS model, why write the REGRESS model? The answer is that TREND gives you only the *a* and *b* coefficients of Equation (7-26), not the additional richness of information about the extent of the association between the variables that can be obtained from the calculations done in the REGRESS model.

Linear regression is also performed by POLYFIT(1). Here, the X values are assumed to correspond to the integers 1, 2, 3,....corresponding to the column numbers. Suppose you have six values of Y and ask for POLYFIT(1) in column 7. IFPS will treat the first six values as a time series (see Section 7.7), fit a regression line through the points and use the regression line to forecast the value in the next time interval. Again, POLYFIT(1) is much more limited than the REGRESS model.

7.5.2 Correlation Analysis

In correlation analyis, the basic objective is to determine the degree of association between variables. The stronger the association, the better able we are to forecast the value of the dependent variable (Y) given the value of the independent variable (X).

In correlation analysis, the usual assumptions made are somewhat stronger than in regression analysis. Specifically, in correlation analysis it is assumed that:

- Both X and Y are random variables.
- Both X and Y are normally distributed; however the two distributions need not be independent.
- The standard deviations of Y are the same for all values of X and the standard deviations of X are the same for all values of Y.

These assumptions differ from the regression model, where only Y is assumed to be a random variable and the Y values are treated as a random sample taken from the conditional probability distribution of Y given X.

The degree of correlation between Y and X is usually expressed in terms of two quantitites: the coefficient of determination, R^2 , and the correlation coefficient, r. As implied by the notation, the coefficient of determination is just the square of the correlation coefficient. The coefficient of determination is a ratio that compares the variation of the Y values around the regression line to the variation of the Y values around the average value of Y. As usual, when we talk about variation in statistics we mean the sum of the squared deviations. In equation terms, the coefficient of determination is given by:

$$R^2 = 1 - \frac{\Sigma (Y - Y_C)^2}{\Sigma (Y - YBAR)^2} \qquad (7\text{-}31)$$

The value of the coefficient of determination is usually interpreted as the fraction of the variation in Y that is accounted for ("explained") by the regression equation that relates X and Y. Note that if Y_C is equal to YBAR for all values of Y then no new information is obtained from the regression equation since no matter what X we specify, we always forecast the same Y. In this case, the coefficient of determination is equal to 0. At the other extreme, if theY value always falls directly on the regression line then knowing X forecasts Y perfectly and the coefficient of determination turns out to be equal to 1. In practice, values of the coefficient of determination of 0 and 1 are almost never observed; rather the values are between 0 and 1.

In calculating the coefficient of determination in Figure 7-12, we have used a slightly different form of Equation (7-31) that is equivalent to it. In this form, we use the coefficients *a* and *b* and the other quantities we have already calculated. Specifically, we compute

$$R^2 = \frac{A*SUMY + B*SUMXY - N*YBAR*YBAR}{SUMYSQUARE - N*YBAR*YBAR} \qquad (7\text{-}32)$$

EXERCISE: Equation (7-32) does not take sample size into account. If you wanted to be precise for small samples you would modify Equation (7-32) by dividing the numerator by (N-2) and the denominator by (N-1). Change Line 280 in Figure 7-12 to this "corrected" sample coefficient of determination.

In calculations, the correlation coefficient, r, is determined by taking the square root of R^2. In taking square roots, we have to make a choice between the positive and negative square root. If the Y value increases with increasing X, the regression line has positive slope and the regression coefficient, *b*, is positive whereas if the Y value decreases as X increases,the slope and *b* are both negative. To indicate the direction of the relation, the + square root is chosen if *b* is positive and the - square root is chosen if b is negative. These two cases are illustrated below for perfect correlation ($r=-1$ and $r=1$):

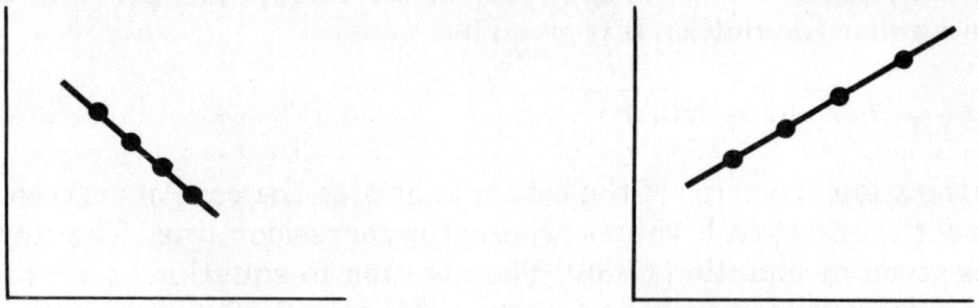

r = −1 r = +1

In IFPS we can pick the positive or negative sign by using the IF ... THEN ....ELSE construct. The XPOWERY function requires a positive input for numbers raised to a fractional power such as 0.5 and always gives a positive output. In Line 300 of Figure 7-12 we use IF...THEN...ELSE to compute a multiplier which has the value 1 if the slope, *b*, is positive and -1 if the slope, *b*, is negative. This multiplier is used in line 290 to obtain the desired result.

7.5.3 Statistical Inferences in Regression

In most statistical analyses we want not only to estimate a particular value such as a mean or standard deviation or correlation coefficient, we also want to measure how good the estimate is. We have seen this once before, in Section 7.1.5, where we computed the confidence interval to measure the quality of the estimate of the mean. In this section we examine the quality of the regression and of the correlation coefficients.

The first case which we consider is the correlation coefficient r. If, based on a sample, we compute a value for r that is non-zero we imply that Y and X are related. We want to protect against the possibility that there is, in fact, no correlation between X and Y even though we computed one on the basis of the sample that we observed. To do so, we must run a hypothesis test. Our null hypothesis is that the correlation of the underlying population is 0 and our alternative hypothesis is that the correlation is not zero. (We have not explained the formalism of hypothesis testing in this chapter; if you are not familiar with it, refer to any standard statistics text.) The usual approach to testing this hypothesis is to compute the statistic:

$$t = r / \sqrt{(1-r*r)/(N-2)} \qquad (7\text{-}33)$$

This statistic has a t distribution with (N-2) degrees of freedom, where N is the number of observations in the sample. Once you have computed t from Equation (7-33), you look up the 5% level of significance for this number of degrees of freedom. If the absolute value of t is greater than the tabulated value, you can reject the hypothesis of no association between X and Y in the population. In Figure 7-12, for example, the value of 10.503 is far larger than the table value of 2.776 for the 5% level of the t distribution with 4 degrees of freedom.

The second case we consider is the regression coefficient *b*. Being a slope of a straight line, b estimates the incremental change in Y for each unit increase in X based on the sample. Computing a confidence interval for *b* allows us to judge the quality of this estimate. The 95% confidence interval is given by:

$$b + t^{*}s_b \qquad (7\text{-}34)$$

where t is the 5% level of the t distribution for (N-2) degrees of freedom and s_b is the estimated standard deviation of the sampling distribution. The problem therefore is to determine this standard deviation. It is given by:

$$s_b = s_{Y,X} \; / \; \sqrt{\Sigma\,(X - XBAR)^2} \qquad (7\text{-}35)$$

where $s_{Y,X}$ is the standard error of the estimate and, in the case of regression, measures the dispersion of the observed Y values around the regression line. The standard error of the estimate is given by equation (7-36). The notation in equation (7-36) conforms to the way the equation is written in IFPS on Line 380 of Figure 7-12.

$$s_{Y,X} = \sqrt{(SUMYSQUARE - A^{*}SUMY - B^{*}SUMXY) / (N\text{-}2)} \qquad (7\text{-}36)$$

All the terms of Equation (7-36) were computed in finding the *a* and *b* coefficients of the regression equation. Thus, first finding the standard error of the estimate, then using the standard error of the estimate to estimate the standard deviation of the sampling distribution of the value of b leads us to finding the upper and lower limits of the confidence interval on b. All of these steps are shown in lines 380 to 431 of Figure 7-12.

7.6 MULTIPLE REGRESSION

In the previous section we considered the problem of finding the straight line which best describes the relation between an independent variable X and a dependent variable Y. Many real situations are more complex, with two or more independent variables, X1, X2 ,... affecting the values of the dependent variable Y. In this section we consider the simple extension of linear regression from one independent variable to two independent variables. This is the simplest form of multiple regression. You will see how the ideas of linear regression extend to two variables. Extension to more variables follows the same patterns. Although it is conceptually not difficult to extend this program to three, four or more variables, it is a time-consuming process. An alternative is to use a multiple linear regression routine available for IFPS. (This is a separate routine that may be purchased at nominal cost; check whether it is available at your installation).

The multiple regression equation for two independent variables is given by:

$$Y_C = a + b1^{*}X1 + b2^{*}X2 \qquad (7\text{-}37)$$

where *a, b1,* and *b2* are the regression coefficients which are selected in such a way as to miminize the difference between the predicted values Y_C and the observed values, Y. For example, we may be relating annual sales in thousands of dollars (Y) to annual advertising expenditures in thousand of dollars (X1) and to percentage of local unemployment (X2).

The procedure for obtaining *a, b1,* and *b2* involves first finding a number of sums, specifically ΣY, ΣX1, ΣX2, ΣX1Y, ΣX2Y, ΣX1X2, ΣYY, Σ X1X1, and Σ X2X2. That is, we find the sums of the individual variables,the sums of the variables taken two at a time and the squares of the variables. We will refer to these as SUMY,SUMX1, etc., just as they are referred to in Figure 7-14. SUMY, SUMX1, and SUMX2 are used to find the average values of Y , X1, and X2, that is, YBAR, X1BAR, and X2BAR respectively.

Unlike linear regression where we use the sums directly, it turns out to be computationally more efficient to compute the deviations of the sums from the means of the corresponding variables. Thus, for example, we compute the deviation from the sum of the Y squared in line 280 as:

SUMYSQUARED = SUMYSQUARE –YBAR*SUMY.

These deviations are referred to in Figure 7-14 with a D at the end of the variable name (e.g., SUMX1YD). The advantage of the deviation format is that it reduces the problem from solving three simultaneous equations to solving two simultaneous equations. That is, the coefficients *b1* and *b2* are defined by the relations:

$$b_1 = \frac{SUMX1YD*SUMX2SQUARED - SUMX2YD*SUMX1X2D}{SUMX1SQUARED*SUMX2SQUARED - SUMX1X2D*SUMX1X2D} \qquad (7\text{-}38)$$

$$b_2 = \text{(SUMX1YD– B1*SUMX1SQUARED) / SUMX1X2D} \qquad (7\text{-}39)$$

These quantities can be determined directly from each of the deviation terms. (Note that each quantity in Equations (7-38) and (7-39) has the letter D at the end of it.) Once the *b* coefficients are known, the a coefficient can be obtained from:

$$a = \text{YBAR} - b1\text{*X1BAR} - b2\text{*X2BAR} \qquad (7\text{-}40)$$

Here *a* depends only on the *b1 and b2* coefficients and on the averages found earlier.

If you have been following the development in this section and in the previous linear regression section you have seen how similar the two models are. This similarity extends to their use. Once you have found the coefficients of the regression equation (i.e., of Equation (7-37)), you can estimate the value of the dependent variable Y for any given pair of values X1 and X2.

The measures of deviation and correlation in multiple regression are quite similar to those in linear regression. We show several of these in Figure 7-14. The standard error of the estimate is the standard deviation of the observed values of Y around the fitted regression line given by Equation (7-37). The coefficient of multiple determination, like the coefficient of determination in the linear case, measures the fraction of the variance in the dependent variable explained by the regression equation. Examining this coefficient

```
MODEL MULREG  VERSION OF  01/12/83  19:45
10 COLUMNS 1-6
20 *
30 * LINEAR MULTIPLE REGRESSION -- THREE VARIABLES
40 *
50 *SUMS
60 *
70 SUMX1=PREVIOUS + X1
80 SUMX2=PREVIOUS+X2
90 SUMY=PREVIOUS+Y
100 SUMX1Y=PREVIOUS + X1*Y
110 SUMX2Y=PREVIOUS +X2*Y
120 SUMYSQUARE=PREVIOUS +Y*Y
130 SUMX1SQUARE=PREVIOUS +X1*X1
140 SUMX2SQUARE=PREVIOUS +X2*X2
150 SUMX1X2 =PREVIOUS +X1*X2
160 *
170 *AVERAGES
180 *
190 YBAR=SUMY/N
200 X1BAR=SUMX1/N
210 X2BAR=SUMX2/N
220 *
230 * CALCULATION OF DEVIATIONS
240 *
250 SUMX1YD=SUMX1Y-X1BAR*SUMY
260 SUMX2YD=SUMX2Y-X2BAR*SUMY
270 SUMX1X2D=SUMX1X2-X1BAR*SUMX
280 SUMYSQUARED=SUMYSQUARE-YBAR*SUMY
290 SUMX1SQUARED=SUMX1SQUARE-X1BAR*SUMX1
300 SUMX2SQUARED=SUMX2SQUARE-X2BAR*SUMX2
310 *
320 *CALCULATION OF COEFFICIENTS OF MULTIPLE REGRESSION LINE
330 *
340 A= YBAR -B1*X1BAR -B2*X2BAR
350 B1= (SUMX1YD*SUMX2SQUARED-SUMX1X2D*SUMX2YD)/'
360(SUMX1SQUARED*SUMX2SQUARED-SUMX1X2D*SUMX1X2D)
370 B2=(SUMX1YD-B1*SUMX1SQUARED)/SUMX1X2D
380 *
390 X1 ESTIMATE = 1.8
400 X2 ESTIMATE = 5.7
410 Y ESTIMATE =0 FOR 2, A+B1*X1 ESTIMATE +B2*X2 ESTIMATE
420 *
430 * STANDARD ERROR OF THE ESTIMATE
440 STD ERROR OF ESTIMATE=0 FOR 3,XPOWERY(NUMERATOR/(N-3),.5)
450 NUMERATOR=SUMYSQUARED-B1*SUMX1YD-B2*SUMX2YD
460 *
470 *COEFFICIENT OF MULTIPLE DETERMINATION
480 RSQUARE = 1-(STD ERROR OF ESTIMATE*STD ERROR OF ESTIMATE)/'
490 VARIANCE OF Y
500 R =XPOWERY(RSQUARE,.5)
```

FIGURE 7-14. LINEAR MULTIPLE REGRESSION
(This Figure Continued on the Next Page)

```
510 *COMPUTATION OF VARIANCE OF Y
520 *
530 VARIANCE OF Y= PREVIOUS +(Y-MATRIX(YBAR,6))*(Y-MATRIX(YBAR,6))'
540 FOR 5,(PREVIOUS +XPOWERY((Y-YBAR),2))/(N-1)
550 *
560 *TWO VARIABLE CORRELATION COEFFICIENTS
570 *
580 RX1X2=XPOWERY(RATIO1,.5)
590 RYX1=XPOWERY(RATIO2,.5)
600 RYX2=XPOWERY(RATIO3,.5)
610 RATIO1=SUMX1X2D*SUMX1X2D/(SUMX1SQUARED*SUMX2SQUARED)
620 RATIO2=SUMX1YD*SUMX1YD/(SUMX1SQUARED*SUMYSQUARED)
630 RATIO3=SUMX2YD*SUMX2YD/(SUMX2SQUARED*SUMYSQUARED)
640 *
650 *DATA
660 *
670 X1=1.7,3.0,2.0,1.5,.6,1.5
680 X2=6,7,5,2,3,4
690 Y= 50,100,75,45,20,50
700 N=1,PREVIOUS+1
END OF MODEL
? solve
MODEL MULREG  VERSION OF  01/12/83  19:45 -- 6 COLUMNS 39 VARIABLES
ENTER SOLVE OPTIONS
? all

                                  1        2        3        4        5        6


 LINEAR MULTIPLE REGRESSION -- THREE VARIABLES
SUMS

SUMX1                         1.700    4.700    6.700    8.200    8.800    10.30
SUMX2                             6       13       18       20       23       27
SUMY                             50      150      225      270      290      340
SUMX1Y                           85      385      535    602.5    614.5    689.5
SUMX2Y                          300     1000     1375     1465     1525     1725
SUMYSQUARE                     2500    12500    18125    20150    20550    23050
SUMX1SQUARE                   2.890    11.89    15.89    18.14    18.50    20.75
SUMX2SQUARE                      36       85      110      114      123      139
SUMX1X2                       10.20    31.20    41.20    44.20       46       52

AVERAGES

YBAR                             50       75       75    67.50       58    56.67
X1BAR                         1.700    2.350    2.233    2.050    1.760    1.717
X2BAR                             6    6.500        6        5    4.600    4.500
```

FIGURE 7-14. LINEAR MULTIPLE REGRESSION
(This Figure Continued on the Next Page)

CALCULATION OF DEVIATIONS

SUMX1YD	0	32.50	32.50	49	104.1	105.8
SUMX2YD	0	25	25	115	191	195
SUMX1X2D	0	.6500	1	3.200	5.520	5.650
SUMYSQUARED	0	1250	1250	1925	3730	3783
SUMX1SQUARED	0	.8450	.9267	1.330	3.012	3.068
SUMX2SQUARED	0	.5000	2	14	17.2	

CALCULATION OF COEFFICIENTS OF MULTIPLE REGRESSION LINE

A	50	-250	35.94	-7.995	-2.871	-2.567
B1	0	0	46.88	37.95	34.51	34.46
B2	0	50	-10.94	-.4594	.0309	.0168
X1 ESTIMATE	1.800	1.800	1.800	1.800	1.800	1.800
X2 ESTIMATE	5.700	5.700	5.700	5.700	5.700	5.700
Y ESTIMATE	0	0	57.97	57.69	59.41	59.56
STD ERROR OF ESTIMAT	0	0	0	10.88	8.128	6.656
NUMERATOR	0	0	0	118.4	132.1	132.9

COEFFICIENT OF MULTIPLE DETERMINATION

RSQUARE	1	1	1	.9505	.9823	.9414
R	1	1	1	.9750	.9911	.9703

COMPUTATION OF VARIANCE OF Y

VARIANCE OF Y	44.44	1922	2258	2394	3739	756.7

TWO VARIABLE CORRELATION COEFFICIENTS

RX1X2	0	1	.7346	.7416	.7669	.7710
RYX1	0	1	.9549	.9684	.9821	.9823
RYX2	0	1	.5000	.7005	.7541	.7578
RATIO1	0	1	.5396	.5499	.5882	.5945
RATIO2	0	1	.9119	.9378	.9646	.9649
RATIO3	0	1	.2500	.4907	.5686	.5743

DATA

X1	1.700	3	2	1.500	.6000	1.500
X2	6	7	5	2	3	4
Y	50	100	75	45	20	50
N	1	2	3	4	5	6

FIGURE 7-14. LINEAR MULTIPLE REGRESSION
(Continued)

can help you judge whether going from one variable to two is worth it. If the coefficient for multiple determination is less than the coefficient of determination then adding the second variable has harmed you not helped you. Furthermore, if you find an increase but the amount of the increase is small, you may be better off just using one variable if the data gathering effort for the second variable is expensive.

Finally, Figure 7-14 shows the correlation coefficients for each pair of variables. If the two independent variables X1 and X2 are highly correlated, then using two variables should not give you much more information than 1 variable; however, you can also tell from the correlation coefficients between Y and X1 and between Y and X2 respectively whether X1 or X2 is a better predictor of Y=.60. Again, plot the results to compare the answers.

7.7 TIME SERIES AND FORECASTING

The term time series refers to a set of values about a specific quantity that was obtained at different points in time. For example, you may have sales data for your department obtained daily or you may be keeping monthly records on the U.S. balance of trade. You can use time series data to forecast future values if you believe that the the trends and patterns observed in the past will continue without changes in the underlying causal relationships. If events occur that change these relations (e.g., a three month strike by your principal supplier or a sharp increase in oil prices) then, no matter how well you apply them, the methods of this section will be useless in obtaining reliable or accurate forecasts.

In this section we will consider both short-term and long-term forecasting based on historical data.

7.7.1 Short-Term Forecasting

By short-term forecasting we mean forecasts that deal only with the next period. The following are five methods of making such forecasts:

1. Arithmetic mean.
2. Moving average
3. Trend extrapolation
4. Exponential smoothing
5. Double exponential smoothing.

Figure 7-15 illustrates the various short-range forecasting methods. We show 12 periods of historical data (sales in thousands of dollars in each of the previous 12 quarters, Line 60). The forecast value is shown in the last column. Note that the value of sales in the last column is the same as in Column 12. This corresponds to a forecast that says the next period will be identical to the present period. Is this a good method of forecasting?

The arithmetic mean and the moving average were discussed in Section 7.1. The arithmetic mean forecast simply assumes that the next period will be the average of all the values observed in the past. The mean of all the historical data is thus used as the forecast for the next period. All previous periods are weighted equally. A quick way of obtaining this forecast is to use POLYFIT(0). As described in Section 3.2.3, POLYFIT(0) computes the mean of all previous values of a variable

```
MODEL FORECAST2  VERSION OF  09/01/82  20:11
10 COLUMNS 1-12,FRCST
20 *
30 * INPUT DATA
40*  ==========
50 *
60 SALES=13.1,12.0,15.8,11.4,14.0,15.3,17.6,13.0,15.2,16.4,19.2,'
61 14.7,0
70*
80*MOVING AVERAGE
85*==============
90*
100 MOVING AVERAGE = 0,0,0,MOVAVG(SALES,.33,.33,.33,0)
110*
120 *FORECASTS USING THE POLYFIT FUNCTION
123*=====================================
130*
140 MEAN = SALES FOR 12,POLYFIT(0)
150 LINEAR REGRESSION = SALES FOR 12,POLYFIT(1)
160 QUADRATIC REGRESSION = SALES FOR 12,POLYFIT(2)
170*
180*EXPONENTIAL SMOOTHING
183*=====================
190*
200 EXPFORECAST = SALES,PREVIOUS SALES,PREVIOUS EXPFORECAST +ALPHA*'
201 (PREVIOUS SALES'-PREVIOUS EXPFORECAST)
210 ALPHA = .2
220*
230*DOUBLE EXPONENTIAL SMOOTHING
235*============================
240*
250DOUBLESMOOTH = SALES,PREVIOUS SALES,2*PREVIOUS EXPFORECAST-'
251 PREVIOUS 2 F2FUNCTION
260 F2FUNCTION=SALES,ALPHA*EXPFORECAST+(1-ALPHA)*PREVIOUS F2FUNCTION
END OF MODEL
ENTER SOLVE OPTIONS
? all

                               1      2      3      4      5      6      7


 INPUT DATA
 ==========

SALES                      13.10     12  15.80  11.40     14  15.30  17.60

MOVING AVERAGE
==============

MOVING AVERAGE                 0      0      0  13.63  13.07  13.73  13.57
```

FIGURE 7-15. VARIOUS FORECASTING METHODS
(This Figure Continued on the Next Page)

```
FORECASTS USING THE POLYFIT FUNCTION
====================================

MEAN                    13.10     12  15.80  11.40     14  15.30  17.60
LINEAR REGRESSION       13.10     12  15.80  11.40     14  15.30  17.60
QUADRATIC REGRESSIO     13.10     12  15.80  11.40     14  15.30  17.60

EXPONENTIAL SMOOTHING
=====================

EXPFORECAST             13.10  13.10  12.88  13.46  13.05  13.24  13.65
ALPHA                   .2000  .2000  .2000  .2000  .2000  .2000  .2000

DOUBLE EXPONENTIAL SMOOTHING
============================

DOUBLESMOOTH            13.10  13.10  13.10  12.66  13.87  12.96  13.36
F2FUNCTION              13.10  13.10  13.06  13.14  13.12  13.14  13.25
                            8      9     10     11     12  FRCST


 INPUT DATA
 ==========

SALES                      13  15.20  16.40  19.20  14.70      0

MOVING AVERAGE
==============

MOVING AVERAGE          15.63  15.30  15.27  14.87  16.93  16.77
 FORECASTS USING THE POLYFIT FUNCTION
====================================

MEAN                       13  15.20  16.40  19.20  14.70  14.81
LINEAR REGRESSION          13  15.20  16.40  19.20  14.70  17.19
QUADRATIC REGRESSION       13  15.20  16.40  19.20  14.70  16.85

EXPONENTIAL SMOOTHING
=====================
EXPFORECAST             14.44  14.15  14.36  14.77  15.66  15.47
ALPHA                   .2000  .2000  .2000  .2000  .2000  .2000

DOUBLE EXPONENTIAL SMOOTHING
============================

DOUBLESMOOTH            14.16  15.64  14.82  15.11  15.77  17.34
F2FUNCTION              13.49  13.62  13.77  13.97  14.31  14.54
```

FIGURE 7-15. VARIOUS FORECASTING METHODS (Continued)

The moving average forecast argues that the further back in time data were obtained the less relevant they are to the future. Thus, in a moving average forecast, choices have to be made of how many previous historical periods to use and how the weights should be assigned to each period used. You might use a moving average forecast if you are forecasting a quantity repetitively, such as next month's sales and believe that only the last few months are relevant. The forecast value is equal to the moving average value. In Figure 7-15, the moving average forecast is based on three periods weighted equally. In the exercise below we ask you to compute moving averages for different periods and unequal weightings.

If there are definite trends in the data (e.g. sales are growing), a simple form of short-term forecasting is to apply the methodology of linear regression (Section 7.5). You find the appropriate regression equation based on the past values and then evaluate the regression equation for the next period. The POLYFIT(1) function can be used for this purpose. Although it uses the identical calculation methods, this approach to forecasting is not simply an application of regression analysis since the assumptions of regression analysis are not satisfied. Rather this form finds the best-fitting line and uses the extrapolation of the line to the next period as the forecast. Figure 7-15 also shows the use of POLYFIT(2) which extrapolates on the basis of the best fitting quadratic equation.

EXERCISE: Modify Figure 7-15 to compute the following quantities:

1. The moving average forecast, based on the last six periods weighted equally.

2. The error in the moving average forecast, based on the difference between the forecast and actual values.

3. The trend forecast for each period. To obtain this forecast you must use the TREND function described in Section 3.2. You may find this a little tricky to do; however, try to find a clever way of making this computation.

4. The error in the trend forecast, based on the difference between the forecast and actual values.

Exponential smoothing is a short-term forecasting method that gives weight to all the historical points, but weights recent points more heavily than old ones. Exponential smoothing is defined by a recursive relationship:

EXPFORECAST = PREVIOUS EXPFORECAST + ALPHA
(PREVIOUS ACTUAL −PREVIOUS EXPFORECAST) (7-41)

That is, the forecast for this period is the same as the forecast for last period but modified by the difference between the observed value and the previous forecast value. ALPHA is a constant of proportionality (between 0 and 1) that determines the extent of the influence of the observed values. For example, if ALPHA is zero, then EXPFORECAST = PREVIOUS EXPFORECAST and actual values are ignored, whereas if ALPHA = 1, the forecast is simply the last observed value. Typically, values between 0.1 and 0.3 are used for ALPHA; a value of 0.2 is used in Figure 7-15. When starting this process, the first data point is used as the first forecast (since we have no history at that time, all we can assume is that the first period will be repeated). The formula is then applied iteratively on all the historical data. The last value computed is the forecast.

EXERCISE: Use WHAT IF statements on the model of Figure 7-15 to observe the effect of ALPHA on the forecasts. Specifically, use ALPHA values of .1, .3, .5, .7, and .9 and print out the exponential smoothing forecast values. For each case, PLOT the observed and forecast values. Which value of ALPHA gives the best forecast?

EXERCISE: It can be shown that exponential smoothing is equivalent to an N period moving average if N is chosen so that

N = (2/ALPHA) - 1 (7-42)

Verify this by using Equation (7-42) to find N for ALPHA values of 0.1, 0.333, 0.4, and 0.5. Use WHAT IF statements to modify Figure 7-15 to find both the moving average and exponential smoothing forecasts for these combinations of ALPHA and N.

Double exponential smoothing, while slightly more difficult to compute (it requires one more line in your IFPS model and has a slightly more complex form than exponential smoothing), provides a way of improving exponential smoothing so that it usually tends to follow actual values more closely. It is widely used in marketing applications. The basic relation for double exponential smoothing is:

DOUBLESMOOTH = 2*PREVIOUS EXPFORECAST
-PREVIOUS 2 F2FUNCTION (7-43)

where DOUBLESMOOTH is the double exponential smoothing forecast and EXPFORECAST is the exponential smoothing forecast as in Equation 7-41. F2FUNCTION is called the double smoothing function. It is computed from the relation:

F2FUNCTION = ALPHA * EXPFORECAST +
(1 - ALPHA) *PREVIOUS F2FUNCTION (7-44)

If you look closely at F2FUNCTION you will see that it requires two periods of historical data. The exponential smoothing forecast depends on the previous period's observed data and hence the PREVIOUS F2FUNCTION depends on data observed two periods ago. Going through the same analysis will show you that the DOUBLESMOOTH forecast uses a minimum of three periods of historical data and hence the first meaningful DOUBLESMOOTH forecast is for period 4.

EXERCISE: Use WHAT IF statements with Figure 7-15 to determine the effect of ALPHA on the DOUBLESMOOTH forecast. Use ALPHA values of .1, .3, .5, .7, .9. In each case, PLOT the actual and forecast values. Does DOUBLESMOOTH provide more accurate forecasts than exponential smoothing? What is the best value of ALPHA for the data shown?

7.7.2 Long-Term Forecasting

If you have a large amount of historical time series data available and you believe that the underlying phenomena will continue into the future, then the classical time series model can be used as a long-term forecasting method. When you plot historical time series you will usually find that the data appear complex and are difficult to interpret. The reason is that many phenomena are occurring and they interact with one another. In the classical time series model, the changes over time are assumed to contain four components:

1. Trend, T.
2. Cyclical fluctuations, C.
3. Seasonal variations, S.
4. Irregular movements, I.

that interact with one another to produce the observed time series. The model attempts to separate these components, obtain forecasts for each of them, and then combine these individual forecasts into a composite forecast of future values.

Trend refers to long-term movements caused by underlying factors (e.g., demographic, technological, taste changes). *Cyclical fluctuations*, such as business cycles, are movements around the trend. Typically, they are several years in duration. *Seasonal variations* are much shorter cycles, completed within a year and repeating from year to year. For example, air conditioner and snow shovel sales exhibit strong seasonal variations. *Irregular movements* refers to the very short-term fluctuations in time series that follow no pattern. They are what is left over when the first three components have been accounted for.

One form of the classical time series model assumes that the values, Y, of a time series are the product of the four components, that is:

$$Y = T * C * S * I \tag{7-45}$$

To find the trend component, the method of least squares is used, that is, the arithmetic of regression analysis. We will consider the simple case of an arithmetic straight line trend. We assume that the trend is of the form:

$$Y_t = a + b*X \tag{7-46}$$

where Y_t is the computed trend value for period X. To simplify the calculations, the time periods are measured with respect to the arithmetic mean (i.e., middle) of the historical data. For example, if we have data on the period 1961-1981, we choose 1970 as X=0, 1971 as X=1, 1972 as X=2, 1969 as X= –1, 1968 as X = –2, etc. Since the average value of X is 0, the equations that define the coefficients *a* and *b* simplify to:

$$a = \text{YBAR} \tag{7-47}$$

$$b = \text{SUMXY/SUMXSQUARED} \tag{7-48}$$

Here YBAR is the average of the observed values, Y; SUMXY is the sum of the products of X and Y, and SUMXSQUARED is the sum of the squares of the X values. Figure 7-16 illustrates the computation of the trend line for a simple set of 11 data points. We have written the model in a general form. Specifically, we have chosen to input the variable NPERIODS to represent the number of periods of data and have computed the initial value of X by taking –(NPERIODS –1)/2. Note that if you want to use this model for a different number of periods, you have to be careful and change the reference to the number of data points everywhere it occurs; specifically in Line 10 (number of columns), , and Line 170 (NPERIODS).

```
MODEL TLINEB  VERSION OF  08/22/82  23:09
10 COLUMNS 1-24
20 *
30* INPUT DATA
40*
50 X=-(NPERIODS -1)/2,PREVIOUS+1
60 Y= 13.1,12.0,15.8,11.4,14.0,15.3,17.6,14.0,15.2,16.4,19.2,14.7,'
61 15.6,15.5,17.2,16.7,16.8,16.5,17.4,14.4,17.0,19.4,19.2,16.7
70*
80 * COMPUTATION OF TREND LINE COEFFICIENTS
90*
100 SUMY=PREVIOUS + Y
110 SUMXSQUARED=PREVIOUS +X*X
120 SUMXY= PREVIOUS + X*Y
130*
140 A= SUMY/NPERIODS
150 B= SUMXY/SUMXSQUARED
160*
170 NPERIODS = 24
END OF MODEL
? solve
MODEL TLINEB  VERSION OF  08/22/82  23:09 -- 24 COLUMNS 8 VARIABLES
ENTER SOLVE OPTIONS
? all

               1    2    3    4    5    6    7    8    9   10   11   12


 INPUT DATA

X         -11.5-10.5-9.50-8.50-7.50-6.50-5.50-4.50-3.50-2.50-1.50-.500
Y          13.1   12 15.8 11.4   14 15.3 17.6   14 15.2 16.4 19.2 14.7

 COMPUTATION OF TREND LINE COEFFICIENTS

SUMY       13.1 25.1 40.9 52.3 66.3 81.6 99.2  113  128  145  164  179
SUMXSQUA    132  243  333  405  461  504  534  554  566  573  575  575
SUMXY      -151 -277 -427 -524 -629 -728 -825 -888 -941 -982-1011-1018

A          .546 1.05 1.70 2.18 2.76 3.40 4.13 4.72 5.35 6.03 6.83 7.45
B         -1.14-1.14-1.28-1.29-1.36-1.45-1.55-1.60-1.66-1.72-1.76-1.77

NPERIODS     24   24   24   24   24   24   24   24   24   24   24   24
```

FIGURE 7-16. COMPUATION OF THE TREND LINE FORECAST
(This Figure Continued on the Next Page)

	13	14	15	16	17	18	19	20	21	22	23	24
INPUT DATA												
X	.500	1.50	2.50	3.50	4.50	5.50	6.50	7.50	8.50	9.50	10.5	11.5
Y	15.6	15.5	17.2	16.7	16.8	16.5	17.4	14.4	17	19.4	19.2	16.7
COMPUTATION OF TREND LINE COEFFICIENTS												
SUMY	194	210	227	244	261	277	294	309	326	345	364	381
SUMXSQUAR	575	578	584	596	616	647	689	745	817	908	1018	1150
SUMXY	-1010	-987	-944	-886	-810	-719	-606	-498	-354	-170	32.1	224
A	8.10	8.74	9.46	10.2	10.9	11.5	12.3	12.9	13.6	14.4	15.2	15.9
B	-1.76	-1.71	-1.62	-1.49	-1.31	-1.11	-.880	-.669	-.433	-.187	.032	.195
NPERIODS	24	24	24	24	24	24	24	24	24	24	24	24

FIGURE 7-16. COMPUTATION OF THE TREND LINE FORECAST (Continued)

We next turn to seasonal variations. To make meaningful comparisons you would like to remove the effects of these variations, that is, to deseasonalize the data. To do so, the most widely used technique is the ratio to moving average method. We will illustrate this method for the case of quarterly data and leave it as an exercise to you to deal with monthly data.

The basic idea in deseasonalizing data is to find a number which represents the ratio between the observed value in a given period and the value that would have been observed if seasonal effects had not been present (that is, the average value for the year). Once these ratios have been found for each quarter, every observed value is divided by the ratio for its quarter. For example, if sales in the fourth quarter are 30% above average sales for the year, then it would be appropriate to divide fourth quarter sales by 1.3. The ratios, called seasonal indices, are found by applying the ratio to moving average method shown in Figures 7-17 and 7-18 . It is easier to use separate models to determine the seasonal indices than to attempt to compute them as an integral part of the forecasting model. (If you do not believe this assertion, write a single IFPS model that performs the entire seasonal index problem and judge the level of difficulty for yourself.)

In Figure 7-17, we convert the observed data for each quarter into a percentage number relative to a four-quarter (i.e., annual) average centered at the observed point. To do so, we perform the following steps:

1. Compute 4-quarter moving totals. These totals are the sum of the current value of the data and the previous three values. If we divide this total by four, we have a 4-quarter average. However, by their definition, these averages lie midway between the 2nd and 3rd quarter of the data. We would like to obtain averages that lie at the same level as the data, that is, a centered moving average.

```
MODEL MOVAVGPCT  VERSION OF  01/12/83  20:06
10 COLUMNS 1-24
20 *
30 SALES = 13.1,12,15.8,11.4,14.0,15.3,17.6,13.0,15.2,16.4,19.2,'
40  14.7,15.6,15.5,17.2,16.7,16.8,16.5,17.4,14.4,17.0,19.4,19.2,16.7
50 MOV TOT=0,0,FUTURE SALES+SALES+PREVIOUS SALES+'
51 PREVIOUS 2 SALES FOR 21,0
60 MOV TOT8=0,0,MOV TOT +FUTURE MOV TOT FOR 20,0
70 MOVING AVG = MOV TOT8/8
80 SALES INDX=0,0, 100*SALES/MOVING AVG FOR 20,0,0
END OF MODEL
? solve
MODEL MOVAVGPCT VERSION OF 01/12/83  20:06 -- 24 COLUMNS 5 VARIABLES
? invert
? all
```

	SALES	MOV TOT	MOV TOT8	MOVING AVG	SALES INDX
1	13.10	0	0	0	0
2	12	0	0	0	0
3	15.80	52.30	105.5	13.19	119.8
4	11.40	53.20	109.7	13.71	83.14
5	14	56.50	114.8	14.35	97.56
6	15.30	58.30	118.2	14.78	103.6
7	17.60	59.90	121	15.13	116.4
8	13	61.10	123.3	15.41	84.35
9	15.20	62.20	126	15.75	96.51
10	16.40	63.80	129.3	16.16	101.5
11	19.20	65.50	131.4	16.43	116.9
12	14.70	65.90	130.9	16.36	89.84
13	15.60	65	128	16	97.50
14	15.50	63	128	16	96.88
15	17.20	65	131.2	16.40	104.9
16	16.70	66.20	133.4	16.68	100.1
17	16.80	67.20	134.6	16.83	99.85
18	16.50	67.40	132.5	16.56	99.62
19	17.40	65.10	130.4	16.30	106.7
20	14.40	65.30	133.5	16.69	86.29
21	17	68.20	138.2	17.28	98.41
22	19.40	70	142.3	17.79	109.1
23	19.20	72.30	0	0	0
24	16.70	0	0	0	0

FIGURE 7-17. SALES INDEX BASED ON MOVING AVERAGES: 24 QUARTERS OF DATA
(This Figure Continued on the Next Page)

```
MODEL SEASONAL  VERSION OF  01/12/83  19:54
10 COLUMNS 1-4
20 *
30 *QUARTERLY INPUT DATA
40 *
50 Q1=.976,.965,.975,.998
60 Q2= 1.035,1.015,.969,.996
70 Q3= 1.163,1.169,1.049,1.067
80 Q4= .844,.899,1.002,.863
90 *
100 *COMPUTATION OF MAXIMUM AND MINIMUM
110 *
120 MAXQ1=Q1,MAXIMUM(PREVIOUS,Q130 MAXQ2=Q2,MAXIMUM(PREVIOUS,Q2)
140 MAXQ3=Q3,MAXIMUM(PREVIOUS,Q3)
150 MAXQ4=Q4,MAXIMUM(PREVIOUS,Q4)
160 MINQ1=Q1,MINIMUM(PREVIOUS,Q1)
170 MINQ2=Q2,MINIMUM(PREVIOUS,Q2)
180 MINQ3=Q3,MINIMUM(PREVIOUS,Q3)
190 MINQ4=Q4,MINIMUM(PREVIOUS,Q4)
200 *
210 *COMPUTATION OF SUM OF QUARTERLY DATA
220 *
230 SUMQ1=PREVIOUS+Q1
240 SUMQ2=PREVIOUS+Q2
250 SUMQ3=PREVIOUS+Q3
260 SUMQ4=PREVIOUS+Q4
270 *
280 *COMPUTATION OF REDUCED MEANS
290 *
300 MEANQ1=0,0,(SUMQ1-MAXQ1-MINQ1)/(N-2)
310 MEANQ2=0,0,(SUMQ2-MAXQ2-MINQ2)/(N-2)
320 MEANQ3=0,0,(SUMQ3-MAXQ3-MINQ3)/(N-2)
330 MEANQ4=0,0,(SUMQ4-MAXQ4-MINQ4)/(N-2)
340 TOTMEAN=SUM(L300 THRU L330)
350 *
360 *COMPUTATION OF SEASONAL INDEXES
370 *
380 ADJ FACTOR=0,0,400/TOTMEAN
390 INDEX1=ADJ FACTOR*MEANQ1
400 INDEX2=ADJ FACTOR*MEANQ2
410 INDEX3 =ADJ FACTOR*MEANQ3
420 INDEX4=ADJ FACTOR*MEANQ4
430 *
440 N=PREVIOUS+1
END OF MODEL
```

FIGURE 7-18. SEASONAL INDEXES

```
? solve
MODEL SEASONAL VERSION OF  01/12/83  19:54 -- 4 COLUMNS 27 VARIABLES
ENTER SOLVE OPTIONS
? all
```

	1	2	3	4
QUARTERLY INPUT DATA				
Q1	.9760	.9650	.9750	.9980
Q2	1.035	1.015	.9690	.9960
Q3	1.163	1.169	1.049	1.067
Q4	.8440	.8990	1.002	.8630
COMPUTATION OF MAXIMUM AND MINIMUM				
MAXQ1	.9760	.9760	.9760	.9980
MAXQ2	1.035	1.035	1.035	1.035
MAXQ3	1.163			
MAXQ4	.8440	.8990	1.002	1.002
MINQ1	.9760	.9650	.9650	.9650
MINQ2	1.035	1.015	.9690	.9690
MINQ3	1.163	1.163	1.049	1.049
MINQ4	.8440	.8440	.8440	.8440
COMPUTATION OF SUM OF QUARTERLY DATA				
SUMQ1	.9760	1.941	2.916	3.914
SUMQ2	1.035	2.050	3.019	4.015
SUMQ3	1.163	2.332	3.381	4.448
SUMQ4	.8440	1.743	2.745	3.608
COMPUTATION OF REDUCED MEANS				
MEANQ1	0	0	.9750	.9755
MEANQ2	0	0	1.015	1.006
MEANQ3	0	0	1.163	1.115
MEANQ4	0	0	.8990	.8810
TOTMEAN	0	0	4.052	3.977
COMPUTATION OF SEASONAL INDEXES				
ADJ FACTOR	0	0	98.72	100.6
INDEX1	0	0	96.25	98.11
INDEX2	0	0	100.2	101.1
INDEX3	0	0	114.8	112.1
INDEX4	0	0	88.75	88.61
N	1	2	3	4

FIGURE 7-18. SEASONAL INDEXES
(Continued)

2. Add the current and next 4 quarter moving total.

3. Divide the number obtained in Step 2 by 8 to obtain a centered moving average.

4. Divide the original data by the centered moving average obtained in Step 3.

The results shown in Figure 7-17 are divided by 100 and used as input data for Figure 7-18. These inputs are labeled Q1, Q2, Q3, and Q4. Note that rather than listing the data sequentially, we have separated it by quarters. The convention in doing these calculations is to remove the largest and the smallest value observed. Such a procedure eliminates outlying values that may be due to unusual conditions in the past (e.g., a heat wave, a strike). In IFPS this means we have to compute the maximum and minumum of the values for each quarter. This is done in Figure 7-18 by using the MAXIMUM and MINIMUM functions. Note that we choose the initial values as the starting values for these calculations and then successively choose either the previously observed maximum (or minimum) or the current value, depending on which is larger. The mean for each quarter is computed in Lines 300 through 330 by using the relation:

$$((\Sigma Q_i) - \text{MAX } Q_i - \text{MIN } Q_i) / (N-2) \quad (7\text{-}49)$$

That is, we add up all the values for quarter i and then subtract the largest and smallest values observed in that quarter. We then divide by the number of observations considered, that is (N-2).

The foregoing mean values look like seasonal indices but they are not. The reason is that if you add them up they do not have an average value of 100, which is what is desired. To obtain an average of 100, we perform the following steps:

1. Add up the means. In our case the total is 3.977.

2. Divide 400 by the sum of the means. The result of this division is an adjustment factor.

3. Multiply each mean by the adjustment factor. The results are the seasonal indices.

Note that the indices just computed are one form of index number, the subject of Section 7.8 which follows.

EXERCISE: For clarity of presentation, Figure 7-18 separates input data, maximum, minimum, sum, and mean by quarters. Although visually helpful, this formulation results in a complex input requirements, a lengthy model and long printout. Write an IFPS program that allows you to write each of these quantities in a single line, with the data input in the sequence of occurrence (e.g., .976, 1.035, 1.163, .844, .965 ...). You will be find PREVIOUS 4 helpful in doing this.

EXERCISE: Modify the previous exercise so that the model is applicable to monthly input data.

Let us review where we now stand. We had defined a model:

$$Y = T * S * C * I. \quad (7\text{-}45)$$

If we divide both sides by the seasonal index S that we have just computed, we obtain a forecast Y/S which has seasonal effects removed from it:

$$Y/S = T * C * I \tag{7-50}$$

We turn now to the cyclical values. If we divide the deseasonalized forecast by the trend line:

$$Y/ST = C*I \tag{7-51}$$

the cyclic component modified by the irregular component remains. If we assume that the irregular component is random, its average value will be 1 and we can approximate the cyclic components by dividing the observed values by the product of the seasonal and trend values. The cyclic component shown in Figure 7-19 is interpreted in the same way as the seasonal index in that values below one indicate a reduction from the trend values while values above one indicate values above the trend due to cyclic effects.

```
MODEL RECOMPOSE  VERSION OF  08/22/82  23:04
10 COLUMNS 1-6
20 TREND = A * B*NCOL
30 SEASONAL = .979,1.016,1.135,.870,PREVIOUS 4 SEASONAL
40 CYCLIC =1.02,1.04,1.06,1.05,1.03
50 *
60 FORECAST = TREND * SEASONAL *CYCLIC
70 *INPUT DATA
80 *
90 A= 12.42
100 B=.3668
110 NCOL=13,PREVIOUS + 1
END OF MODEL
MODEL RECOMPOSE VERSION OF  08/22/82  23:04 -- 6 COLUMNS 7 VARIABLES
ENTER SOLVE OPTIONS
? all
```

	1	2	3	4	5	6
TREND	59.22	63.78	68.33	72.89	77.45	82.00
SEASONAL	.9790	1.016	1.135	.8700	.9790	1.016
CYCLIC	1.020	1.040	1.060	1.050	1.030	1.030
FORECAST	59.14	67.39	82.21	66.59	78.09	85.81
INPUT DATA						
A	12.42	12.42	12.42	12.42	12.42	12.42
B	.3668	.3668	.3668	.3668	.3668	.3668
NCOL	13	14	15	16	17	18

FIGURE 7-19. FORECASTS BASED ON TREND, SEASONAL AND CYCLIC FACTORS

Using the historical cyclic data to infer a general form for the cyclic pattern is a relatively complex art which is made more difficult by the fact that the data are based on the product C*I which contains the irregular component. We will not attempt to discuss the intricacies here. Rather we will assume that the cyclic component has been established based on the historical data. (If pressed to do it, you may simply have to draw a smooth curve through the historical cyclic data and then extrapolate it into the future by eye. An alternative is to attempt to fit a simple sine wave to the data based on the time from peak to peak and the swing in amplitude from peak to trough.

Thus far we have spent considerable time to decompose the observed data into trend, seasonal, and cyclic components. Once we know these components, we can recompose these results to obtain forecasts. This is done in Figure 7-19 where we show a forecast for six quarters based on the analysis of the time series data used in Figures 7-16 through 7-18. To compute the trend, we use the a and b coefficients of the trend line $a + b$*X. The initial value is for quarter 13 (shown as the initial value of NCOL). Since the trend line is linear with slope b, we increase by b from quarter to quarter to quarter. The seasonal index (Line 30) is given numerically for the first four quarters and then uses the value four quarters previously because the seasonal index repeats every four quarters. We have approximated the cyclic factor and simply provided input values; you might want to do a more substantial analysis for your own problems. Finally, we have multiplied the three factors together (assuming the irregular factor, which cannot be forecast anyway, to be equal to 1) to obtain the forecast values.

7.8 INDEX NUMBERS

Index numbers are pervasive in our society. The evening news tells us about the latest values of the consumer price index, the wholesale price index, the Dow Jones Average, and many others. These index numbers provide a handy shorthand for understanding the movement of economic trends over time. In this section, we will describe the underlying concept of index numbers and show how to compute them using IFPS.

An index number is a ratio that relates prices (or other quantities) at two different points in time. Typically, a particular year (or group of years) is chosen as the base year and current values are compared to the values in the base year. For example, the consumer price index for all urban consumers has used 1967 as the base year. This index stood at 242.5 in April 1980, indicating that prices were 2.425 times as great in April 1980 than in the base year of 1967. Note that the index multiplies the ratio by 100 (242.5 rather than 2.425).

Indexes typically measure the change in a group of items, often referred to as a market basket. For illustrative purposes, we will consider the simplified market basket shown in Table 7-1. This market basket might reflect a high school student's weekly snack diet.

Figure 7-20 shows the IFPS model using this price and purchase information to generate various index numbers. We begin by considering "aggregative index numbers", that is index numbers that consider only the total price. If we add up the values in the price column in 1980 ($1.90) and the values in the price column in 1970 ($1.20) and take their ratio times 100 we obtain:

$$\text{Aggregative price index} = 100 * (1.90/1.20) = 158.33$$

This is an unweighted index since it does not take into account how much of each item was consumed.

TABLE 7-1

MARKET BASKET

COMMODITY	PRICE 1970	PRICE 1980	AMOUNT 1970	AMOUNT 1980
Coffee	.10	.25	20	15
Hamburgers	.50	.65	5	6
French Fries	.20	.40	5	4
Ice Cream Cone	.25	.40	3	3
Chocolate Bar	.15	.20	1	2

```
MODEL INDEX  VERSION OF  01/12/83  20:17
10 COLUMNS 1-5
20 *
30 * COMMODITY PRICES
40 *
50 PRICES 1970 = .1,.5,.2,.25,.15
60 PRICES 1980 = .25,.65,.4,.4,.2
70 *
80 TOTAL 1970 COST = PREVIOUS + PRICES 1970
90 TOTAL 1980 COST = PREVIOUS + PRICES 1980
100 *
110 UNWEIGHTED AGGREGATIVE INDEX=100*TOTAL 1980 COST/TOTAL 1970 COST
120 *
130 PRICE RATIO 1980 TO 1970 = PRICES 1980/PRICES
140 CUMULATIVE 1980 TO 1970 PRICE RATIO=PREVIOUS+'
141 PRICE RATIO 1980 TO 1970

150 UNWEIGHTED INDEX OF PRICE RELATIVES = '
160 CUMULATIVE 1980 TO 1970 PRICE RATIO *100/NCOL
170 *
180 * PURCHASES
190 *
200 PURCHASES 1970 = 20,5,5,3,1
210 PURCHASES 1980 =15,6,4,3,2
220 *
230 *LASPEYRES INDEX
240 *
250 COSTS 1980 = PRICES 1980* PURCHASES 1970
260 COSTS 1970 = PRICES 1970 * PURCHASES 1970
270 CUMULATIVE 1980 COSTS = PREVIOUS + COSTS 1980
280 CUMULATIVE 1970 COSTS = PREVIOUS + COSTS 1970
290 LASPEYRES INDEX=100*CUMULATIVE 1980 COSTS/CUMULATIVE 1970 COSTS
300 *
```

FIGURE 7-20. INDEX NUMBERS
(This Figure Continued on the Next Page)

```
310 *PAASCHE INDEX
320 *
330 COST 1980 = PRICES 1980 * PURCHASES 1980
340 COST 1970 = PRICES 1970 * PURCHASES 1980
350 CUMULATIVE 1980 COST = PREVIOUS + COST
360 CUMULATIVE 1970 COST = PREVIOUS + COST 1970
370 PAASCHE INDEX = 100*CUMULATIVE 1980 COST /CUMULATIVE 1970 COST
380 *
390 NCOL=PREVIOUS + 1
END OF MODEL
? solve
ENTER SOLVE OPTIONS
? all

                                           1       2       3       4       5
 COMMODITY PRICES

PRICES 1970                              .10     .50     .20     .25     .15
PRICES 1980                              .25     .65     .40     .40     .20

TOTAL 1970 COST                          .10     .60     .80    1.05    1.20
TOTAL 1980 COST                          .25     .90    1.30    1.70    1.90

UNWEIGHTED AGGREGATIVE INDEX          250.00  150.00  162.50  161.90  158.33

PRICE RATIO 1980 TO 1970                2.50    1.30    2.00    1.60    1.33
CUMULATIVE 1980 TO 1970 PRICE RAT       2.50    3.80    5.80    7.40    8.73
UNWEIGHTED INDEX OF PRICE RELATIV     250.00  190.00  193.33  185.00  174.67

 PURCHASES

PURCHASES 1970                         20.00    5.00    5.00    3.00    1.00
PURCHASES 1980                         15.00    6.00    4.00    3.00    2.00

LASPEYRES INDEX

COSTS 1980                              5.00    3.25    2.00    1.20     .20
COSTS 1970                              2.00    2.50    1.00     .75     .15
CUMULATIVE 1980 COSTS                   5.00    8.25   10.25   11.45   11.65
CUMULATIVE 1970 COSTS                   2.00    4.50    5.50    6.25    6.40
LASPEYRES INDEX                       250.00  183.33  186.36  183.20  182.03

PAASCHE INDEX

COST 1980                               3.75    3.90    1.60    1.20     .40
COST 1970                               1.50    3.00     .80     .75     .30
CUMULATIVE 1980 COST                    3.75    7.65    9.25   10.45   10.85
CUMULATIVE 1970 COST                    1.50    4.50    5.30    6.05    6.35
PAASCHE INDEX                         250.00  170.00  174.53  172.73  170.87

NCOL                                    1.00    2.00    3.00    4.00    5.00
```

FIGURE 7-20. INDEX NUMBERS
(Continued)

EXERCISE: Add gasoline to the market basket in Table 7-1. Its price was $0.42 in 1970 and $1.23 in 1980. Consumption went from 6 gallons to 4 gallons during that time. Determine the aggregative price index for this augmented market basket.

An alternate way of computing an unweighted index is to consider the relative prices of each item and average these relative prices. The relative price of an item is the ratio of its current price to its price in the base year. For example, for coffee in Table 7-1, the relative price of coffee in 1980 compared to 1970 is 250 (i.e., 100*(.25/.10)). This form of index is called the unweighted index of price relatives. Note that for our market basket it is 100*(8.73/5) or 174.60. Here, 8.73 is the sum of the price ratios and we divide by 5 to obtain the average of a market basket containing 5 items. In general, the two types of unweighted indexes give different answers.

Neither of these simple indexes is appropriate when the amount purchased differs for each item. What we would like to know is how much actual expenditures have risen. Therefore, we have to multiply the unit cost by the amount purchased. For example, in 1970 20*0.20 = $4.00 was spent on coffee. At this point we have to decide which consumption pattern we will compare: the 1970 market basket or the 1980 market basket. The first case, called the Laspeyres index, assumes that we want to know how much a 1970 market basket would cost us if we bought it today. It takes the ratio of the the total cost of the 1970 market basket in 1980 to its cost in 1970. (See Lines 230 through 290 of Figure 7-20). The second case, called the Paasche index, assumes that we don't care about consumption patterns in the past but are interested in how much more today's market basket costs us compared to a point in the past. It takes the ratio of the total cost of the 1980 market basket in 1980 to its cost in 1970. (See Lines 310 through 370 of Figure 7-20) The results, for the Laspeyres index and the Paasche indices, respectively, as shown in Figure 7-20, are 182.03 and 170.87. The advantage of the Laspeyres index is that it always measures the same basket thereby providing continuity and requiring no data gathering on changing tastes. The Paasche index accounts for taste changes and includes substitutions made by consumers that reflect different rates of inflation on different items but requires new data to be gathered each time on the market basket.

EXERCISE: Compute the Laspeyres index for a weighted index of price relatives for the market basket of Table 7-1. That is, multiply the price relative of each item in 1980 by the total cost in 1970 (unit cost times number of units) for each item to obtain the current cost. Show that the Laspeyres index is the same for both methods of computation.

EXERCISE: Compute the Paasche index for a weighted index of price relatives for the market basket of Table 7-1.

EXERCISE: Compute the Laspeyres and Paasche indices with gasoline added to the market basket as in the first exercise in this section.

[illegible]

[illegible]

[illegible]

[illegible]

[illegible]

[illegible]

[illegible]

[illegible]

CHAPTER VIII
APPLICATIONS IN PRODUCTION AND OPERATIONS MANAGEMENT

8.1 Break-Even Analysis

8.2 Aggregate Scheduling

8.2.1 Production Forecasting
8.2.2 Standard Units of Work
8.2.3 Trading Off Overtime, Workforce, and Inventory
8.2.4 The HMMS Model

8.3 Inventory

8.3.1 Simple EOQ Model
8.3.2 Economic Lot Size Model--Continuous Delivery
8.3.3 Quantity Discounts
8.3.4 Order Point Systems
8.3.5 Simulating Inventory Requirements

8.4 Material Requirements Planning

8.5 Equipment Replacement

8.5.1 One-Time Purchase
8.5.2 Purchase with Replacement

8.6 Quality Control

8.6.1 Operating Characteristic Curves
8.6.2 Producers Risk and Consumers Risk
8.6.3 P-Chart

CHAPTER VIII
APPLICATIONS IN PRODUCTION AND OPERATIONS MANAGEMENT

This chapter shows you how to apply IFPS to problems in production and operations management (P/OM). The area of production and operations management has become increasingly important in recent years throughout the world as competition makes improvements in productivity necessary for survival. Many of the management techniques of P/OM involve financial analysis and can be well modeled in IFPS. In this chapter we present two such methods (break-even analysis and equipment replacement analysis). Some problems involve statistical techniques (particularly forecasting) and simulation which have been discussed earlier in this book. We present examples of these problems and of others which are unique to P/OM, such as inventory models and material requirements planning (MRP).

As in Chapters VI and VII, we have taken many of the examples from an existing text. In this case, *OPERATIONS MANAGEMENT* by Martin K. Starr (Prentice-Hall, 1978) is used. If you need more information about a particular method or topic you can refer to the Starr book or to any similar introductory text in P/OM. We have tried, however, to present the sampling of topics from P/OM in such a way that if you have a working understanding of the underlying concepts you can use this chapter to solve P/OM problems without having to refer to outside sources.

8.1 BREAK-EVEN ANALYSIS

In making decisions involving production and operations management, financial considerations are equally important to technical considerations. Break-even analysis, described in Section 6.6 in the chapter on Financial Applications, is so fundamental to financial decision making in P/OM that we present a second discussion here. Simply put, break-even occurs when present value of revenue equals present value of expenses, that is, profit equals zero.

Consider a simple situation in which a company is trying to decide whether to invest $5 million into automation equipment for a portion of its production line. The situation of the company is as follows:

Annual sales	$40.0 million
Current expenses	$25.4 million
Annual production volume	100,000 units

Of its current expenses, $5.4 million are fixed costs. Its current break-even quantity can be obtained from the formula:

$$BREAKEVEN\,VOLUME = \frac{FIXED\,COST}{UNIT\,PRICE - UNIT\,VARIABLE\,COST} \qquad (8-1)$$

This formula expresses the usual idea that the profit is zero when the markup (excess of price over variable cost) times the volume of sales is just sufficient to cover the fixed cost. As shown in Figure 8-1, before investment, the company actually breaks even at annual sales of 27,000 units.

```
MODEL EVEN  VERSION OF  08/31/82  08:29
10 COLUMNS 1-5
20 *
25*     ALL DOLLAR VALUES IN (000'S)
27*
30 *     BEFORE INVESTMENT
40 *
50 SALES=40000
60 EXPENSES=25400
70 ANNUAL PRODUCTION = 100
80 FIXED COST = 5400
90 *
100 VARIABLE COST = EXPENSES - FIXED COST
110 UNIT VARIABLE COST = VARIABLE COST/ANNUAL PRODUCTION
120 UNIT PRICE = SALES/ANNUAL PRODUCTION
130 PROFIT=SALES-EXPENSES
140 BREAKEVEN VOLUME = FIXED COST/(UNIT PRICE - UNIT VARIABLE COST)
150 *
160 *      AFTER INVESTMENT -- NO TAX CASE
170 *
180 DEPRECIATION=1000
190 VARIABLE COST SAVING = 3000
200 UNIT VARIABLE COST SAVING=VARIABLE COST SAVING/ANNUAL PRODUCTION
210 BREAK EVEN = (FIXED COST +DEPRECIATION)/(UNIT PRICE - '
211 UNIT VARIABLE COST + UNIT VARIABLE COST SAVING)
220 *
230 *    FINANCIAL MEASURES
240 *
250 INVESTMENT=5000,0
260 TOTAL SAVINGS=VARIABLE COST SAVING + DEPRECIATION
270 DISCOUNT RATE = .30
280 PRESENT VALUE=NPVC(TOTAL SAVINGS,DISCOUNT RATE,INVESTMENT)
290 RATE OF RETURN=IRR(TOTAL SAVINGS,INVESTMENT)
300 *
310 *      AFTER INVESTMENT -- 46 PERCENT TAX RATE CASE
320 *
330 TAX RATE =.46
340 NET SAVINGS=DEPRECIATION*TAX RATE+VARIABLE COST SAVING*'
341 (1-TAX RATE)
350 NET PRESENT VALUE=NPVC(NET SAVINGS,DISCOUNT RATE,0)
360 NET RATE OF RETURN=IRR(NET SAVINGS,INVESTMENT)
END OF MODEL
```

FIGURE 8-1.BREAK-EVEN ANALYSIS
(This Figure continued on the Next Page)

```
? solve

MODEL EVEN  VERSION OF  08/31/82  08:29 -- 5 COLUMNS 22 VARIABLES
ENTER SOLVE OPTIONS
? all
```

	1	2	3	4	5
ALL DOLLAR VALUES IN (000'S)					
BEFORE INVESTMENT					
SALES	40000	40000	40000	40000	40000
EXPENSES	25400	25400	25400	25400	25400
ANNUAL PRODUCTION	100	100	100	100	100
FIXED COST	5400	5400	5400	5400	5400
VARIABLE COST	20000	20000	20000	20000	20000
UNIT VARIABLE COST	200	200	200	200	200
UNIT PRICE	400	400	400	400	400
PROFIT	14600	14600	14600	14600	14600
BREAKEVEN VOLUME	27	27	27	27	27
AFTER INVESTMENT -- NO TAX CASE					
DEPRECIATION	1000	1000	1000	1000	1000
VARIABLE COST SAVING	3000	3000	3000	3000	3000
UNIT VARIABLE COST S	30	30	30	30	30
BREAK EVEN	27.83	27.83	27.83	27.83	27.83
FINANCIAL MEASURES					
INVESTMENT	5000	0	0	0	0
TOTAL SAVINGS	4000	4000	4000	4000	4000
DISCOUNT RATE	.3000	.3000	.3000	.3000	.3000
PRESENT VALUE	-1923	443.8	2264	3665	4742
RATE OF RETURN		.3798	.6074	.7054	.7515
AFTER INVESTMENT -- 46 PERCENT TAX RATE CASE					
TAX RATE	.4600	.4600	.4600	.4600	.4600
NET SAVINGS	2080	2080	2080	2080	2080
NET PRESENT VALUE	1600	2831	3778	4506	5066
NET RATE OF RETURN			.1195	.2401	.3069

FIGURE 8-1. BREAK-EVEN ANALYSIS
(Continued)

The $5 million investment would result in annual variable cost savings of $3 million at the current volume of 100,000 units. The company will depreciate the equipment on a straight line basis over 5 years (i.e., at $1 million/year). It insists on a 30% rate of return on its investments. Figure 8-1 also shows the analysis with the investment. First we compute the break-even volume with the investment, adding the depreciation to our fixed cost and reducing the variable cost by the variable cost saving. The results show that the break-even volume is increased slightly to 27830, still well below the annual production.

We next consider the investment of $5 million which is to be offset by the savings in variable cost and the depreciation. The measures of effectiveness are the net present value and the internal rate of return. The results show that financial break-even occurs during the second year (since present value becomes positive) and the rate of return on the investment is 75% for the five-year time horizon.

These results are quite favorable for the investment; however, they do not present the whole picture. To be more realistic, we must consider tax effects. The company's marginal tax rate is 46%. The savings from depreciation must therefore be multiplied by the tax rate since only the taxes are saved, while the variable cost savings must be multiplied by (1 - tax rate) since only the after-tax savings accrue to the company. With taxes included the project still passes the company's criteria, but just barely since the rate of return is 30.69 percent. The present value of the investment is approximately $66 thousand.

Note that Figure 8-1 also allows you to determine the payback period with discounting taken into account. Specifically, the present value exceeds the 5 million dollar investment during Year 5.

The sequence of steps followed in Figure 8-1 is by no means the only way to analyze the problem. Figure 8-2 shows the same problem organized in the way accountants think about the problem. In this form of the analysis, we first compute the current value of the operation (i.e., the profit on sales, Line 90). We then compute the value with the investment (labeled INVESTMENT VALUE) and, after a series of steps (read these over and make sure you understand lines 160 through 190) arrive at the net after taxes, which is used to compute the present value net after-tax of the stream of savings. Since this net present value is $5.066 million, if we subtract the required $5 million investment, we again find the $66 thousand value we obtained in Figure 8-1.

EXERCISE:Consider the following revenue stream associated with a new product:

Year After Release	1	2	3	4	5	6	7
Revenue (million $)	0.2	0.5	1.2	1.8	2.0	1.0	0.6

If your company requires a 15% rate of return on its investments, what is the maximum you should be willing to spend for design, tooling, introductory advertising, and similar initial investment expenses? This is a straightforward application of the IFPS NPVC function. The answer is that the maximum investment you would be willing to make is $4.02 million.

EXERCISE: Use IFPS to determine for what lease period you should be indifferent between buying an automobile for personal use at $10,000 or leasing it at $550 per month. Assume you can invest in a money fund that guarantees you 1% per month after taxes. Assume further that all other expenses will be the same in either case.

EXERCISE: Reformulate the model of Figure 8-1 so that break-even volume is not computed directly. Rather, use GOAL SEEKING to find the break-even volume. Note that you will have to formulate the problem in such a way that profit depends on the annual production.

```
MODEL EVEN2  VERSION OF  08/31/82  08:29
10COLUMNS 1-5
20*
30*BREAKEVEN ANALYSIS DONE IN ACCOUNTING STYLE
40*
50 SALES = 40000
60 FIXED COST =5400
70 INITIAL DEPRECIATION =0
80 VARIABLE COST = 20000
90 CURRENT VALUE = SALES -FIXED COST - VARIABLE COST
100*
110* WITH INVESTMENT
120*
130 INVESTMENT DEPRECIATION =1000
140 INVESTMENT VARIABLE COST = 17000
150 INVESTMENT VALUE = SALES -FIXED COST -INVESTMENT VARIABLE COST
160 VALUE DIFFERENCE = INVESTMENT VALUE - CURRENT VALUE
170 DIFFERENCE WITH DEPRECIATION = VALUE DIFFERENCE'
171 -(INVESTMENT DEPRECIATION - INITIAL DEPRECIATION)
180 TAX INCREASE = DIFFERENCE WITH DEPRECIATION *0.46
190 NET AFTER TAXES = VALUE DIFFERENCE -TAX INCREASE
200 PRESENT VALUE NET AFTER TAXES = NPVC(NET AFTER TAXES,0.30,0)
END OF MODEL
? solve
MODEL EVEN2  VERSION OF  08/31/82  08:29 -- 5 COLUMNS 13 VARIABLES
ENTER SOLVE OPTIONS
? all

                                      1       2       3       4       5


BREAKEVEN ANALYSIS DONE IN ACCOUNTING STYLE

SALES                             40000   40000   40000   40000   40000
FIXED COST                         5400    5400    5400    5400    5400
INITIAL DEPRECIATION                  0       0       0       0       0
VARIABLE COST                     20000   20000   20000   20000   20000
CURRENT VALUE                     14600   14600   14600   14600   14600

 WITH INVESTMENT

INVESTMENT DEPRECIATION            1000    1000    1000    1000    1000
INVESTMENT VARIABLE COST          17000   17000   17000   17000   17000
INVESTMENT VALUE                  17600   17600   17600   17600   17600
VALUE DIFFERENCE                   3000    3000    3000    3000    3000
DIFFERENCE WITH DEPRECIATION       2000    2000    2000    2000    2000
TAX INCREASE                        920     920     920     920     920
NET AFTER TAXES                    2080    2080    2080    2080    2080
PRESENT VALUE NET AFTER TAXES      1600    2831    3778    4506    5066
```

FIGURE 8-2. BREAK-EVEN ANALYSIS IN ACCOUNTING FORMAT

8.2 AGGREGATE SCHEDULING

In a job shop, planning is done at three levels: aggregate scheduling, shop loading, and sequencing. Aggregate scheduling involves determining the total resources (labor, raw materials, supplies, facilities) that have to be available for a given period (e.g., a quarter). Shop loading involves the assignment of actual work on hand to individual facilities. Sequencing determines the order in which work is to be done at each facility. Both shop loading and sequencing must be done much more often than aggregate scheduling because they have to take into account day-to-day changes that occur. These three levels of planning are interrelated. In this section, we shall be concerned with the first level, aggregate scheduling.

8.2.1 Production Forecasting

Aggregate scheduling involves predicting the demand for resources. Therefore, the aggregate scheduling process begins with forecasts of these demands. Usually, some of the information is on hand from orders already in process or booked. However, we can anticipate that new orders will come into the job shop, some of which will have to be started during the planning period. The short-range forecasting methods described in Section 7.7 are usually employed to make the needed forecasts. The following four exercises describe a simple operations management situation. You are asked to use the methods of moving averages, weighted moving averages, exponential smoothing, and regression respectively to obtain forecasts for this situation. You should write IFPS models for each method. Refer to Chapter 7 for the details of the methods and for sample IFPS models.

EXERCISE: The Parks Department assigns crews to different tasks. These task are completed in batches before another task in undertaken. For example, tree care last year required the following number of crew hours:

Month	Crew Hours	Month	Crew Hours	Month	Crew Hours
Jan	110	May	250	Sept	280
Feb	120	June	200	Oct	120
March	140	July	200	Nov	100
Apr	180	Aug	220	Dec	80

Use a moving average based on six- month history to "predict" the crew requirements for July of last year through January of this year. Determine the magnitude of the error in the "forecast" by comparing your prediction for July though December with the actual crew hours.

What if you used a three-month moving average? Are the results more accurate?

EXERCISE: If you examine the Parks Department data given in the previous exercise you can see that recent months requirements are closer to next month's than those several months ago. A weighted moving average might be more appropriate. Use a weighted six-month moving average on the Parks Department data with weights of 0.1, 0.1, 0.1, 0.2, 0.2, and 0.3. Again determine the magnitude of the error and compare with the error obtained with unweighted moving averages for six months and for three months.

EXERCISE: Use exponential smoothing (Section 7.7.1) on the Parks Department data.

Use WHAT IF statements to find the value of ALPHA that most closely predicts the values for July through December. Use this value of ALPHA as your forecast for January.

EXERCISE: Use POLYFIT(1) and POLYFIT(2) to forecast January. To check the validity of these methods, use POLYFIT(1) and POLYFIT(2) to forecast each month from August to December. Determine the error between the regression forecasts defined by the POLYFIT functions and the observed values. Are these errors acceptable? (Sections 3.2.3 and 7.7.1 discuss POLYFIT.)

8.2.2 Standard Units of Work

In aggregate scheduling, individual availabilities and requirements are put on common scales so that judgments can be made as to whether shortages or surpluses exist. These common scales are referred to as standard units of work. As a simple example, consider a plant that has four machines that produce at different rates and which must produce five jobs during the next week. The machine data are shown in Table 8-1. We follow the usual practice of picking one machine as the standard (e.g., Machine 2) and showing the production of other machines as an index that indicates relative output. In this way, although Machine 1 has 36 hours available it is eqivalent to only 18 hours of the standard machine (Machine 2 with index 1.0) because it produces half as much per unit time.

TABLE 8-1

STANDARD MACHINE HOURS

MACHINE	1	2	3	4	TOTAL
HRS AVAILABLE	36	54	80	33.3	
PRODUCTION INDEX	0.5	1.0	0.8	0.6	
STD.MACH. HRS	18	54	64	20	156

EXERCISE: Write an IFPS program to generate the standard machine hours given in Table 8-1.

Next consider the demand. For each job, we know the number of units that have to be produced and the number of units produced per standard machine hour. The data are shown in Table 8-2.

TABLE 8-2

DEMAND DATA

JOB	A	B	C	D	E
UNITS DEMAND	300	210	240	1800	400
UNITS PER STD. MACH. HR.	6	7	6	30	25

Figure 8-3 shows the IFPS program that converts the data in Table 8-2 to standard machine hours required. The calculations involve dividing the demand by the units produced per standard machine hour to obtain standard machine hours needed for each job and then adding the resulting demands for machine time. In this particular example, the demand of 196 standard machine hours exceeds the supply of 156 and you, as manager, must decide what to do. Do you work overtime? Subcontract? Delay a job (e.g. job C) to the following week? Although the calculations in Figure 8-3 are very simple, they must be done if you are to become aware of problems before they happen. Preparing a simple model such as Figure 8-3 may seem like overkill; however, if you have it and, more important, use it regularly you will find your job easier.

```
MODEL STDHRS   VERSION OF   08/31/82   08:28
10 COLUMNS A,B,C,D,E
20 *
30* INPUT DATA FOR JOBS A THROUGH E
40*
50 UNITS DEMAND = 300,210,240,1800,400
60 UNITS PER STD MACH HR =6,7,6,30,25
70*
80*CALCULATIONS
90*
100 STD MACH HRS PER JOB = UNITS DEMAND/UNITS PER STD MACH HR
110 TOTAL MACHINE TIME =STD MACH HRS PER JOB + PREVIOUS
120*
130*STD MACH HRS   = STANDARD MACHINE HOURS
END OF MODEL
? solve
MODEL STDHRS   VERSION OF   08/31/82   08:28 -- 5 COLUMNS 4 VARIABLES
ENTER SOLVE OPTIONS
? all
                              A        B        C        D        E

 INPUT DATA FOR JOBS A THROUGH E

UNITS DEMAND                300      210      240     1800      400
UNITS PER STD MACH HRS        6        7        6       30       25

CALCULATIONS

STD MACH HRS PER JOB         50       30       40       60       16
TOTAL MACHINE TIME           50       80      120      180      196

STD MACH HRS   = STANDARD MACHINE HOURS
```

FIGURE 8-3. MODEL FOR DETERMINING STANDARD MACHINE HOURS

8.2.3 Trading Off Overtime, Work Force, and Inventory

Demand is almost never constant over time. It fluctuates week to week. You have several policy options available to you, including:

- Policy 1: trying to match work force to demand.

- **Policy 2**: keeping a constant work force that produces exactly the amount required over the time horizon.
- **Policy 3**: keeping a constant work force larger than in Policy 2 and thereby producing for inventory.

These three policies are illustrated in Figure 8-4. The planning period is six weeks. The demand fluctuates between 340 and 420 units. Each worker produces 10 units per week. In Policy 1, exactly as many workers are hired as needed and, although there is no inventory, workers have to be hired or fired each week. There are usually costs associated with both hiring and firing (e.g., recruiting, unemployment insurance). In Policy 2 (WHAT IF CASE 1), the work force is kept constant at 38 and there is no inventory left over at the end of the six weeks and there are no hire or fire costs. However, the policy results in backlogs four weeks out of six and, as we discuss in Section 8.3, such inventory shortages have costs associated with them. Policy 3, shown as WHAT IF CASE 2 in Figure 8-4, tries to overcome these shortages by increasing the work force to 39. Here we wind up with both the cost of an additional worker and the cost of holding inventory.

EXERCISE: Suppose the demand in Figure 8-4 is incurred in reverse order, that is, 340, 420, 350, 390, 360, 420. Which of the three policies is preferred? Run the calculations using the IFPS model and justify your answer.

Thus far, we have only considered trading off work force size and inventory. You can usually stretch your work force by overtime, which adds another trade-off dimension to the problem. A standard model that allows you to consider such tradeoffs was developed by Holt, Modigliani, Muth, and Simon and is known as the HMMS quadratic cost model. (Incidentally, Simon is Prof. Herbert A. Simon who later won the Nobel Prize in Economics).

8.2.4 The HMMS Model

The HMMS model involves adding up six components of cost. These components and their definitions are given in Table 8-3, where C1 through C9 represent various constants in the model.

TABLE 8-3

COST COMPONENTS OF THE HMMS MODEL

PAYROLL	C1 * WORKFORCE
HIRING COST	C2 * (CHANGE IN WORK FORCE)^2
OVERTIME1	C3 * (PRODUCTION -C4*WORKFORCE) ^{2}
OVERTIME2	C5 * PRODUCTION
OVERTIME3	–C6*WORKFORCE
INVENTORY	C7*(TOTAL INVENTORY–C8–C9*DEMAND) ^{2}

```
MODEL TRADEOFF  VERSION OF  08/31/82  08:28
10 COLUMNS 1-6
20 DEMAND=420,360,390,350,420,340
30 PRODUCTION=DEMAND
40 WORK FORCE=PRODUCTION/10
50 CHANGE IN WORK FORCE=0,WORK FORCE - PREVIOUS WORK FORCE
60 CURRENT INVENTORY=PRODUCTION-DEMAND
70 TOTAL INVENTORY=CURRENT INVENTORY,PREVIOUS TOTAL INVENTORY'
71 +CURRENT INVENTORY
END OF MODEL
? solve
MODEL TRADEOFF  VERSION OF  08/31/82  08:28 -- 6 COLUMNS 6 VARIABLES
ENTER SOLVE OPTIONS
? all
```

	1	2	3	4	5	6
DEMAND	420	360	390	350	420	340
PRODUCTION	420	360	390	350	420	340
WORK FORCE	42	36	39	35	42	34
CHANGE IN WORK FORCE	0	-6	3	-4	7	-8
CURRENT INVENTORY	0	0	0	0	0	0
TOTAL INVENTORY	0	0	0	0	0	0

```
ENTER SOLVE OPTIONS
?what if
WHAT IF CASE 1
ENTER STATEMENTS
? production = 380
? solve
ENTER SOLVE OPTIONS
? all

***** WHAT IF CASE 1 *****
1 WHAT IF STATEMENT PROCESSED
```

	1	2	3	4	5	6
DEMAND	420	360	390	350	420	340
PRODUCTION	380	380	380	380	380	380
WORK FORCE	38	38	38	38	38	38
CHANGE IN WORK FORCE	0	0	0	0	0	0
CURRENT INVENTORY	-40	20	-10	30	-40	40
TOTAL INVENTORY	-40	-20	-30	0	-40	0

FIGURE 8-4. TRADE-OFFS AMONG OVERTIME, WORK-FORCE AND INVENTORY IN AGGREGATE SCHEDULING

(This Figure is Continued On the Next Page)

```
ENTER SOLVE OPTIONS
? what if
WHAT IF CASE 2
ENTER STATEMENTS
? production =390
? solve
ENTER SOLVE OPTIONS
?all

***** WHAT IF CASE 2 *****
1 WHAT IF STATEMENT PROCESSED
```

	1	2	3	4	5	6
DEMAND	420	360	390	350	420	340
PRODUCTION	390	390	390	390	390	390
WORK FORCE	39	39	39	39	39	39
CHANGE IN WORK FORCE	0	0	0	0	0	0
CURRENT INVENTORY	-30	30	0	40	-30	50
TOTAL INVENTORY	-30	0	0	40	10	60

FIGURE 8-4. TRADE-OFFS AMONG OVERTIME, WORK-FORCE AND INVENTORY IN AGGREGATE SCHEDULING (Continued)

If you examine Table 8-3, you will see that each of the quantities (but not the constants) on the right was defined in the model shown in Figure 8-4. Therefore, we can expand Figure 8-3 to create Figure 8-5 which implements HMMS as an IFPS model. The components of the HMMS cost model are shown in Lines 90 through 140. Values are assigned to the constants in lines 170 through 250. These constants represent unit costs associated with payroll, hiring and firing, overtime, and inventory. The total costs for each week and the cumulative costs are shown in Lines 270 and 280.

The demand and conditions in Figure 8-5 are identical to those in Figure 8-4, with cost coefficient values added.

EXERCISE: Use WHAT IF statements to modify Figure 8-5 for the following conditions:

1. A constant work force of 39 with no overtime allowed.

2. A constant work force of 38 but 40 hours allowed each week for the first 3 weeks.

3. A policy of your own devising that has as small a total cost as you can find.

```
MODEL HMMS  VERSION OF  08/31/82  08:28
10 COLUMNS 1-6
20 DEMAND = 420,360,390,350,420,340
30 PRODUCTION = 380
40 WORK FORCE=PRODUCTION/10
50 CHANGE IN WORK FORCE=0,WORK FORCE - PREVIOUS WORK FORCE
60 CURRENT INVENTORY=PRODUCTION-DEMAND
70 TOTAL INVENTORY=CURRENT INVENTORY,PREVIOUS TOTAL INVENTORY +'
71 CURRENT INVENTORY
80 *
90 PAYROLL=C1*WORKFORCE
100 HIRING COST=C2*CHANGE IN WORK FORCE*CHANGE IN WORK FORCE
110 OVERTIME1=C3*(PRODUCTION-C4*WORKFORCE)*(PRODUCTION'
111 -C4*WORK  FORCE)
120 OVERTIME2=C5*PRODUCTION
130 OVERTIME3=(-C6*WORK FORCE)
140 INVENTORY=C7*(TOTAL INVENTORY-C8-C9*DEMAND)*(TOTAL INVENTORY'-
141 C8-C9*DEMAND)
160 *
170 C1=100
180 C2=3
190 C3=0.2
200 C4=10
210 C5=2
220 C6=20
230 C7=0.1
240 C8=60
250 C9=.2
260 *
270 COST=SUM(L90,L140)
280 TOTAL COST = PREVIOUS TOTAL COST + COST
END OF MODEL
```

FIGURE 8-5. HMMS MODEL
(This Figure Is Continued on the Next Page)

```
? solve
MODEL HMMS  VERSION OF  08/31/82  08:28 -- 6 COLUMNS 23 VARIABLES
ENTER SOLVE OPTIONS
? all
```

	1	2	3	4	5	6
DEMAND	420	360	390	350	420	340
PRODUCTION	380	380	380	380	380	380
WORK FORCE	38	38	38	38	38	38
CHANGE IN WORK FORCE	0	0	0	0	0	0
CURRENT INVENTORY	-40	20	-10	30	-40	40
TOTAL INVENTORY	-40	-20	-30	0	-40	0
PAYROLL	3800	3800	3800	3800	3800	3800
HIRING COST	0	0	0	0	0	0
OVERTIME1	0	0	0	0	0	0
OVERTIME2	760	760	760	760	760	760
OVERTIME3	-760	-760	-760	-760	-760	-760
INVENTORY	3386	2310	2822	1690	3386	1638
C1	100	100	100	100	100	100
C2	3	3	3	3	3	3
C3	.2000	.2000	.2000	.2000	.2000	.2000
C4	10	10	10	10	10	10
C5	2	2	2	2	2	2
C6	20	20	20	20	20	20
C7	.1000	.1000	.1000	.1000	.1000	.1000
C8	60	60	60	60	60	60
C9	.2000	.2000	.2000	.2000	.2000	.2000
COST	7186	6110	6622	5490	7186	5438
TOTAL COST	7186	13296	19918	25408	32594	38032

FIGURE 8-5. HMMS MODEL
(continued)

8.3 INVENTORY

Inventory refers to keeping items needed in the production process or for sale in stock. A very simple case is shown in the following drawing:

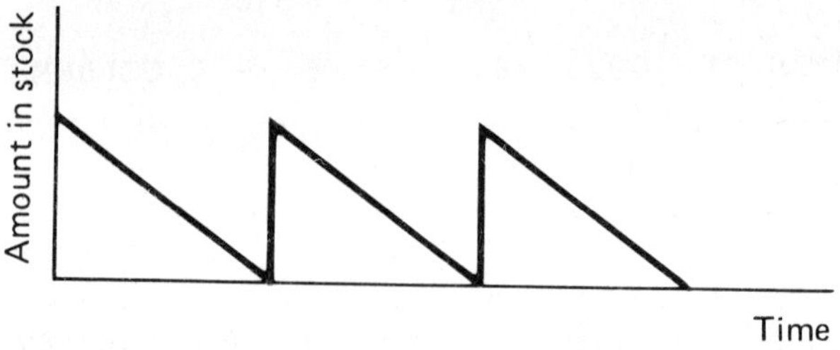

Here an order is placed at time 0, and received instantaneously. Demand results in withdrawal at a constant rate. At time T, the initial supply is exhausted and another order is placed. Restocking is again instantaneous. This process can be assumed to repeat itself. The decision problem you have is how many to order, that is, what is the optimum order quantity? Knowing the demand, the order quantity also determines the time between reorders.

This seemingly simple problem is an economic one because there are costs associated with both the ordering and the holding of inventory. In fact, if we consider more general inventory situations, we have the following economic structure:

1. Carrying cost: Cost of storing, financing, guarding inventory ($/item-year)

2. Reorder cost: Fixed cost of placing an order ($/order)

3. Shortage cost: Cost of not meeting demand due to stockout ($/unit-year)

4. Price break: Discounts due to quantity purchases.

More complex models allow for producing (or delivery of) goods at the same time that they are used up, salvage value for items not sold, lead time to account for the time between placing an order and receiving it, uncertain demand patterns, etc. Many problems that do not at first appear to be inventory models really are. One example is the amount of cash kept in the till by a supermarket or a bank. Here the carrying cost is lost interest, order cost is armored car delivery, and stockout costs are lost sales. Another example is flight attendants for airlines. Since these are hired in groups there will often be a surplus when a new class graduates. Thus, carrying costs are wages and fringes, order costs are training costs for a class, and shortage cost are the costs of cancelled flights if flight attendants are not available. In this section we will consider several simple inventory models to demonstrate how IFPS can be used to help in understanding the inventory process and in computing the optimal policy based on an inventory model. We will discuss the following situations:

- No shortages allowed, instant replenishment, constant withdrawal.

- No shortages allowed, constant delivery, constant withdrawal.

- The first case above with quantity discounts.

- Shortages and lead time

- Uncertain demand patterns.

8.3.1 Simple EOQ Model

This case, described by the drawing above, assumes instant delivery, no shortages allowed, and a constant withdrawal rate. The total inventory cost is the sum of the carrying cost and the order cost. The components that go into the total cost are:

1. The average number of units carried in stock, which is equal to half the number of units purchased per order, that is, the order quantity, x.

2. The average dollar inventory, which is the unit price times the average number of units carried in stock, i.e., cx/2.

3. The annual carrying cost per unit, CC, which is expressed as a percentage of the price. Multiplying this quantity by the average inventory gives the carrying cost.

4. The number of orders placed per year, which is obtained by dividing the annual demand, z, by the order quantity.

5. The cost per order placed, CR. Multiplying the cost per order placed by the number of orders yields the order cost.

In equation terms, the total cost is given by:

$$TC = 0.5 * c*x*CC + CR*z/x \tag{8-2}$$

All quantities on the right side of equation (8-2) are known except the order quantity, x. It can be shown that the optimal size of the order quantity is given by:

$$x = 2*z*CR/c*CC \tag{8-3}$$

It turns out that for this optimal value of x, (called the Economic Order Quantity, or EOQ), the order cost and the carrying cost are equal. These results are implemented in the model shown in the top half of Figure 8-6 (lines 20 through 70.) The numerical results shown are based on the folloing input assumptions: an item (e.g., a bolt) costs six cents, has a 15% carrying cost per unit, and an annual demand of 200,000 units.

EXERCISE: Check that the order quantity computed in Line 40 in Figure 8-6 is optimal. Expand the model shown in Lines 40 through 90 so that it uses 11 columns that specify order quantities spaced at intervals of 500 starting at 27,500. You should find that the total costs are larger, but only slightly, even for order quantities well away from the optimum.

```
MODEL INVENTORY  VERSION OF  08/31/82  08:28
10 COLUMNS 1
20 * SIMPLE EOQ MODEL
30*
40 ORDER QUANTITY = XPOWERY((2*ANNUAL DEMAND*COST PER ORDER)/'
41 (PRICE *CARRYING COST PER UNIT),0.5)
50 CARRYING COST=0.5*PRICE * ORDER QUANTITY*CARRYING COST PER UNIT
60 ORDER COST =(ANNUAL DEMAND /ORDER QUANTITY)*COST PER ORDER
70 TOTAL COST = CARRYING COST + ORDER COST
80*
90* CONTINUOUS DELIVERY (CD)
100 *
110 CD FACTOR =(DAILY PRODUCTION - DAILY DEMAND)/DAILY PRODUCTION
120 CD ORDER QUANTITY = XPOWERY((2*ANNUAL DEMAND*COST PER SETUP)'
121 /(PRICE * CARRYING COST PER UNIT * CD FACTOR),0.5)
130 CD CARRYING COST = 0.5* PRICE*CD ORDER QUANTITY*CD FACTOR'
131 *CARRYING COST PER UNIT
140 CD ORDER COST =(ANNUAL DEMAND/CD ORDER QUANTITY)*COST PER SETUP
150 TOTAL CD COST = CD CARRYING COST + CD ORDER COST
160*
170 LENGTH OF PRODUCTION RUN IN DAYS = CD ORDER QUANTITY/'
171 DAILY PRODUCTION
180 TIME BETWEEN PRODUCTION RUNS = CD ORDER QUANTITY*CD FACTOR'
181 /DAILY DEMAND
185 TOTAL CYCLE TIME = L170 +L180
190 AVERAGE CD INVENTORY =0.5*CD ORDER QUANTITY *CD FACTOR
200 MAXIMUM CD INENTORY = 2*AVERAGE CD INVENTORY
300 *
310 *INPUT DATA
320*
330 PRICE = 0.06
340 CARRYING COST PER UNIT =.15
350 COST PER ORDER = 20.00
360 ANNUAL DEMAND =200000
370 DAILY PRODUCTION = 1800
380 DAILY DEMAND = ANNUAL DEMAND/250
390 COST PER SETUP =20.00
END OF MODEL
```

FIGURE 8-6. SIMPLE EOQ AND CONTINUOUS DELIVERY INVENTORY MODELS
(This Figure is Continued on the Next Page)

```
? solve
MODEL INVENTORY  VERSION OF  08/31/82  08:28--1 COLUMNS 21 VARIABLES
ENTER SOLVE OPTIONS
? all
                                     1

 SIMPLE EOQ MODEL

ORDER QUANTITY                   29814
CARRYING COST                    134.2
ORDER COST                       134.2
TOTAL COST                       268.3

 CONTINUOUS DELIVERY (CD)

CD FACTOR                        .5556
CD ORDER QUANTITY                40000
CD CARRYING COST                   100
CD ORDER COST                      100
TOTAL CD COST                      200

LENGTH OF PRODUCTION RUN         22.22
TIME BETWEEN PRODUCTION          27.78
TOTAL CYCLE TIME                    50
AVERAGE CD INVENTORY             11111
MAXIMUM CD INENTORY              22222

INPUT DATA

PRICE                            .0600
CARRYING COST PER UNIT           .1500
COST PER ORDER                      20
ANNUAL DEMAND                   200000
DAILY PRODUCTION                  1800
DAILY DEMAND                       800
COST PER SETUP                      20
```

FIGURE 8-6. SIMPLE EOQ AND CONTINUOUS DELIVERY INVENTORY MODELS
(Continued)

8.3.2 Economic Lot Size Model - Continuous Delivery

As a second case, consider a situation which is identical to the previous one except that you can produce the item in your own shop. Assume that you can produce at a constant rate, which is greater than the demand for the product. Thus, as shown below, an inventory builds up and you alternate between producing and not producing. The decision you now have to make is how big the production run should be.

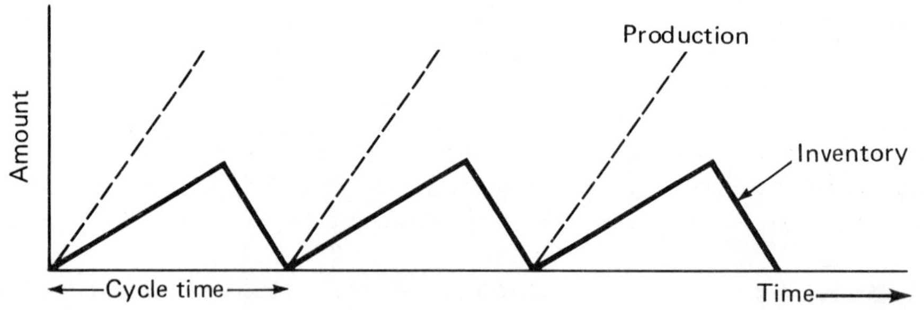

In evaluating this situation,the results are have the same form as the EOQ model except for a factor, which we have called the "CD Factor" of Figure 8-6 (line 110), which describes the excess of daily production over daily demand:

CD FACTOR = (PRODUCTION –DEMAND)/PRODUCTION (8-4)

A second difference is that rather than incurring a cost per order placed, we incur a setup cost, CS, every time we restart production. In this case, the optimal order quantity is given by:

x = (2*z*CS/c*CR) * CD FACTOR (8-5)

As shown in Figure 8-6, as a result of production, the order quantity increases (from 29814 to 40000) and the inventory cost decreases (from 134.2 to 100) compared to the EOQ case. This results from the fact that you use up some of the items as they are produced. Hence, the average inventory and the maximum inventory are less than for EOQ. Figure 8-6 also shows the length of the production run in days, the time between production runs and the cycle time, which is the time from the start of one production cycle to the next. The data used to illustrate continuous delivery are based on the same situation as for the EOQ model. It is assumed that there is a cost of $20 per setup, that there is daily production of 1800 units, and 250 working days per year.

8.3.3 Quantity Discounts

The EOQ model is based on the assumption of a fixed price. If a supplier offers a discount when large quantities are ordered, then it is possible to trade off additional inventory cost (resulting from ordering a non-optimal quantity) for the cost saving. Thus, the decision to be made is whether to order the EOQ or the minimum quantity for which the price break is obtained. The steps followed are:

1. Compute the economic order quantity and total inventory cost for the undiscounted price as in Section 8.3.1 above.

2. Compute the economic order quantity with the discounted price. (Note that this quantity will typically be larger than without the discount. Can you see

why from Equation 8-2?). If this quantity is less than the minimum quantity required for the discount, then recognize that you will have to order the minimum.

3. Compute the total inventory cost for the discounted quantity.

4. Compare the total costs: for the two cases and pick the lower one. The total cost is defined by Equation (8-6).

$$\text{Total Cost} = \text{Inventory Cost} + \text{Cost of Goods} \qquad (8\text{-}6)$$

This procedure is illustrated in Figure 8-7. You will see the model uses the IF...THEN...ELSE construct to make choices as to which quantity is best with the discount and which quantity to select based on total cost.

EXERCISE: In Figure 8-7, a discount is offered for quantities in excess of 50,000. Suppose the supplier offers to sell at 4 cents if you order at least 100,000 and at 3.7 cents if you order 200,000. Modify the model in Figure 8-7 and determine the optimal inventory policy.

8.3.4 Order Point Systems

In this section we consider a slightly more complex model. We will relax three of the assumptions made previously. Specifically,

- Delivery need not be instantaneous. There is a known lead time between placing and receiving an order.
- Demand need not be uniform but can vary in a known manner.
- Shortages can occur but there is a cost associated with them.

In this more complex situation, the optimization of inventory leads to a reorder point policy. In this policy, whenever the inventory level goes to or below a specified level (the reorder point, s), an order is placed. The order may either be fixed in size or may be designed to bring inventory up to a desired level, S.

Figure 8-8 illustrates the forecast level of inventory and the costs incurred month by month over a 12-month period. Here we model the following relations:

1. A month-by-month demand forecast is supplied as input.

2. The inventory at the beginning of a month is equal to the inventory at the end of the previous month plus the number of units received from an order placed two periods ago. (i.e., we assume a two-month lead time and delivery at the beginning of the month).

3. The number of units sold is equal to the smaller of the demand or the beginning inventory. Costs are associated with shortages if they occur.

4. If the ending inventory is less than or equal to the reorder point, an order of fixed size is placed.

```
MODEL DISCOUNT  VERSION OF  08/31/82  08:27
10 COLUMNS 1
20 * SIMPLE EOQ MODEL
30 *
40 ORDER QUANTITY = XPOWERY((2*ANNUAL DEMAND*COST PER ORDER)/(PRICE'
41 *CARRYING COST PER UNIT),0.5)
50 CARRYING COST=0.5 *  PRICE*ORDER QUANTITY*CARRYING COST PER UNIT
60 ORDER COST =(ANNUAL DEMAND /ORDER QUANTITY)*COST PER ORDER
70 TOTAL INVENTORY COST = CARRYING COST + ORDER COST
80*
90* EOQ WITH DISCOUNT
100*
110 DISCOUNT EOQ = XPOWERY((2*ANNUAL DEMAND*COST PER ORDER)/'
111 (DISCOUNT PRICE*CARRYING COST PER UNIT),0.5)
120 DISCOUNT ORDER QUANTITY = IF DISCOUNT EOQ .GT.'
121 DISCOUNT MINIMUM QUANTITY THEN DISCOUNT EOQ'
122 ELSE DISCOUNT MINIMUM QUANTITY
130 DISCOUNT CARRYING COST=0.5*DISCOUNT PRICE*'
131 DISCOUNT ORDER QUANTITY*CARRYING COST PER UNIT
140 DISCOUNT ORDER COST=(ANNUAL DEMAND/DISCOUNT ORDER QUANTITY)*'
141 COST PER ORDER
150 DISCOUNT TOTAL INVENTORY COST=DISCOUNT CARRYING COST+DISCOUNT'
151 ORDER COST
160*
170* OPTIMAL POLICY
175*
180 EOQ TOTAL COST =TOTAL INVENTORY COST + ORDER QUANTITY*PRICE
185 DISCOUNT TOTAL COST=DISCOUNT TOTAL INVENTORY COST+'
186 DISCOUNT ORDER QUANTITY'
186* DISCOUNT PRICE
190 OPTIMAL ORDER QUANTITY = IF DISCOUNT TOTAL COST  .LT.'
191 EOQ TOTAL COST' THEN DISCOUNT ORDER QUANTITY ELSE ORDER QUANTITY
200 OPTIMAL TOTAL COST = IF DISCOUNT TOTAL COST .LT.'
201 EOQ TOTAL COST THEN DISCOUNT TOTAL COST ELSE EOQ TOTAL COST
300 *
310 *INPUT DATA
320*
330 PRICE = 0.06
340 CARRYING COST PER UNIT =.15
350 COST PER ORDER = 20.00
360 ANNUAL DEMAND =200000
370 DISCOUNT PRICE =.05
380 DISCOUNT  MINIMUM QUANTITY =50000
390 COST PER SETUP =20.00
END OF MODEL
```

FIGURE 8-7. OPTIMAL INVENTORY WITH QUANTITYT DISCOUNTS
(This Figure Continued on the Next Page)

```
? solve
MODEL DISCOUNT   VERSION OF   08/31/82   08:27 -- 1 COLUMNS 20
VARIABLES
ENTER SOLVE OPTIONS
? all

                                          1

 SIMPLE EOQ MODEL

ORDER QUANTITY                        29814
CARRYING COST                         134.2
ORDER COST                            134.2
TOTAL INVENTORY COST                  268.3

 EOQ WITH DISCOUNT

DISCOUNT EOQ                          32660
DISCOUNT ORDER QUANTITY               50000
DISCOUNT CARRYING COST                187.5
DISCOUNT ORDER COST                      80
DISCOUNT TOTAL INVENTORY              267.5

 OPTIMAL POLICY

EOQ TOTAL COST                         2057
DISCOUNT TOTAL COST                    2768
OPTIMAL ORDER QUANTITY                29814
OPTIMAL TOTAL COST                     2057

INPUT DATA

PRICE                                 .0600
CARRYING COST PER UNIT                .1500
COST PER ORDER                           20
ANNUAL DEMAND                        200000
DISCOUNT PRICE                        .0500
DISCOUNT  MINIMUM QUANTITY            50000
COST PER SETUP                           20
```

FIGURE 8-7.OPTIMAL INVENTORY WITH QUANTITY DISCOUNT
(Continued)

```
MODEL REORDERPT  VERSION OF  08/31/82  08:27
5 COLUMNS 1-24
10*
15*INVENTORY LEVELS
20*
30 BEGINNING INVENTORY =ORDER SIZE,PREVIOUS ENDING INVENTORY +'
31 PREVIOUS 2 UNITS ORDERED
60 UNITS SOLD =IF DEMAND .LE. BEGINNING INVENTORY THEN DEMAND'
61 ELSE BEGINNING INVENTORY
70 ENDING INVENTORY =BEGINNING INVENTORY - UNITS SOLD
80 LOST SALES =MAXIMUM (DEMAND-BEGINNING INVENTORY,0)
90 UNITS ORDERED=IF ENDING INVENTORY + PREVIOUS UNITS ORDERED'
91 .LT.REORDER POINT THEN ORDER SIZE ELSE 0
100 AVERAGE UNITS ON HAND=(BEGINNING INVENTORY+ENDING INVENTORY)/2
105*
110*COMPUTATION OF INVENTORY COST
120*
130CARRYING COST =CARRYING COST RATE*AVERAGE UNITS ON HAND*'
131 PURCHASE PRICE
140 ORDER COST=IF UNITS ORDERED .GT.0 THEN COST PER ORDER ELSE 0
150 COST OF LOST SALES=LOST SALES*LOST SALE PENALTY
160 INVENTORY COST =CARRYING COST + ORDER COST +COST OF LOST SALES
170*
180*COMPUTATION OF TOTAL COSTS
190*
200 PURCHASING COST =UNITS ORDERED*PURCHASE PRICE
210 TOTAL COST =INVENTORY COST + PURCHASING COST
215*
220 AVERAGE INVENTORY COST='
221 MEAN(MATRIX(INVENTORY COST,1),INVENTORY COST)
230AVERAGE TOTAL COST = MEAN(MATRIX(TOTAL COST,1),TOTAL COST)
240*
250*INPUT DATA
260*
265 DEMAND=27
270 PURCHASE PRICE =20
280 COST PER ORDER=500
290 CARRYING COST RATE = .20/TIME PERIODS PER YEAR
300 LOST SALE PENALTY = 15
310 TIME PERIODS PER YEAR = 12
320*
330* DECISION VARIABLES
340*
350 ORDER SIZE = 100
360 REORDER POINT = 30
END OF MODEL
```

a. Model

Figure 8-8. REORDER POINT SYSTEM
(This Figure Continued on the Next Page)

```
? plot
MODEL REORDERPT VERSION OF  08/31/82  08:27--24 COLUMNS 22 VARIABLES
ENTER PLOT OPTIONS
? grid 36,64,8
? plot reorder point,beginning inventory


100 2       2       2       2       2       2


 90


 80

      2       2       2       2       2       2
 70


 60


 50
        2       2       2       2       2       2

 40


 30 1 1 1 1 1 1 1 1 1 1 1 1 1 1 1 1 1 1 1 1 1 1 1 1


 20       2       2       2       2       2       2

    1   3   5   7   9   11  13  15  17  19  21  23

    1 - REORDER POINT
    2 - BEGINNING INVENTORY
```

b. Plot of Reorder Point and Beginning Inventory

FIGURE 8-8. REORDER POINT SYSTEM
(This Figure Continued on the Next Page)

```
? solve
ENTER SOLVE OPTIONS
?columns 1-9,24
?all
```

	1	2	3	4	5	6	7	8	9	24
INVENTORY LEVELS										
BEGINNING INVENTOR	100	73	46	19	100	73	46	19	100	19
UNITS SOLD	27	27	27	19	27	27	27	19	27	19
ENDING INVENTORY	73	46	19	0	73	46	19	0	73	0
LOST SALES	0	0	0	8	0	0	0	8	0	8
UNITS ORDERED	0	0	100	0	0	0	100	0	0	0
AVERAGE UNITS ON H	86.5	59.5	32.5	9.50	86.5	59.5	32.5	9.50	86.5	9.50
COMPUTATION OF INVENTORY COST										
CARRYING COST	28.8	19.8	10.8	3.17	28.8	19.8	10.8	3.17	28.8	3.17
ORDER COST	0	0	500	0	0	0	500	0	0	0
COST OF LOST SALES	0	0	0	120	0	0	0	120	0	120
INVENTORY COST	28.8	19.8	511	123	28.8	19.8	511	123	28.8	123
COMPUTATION OF TOTAL COSTS										
PURCHASING COST	0	0	2000	0	0	0	2000	0	0	0
TOTAL COST	28.8	19.8	2511	123	28.8	19.8	2511	123	28.8	123
AVERAGE INVENTORY	28.8	24.3	187	171	142	122	177	171	155	171
AVERAGE TOTAL COST	28.8	24.3	853	671	542	455	749	671	599	671
INPUT DATA										
DEMAND	27	27	27	27	27	27	27	27	27	27
PURCHASE PRICE	20	20	20	20	20	20	20	20	20	20
COST PER ORDER	500	500	500	500	500	500	500	500	500	500
CARRYING COST RATE	.017	.017	.017	.017	.017	.017	.017	.017	.017	.017
LOST SALE PENALTY	15	15	15	15	15	15	15	15	15	15
TIME PERIODS PER Y	12	12	12	12	12	12	12	12	12	12
DECISION VARIABLES										
ORDER SIZE	100	100	100	100	100	100	100	100	100	100
REORDER POINT	30	30	30	30	30	30	30	30	30	30

c. Results for Periods 1 Through 9 and 24

Figure 8-8. REORDER POINT SYSTEM
(This Figure Continued on the Next Page)

```
ENTER SOLVE OPTIONS
? plot inventory cost, average inventory cost, average total cost

        3

800

                3
                        3
700                             3       3       3
          3       3       3       3       3       3
                                            3
                            3       3
600                 3                 3       3
                              3
            3         3

500     1       1       1       1       1       1

              3

400



300



200
        2 2     2 2     2 2     2 2     2 2 2   2 2
            2       2 2     2 2     2 2       2
          1   2   1       1       1       1       1
100


    * *     1 1     1 1     1 1     1 1     1 1
  0 +---+---+---+---+---+---+---+---+---+---+---+---+--

    1   3   5   7   9  11  13  15  17  19  21  23

    1 - INVENTORY COST
    2 - AVERAGE INVENTORY COST
    3 - AVERAGE TOTAL COST
```

d. Plot of Inventory Cost for Each Period, Averrage Inventory Cost, Average Total Cost

FIGURE 8-8. REORDER POINT SYSTEM
(Continued)

The model in Figure 8-8 shows the inventory, sales, and lost sales. It also computes the inventory costs by the same methods as Figures 8-6 and 8-7. The inventory costs are added to the purchase costs to obtain total cost. The decision variables are the size of the order to be placed and the reorder point.

In addition to showing the model and the solution, we show two plots; one shows the monthly inventory level and the reorder point while the other shows the associated costs. These plots cover a 24-month time period.

EXERCISE: Modify Figure 8-8 so that the amount ordered will just bring the starting inventory to 250 when the order arrives.

EXERCISE: Investigate the effects of different reorder points. Assume that you can place orders of either 200 or 400 and that there is a discount of 1.50 per unit if you place the larger order. Find the minimum cost combination of order quantity and reorder point (to the nearest 10, i.e., 40,50,60, etc.).

8.3.5 Simulating Inventory Requirements

The model shown in Figure 8-8 is based on deterministic demand. As we have seen from Chapter V on simulation and the simulation examples in Section 6.11, it is a relatively simple matter to introduce uncertainty into models. Figure 8-9 is an example for inventory systems. Here a WHAT IF statement is used to introduce uncertainty in demand (i.e., demand can be anywere from 23 to 30) into Figure 8-8 and the effect of this uncertainty on average inventory cost and average total cost is shown.

In many inventory analyses, there are a number of uncertainties about the future values of various assumed data including demand, cost of lost sales, price to be paid when purchasing the inventory item, and the actual lost sale penalty. If we can estimate probability distributions for these quantities, MONTE CARLO analysis can be performed to determine the implications of these uncertainties. In addition, as was pointed out in Chapter V, you can also create scenarios for most likely, best, and worst cases.

EXERCISE: Suppose that in addition to being uncertain about demand, you expect the purchase price to inflate at between 9 and 18% per year (i.e. between 0.75 and 1.5% per month) with the most likely value being 15% per year and the uncertainty triangularly distributed. Furthermore, ordering cost is expected to increase between $5 and $10 a month, uniformly. Run a MONTE CARLO simulation that takes all of these uncertainties into account. Determine the distribution of the present worth at the end of two years. Include a plot of the distribution of present worth in your output.

EXERCISE: Determine the most likely, best, and worst case results for the conditions outlined in the previous exercise.

```
?what if
WHAT IF CASE 1
ENTER STATEMENTS
?demand = unirand(23,30)
? monte carlo 200
ENTER MONTE CARLO OPTIONS
? hist inventory cost,hist average total cost
ENTER MONTE CARLO OPTIONS
? none


***** WHAT IF CASE 1 *****


                    FREQUENCY TABLE

     PROBABILITY OF VALUE BEING GREATER THAN INDICATED

          90      80      70      60      50      40      30      20      10

    INVENTORY COST
   24   15.8    43.1    60.5    75.1    88.3   101.1   116.2   139.4   169.9

    AVERAGE TOTAL COST
   24    656     658     660     662     663     665     667     669     672


                    SAMPLE STATISTICS

             MEAN    STD DEV SKEWNESS KURTOSIS   10PC CONF MEAN   90PC

    INVENTORY COST
     24      93.78     62.78        1.7      11.4        88.10        99.46

    AVERAGE TOTAL COST
     24      663.7     6.092         .1       2.5        663.1        664.2
```

FIGURE 8-9. REORDER POINT MODEL WITH UNCERTAIN DEMAND
(This Figure Continued on the Next Page)

```
      HISTOGRAM FOR COLUMN        24 OF INVENTORY COST
    49- 52        *
    45- 48        *
    41- 44      * *
    37- 40      * *
    33- 36      * * *
    29- 32    * * * *
    25- 28    * * * *
    21- 24    * * * * *
    17- 20    * * * * *
    13- 16    * * * * * *
     9- 12    * * * * * *
     5-  8    * * * * * * *
     1-  4    * * * * * * *               *
              -----------------------------
                    1     2     3     4
              1     2     2     2     3
              7     1     5     9     3
START           .0 STOP     520.0 SIZE OF INTERVAL      34.67


      HISTOGRAM FOR COLUMN        24 OF AVERAGE TOTAL COST
    31- 33                  *
    28- 30                  *
    25- 27                  *
    22- 24                * * *
    19- 21            * * * * *
    16- 18            * * * * *
    13- 15            * * * * * * * *
    10- 12          * * * * * * * * * *
     7-  9          * * * * * * * * * *
     4-  6        * * * * * * * * * * * *
     1-  3    * * * * * * * * * * * * * * *
              -----------------------------
              6     6     6     6     6
              4     5     6     6     7
              9     5     1     7     3
              .     .     .     .     .
              0     2     4     6     8
START         648.0 STOP      679.0 SIZE OF INTERVAL      2.07
```

FIGURE 8-9. REORDER POINT MODEL WITH UNCERTAIN DEMAND
(Continued)

8.4 MATERIAL REQUIREMENTS PLANNING

Material Requirements Planning (MRP) is an information systems approach to keeping track of demands in a complex, hierarchical production system. It is particularly useful where demand is in batches rather than continuous and where there are complex relations among materials, semi-finished components, components, and end products.

MRP requires three sets of inputs:

1. A master production schedule
2. A record of product structure
3. Inventory on hand and on order, and an order policy

These three inputs are organized by MRP to produce a schedule of orders and production. To achieve this organization, MRP uses the concepts of:

- dependent demand
- net requirement
- lead time offsetting

which we will now describe. Dependent demand can be seen from an example. Suppose you offer a lettuce and tomato salad in your restaurant with each entree. The demand (and the portion) determines the number of heads of lettuce and the number of tomatoes needed. However, what do you do if your customers can order entrees with salad, chef's salads and budget blue plates which contain a wedge of lettuce? The demand for lettuce thus is a function of all menu items that contain lettuce. In definitional terms:

Dependent Demand = total demand for an ingredient, material, or part

Net requirement refers to the amount that has to be ordered. It is determined by the accounting relation:

Net Requirement = Total Required – On Hand – In Process – Receipts

For example, consider truck engines. The net number required is equal to the total number required for final truck assembly less those in inventory, those on the assembly line being completed, and those scheduled to be received from subcontractors.

Lead time is the time between placing and order and receiving it. Offsetting by the lead time involves placing orders at (need time – lead time). Lead times may differ. For example, you may have to order labels one week, wrappings two weeks, and crates three weeks before you can ship an order.

As an example of MRP, consider the production of electric light bulbs. (This example is based on Richard Tellier, *OPERATIONS MANAGEMENT* (Harper and Row,l978).) Suppose your factory makes 60 and 100 watt bulbs. The following information is available: 60 watt bulbs are shipped at 3-week intervals, 100 watt bulbs at 4-week intervals. Demand (in 1000's) over the next 12 weeks is 10, 8, 12, 10 for 60 watt bulbs and 15, 14, and 16 for 100 watt bulbs. The parts list is as follows:

- Filament (60w or 100w)
- Glass bulbs (same for both)

- Base (purchased)

The product structure record is:

Product	Part	Materials(for each 1000 units)
100 watt glass bulb base	100w filament	500 oz. tungsten alloy 1000 oz sand-silica mix
60 watt glass bulb base	60w filament	250 oz. tungsten alloy 1000 oz sand-silica mix

Other basic data are:

	On Order	On Hand	EOQ	Lead Time(weeks)
100w filaments	0	5	20	1
60w filaments	0	0	20	1
Glass bulbs	0	10	30	2
Bases	35	7.5	35	3
Tungsten alloy	15	0	15	3
Sand-silica	0	15	30	1

The orders for bases and alloys will be delivered in the lead time. EOQ is the economic order quantity (see Section 8.3.1). Figure 8-10 shows the MRP formulation for filaments, bulbs and bases. The requirements for finished product are the basic input. For each item, the amount required is determined by the products it is used in. The amount on order is determined by the initial data. The amount on hand is the initial inventory plus the amounts ordered a lead time ago less the amount required (which is assumed to be used up). An order of size EOQ is placed whenever the amount on hand is less than the amount required, offset by the lead time. For simplicity we have labeled the items A, B, D, E in Figure 8-10. (C is not used since a single C at the start of an IFPS line is treated as a comment rather than as part of a name).

EXERCISE: Extend the model in Figure 8-10 to include the tungsten alloy and the sand-silica. The data given are for 1000's of ounces.

EXERCISE: Suppose an additional order is received for 8000 100 watt bulbs and 13000 160 watt bulbs to be delivered during Week 4 and again in Weeks 7 and 11. Use the model in the previous exercise for these additional requirements. Note the cascading effects that these changed requirements impose.

Software packages specifically designed for MRP are available commercially. These packages provide capabilities for handling many hundreds of items using a firm's own numbering systems for parts, materials, etc. The purpose of presenting the MRP model in Figure 8-10 was to illustrate the MRP concept and to show how IFPS can be used to keep track of small products.

```
MODEL MRP  VERSION OF  12/27/82  21:27
10 COLUMNS 1-12
20 *
30 *REQUIREMENTS FOR FINISHED PRODUCT
40 *
50 HUNDRED WATT BULBS =0,0,10,0,0,8,0,0,12,0,0,10
60 SIXTY WATT BULBS = 0,0,0,15,0,0,0,14,0,0,0,16
70 *
80 * 100 WATT FILAMENTS (=A)
90 *
100 A REQUIRED = HUNDRED WATT BULBS
110 A ON ORDER = 0
120 A ON HAND = 5,PREVIOUS + PREVIOUS A ORDERED -A REQUIRED
130 A ORDERED=IF A ON HAND-FUTURE A REQUIRED .LT.0 THEN A EOQ ELSE 0
140 A EOQ = 20
150 *
160 * 60 WATT FILAMENTS (=B)
170 B REQUIRED = SIXTY WATT BULBS
180 B ON ORDER = 0
190 B ON HAND = 0,PREVIOUS + PREVIOUS B ORDERED - B REQUIRED
200 B ORDERED=IF B ON HAND-FUTURE B REQUIRED .LT.0 THEN B EOQ ELSE 0
210 B EOQ = 20
220 *
230 *GLASS BULBS (=D)
240 *
250 D REQUIRED = A REQUIRED + B REQUIRED
260 D ON ORDER = 0
270 D ON HAND =10,PREVIOUS + PREVIOUS 2 D ORDERED - D REQUIRED
280 D ORDERED=IF D ON HAND-FUTURE 2 D REQUIRED.LT.0 THEN D EOQ'
281 ELSE 0
290 D EOQ = 30
300 *
310 *BASES ( =E)
320 *
330 E REQUIRED = A REQUIRED + B REQUIRED
340 E ON ORDER = 0 FOR 2,35,0
350 E ON HAND = 7.5,PREVIOUS + PREVIOUS 3 E ORDERED + E ON ORDER '
351 - E REQUIRED
360 E ORDERED =IF E ON HAND - FUTURE 3 E REQUIRED .LT.0 THEN '
361 E EOQ ELSE 0
370 E EOQ = 35
END OF MODEL
```

FIGURE 8-10. MATERIALS REQUIREMENT PLANNING
(This Figure Continued on the Next Page)

```
? solve
MODEL MRP  VERSION OF  12/27/82  21:27 -- 12 COLUMNS 22 VARIABLES
ENTER SOLVE OPTIONS
?all
```

	1	2	3	4	5	6	7	8	9	10	11	12
REQUIREMENTS FOR FINISHED PRODUCT												
HUNDRED WATT BULBS	0	0	10	0	0	8	0	0	12	0	0	10
SIXTY WATT BULBS	0	0	0	15	0	0	0	14	0	0	0	16
100 WATT FILAMENTS (=A)												
A REQUIRED	0	0	10	0	0	8	0	0	12	0	0	10
A ON ORDER	0	0	0	0	0	0	0	0	0	0	0	0
A ON HAND	5	5	15	15	15	7	7	7	15	15	15	5
A ORDERED	0	20	0	0	0	0	0	20	0	0	0	0
A EOQ	20	20	20	20	20	20	20	20	20	20	20	20
60 WATT FILAMENTS (=B)												
B REQUIRED	0	0	0	15	0	0	0	14	0	0	0	16
B ON ORDER	0	0	0	0	0	0	0	0	0	0	0	0
B ON HAND	0	0	0	5	5	5	5	11	11	11	11	15
B ORDERED	0	0	20	0	0	0	20	0	0	0	20	0
B EOQ	20	20	20	20	20	20	20	20	20	20	20	20
GLASS BULBS (=D)												
D REQUIRED	0	0	10	15	0	8	0	14	12	0	0	26
D ON ORDER	0	0	0	0	0	0	0	0	0	0	0	0
D ON HAND	10	10	0	15	15	7	7	23	41	41	41	15
D ORDERED	0	30	0	0	0	30	30	0	0	0	0	0
D EOQ	30	30	30	30	30	30	30	30	30	30	30	30
BASES (=E)												
E REQUIRED	0	0	10	15	0	8	0	14	12	0	0	26
E ON ORDER	0	0	35	0	0	0	0	0	0	0	0	0
E ON HAND	7.5	7.5	33	53	53	45	45	31	19	19	19	28
E ORDERED	35	0	0	0	0	0	0	0	35	0	0	0
E EOQ	35	35	35	35	35	35	35	35	35	35	35	35

FIGURE 8-10. MATERIALS REQUIREMENT PLANNING (Continued)

8.5 EQUIPMENT REPLACEMENT

One of the more important capital budgeting decisions faced by firms is the replacement of major pieces of equipment, be they drill presses in a job shop or copying equipment in an office. Some equipment has a fixed life because it eventually wears out. However, there are many types of equipment which could be kept in operation essentially forever by repairing or replacing parts. Of course, the longer the equipment is kept, the less efficient (and hence more costly and less productive) it becomes. In this section we consider the possibility of replacing equipment which deteriorates but does not wear out.

The simplest assumption is that the present piece of equipment will be kept for a period that will maximize its net present value but will not be replaced thereafter. We will analyze this simple case first. However, recognize that this assumption is overly simple. The second case we consider is a sequence of replacements, each at the optimal time. That is, the present equipment is kept for an optimum time. It is replaced by new equipment, which is also kept for an optimum time and so on. The assumption made is that each replacement is identical to the present equipment. More complex analyses (which we present as Exercises) introduce the ideas of technological improvement and accounting for anticipated inflation.

8.5.1 One-Time Purchase

Suppose a new piece of equipment is to be bought. The following conditions are estimated for this equipment:

- Initial investment cost = $10000

- Revenue generated by equipment = $7000 in the first year, decreasing by $500 per year thereafter.

- Operating and maintenance expenses = $2000 in the first year and increasing by $400 per year thereafter.

- The salvage value = $7500 in the first year and decreasing by 25% of its value each year until it reaches its scrap value of $1000.

- The discount rate = 18%.

The problem is to determine how long to keep this equipment to maximize its present worth. You will notice that the problem we have formulated involves the optimal timing of the sale of an investment, a topic discussed in Section 6.5. An IFPS model to solve this problem is shown in Figure 8-11. The measure of effectiveness is the net present value of the stream of returns for the initial investment. The net present value has two components:

1. The difference between revenue and expenses. This return is realized each year the equipment is kept.

2. The salvage value of the equipment when it is disposed of. The return from salvage is realized only at the time of sale. We assume that the sale for salvage occurs at the end of a year.

```
MODEL REPLACE1  VERSION OF  08/31/82  08:26
10 COLUMNS 1-12
20*EQUIPMENT REPLACEMENT - 1 TIME PURCHASE ONLY
30*
40*INPUT DATA
50*
60 INVESTMENT = 10000,0
70 REVENUE = 7000,PREVIOUS-500
80 EXPENSES = 2000,PREVIOUS+400
90 SALVAGE=7500,IF PREVIOUS .LT.1333 THEN 1000 ELSE PREVIOUS*.75
100 DISCOUNT RATE = 0.18
110*
120*CALCULATION OF SALVAGE PV
130*
140 CUMULATIVE PV = NPVC(SALVAGE,DISCOUNT RATE,0)
150 SALVAGE PV = CUMULATIVE PV - PREVIOUS CUMULATIVE PV
160 *
170*RESULTS
180*
190 NPV WITHOUT SALVAGE=NPVC(REVENUE-EXPENSES,DISCOUNT RATE,'
191 INVESTMENT)
200 NET PRESENT VALUE = NPV WITHOUT SALVAGE + SALVAGE PV
END OF MODEL
```

a. Model

```
? solve
MODEL REPLACE1  VERSION OF  08/31/82 08:26 -- 12 COLUMNS 9 VARIABLES
ENTER SOLVE OPTIONS
?invert
?revenue,expenses,salvage,salvage pv,net present value
```

	REVENUE	EXPENSES	SALVAGE	SALVAGE P	NET PRESE
1	7000	2000	7500	6356	593.2
2	6500	2400	5625	4040	1222
3	6000	2800	4219	2568	1697
4	5500	3200	3164	1632	1948
5	5000	3600	2373	1037	1965
6	4500	4000	1780	659.3	1772
7	4000	4400	1335	419.0	1406
8	3500	4800	1001	266.3	907.9
9	3000	5200	1000	225.5	371.0
10	2500	5600	1000	191.1	-255.7
11	2000	6000	1000	161.9	-932.5
12	1500	6400	1000	137.2	-1630

b. Results Using Vertical Format Based on INVERT Solve Option

FIGURE 8-11. EQUIPMENT REPLACEMANET: One-Time Purchase Only
(This Figure Continued on the Next Page)

```
MODEL  REPLACE1    VERSION  OF    08/31/82    08:26  --  12  COLUMNS  9
VARIABLES
ENTER SOLVE OPTIONS
? all
```

	1	2	3	4	5	6
EQUIPMENT REPLACEMENT - 1 TIME PURCHASE ONLY						
INPUT DATA						
INVESTMENT	10000	0	0	0	0	0
REVENUE	7000	6500	6000	5500	5000	4500
EXPENSES	2000	2400	2800	3200	3600	4000
SALVAGE	7500	5625	4219	3164	2373	1780
DISCOUNT RATE	.1800	.1800	.1800	.1800	.1800	.1800
CALCULATION OF SALVAGE PV						
CUMULATIVE PV	6356	10396	12963	14595	15633	16292
SALVAGE PV	6356	4040	2568	1632	1037	659.3
RESULTS						
NPV WITHOUT SALVAGE	-5763	-2818	-870.5	315.8	927.7	1113
NET PRESENT VALUE	593.2	1222	1697	1948	1965	1772

	7	8	9	10	11	12
EQUIPMENT REPLACEMENT - 1 TIME PURCHASE ONLY						
INPUT DATA						
INVESTMENT	0	0	0	0	0	0
REVENUE	4000	3500	3000	2500	2000	1500
EXPENSES	4400	4800	5200	5600	6000	6400
SALVAGE	1335	1001	1000	1000	1000	1000
DISCOUNT RATE	.1800	.1800	.1800	.1800	.1800	.1800
CALCULATION OF SALVAGE PV						
CUMULATIVE PV	16711	16977	17203	17394	17556	17693
SALVAGE PV	419.0	266.3	225.5	191.1	161.9	137.2
RESULTS						
NPV WITHOUT SALVAGE	987.4	641.5	145.5	-446.8	-1094	-1767
NET PRESENT VALUE	1406	907.9	371.0	-255.7	-932.5	-1630

c. Results in Conventional Format

FIGURE 8-11. EQUIPMENT REPLACEMENT; One-Time Purchase Only (Continued)

To compute the contribution to net present value from salvage value we have to consider the fact that the salvage value is realized only once. Hence the strategy followed in Figure 6-10 in Section 6.5 applies. To compute the net present value of salvage in some period, say k, we first compute the net present value of all salvage payments in the k periods and then subtract the net present value of all salvage payments during the first k-1 periods (after all, we don't receive them). The difference between these two cumulative net present values must be the net present value from the kth period.

EXERCISE: Modify Figure 8-11 to compute the contribution of salvage value to net present worth directly from the formula that:

$$\text{NPV OF SALVAGE} = \text{SALVAGE(K)/(1 + DISCOUNT RATE)}^{K}$$

We present the output in Figure 8-11 in two ways, based on different SOLVE options. Note that in the conventional horizonal format we see complete detail but have to search through the detail to find the critical piece of information, namely the optimal lifetime of the equipment. In the vertical format, obtained by using the INVERT command, four quantities (revenue, expenses, salvage, and net present value) are shown. The vertical format allows you to obtain as many periods as you want in a neat format at the expense of printing out fewer quantities and hence providing less detail. In either case, if we scan the results for net present value (i.e., NPV in the model) we see that the maximum present worth occurs after five years.

8.5.2 Purchase With Replacement

If we assume that we are in business to stay, then the piece of equipment being considered (be it drill press or copier) will be replaced by another piece of equipment that performs the same function, which in turn will eventually be replaced by another and by another and another in perpetuity. As a first step, we can create a simplified model in which we assume that the replacements are identical in characteristic to the original and have the same cost, revenue, expense, and salvage. To be able to make sense out of such an infinite sequence of cash flows, it turns out to be easiest to try to find an equivalent annual cash flow in which the flows are identical. That is, to find the equivalent annuity associated with the present value.

If we know that the life of the equipment is T years, then we can compute an annual annuity payment that has the same present value (PV in formula below) as the equipment and is received for T years. The formula for this computation is:

$$ANNUAL\ ANNUITY = \frac{PV*(1 + DISCOUNT\ RATE)^{T} * DISCOUNT\ RATE}{(1 - DISCOUNT\ RATE)^{T} - 1} \qquad (8-7)$$

Since we will replace the present equipment with identical equipment every T years, we will receive this equivalent annual annuity in perpetuity. The formula for finding the present worth of a perpetual annual annuity is:

$$\text{PV OF PERPETUAL ANNUITY} = \text{ANNUAL ANNUITY/DISCOUNT RATE)} \qquad (8\text{-}8)$$

If we substitute the value of the ANNUAL ANNUITY from Equation (8-7) into Equation (8-8), we obtain the formula for the present value with replacement:

$$PV\ WITH\ REPLACEMENT = \frac{PV*(1+DISCOUNT\ RATE)^{T}}{(1+DISCOUNT\ RATE)^{T}-1} \qquad (8-9)$$

Equation (8-9) is used in Figure 8-12 to find the present value of an infinite string of identical replacements for the equipment considered above in Section 8.5.1. Since we began with the assumption that we do not know the optimal life of the equipment under these conditions, we compute the present value with replacement for individual equipment lifetimes of 1, 2, 3, 4,.... years and select as the optimum time between equipment replacements the one for which the present value with replacement is maximum.

```
WHAT IF CASE 1
ENTER STATEMENTS
? discount factor = 1 +discount rate,previous*(1+discount rate)
WARNING - NEW VARIABLE WAS CREATED
? annuity factor  = discount factor/(discount factor -1)
WARNING - NEW VARIABLE WAS CREATED
? npv with replacement = net prevent value*annuity factor
WARNING - NEW VARIABLE WAS CREATED
? solve
ENTER SOLVE OPTIONS
? invert
?revenue,expenses,salvage pv,net present value,npv with replacement

***** WHAT IF CASE 1 *****
3 WHAT IF STATEMENTS PROCESSED
```

	REVENUE	EXPENSES	SALVAGE P	NET PRESE	NPV WITH
1	7000	2000	6356	593.2	3889
2	6500	2400	4040	1222	4335
3	6000	2800	2568	1697	4336
4	5500	3200	1632	1948	4023
5	5000	3600	1037	1965	3491
6	4500	4000	659.3	1772	2815
7	4000	4400	419.0	1406	2050
8	3500	4800	266.3	907.9	1237
9	3000	5200	225.5	371.0	479.0
10	2500	5600	191.1	-255.7	-316.1
11	2000	6000	161.9	-932.5	-1113
12	1500	6400	137.2	-1630	-1889

FIGURE 8-12. EQUIPMENT REPLACEMENT; Infinite Replacements

(In Figure 8-12, the column headings for NET PRESENT VALUE AND NPV WITH REPLACEMENT are abbreviated because of a lack of space.) If you examine the output in Figure 8-12, you will see that the optimal time to selling the equipment for salvage is shorter with replacement than in the one-time purchase case (three years rather than five). This shortening of the optimal economic life is generally true when replacement is introduced.

EXERCISE: To help you understand why the economic life is shortened, create a version of the model in Figure 8-11 in which the lifetime is known and the replacement cycle is shown explicitly. Thus, for example, if you assume the lifetime is five years, your investment would be modeled as:

```
INVESTMENT = 10000, 0 FOR 4,PREVIOUS 5 INVESTMENT
```

Run this model once under the assumption of a five-year cycle and once under the assumption of a three-year cycle. In both cases, run for 60 years and compute the net present value for the 60-year period. Prepare a short write-up that explains the general phenomenon, and save this exercise for later use.

Figure 8-12 modified Figure 8-11 through the use of WHAT IF statements which add Equation (8-9) to the model. This is a perfectly legitimate way of updating a model and we have used it here to highlight the change that has been made to take replacement into account. Although useful for modifications made in a model only at one time, it is a poor way of making a modification if you are going to use the modification over and over. If you want to keep both models (e.g., the models of Figure 8-11 and 8-12) in your file, a way of doing so is to use the COPY command available in IFPS. (See Section 4.5.4 for a more detailed discussion of COPY). This command is of the form:

COPY MODEL name of model TO name of copy

For example, you might type:

```
COPY MODEL REPLACE1 TO REPLACE2
```

Note that you have to use the word MODEL for the original but not for the copy. Once you have made the copy, two models exist in your file. To obtain the copy you have to ask for it. In our example, you would type:

```
MODEL REPLACE2
```

EXERCISE: Duplicate the results of Figure 8-12 by writing and running a complete model rather than using WHAT IF.

EXERCISE: Suppose the replacements can be expected to have increased productivity. Assume that productivity shows up in the form of leaving the investment (i.e., the price paid for the replacement) and expenses fixed, but increasing revenue by 3% per year. Thus, a replacement bought after four years will generate revenues that are $(1.03)^4$ greater than equipment bought now. Model this situation. You will find it easiest to modify the exercise we asked you to save above to take this growth of productivity into account.

EXERCISE: Suppose that, in addition to the productivity gain introduced in the previous exercise, you want to add the sophistication of inflation accounting into the model. You recognize that different rates of inflation govern the various components of revenue and expense, some moving at the general inflation rate given by the consumer price index and others moving either more quickly or more slowly. Modify the model of the previous exercise so that it includes replacement, productivity growth, and inflation. To obtain numerical results, assume that the investment (purchase price of the equipment) will remain fixed. Assume that revenue from productivity growth will increase 3% per year in constant dollar terms (i.e., relative to the consumer price index). However, market prices for products produced by the machine will be increasing at 1% below the inflation rate each year because of competition. Historically, the expenses associated with the machine have increased by 2% per year in constant dollar terms. Furthermore, because of the increase in productivity the salvage value after one year has increased by 3% per year in constant dollar terms; however, salvage value at the end of the first year is not expected ever to go above $9000.

8.6 QUALITY CONTROL

Quality control can be divided into:

- input quality control
- output quality control

In input quality control you are, in effect, a consumer who is inspecting materials or parts that you have purchased and plan to use in some process. In output quality control you are the producer who is shipping goods to the customer and checking goods before they are shipped. In this section we will be concerned with quality control for large lot sizes, that is shipments received or shipments to be made that involve a large number of identical items (be they screws, industrial diamonds, or customer responses to a satisfaction survey). The ideal of 100% inspection, in which every item is checked, can be prohibitively expensive or, if the inspection involves destructive testing, impossible. Therefore, for large lot sizes, quality control involves sampling. If you are sampling, you have to apply the concepts of statistics. In the models discussed in this section, we will apply the ideas of average, standard deviation, and binomial distribution which were discussed in Chapter VII. Quality control lies at the intersection between operations management and statistics and ideas from both disciplines are required.

The following three subsections present representative ideas from quality control. You will find that many problems in quality control lend themselves readily to computation using IFPS.

8.6.1 Operating Characteristic Curves

In simplest terms, an operating characteristic curve (referred to as an OC curve) shows the relation between accepting a lot and the fraction defective in it for a given sampling plan. The sampling plan is defined by three characteristics:

lot size	total items in a shipment
sample size	number of items inspected
sample criterion	the maximum number of defectives allowed

That is, you choose a sample from the lot and inspect each item in the sample. If the number of defectives is at or below the sample criterion, you accept the lot; otherwise you reject it. For example, if you take a sample of 20 from a lot of 100 and your sample criterion is 1, then you would reject the entire lot of 100 if you found two defectives among your sample of 20.

OC curves can be computed directly. If the lot size is small, you have to consider the fact that you keep reducing the lot with each sample(e.g., a sample of taken from a lot of 20 reduces the lot size to 19, 18, 17,...as each sample is removed). In this case, a hypergeometric probability distribution must be used. If the lot size is large, (of the order of a 1000 or more), the sampling process does not reduce the lot size appreciably and it is therefore possible to approximate the sampling procedure with a binomial probability distribution (see Section 7.3.1).

Figure 8-13 illustrates the computation of the OC curve under the assumption of a large sample size. Each column in Figure 8-13 represents a 1% increment in the actual number of defectives in the lot. The sample size is 100. In general, the probability of finding exactly k defectives in a sample of 100 is given by the binomial probability of k successes in 100 trials. If your criterion is 0 defectives, then

$$\text{Probability (0 defectives)} = (1\text{-p})^{100}$$

This is shown in the PROB ACCEPT CRITERION0 line of Figure 8-13. If your criterion is up to 1 defective allowed, then you have will accept the lot if there are 0 or 1 defective. Therefore, you have to add up the probability of 0 defectives and the probability of 1 defective (see Line 60). Similarly for up to two defectives, you have to add up the probability of 0 or 1 defective. If you examine the results, you will see, for example, that if the actual fraction of defectives is 3% (i.e., 30 in a lot of 1000), you have a 4.8% chance of finding no defectives, a 19.5% chance of finding at most 1 defective, and a 42% chance of finding at most 2 defectives in the sample of 100. In general, as your sample criterion gets larger (from 0 to 1 to 2 defectives allowed), you have a much higher chance of accepting a sample with a given percentage of defectives.

```
MODEL OCCURVE  VERSION OF  08/31/82  08:26
10 COLUMNS 0-50
20*OPERATING CHARACTERISTIC CURVES BASED ON BINOMIAL DISTRIBUTION
30*
40 FRACTION DEFECTIVE =0,PREVIOUS +0.01
50 PROB ACCEPT CRITERION0=XPOWERY((1-FRACTION DEFECTIVE),'
51 SAMPLE SIZE)
60 PROB ACCEPT CRITERION1=L50+L50*SAMPLE SIZE*FRACTION DEFECTIVE/'
61 (1-FRACTION DEFECTIVE)
70 PROB ACCEPT CRITERION2=L60 +.5*SAMPLE SIZE*(SAMPLE SIZE -1)*'
71 (FRACTION DEFECTIVE*FRACTION DEFECTIVE)'
72 XPOWERY((1-FRACTION DEFECTIVE),(SAMPLE SIZE-2))
100*
110*ASSUMPTIONS
120*
130 LOT SIZE =1000
140 SAMPLE SIZE = 100
END OF MODEL
```

FIGURE 8-13. OPERATING CHARACTERISTIC CURVES BASED ON BINOMIAL DISTRIBUTION
(This Figure is Continued on the Next Page)

```
? solve
ENTER SOLVE OPTIONS
? all

                               0       1       2       3       4       5

OPERATING CHARACTERISTIC CURVES BASED ON BINOMIAL DISTRIBUTION

FRACTION DEFECTIVE             0   .0100   .0200   .0300   .0400   .0500
PROB ACCEPT CRITERION0         1   .3660   .1326   .0476   .0169   .0059
PROB ACCEPT CRITERION1         1   .7358   .4033   .1946   .0872   .0371
PROB ACCEPT CRITERION2         1   .9206   .6767   .4198   .2321   .1183

ASSUMPTIONS

LOT SIZE                    1000    1000    1000    1000    1000    1000
SAMPLE SIZE                  100     100     100     100     100     100

                              10      15      20      30      40      50

OPERATING CHARACTERISTIC CURVES BASED ON BINOMIAL DISTRIBUTION

FRACTION DEFECTIVE         .1000   .1500   .2000   .3000   .4000   .5000
PROB ACCEPT CRITERION0         0       0       0       0       0       0
PROB ACCEPT CRITERION1     .0003       0       0       0       0       0
PROB ACCEPT CRITERION2     .0019       0       0       0       0       0

ASSUMPTIONS

LOT SIZE                    1000    1000    1000    1000    1000    1000
SAMPLE SIZE                  100     100     100     100     100     100
```

FIGURE 8-13. OPERATING CHARACTERISTIC CURVES BASED ON BINOMIAL DISTRIBUTION (Continued)

EXERCISE: Modify Figure 8-13 so that it also approximates the probabilities with a Poisson distribution. Compare the two sets of results.

EXERCISE: Modify Figure 8-13 so that it computes the operating curve from a hypergeometric distribution. Run the model for a lot size of 50, a sample size of 10, and for a fraction of defectives between 0 and 20%.

8.6.2 Producers Risk and Consumers Risk

Producers risk and consumers risk refer really to two kinds of errors which can occur (technically referred to by statisticians as errors of the first kind and errors of the second kind.) In producers risk a lot that really meets the quality standard is rejected (e.g., you are willing to accept 1% defectives and happen to find the nine bad items in a lot of 1000 in your sample of 100). In consumers risk, a lot that really fails the quality standard is accepted (e.g., you take a sample of 100 and find none of the 250 defectives). The term "lot tolerance fraction defective" (or LTFD) is used to refer to the maximum fraction defectives that the consumer is willing to tolerate in each lot. Another consideration used in these analyses is the historical "process average" for defectives. The term process average refers to the long-run fraction of defectives from the manufacturer's production process.

The values of producers risk and consumers risk are typically a matter of negotiation between seller and buyer. When a lot is received, a sample is inspected. Typically, if more defectives than the sample criterion are observed, then the entire lot is inspected and the defectives removed. The key is to find a sampling procedure that minimizes cost.

We will not go through the entire costing process here. However, we will illustrate the ideas by considering the following situation : A credit card manufacturer sells credit card blanks in lots of 20,000 to a credit card issuer (e.g., department store). Through negotiation, the consumers risk is set at 6% and the producers risk at 8%. The manufacturer's historical data show that the process average of defectives is .003. Since each sample taken increases the cost, the objective is to find the minimum size sample within the producers risk and to find the lot tolerance fraction defective associated with this minimum sample size. The minimum sample size will also depend on the sample criterion. We use a criterion of 0. This example is Problem 16 on p. 555 of *OPERATIONS MANAGEMENT* by Starr (Prentice Hall, 1978)

The IFPS model for this situation is shown in Figure 8-14. With n trials (that is, a sample of size n) and a probability p of a defective on each trial, the probability of accepting the lot because no defectives were found is:

$$\text{Prob(Acceptance)} = (1\text{–Process Average})^{n}$$

In our case, the process average is .003 and the allowed producers risk is .08. Hence, we want a 92% probability of acceptance; that is, we want to solve the equation:

$$(1\text{–Producers Risk}) = (1\text{–Process Average})^{n}$$

for n. One way of finding n is by search. That is, we choose a sample size, n, and determine the associated probability of acceptance. As shown in Figure 8-14, as sample size goes up, the probability of 0 defectives goes down. We terminate the search when the probability goes from above the criterion to below the criterion. In Figure 8-14 we show only the region where this transition occurs. (Note that search procedures such as in this figure are often a very simple way of solving complex mathematical relations.)

Figure 8-14 also shows the computation of the lot tolerance fraction defective for each sample size. The relation used is that:

$$\text{Consumer Risk} = (1 - \text{Probability(LTDF)})^{n}$$

and hence:

$$\text{Probability(LTDF)} = 1 - (\text{Consumer Risk})^{1/n}$$

The results indicate that with a sample of 28, we will be within the producers risk of 8% but that the lot tolerance defective fraction is 9.6%.

```
MODEL CREDCARD  VERSION OF  08/31/82  08:25
10 COLUMNS 1-50
20 *CREDIT CARD PROBLEM
30*
40*SAMPLE SIZE DETERMINATION
45 SAMPLE SIZE =1,PREVIOUS+1
50 PROBABILITY OF ACCEPTANCE = XPOWERY((1-FRACTION DEFECTIVE),'
51 SAMPLE SIZE)
60*
70*NOTE CHOOSE SAMPLE SIZE SO THAT PROBABILITY OF ACCEPTANCE IS JUST
71*LESS THAN OR EQUAL TO THE PROBABILITY OF ACCEPTANCE CRITERION
100*
110*LOT TOLERANCE FRACTION DEFECTIVE(LTFD)
120*
130LTFD = 1- XPOWERY(CONSUMER RISK,1/SAMPLE SIZE)
200*
210*ASSUMPTIONS
220*
230 FRACTION DEFECTIVE =.003
240 CONSUMER RISK =.06
250 PRODUCERS RISK =.08
260 ACCEPTANCE CRITERION=1-PRODUCERS RISK
270 SAMPLE CRITERION = 0
END OF MODEL
? solve
MODEL CREDCARD VERSION OF  08/31/82  08:25 -- 50 COLUMNS 8 VARIABLES
ENTER SOLVE OPTIONS
?columns 23-28
? all

                               23      24      25      26      27      28

CREDIT CARD PROBLEM


SAMPLE SIZE DETERMINATION
SAMPLE SIZE                    23      24      25      26      27      28
PROBABILITY OF ACCEPTANCE .9332   .9304   .9276   .9249   .9221   .9193

NOTE CHOOSE SAMPLE SIZE SO THAT PROBABILITY OF ACCEPTANCE IS JUST
LESS THAN OR EQUAL TO THE PROBABILITY OF ACCEPTANCE CRITERION

LOT TOLERANCE FRACTION DEFECTIVE(LTFD)

LTFD                      .1151   .1106   .1064   .1026   .0990   .0956

ASSUMPTIONS

FRACTION DEFECTIVE        .0030   .0030   .0030   .0030   .0030   .0030
CONSUMER RISK             .0600   .0600   .0600   .0600   .0600   .0600
PRODUCERS RISK            .0800   .0800   .0800   .0800   .0800   .0800
ACCEPTANCE CRITERION      .9200   .9200   .9200   .9200   .9200   .9200
SAMPLE CRITERION              0       0       0       0       0       0
```

FIGURE 8-14. PRODUCERS AND CONSUMERS RISK

8.6.3 P-Chart

The previous two subsections dealt with using sampling for input quality control. In this section, we discuss p-charts which are used for output quality control. The p-chart is a control chart for fraction defectives and is also based on sampling. Here we will use the ideas of standard deviation and confidence intervals. The confidence intervals in this case correspond to control limits within which we will accept the lot and outside of which we will reject the lot.

The basic idea is to take several samples from a production run. Each sample is 100% inspected and the number of defectives noted. For example, we may take 6 samples from a run of 1800 and find:

Sample No.	1	2	3	4	5	6
Sample Size	25	25	36	64	25	25
Defectives in Sample	1	2	3	4	4	2

If you add up the total number of items inspected and the number of defectives found you find that there were 16 failures in the 200 samples, or 8%. This value is the process average. To determine the control limits for each sample of size n, you must first compute the standard deviation from the relation:

STANDARD DEVIATION = √PROCESS AVERAGE * (1-PROCESS AVERAGE / n

You must next choose the number of standard deviations that define the control limits. In the example shown in Figure 8-15, one standard deviation is used. The result is to define upper and lower control limits that are one standard deviation on either side of the process average.

Because the standard deviation depends on the sample size, the control limits change with n. By observing the samples, you can determine whether the process is out of control. In the example shown in Figure 8-15, the 5th sample is outside the control limits (indicated with a control limit warning on the printout).

From the point of view of using IFPS, note the use of the IF...THEN...ELSE statement in lines 130, 131 and 132. We first test whether the observed fraction is greater than the upper control limit. If it is not, we test if the observed fraction is smaller than the lower limit. If both tests are passed, we print out a 0, if one test is failed we print out a value of a 1000 to warn of the out-of-bounds condition.

```
MODEL PCHART  VERSION OF  08/31/82  08:25
10 COLUMNS 1-6
20*P-CHART PROBLEM
30*
40 SUBGROUP SAMPLE =1,PREVIOUS+1
50 NUMBER INSPECTED =25,25,36,64,25,25
60 NUMBER DEFECTIVE = 1,2,3,4,4,2
70 VARIANCE=PROCESS AVERAGE*(1-PROCESS AVERAGE)/NUMBER INSPECTED
80 STANDARD DEVIATION = XPOWERY(VARIANCE,.5)
90 UPPER CONTROL LIMIT =PROCESS AVERAGE+STANDARD DEVIATION
100 LOWER CONTROL LIMIT =PROCESS AVERAGE-STANDARD DEVIATION
110 ACTUAL FRACTION DEFECTIVE=NUMBER DEFECTIVE/NUMBER INSPECTED
120*
130 CONTROL LIMIT WARNING=IF ACTUAL FRACTION DEFECTIVE .GT.
131 UPPER CONTROL LIMIT THEN 1000 ELSE IF ACTUAL FRACTION DEFECTIVE'
132 .LT. LOWER CONTROL LIMIT THEN 1000 ELSE 0
140*
150*NOTE:CONTROL LIMIT WARNING = 1000 DENOTES CONTROL LIMIT EXCEEDED
160*
170 TOTAL INSPECTED =PREVIOUS + NUMBER INSPECTED
180 TOTAL DEFECTIVE =PREVIOUS + NUMBER DEFECTIVE
190 PROCESS AVERAGE =MATRIX(TOTAL DEFECTIVE,6)/'
191 MATRIX(TOTAL INSPECTED,6)
END OF MODEL
?solve
ENTER SOLVE OPTIONS
? all
```

	1	2	3	4	5	6
P-CHART PROBLEM						
SUBGROUP SAMPLE	1	2	3	4	5	6
NUMBER INSPECTED	25	25	36	64	25	25
NUMBER DEFECTIVE	1	2	3	4	4	2
VARIANCE	.0029	.0029	.0020	.0012	.0029	.0029
STANDARD DEVIATION	.0543	.0543	.0452	.0339	.0543	.0543
UPPER CONTROL LIMIT	.1343	.1343	.1252	.1139	.1343	.1343
LOWER CONTROL LIMIT	.0257	.0257	.0348	.0461	.0257	.0257
ACTUAL FRACTION DEFECTIV	.0400	.0800	.0833	.0625	.1600	.0800
CONTROL LIMIT WARNING	0	0	0	0	1000	0
NOTE: CONTROL LIMIT WARNING = 1000 DENOTES CONTROL LIMIT EXCEEDED						
TOTAL INSPECTED	25	50	86	150	175	200
TOTAL DEFECTIVE	1	3	6	10	14	16
PROCESS AVERAGE	.0800	.0800	.0800	.0800	.0800	.0800

FIGURE 8-15. P-CHART

(NOTE: This Figure is Continued on the Next Page)

```
ENTER SOLVE OPTIONS
?plot upper   control  limit,lower  control  limit,  actual  fraction
defective



   .16                                                        3


   .14
      1         1                                             1
                          1
   .12
                                     1

   .10
                          3
   .08          3

                                     3
   .06

                                     2
   .04 3
                          2
      2         2                                             2
   .02
      1         2         3          4                        5


      1 - UPPER CONTROL LIMIT
      2 - LOWER CONTROL LIMIT
      3 - ACTUAL FRACTION DEFECTIVE
```

FIGURE 8-15. P-CHART
(Continued)

APPENDIX I
HELP COMMANDS

This Appendix describes the HELP commands available in IFPS. It is an expansion of Section 2.10. You should read and be familiar with Section 2.10 before starting to use this Appendix as a reference.

A1.1 HELP and HELP HELP

If you type HELP or if you type HELP HELP you will receive the following index:

```
? help

HELP COMMAND
FORM(S)
 (1)    HELP
 (2)    HELP HELP
 (3)    HELP WHERE
 (4)    HELP CONTENTS
 (5)    HELP *
 (6)    HELP KEYWORD
USAGE
      "HELP" AND "HELP HELP" PROVIDE THIS MESSAGE TELLING HOW TO
      USE THE HELP COMMAND.
      "HELP WHERE" IDENTIFIES WHICH SUBSYSTEM THE USER IS CURRENTLY
      IN, ALONG WITH  THE  CURRENTLY  ACTIVE  FILE,  AND  SPECIFIC
      MODEL, REPORT,  OR STRUCTURE, AS APPROPRIATE.
      "HELP CONTENTS" PRODUCES A TABLE OF CONTENTS OUTLINING MAJOR
      CATEGORIES WITHIN IFPS.  INSTRUCTIONS ARE ALSO GIVEN FOR A
      SUBSEQUENT HELP COMMAND FOR EACH CATEGORY, TO LIST ALL
      CORRESPONDING KEYWORDS FOR WHICH HELP IS AVAILABLE.
      "HELP *" PRINTS A LIST OF ALL KEYWORDS AVAILABLE WITH THE HELP
      COMMAND.
      "HELP KEYWORD" PRINTS THE HELP MESSAGE FOR THE SPECIFIED
      KEYWORD,VALID FROM ANY LEVEL OF IFPS.  CONTROL WILL REMAIN AT
      THE LEVEL WHERE HELP WAS ENTERED.

READY FOR MODELING LANGUAGE COMMAND
```

A1.2 HELP WHERE

HELP WHERE tells you where you are in IFPS. For example, if you are in a file named SAMPLE and are working on a model named GRAY, you would see the following three lines in response to HELP WHERE:

```
? help where

SUBSYSTEM: MODELING
MODEL NAME: GRAY
MODELS AND REPORTS FILE : SAMPLE
READY FOR MODELING LANGUAGE COMMAND
```

A1.3 HELP CONTENTS

HELP CONTENTS divides IFPS into ten categories and allows you to obtain a list of keywords that apply to each category. HELP CONTENTS results in the following printout:

```
? help contents

CONTENTS OF HELP FILE
THE IFPS  HELP  FILE  IS  ORGANIZED  INTO  THE  CATEGORIES SHOWN
BELOW. FOR A LISTING OF THE COMMANDS/OPTIONS IN ANY CATEGORY, ENTER
HELP CATEGORY WHERE  "CATEGORY" IS THE KEYWORD IDENTIFIER SHOWN TO
THE LEFT OF  THE  DESIRED CATEGORY (FOR INSTANCE, HELP REL8).

      UC        UNIVERSAL CONSOLIDATION
      REL8      OTHER RELEASE 8.0 COMMANDS/OPTIONS
      SROPTS    SOLVE/REPORT OPTIONS
      EXECS     EXECUTIVE LEVEL COMMANDS
      MODS      MODELING LANGUAGE COMMANDS
      CMDS      COMMAND FILE COMMANDS
      DATA      DATAFILE SUBSYSTEM COMMANDS; STORE/STORENT OPTIONS
      FUNCS     IFPS FUNCTIONS & SUBROUTINES
      STMTS     SPECIAL MODELING STATEMENTS
      SYS       SYSTEM-DEPENDENT CHARACTERISTICS & SPECIAL HELPS
```

HELP CONTENTS is a subject index. If you want to see the keywords in each category you simply type HELP followed by the category's name. For example, HELP FUNCS gives you a list of all the built-in functions and subroutines in IFPS. A list of the keywords in six of these categories (SROPTS, EXECS, MODS, DATA, FUNCS, and SYS) follows.

```
SROPTS - SOLVE/REPORT OPTIONS
* TOPICS VALID AS SOLVE OPTIONS AND REPORT DIRECTIVES
CASELIST   CURRENCY NAMEINDENT   NOCOMMENTS  OVERLAY    SORT
COLUMNS    DOUBLE   NAOUTPUT     NOINDENT    PAGE       SPACE
COMDEC     FORMAT   NAPRINT      NOPAGE      PLOT       WIDTH
COMMAS     INDENT   NEGOPT       NORMAL      POSOPT     ZEROPRINT
COMMENT    INVERT   NOCOMMAS     NOSCALE     SCALE      ZEROSP
COMMENTS   LEFTMARGIN NOCOMMENT  OPT         SINGLE
```

```
* TOPICS VALID AS REPORT DIRECTIVES ONLY
CENTER      COLTITLES NEWPAGE      PROMPT       SKIPZERO      TIME
CENTRE      DATE      PAGELENGTH   SKIPNONZERO  TAB           UNDERLINE
* TOPICS VALID AS PLOT OPTIONS (INTERACTIVELY OR IN A REPORT)
GRID         LEGEND       NORMAL       RANGE        SOVER        VS
INVERT       NOLEGEND     PLOT         SCALE        TITLE
* TOPICS VALID AS SOLVE OPTIONS OR MODELING LANGUAGE COMMANDS
  FOR VALUE CONTROL OF PROBABILISTIC FUNCTIONS
HIGH         LOW          MEAN         MOSTP
```

```
EXECS - EXECUTIVE COMMANDS
* LIST OF EXECUTIVE LEVEL COMMANDS
CATALOG      COPY         EXECUTE      MODEL        QUIT
CMDFILE      CROSSREF     FILE         NORECORD     RECORD
COMBINE      DATAFILE     FORMULA      OPTION       REPORT
COMMANDS     DATASELECT   HELP         OPTIONA      RESEQUENCE
CONSOLDF     DELETE       LIST          THRU        SAVE
CONSOLIDATE  DFNAME       MERGE        OPTIONL      SPOOL
```

```
MODS - MODELING LANGUAGE COMMANDS
* LIST OF MODELING LANGUAGE COMMANDS
ANALYZE     COMPILESAVE IMPACT      OPTIONA     RECORD      STORE
AUTO        DFNAME      LIST         THRU       SAVE        STORENT
BASE MODEL  END         MONTE       OPTIONL     SENSITIVITY USING
COMMANDS    GENREPORT   NORECORD    PLOT        SOLVE       WHAT IF
COMPILEGET  GOAL        OPTION      RECOMPILE   SPOOL
```

```
DATA - DATAFILE COMMANDS;  STORE/STORENT OPTIONS
* DATAFILE SUBSYSTEM COMMANDS & OPTIONS
COLUMNS      LIST         OPTIONG      SOLVE        STORENT
GENREPORT    OPTIOND      SELECT       STORE
* OPTIONS VALID UNDER STORE OR STORENT
COLUMNS      LINENUM      NAOUTPUT     SCALE        TAG
INVERT       LINENUMNOL   NAPRINT      STOREOPT     ZEROSUP
```

```
FUNCS - IFPS FUNCTIONS & SUBROUTINES
* LIST OF IFPS FUNCTIONS AND SUBROUTINES
ABS        GENDECBAL    MDIRR        NATEXP       ROUND        TREND
ACRS DEPR  GENRAND      MEAN         NATLOG       STDDEV       TRIRAND
AMORT      INTERPOLATIOMEDIAN        NORRAND      STEP         TRUNCATE
BCRATIO    IRR          MINIMUM      NPV          STLINE       UNIRAND
CIRR       LOG10        MIRR         NPVC         SUM          VMATRIX
CUMRAND    MATRIX       MOVAVG       NTV          SUMDEPR      XPOWERY
DECBAL     MAXIMUM      NATEST       POLYFIT      T1090RAND
```

```
SYS - SYSTEM CHARS;  HELPS
* SYSTEM-DEPENDENT CHARACTERISTICS & SPECIAL HELPS
FILENAMES    MODELNAMES    PRINT varbls    SPECIAL chars
```

A1.4 HELP *

HELP * provides you with a list of all the key words available within the HELP command. This is a table of contents for HELP.

A1.5 HELP KEYWORD

You can obtain an explanation for each keyword contained in HELP * by typing the word HELP followed by the keyword. We show two typical examples below: HELP ABS and HELP SOLVE. The first is a mathematical function that gives the absolute value of a number or expression. The second describes the SOLVE command. Here you will notice that all uses of SOLVE are discussed, including some, such as SUMBTASK, with which you may not be familiar or not be interested in. This is typical of what you will find in HELP. You will have to decide what is relevant and what is not relevant. *Hint:* Don't spend a lot of time trying to trace down portions of a HELP explanation that seems obscure to you. It usually (but unfortunately, not always) refers to a part of IFPS that is not of concern to you at that moment.

```
? help abs
ABS FUNCTION
FORM(S)
       ABS(EXPRESSION)
WHERE  "EXPRESSION" IS A VARIABLE NAME OR AN INDICATED  CALCULATION
INVOLVING SOME VARIABLE(S).
USAGE
   COMPUTES   THE   ALGEBRAIC   ABSOLUTE   VALUE   OF   THE   DESIGNATED
EXPRESSION. VALID IN A COMPUTATIONAL STATEMENT.

? help solve
SOLVE COMMAND
FORM(S)
       SOLVE
USAGE
   DIRECTS IFPS  TO  SOLVE  (EXECUTE)  THE  CURRENTLY  ACTIVE  MODEL
OR TO DISPLAY A DATA FILE WITH ITS VALUES IN COLUMNS.  NUMEROUS
SOLVE OPTIONS ARE THEN AVAILABLE TO SELECT/FORMAT PRINTED OUTPUT OF
THE SOLUTION.
   VALID IN THE MODELING SUBSYSTEM, WITH A FORMULA OR SUBTASK, OR
IN  THE DATAFILE SUBSYSTEM.
```

```
? help*
*   LIST OF TOPICS
ABS           COPY           INDENT        NAPRINT       !PAUSE        STATUSLIST
ACCESS        CROSSREF       !INPUT        NATEST        PERIODS       STDDEV
ACRS          !CSETPARAM     !INPUTC       NATEXP        PLOT          STEP
ALLOCATE      CUMRAND        INPUTS        NATLOG        POLYFIT       STLINE
ALTER         CURRENCY       INTERPOLATIO  NEGOPT        POSOPT        STMTS
ALTERLIST     DATA           INVERT        NEWPAGE       PRESERVE      STORE
AMORT         DATAFILE       IRR           NOCOMMAS      PRINT         STORENT
ANALYZE       DATASELECT     KEY           NOCOMMENTS    PROMPT        STOREOPT
AUTO          DATE           LEFTMARGIN    NOINDENT      PROTECT       STRUCTURE
BASE          DECBAL         LEGEND        NOLEGEND      QUIT          SUBROUTINE
BCRATIO       DEFINE         LINENUM       NOPAGE        RANGE         SUBTASK
!CALL         DEFINESTATUS   LIST          NORECORD      RECALCULATE   SUM
CASELIST      DELETE         LOG10         NORMAL        RECOMPILE     SUMDEPR
CATALOG       DFNAME         LOW           NORRAND       RECORD        !SUPPRESS
CENTER        DOUBLE         MATRIX        NOSCALE       REL8          SYS
CENTRE        END            MAXIMUM       NPV           REPORT        T1090RAND
CIRR          EXECS          MDIRR         NPVC          RESEQUENCE    TAB
!CLEARRC      EXECUTE        MEAN          NTV           !RETURN       TAG
CMDFILE       !EXIT          MEDIAN        !ONERROR      ROUND         TIME
CMDS          EXPAND         !MENU         OPT           SAVE          TITLE
COLTITLES     FILE           MERGE         OPTION        SCALE         TREND
COLUMN        FILENAMES      !MESSAGE      OPTIONA       SCALEUC       TRIRAND
COLUMNS       FORMAT         MICRO         OPTIONB       SELECT        TRUNCATE
COMBINE       FORMULA        MICROCOMPUTE  OPTIONC       SENSITIVITY   UC
COMDEC        FUNCS          MINIMUM       OPTIOND       !SETPARAM     UNDERLINE
COMMANDS      FUNCTION       MIRR          OPTIONE       SIMULTANEOUS  UNIRAND
COMMAS        GENDECBAL      MODEL         OPTIONF       SINGLE        USING
COMMENT       GENERATE       MODELNAMES    OPTIONG       !SKIP         VMATRIX
COMMENTS      GENRAND        MODIFIED      OPTIONH       SKIPNONZERO   VS
COMPILEGET    GENREPORT      MODS          OPTIONI       SKIPZERO      WHAT
COMPILESAVE   GOAL           MONTE         OPTIONJ       SOLVE         WIDTH
!COND         !GOTO          MOSTP         OPTIONK       SORT          XPOWERY
!CONDS        GRID           MOVAVG        OPTIONL       SOVER         ZEROPRINT
CONSOLDF      HELP           NA            OUTPUTS       SPACE         ZEROSUP
CONSOLIDATE   HIGH           NAIS          OVERLAY       SPECIAL
CONSUC        !IFRC          NAMEINDENT    PAGE          SPOOL
CONTENTS      IMPACT         NAOUTPUT      PAGELENGTH    SROPTS
```

APPENDIX II
IFPS COMMANDS

This appendix contains a list of all commands available to you in IFPS. The appendix is a reference guide to the commands and their syntax. Not all of the commands shown in this appendix are discussed in the text. To help you find out more about those commands that are explained in this book, the section number(s) where the command is covered is listed in parenthesis to the right of the command. For example,

```
    CATALOG                                                        (2.3)
```

indicates that the CATALOG command is discussed in Section 2.3.

Required words in the command are indicated by boldface, CAPITAL letters. Parameters that are optional are enclosed in brackets, ( ). Entries that you select (such as the names of models or files) are printed in small letters. If you have to choose one of several options, all the possible options are listed under one another and they are shown in braces. For example,

```
            MODEL
            REPORT
            FILE
COPY        STRUCTURE    name   [TO]   newname                   (4.5.4)
            FORMULA
            SUBTASK
```

tells you that in using the copy command, you must specify what type of information is to be copied (you have six choices), what the name of the original is and, following the optional word, TO, what name the copy is to have. You are also told that the copy command is discussed in Section 4.5.4. Thus, for example,

```
    COPY MODEL ONE  TO  TWO
```

is a valid use of the COPY command.

For a command having several parts, you separate the parts by spaces, as is done above for COPY. You can use commas in place of spaces. You MUST use commas for separating lists of variable names or column names.

If you command requires more than one line, use an apostrophe (') at the end of the first line and continue the command on the next line

This appendix reproduces the *IFPS Pocket Reference Guide Release 8.0,* which is copyright 1982 by EXECUCOM Systems Corporation and is used by permission.

Executive Commands

CATALOG (2.1.4, 2.3)
CMDFILE file
COMBINE [SAVE] model$_1$ model$_2$ model$_3$ . . .'
  [AS model**]**
COMMAND[S] file [startline [endline]] [parameters]
CONSOLDF file$_1$ [(c_1)] file$_2$ [(c_2)] . . . **NONE** (4.8.6)
CONSOLIDATE model$_1$ [(c_1)] model$_2$ [(c_2)]'
  . . . **[WITH** model **[USING** file**]]** (4.9)

CONSOLIDATE model **USING**' (4.8.5)
  file$_1$[(C_1)] file$_2$[(C_2)] ... **[WITH** model'
  [USING file**]]**

COPY { **MODEL** / **REPORT** / **FILE** / **STRUCTURE** / **FORMULA** / **SUBTASK** } name **[TO]** newname (4.5.4, 4.6.8)

CROSSREF modelname (4.4.1, 4.5.6)
DATAFILE file (4.6)
DATASELECT (4.6.8, 4.9)

DELETE { **MODEL** / **REPORT** / **FILE** / **STRUCTURE** / **FORMULA** / **SUBTASK** } name

DFNAME file

EXECUTE subroutine

FILE { b̸ / **YES** / **NO** } (2.3)

FORMULA name **[USING** df1, [df2,...]]

HELP { b̸ / * / **CONTENTS** / **HELP** / keyword / **WHERE** } (2.10, Appendix I)

KEY File Encryption:
[command] filename { /**KEY** = dddddd/ | (**KEY** = dddddd) }

LIST { **MODEL** | **REPORT** | **FILE** | **CMDFILE** | **DATAFILE** | **STRUCTURE** | **FORMULA** | **SUBTASK** } name [[**EXPAND**] [**GENERATE**]' (2.2.3, 4.4.1, 4.6.5)
[[**APPEND**] [**ONLY**]'
ONTO { file | **SPOOL** }]]

(The options EXPAND and GENERATE apply only with a MODEL, FORMULA, or SUBTASK.)

MERGE file$_1$ file$_2$ file$_3$ . . . **NONE**

MODEL name [**USING** file$_1$ [file$_2$ . . . file$_n$]] (2.3, 4.6.3)

NORECORD (2.6)

OPTION { **A 1** | **A 2** }

OPTION { **B 1** | **B 2** | **B 3** | **B 4** }

OPTION C linewidth

OPTION { **D 1** | **D 2** }

OPTION { **E 1** | **E 2** }

OPTION { **F 1** | **F 2** }

OPTION { **G 1** | **G 2** | **G 3** }

OPTION { **H 1** | **H 2** } (7.5)

OPTION { **I 1** | **I 2** }

OPTION { **J 1** | **J 2** }

OPTION { **K 1** | **K 2** }

OPTION { **L** ø | **L** colnumber }

QUIT { ƀ | **YES** | **NO** } (2.4)

RECORD (2.6)
REPORT name (4.7.1)

RESEQUENCE { **MODEL** | **REPORT** | **CMDFILE** | **STRUCTURE** | **FORMULA** | **SUBTASK** } name [start [incr]] (4.4.1, 4.5.3)

SAVE (2.2.4)

SPOOL { file | **CLOSE** }

STRUCTURE name
SUBTASK name [**USING** df1 [df2 . . .]]

Modeling Language Commands

ANALYZE variable-reference (3.1.4)

AUTO [start [incr]] { ƀ | **S** | **SUPPRESS** } (2.2.2, 2.5.2)

BASE [MODEL] (3.1.1)

COMMAND[S] file [startline [endline]] [parameters]

COMPILEGET file (4.5.5)

COMPILESAVE file (4.5.5)

END (2.2.2)

GENERATE temp-list **AT** start-line **[BY** incr]'
  FOR symbol-list

GENREPORT name [**[APPEND] [ONLY]**' (4.7)
  ONTO { file | **SPOOL** }]

GOAL [SEEKING] (3.1.3)

IMPACT [ON] variable-reference [, **BY** pct]

LIST [EXPAND] [GENERATE] (2.2.3, 4.4.1, 4.6.5)

MONTE CARLO n (5.2 ,5.8, 5.9, 5.10)

NORECORD (2.6)

OPTION letter code
  (All OPTIONS listed in Section 1 are valid in the MODEL subsystem.)

PLOT [variable-reference [/plot-character/],. . .] (4.3)

RECOMPILE

RECORD (2.6)

SAVE (2.2.4)

SENSITIVITY [TO] variable-reference (3.1.2)

SOLVE (2.2.5)

SPOOL { file | **CLOSE** }

STORE file (2.2.5, 3.1.1, 4.1)
  (See Section 9B for valid STORE/STOREP options.)

STOREP file

STORENT file (4.6.7, 4.9)
  (See Section 9B for valid STORENT options.)

USING $file_1$ [$file_2$ . . . $file_n$] . (4.6.3)

WHAT IF [CONTINUE] (3.1.1)

SOLVE/REPORT/PLOT Options

A. *Valid as SOLVE options and REPORT directives:*

CASELIST [BASESUP] (3.1.5)
COLUMN[S] columnlist (2.2.1, 2.8.1, 4.1)

COMDEC $\left\{\begin{matrix}\textbf{A}\\ \textbf{E1}\\ \textbf{E2}\end{matrix}\right\}$

COMMAS
COMMENT[S] (4.1.4)
CURRENCY symbol
DOUBLE (4.1.4)
FORMAT specifications and replications
    Valid column descriptors are 9, B, D, and #. (4.7.5)
    Periods are used for the name field, N's for the
    line number field.
FORMAT. . . n[(D,DDD)] (4.7.5)
INDENT (4.1.4)
INVERT [NOVAR] (4.1.4, 4.3.2)
LEFTMARGIN n
NAMEINDENT number

NAOUTPUT $\left\{\begin{matrix}\not{b}\\ \text{text}\\ \textbf{NULL}\end{matrix}\right\}$

NAPRINT [NO]

NEGOPT $\left\{\begin{matrix}\textbf{PAREN}\\ \textbf{—}\\ \textbf{—A}\\ \textbf{DB}\\ \textbf{CR}\end{matrix}\right\}$ (4.1.4)

NOCOMMAS
NOCOMMENT[S] (4.1.4)
NOINDENT (4.1.4)
NOPAGE
NORMAL

NOSCALE
OPT namewidth columnwidth [decimal-places] (4.2)
OVERLAY [position] text
PAGE
PLOT [variable-reference [/plot-character/], . . .]
    (PLOT options are shown in Section 3C.)   (4.3)

POSOPT $\left\{\begin{matrix}\textbf{+}\\ \textbf{CR}\end{matrix}\right\}$ (4.1.4)

SCALE [MULTIPLY] $\left\{\begin{matrix}\text{constant}\\ \text{variable}\\ \text{constant*variable}\end{matrix}\right\}$ (4.3)

SINGLE (4.1.4)

SORT $\left\{\begin{matrix}\not{b}\\ \textbf{A}\\ \textbf{D}\end{matrix}\right\}$ **ON** $\left\{\begin{matrix}\text{col-refs}\\ \textbf{NAME}\end{matrix}\right\}$ (var-refs)

SPACE [n]

WIDTH linewidth [namewidth columnwidth' (4.2, 4.73)
    [decimal places]]
ZEROPRINT (4.1.4)
ZEROSUP (4.1.4)

B. *REPORT Directives Only:*

CENTER [PROMPT] text (4.7.2)
CENTRE [PROMPT] text
COLUMN[S] TITLE[S] [$title_1$, $title_2$, . . .] (4.7.4)
Date
The current date may be generated with **&DATE&** or ***DATE*** on a comment line.

NEWPAGE $\begin{bmatrix} 1 \\ FF \end{bmatrix}$

Page
The current page number may be generated with ***PAGE*** on a comment line or after the directive CENTER.
PAGELENGTH toplines bodylines bottomlines'
[[newpage key] [repeatlines]]
PROMPT [text]
SKIPNONZERO variable-reference, reportline
SKIPZERO variable-reference, reportline

Tab
/text/**TAB** n, variable (column)'
[, **TAB** n2, variable (column), . . .]

Time
The current time may be generated with **&TIME&** or ***TIME***.
UNDERLINE [character] (4.7.2)

Special Characters
/ Slashes are used for variable name replacement (renaming a variable in the report at print time).

* Any report line starting with an asterisk will be printed verbatim in the report. (*PROMPT will prompt for the line's text before the report is generated.)

C. *Plot Options*

GRID vert-lines horiz-chars gridoption (4.3)
INVERT (4.1.4, 4.3.2)
LEGEND
NOLEGEND
NORMAL
PLOT variable-reference [/plot-character/], . . . (4.3)
RANGE y-minimum y-maximum x-minimum' (4.3.2)
x-maximum
SCALE scalefactor (4.3.2)

SOVER $\left\{\begin{matrix} \text{character} \\ \textbf{LAST} \end{matrix}\right\}$ (4.3.2)

TITLE number $\left\{\begin{matrix} \textbf{TOP} \\ \textbf{LEFT} \\ \textbf{BOTTOM} \end{matrix}\right\} \left\{\begin{matrix} \textbf{CENTER} \\ \textbf{CENTRE} \\ \textbf{MARGIN} \end{matrix}\right\}$ /text (4.3.2)

VS $\left\{\begin{matrix} \text{variable} \\ \textbf{COLUMN} \end{matrix}\right\}$ (4.3.2)

D. *SOLVE Options for Probabilistic Value Control*

HIGH variable list (5.7)
LOW variable list (5.7)
MEAN variable list (5.7)
MOSTP variable list (5.7)
The preceding options may be reset to the default with a BASE [MODEL] command.

Special Modeling Language Statements & Identifiers

ACCESS {**FORMULA** | **SUBTASK**} name, filename

COLUMN[S] {1-n, [, name1 [, name2, . . .]] | 19nn [-19mm] | name1 [, name2, . . .]} (2.2.1, 2.8.1, 4.1.2, 4.1.3)

FUNCTION name, file

NA IS {text | **NULL**}

PERIODS number (2.8.7, 3.2.2, 6.2.4)
PROTECT [OFF]
Relational Operators:
variable = **IF** relational-test'
THEN true-expression' (4.4.3)
ELSE false-expression
for operators:

.EQ. **.NE.**
.LT. **.LE.** (4.4.3)
.GT. **.GE.**

SIMULTANEOUS {**AUTO** | variable-list} (6.15)

SUBROUTINE name, file
Variable-definition Matrix Identifiers:
FUTURE [n] variable-reference. (2.8.5, 3.2.3)
PREVIOUS [n] variable-reference (2.2.1, 2.8.5)

IFPS Functions

Discounted Cash Flow Functions

BCRATIO (cash inflow, discount rate,' (3.2.1)
cash outflow)
CIRR (cash inflow, cash outflow)
IRR (cash inflow, cash outflow) (2.7, 3.2.1, 6.4.3)
MDIRR (cash inflow, cash outflow)
MIRR (cash inflow, discount rate,' (6.4.3)
cash outflow)
NPV (cash inflow, discount rate, life, investment) (6.2)
NPVC (cash inflow, discount rate, cash outflow) (2.7, 3.2, 6.2)
NTV (cash inflow, compound rate, cash outflow) (3.2.1, 6.2)

Mathematical Functions

ABS (value) (3.2.4)
INTERPOLATION ON (variable reference,' (3.2.4, 6.12)
x_1,y_1, x_2,y_2,. . .)
LOG10 (value)
MATRIX (var-ref, col-ref) (2.8.8, 3.2.3, 4.4.2)
MAXIMUM ($value_1$, $value_2$, $value_3$,. . .) (3.2.4, 6.14)
MEAN (reference1, reference2) (3.2.3, 6.7, 7.1)
MEDIAN (reference1, reference2) (3.2.3, 7.1.4)
MINIMUM ($value_1$, $value_2$, $value_3$,. . .) (3.2.4, 6.14, 7.1.5)
NATEST (var-ref)
NATEXP (value) (3.2.4)
NATLOG (value) (3.2.4)
ROUND (value) (3.2.4)
ROUNDUP (value) (3.2.4)
STDDEV (reference1, reference2) (3.2.3, 7.1.5)
STEP (variable-reference, x_1,y_1, x_2,y_2,. . .) (3.2.4)

$$\text{SUM(}\begin{Bmatrix} \text{var-ref} \begin{Bmatrix}\text{THRU}\\ ,\end{Bmatrix} \text{var-ref} \\ \text{col-ref} \begin{Bmatrix}\text{THRU}\\ ,\end{Bmatrix} \text{col-ref}\end{Bmatrix}\text{) (4.4.4)}$$

TRUNCATE (value) (3.2.4)
VMATRIX ([FUTURE] var-ref, col-ref)
XPOWERY (x, y) (3.2.4, 6.12)

Extrapolation Functions

MOVAVG (variable-reference, wt_1, wt_2, wt_3,. . .) (3.2.3, 7.1.1, 7.7)
POLYFIT (k) (3.2.3, 7.7.1)
TREND (variable-reference) (3.2.3)

Probability Distribution Functions

CUMRAND[R] (0%, 10%,. . .100%) (5.3, 5.4)
GENRAND[R] (x_1, y_1, x_2, y_2,. . .) (5.3, 5.4)
NORRAND[R] (mean, std-deviation) (5.3)
TRIRAND[R] (low, most-probable, high) (5.3)
T1090RAND[R] (10%, most-probable, 90%) (5.3)
UNIRAND[R] (low, high) (5.3)

The R form of each distribution implies serial independence of columns. Without the R, the columns are completely correlated.

IFPS Subroutines

A subroutine differs from other variable definition statements in that several variables may be defined on one line of logic. The variables have no line number associated with their values. In the following descriptions, subroutine output variables will be underlined:

ACRS [DEPR] (category, start, cost, period-depreciation, book-value, cumulative depreciation) (3.3)

AMORT (amortized loan, demand loan, interest rate, life, start column, payments per column, payment, interest, principal, balance) (3.3)

DECBAL [DEPR] (asset value, salvage fraction, life, acceleration constant, switch key, period depreciation, book value, cumulative depreciation) (3.3)

GENDECBAL [DEPR] (asset value, salvage fraction, life, acceleration constant, switch key, allocation, period depreciation, book value, cumulative depreciation) (3.3)

STLINE [DEPR] (asset value, salvage fraction, life, period depreciation, book value, cumulative depreciation) (3.3)

SUM [DEPR] (asset value, salvage fraction, life, period depreciation, book value, cumulative depreciation) (3.3)

User-Defined Operations

A. To activate the **FORMULA** or **SUBTASK** subsystem, enter one of the following:
FORMULA name [**USING** df1 [, df2, . . .]]
SUBTASK name [**USING** df1 [, df2, . . .]]

B. Before utilizing a user-defined operation, a model must contain the statement:
ACCESS {**FORMULA** | **SUBTASK**} name, filename

C. Statements required at the beginning of an operation (OUTPUTS valid in a SUBTASK only):
INPUTS input1 [, input2, . . .]
OUTPUTS output1 [, output2, . . .]

D. Commands used when building/solving operations:
LIST
PRESERVE filename
PROMPT
SAVE
SOLVE

Most modeling language commands of Section 2 and the **SOLVE** options of Section 3 are valid for user-defined operations. Executive level commands are also recognized.

Command File Directives

To activate the CMDFILE subsystem and build/edit a command file:

CMDFILE filename

To execute a command file from the Executive level or MODEL subsystem:

COMMAND[S] filename [startline [stopline]]'
[param1 [, param2, . . .]]

!CALL filename [startline [endline]] [parameters]
!CLEARRC
!COMMENT [text]
!COND statement [text]
!CONDS statement [text]
!CSETPARAM number substitution
!END
!EXIT
!GOTO n
!IFRC {.EQ. code / .NE. code} statement
!INPUT [text]
!INPUTC [text]
!MENU[S] number, . . ., number
!MESSAGE [text]
!ONERROR code statement
!PAUSE [text]
!RETURN [n]
!SETPARAM number substitution
!SKIP n
!SUPPRESS
!SUPPRESS OFF

DATAFILE Commands and Options

To activate the **DATAFILE** subsystem to build/edit/execute a data file:

DATAFILE filename (4.6)

A. *Datafile Commands*

COLUMNS n (2.2.1, 2.8.1, 4.1.2, 4.1.3)
GENREPORT name [[**APPEND**][**ONLY**]' (4.7, 4.9)

ONTO { file | **SPOOL** }

LIST (2.2.3, 4.4.1)
SAVE (2.2.4)

SELECT { **TAG** tagname | **VARIABLE** var-name | **COLUMN** col-number }

SOLVE
(The SOLVE options presented in Section 3 are also valid in the DATAFILE subsystem.) (2.2.5, 3.1.1, 4.1, 4.6.5, 4.7)
(OPTIONS D and G are valid in the DATAFILE subsystem—See Section 1.)

STORE file
STOREP file
STORENT file (4.6.7, 4.9)
(See Section 9B for STORE, STOREP, and STORENT options.)

B. *STORE/STORENT/STOREP Options*

COLUMN[S] columnspecs
INVERT
LINENUM[NOL]
(Valid under STORENT only)
MICROSTORE

NAOUTPUT { text | **NULL** | ƀ }

NAPRINT { ƀ | **NO** }
NOAUTOST
NOSTORE

SCALE [MULTIPLY] { constant | variable | constant*variable }
STOREOPT sf dp
TAG tagname
(Valid under STORE and STOREP)
ZEROSUP

Data Editing—See Section 12B

Universal Consolidation

To activate the **STRUCTURE** subsystem to build/edit/execute a structure:

STRUCTURE filename

A. *STRUCTURE* Directives

ALLOCATE dfname
list of distinct variable names

{**COMMENT** / * / **C**} text

DEFINE nodefile **AS** modname'
USING df1 [(fac1)] [, df2 [(fac2)], . . .]'
[**WITH** postmod [**USING** ppdf]]'
[[**ONLY**] **ONTO** rptfile]
DEFINESTATUS filename
GENREPORT rpt1 [, rpt2, . . .] **FROM** [**MODEL**]'
modname [**USING** df1 [, df2, . . .]]
GENREPORT rpt1 [, rpt 2, . . .]'
FROM DATAFILE nodefile
SCALE [**MULTIPLY**] [**BY**] var-name [**EXCLUDE**'
variable-list]
STORE dfname [**FROM** modname]
variable-list
STORENT FROM modname
variable-list

B. *Universal Consolidation Commands*

ALTER {nodefile / **ALL**} [**FROM** dfname1]'
[, {nodefile / **ALL**} [**FROM** dfname2], . . .]
ALTERLIST
AUTO [start [incr]]
BASE
CONSOLIDATE [**THRU** nodefile]'
[**RECALCULATE**]
END
LIST
MODIFIED {dfname1 [, dfname2,...] / **ALL**}
RECALCULATE
RECOMPILE
SAVE
STATUSLIST

Editing Commands

A. *Line Editing Commands*

AUTO (2.2.2, 2.5.2)
END (2.2.2)

Print

To print a line or lines, enter the number, optionally followed by the letter **P**:

```
10P
10
10,40
10,40P
```

Delete

To delete a line or lines, enter the number or the range immediately followed by the letter **D**: (2.5)

```
10D
10,40D
```

Change**

To change the first occurrence of text on a line, any of the following forms may be used. The C form then prints the changed lines; the CS form does not: (2.5.3)

```
10C/old text/new text/
10,60C/old text/new text/
10C "old text" new text"
10,60 "old text" new text"

10CS/old text/new text/
10,60CS/old text/new text/
10CS "old text"new text"
10,60CS "old text" new text"
```

Global Change**

To change every occurrence of text on a line or lines, any of the forms below may be used. The G form then prints the changed lines; the GS form does not: (2.5, 4.10.2)

```
10G/old text/new text/
10G "old text"new text"
10,60G/old text/new text/
10,60G "old text"new text"

10GS/old text/new text/
10GS "old text"new text"
10,60GS/old text/new text/
10,60GS "old text"new text"
```

Insert or Replace

To insert or replace a line of text enter the number of the line, followed by the text of the line: (4.10.3)

```
10 text
```

** On some systems, the backslash character (\) may be used instead of the quote character (").

B. *Data Editing Commands*

CHANGE col-number [**FOR** variable-list[= $\left\{\begin{matrix}\text{values}\\ \text{filename}\end{matrix}\right\}$]]

CHANGE variable [**FOR** column-list [= $\left\{\begin{matrix}\text{values}\\ \text{filename}\end{matrix}\right\}$]]

INSERT col-number [**FOR** variable-list [= $\left\{\begin{matrix}\text{values}\\ \text{filename}\end{matrix}\right\}$]] (4.10.4)

REMOVE col-number [**FOR** variable-list] (4.10.4)

The line editing commands shown in Section 12A are also valid with data entries.

APPENDIX III
RESERVED WORDS

IFPS imposes few limits on you when it comes to labeling or naming files, models, report, and variables. There are, however, a few words which cannot be used to name files, models or reports. These words are called "reserved" words. Some words cannot form part of a compound (i.e., two or more word) variable name. Some words cannot be used by themselves as variable names. That is, IFPS assumes that these words have their specific meaning in the language rather than being one of the names you assigned. The reserved words and variable naming restrictions of IFPS are explained in detail in this Appendix.

MODELS AND REPORTS

The names

END	NONE	USING
NO	STOP	WITH

cannot be used as names for models or reports.

VARIABLES

1. Variables in IFPS models cannot *begin* with the following words:

COLUMN or COLUMNS	FUTURE	PERIODS
COMMENT	IF	PREVIOUS
DATA	MATRIX	SUBROUTINE
END	NO	SIMULTANEOUS
FUNCTION	NONE	USING

This restriction means, for example, that you cannot write:

```
30 FUTURE SAVINGS = 110
```

but you can write:

```
30 FUTURESAVINGS = 110.
```

That is, if any of the above words (e.g., FUTURE) appears as the first word of a multi-word variable name, IFPS will reject it and give you an error message. However, if the word is part of a longer word (e.g., FUTURESAVINGS) it is acceptable.

2. Several restrictions apply because of the need to distinguish comments and line numbers. Specifically:

- Variable names may not begin with C followed by a blank
- Variable names may not begin with an L followed by a number.
- Variable names may not begin with LINE followed by a number.
- Variable names may not begin with RL followed by a number.

Thus,

```
C ALL
L3TWO
LINE2TWO
RL3
```

are all examples of names that *cannot* be used because of their confusion with comments, line numbers, or report line numbers.

Similarly, because the words THRU and FOR are used, respectively, to indicate collections of variables and number of periods, they cannot be used by themselves in the middle of variable names. Thus,

```
A  FOR  B
PROFIT  THRU  INVESTMENT
```

are invalid; however,

AFOR B
PROFITTHRUINVESTMENT

are valid. The operating rule is that FOR and THRU cannot have a blank space on both sides of them.

3. If you use a report with your model, you will run into trouble if a variable name is identical to a report directive. Since it is not unusual in practice to decide that you want to create a report format for presenting your results after you have developed a model, you will find it good practice to avoid using the following names for variables:

CENTER	FORMAT	NOINDENT	SKIPZERO
CENTRE	INDENT	NOPAGE	TAB
COMDEC	INVERT	OPT	UNDERLINE
COMMAS	NEGOPT	PAGE	WIDTH
COMMENT	NOCOMMAS	POSOPT	ZEROPRINT
CURRENCY	NOCOMMENT	SKIPONZERO	ZEROSUP

4. Finally, although you can use the names of commands (e.g., LIST, MODEL, SOLVE) as a variable name or as the first word of a variable name, you cannot change the value of that variable under WHAT IF. The reason is that IFPS treats the name as a command and does not recognize it as a variable to be modified.

FILE NAMES

The following names should not be used for files:

END	NONE	USING
NO	STOP	WITH

APPENDIX IV
20 MOST COMMON ERROR MESSAGES IN IFPS

This appendix lists the more common error messages that you may encounter in using IFPS. The list given is *not* complete. There are many more error messages than we have space for here. We have included those error messages that apply to commands described in this book. If you encounter an error message not listed in this appendix which you cannot figure out, consult the *IFPS USER'S MANUAL*.

UNDEFINED VARIABLE

The variable is not defined on the LEFT-HAND side of an equal sign. You either: (1) spelled the name of the variable differently on the right hand side than on the left hand side, or (2) you didn't define it at all. Look for the variable on the left-hand side. If it isn't there, add a line to your model defining the variable. If it is there, compare the spelling on the two sides.

VARIABLE NOT DEFINED

Similar to UNDEFINED VARIABLE. You referred to a variable on the right hand side of an equal sign and IFPS did not find its definition anywhere on the left side of an equal sign.

UNRECOGNIZED COMMAND

This error typically occurs when you misspell a command such as writing KIST for LIST. To correct, retype the command. However, this error message also occurs if you forget to put an equal sign on a line. In this case, IFPS thinks your modeling instruction is a command and can't understand you. Retype the line.

This error message also occurs after a RESEQUENCE command if you do not specify the MODEL or REPORT that you want. When you give a RESEQUENCE command, your current model or report is no longer available to you. You therefore have to use the MODEL or REPORT command (Section 2.3) to go back to where you were.

FILE NAME MUST BE __ OR FEWER CHARACTERS

You get this message whenever you try to give an IFPS file a name that is longer than maximum allowed on your machine. IFPS is smart enough to tell you the maximum number allowed on your computer. Choose a different name which fits within the maximum allowed.

NUMBER OF EXPRESSIONS IS GREATER THAN NUMBER OF COLUMNS

If you define more columns of information than in your COLUMNS statement, IFPS asks you to correct the line. For example,

```
10 COLUMNS 1-3
20 X=1,2,3,4
```

leads to this message. Remember that if you define too few columns, you do not get an error message. IFPS simply assumes the last column value given is true for all subsequent columns. For example,

```
10 COLUMNS 1-3
20 X=1,2
```

is OK. IFPS assumes the values of X are 1, 2, and 2.

LINE __ NEEDS CORRECTING

This message tells you where your error occurred. Look there first. However, in some cases, the mistake may be at a different place. For example, if you said:

```
10 PROFIT = REVENUE - COST
20 REVINU = 100
```

you may want to change the spelling of REVINU in line 20 even though IFPS tells you that line 10 needs correcting since REVENUE is undefined.

IF LINE EXISTS, IT DOES NOT DEFINE A VARIABLE

You referenced a line in your model by a line number which is empty. For example,

```
10 X=3
20 Y= SUM(L10,L15)
```

would lead to this error.

MODEL NOT FOUND

This message results if you ask for a model in your file by the wrong name or you misspell the name of the file. It also occurs if you are ready to create a new model. IFPS will follow this message immediately with another message: NEW MODEL WILL BE CREATED. If you want to create a new model, ignore the message and begin entering your new model. If you thought you already had a model with that name, first check the spelling. If the spelling seems all right, use CATALOG in response to a question mark to obtain a list of the models in that file.

DIVISION BY ZERO IN COMPUTATION OF VARIABLE

Your model resulted in a zero in the denominator of a fraction. Division by zero does not stop the computation. Rather, IFPS prints a string of 9's in your output at the location where this division was attempted. Be sure to check your output to find out *why* you received this message. It usually means you made a modeling mistake. This error can propagate through your results if you refer to the location by PREVIOUS, FUTURE, or

MATRIX.

ILLEGAL COLUMN NAME OR NUMBER

You referred to a column either by name or by number which does not exist in your model. This message often occurs in editing your model.

COLUMN NUMBER IS GREATER THAN THE NUMBER OF COLUMNS IN MODEL

You referred to a column number that is larger than the number of columns in your model. This error is typically encountered when using the special COLUMN commands.

COLUMN STATEMENT MUST PRECEDE ALL VARIABLE DEFINITIONS

You have to define the number or names of your columns as the first statement in your model. This means that, for example, if you write:

```
10 COLUMNS 1-12
```

you cannot have any lines numbered lower than 10. You can also receive this message if you make a mistake in a special COLUMN command and IFPS thinks you are trying to define the number of columns in your model.

COLUMN NAME OR NUMBER MUST BE FOLLOWED BY FOR

If you use the special COLUMN commands to refer to a specific variable, you have to use the word FOR right after the column name. For example,

```
20 COLUMN 5 OF PRICE = 3
```

is incorrect. You should write:

```
20 COLUMN 5 FOR PRICE = 3.
```

THIS WHAT IF STATEMENT NOT ACCEPTED

If you make a mistake in format writing a WHAT IF statement, IFPS may reject it. You have to start over. Retype WHAT IF and then follow it with the changes you want. If IFPS gives you this message again, review what you just typed and try to see what format error you made.

GOAL UNATTAINABLE - COLUMN _

IFPS tried to achieve your goal but could not. Usually this means that you have relations in your model that do not allow you to satisfy the goal criterion. You will find it useful to use the ANALYZE command for both the variable to be adjusted and the variable in your goal when you try to trace down the error.

NO CONVERGENCE FOR SIMULTANEOUS EQUATIONS IN COLUMN

If you have a set of simultaneous equations in your model, IFPS will try to solve them by an iterative method called Gauss-Seidel. This method terminates when all equations are satisfied simultaneously. If you define impossible relations, for example

```
10 X + Y = 3
20 X + Y = 6
```

then IFPS will tell you that your model is wrong. For complicated sets of simultaneous equations, IFPS may not be able to reach an answer in 50 iterations even though one exists. In this case, you also receive this message. Use the prompts for examining simultaneous equations and check the simultaneous equations by hand, if necessary.

MISSING (or OPERAND

Check for a different number of right-hand and left-hand parentheses or for a missing arithmetic operator (+, –, *, /) or a missing THEN or ELSE in an IF statement.

RESEQUENCE NOT FOLLOWED BY MODEL, REPORT, OR CMDFILE

When you ask IFPS to resequence line numbers, you must specify whether it is a MODEL, REPORT or command file that is to be resequenced and you must give the proper name. Repeat the resequence command giving the correct information.

STARTING NUMBER MUST BE LARGER THAN LAST LINE NUMBER

If you give an AUTO command when revising an existing model, you can only start after the last line of the existing model.

INDEX

ABS, 89
Accuracy, 13
ACRS, 95-96
Aggregate scheduling, 326-333
Aggragation, 13
ALL, 101-105, 175
Allocation fraction, 95
Alpha, 304-305
AMORT, 96-97
Amortization, 93,96-97
ANALYZE, 78-79
Arithmetic operations, 55, 253
Assumptions, role of, 18,235-236, 239-240, 255
AUTO, 38-39, 44
Average deviation, 277
Average return on book value, 218
Balance sheet, 255-256
Base model, 71-72
BCRATIO, 81-83, 219
Benefit/cost ratio,81-83, 219
Best case-worst case estimates, 159-160, 171-174, 239-240
Beta, 228-231
Binomial distribution,281-282, 360-361
Black-Scholes Formula,244-248
Blank lines, 54
Blank spaces, 93
Bonds, 205-206
Book value, 93, 218
Break-even analysis, 231, 236-238, 323-327
Brealey,Richard, 201
Built-in functions, 22, 80-93, 93-97, 165-167
C (edit), 45-46
Call options 244-248
Capital asset pricing model, 228-231
Capitalization rate, 208-213
CASELIST, 79-80
Cash management model, 253-254
CATALOG, 35, 41-42
CENTER, 130
Centering text, 130
CHANGE, 154-155
Changing phrases, 153
Chi-square test, 283-289
Coefficient of determination, 294-295, 297
Coefficient of variation, 278
COLUMN (computational statement),116-118, 143
COLUMN TITLES, 133
COLUMNS, 37-54, 103-104, 175-176
Combinations, 278-280
Combining data from several files, 125-129, 138-147
Commas (in MONTE CARLO), 179
COMMENT, 104
COMPILEGET, 121
COMPILESAVE, 120-121
Confidence intervals, 164-165, 181, 182, 277-278, 364
CONSOLDF, 144
CONSOLIDATE, 22, 138-145, 145-151
CONSOLIDATE...USING, 143-144
CONSOLIDATE...WITH, 146, 150
Consolidation, 22, 138-151
Consumers risk, 361-363
COPY, 120, 128, 360
Correlation analysis, 294-295
Correlation coefficient, 227, 294-296
CROSSREF, 113, 121-122
CUMRAND, 165, 168-169
Cyclical fluctuations, 306, 313-314
D (edit), 46
Data files, 122-129, 144-145, 145-151, 154-155
DATAFILE, 124-125, 145-151
DATASELECT, 125-129, 145-151
DECBAL, 94
Decimal form of percentages, 82
Decision support systems, 15-20
DEFAULT (Monte Carlo), 179
Dependent demand, 349
Depreciation, 93-96, 224-225
Deseasonalizing data, 308-314
Directive, 128-129
Discount rate, 208-211
Discounts (quantity), 338-339

Dispersion measures, 273-278
DOUBLE, 104
Doublesmooth, 305
Dummy model, 122, 149
Economic lot size model, 338
Economic order quantity, 335-337
Editing commands, 44-47, 133-135, 151-155
Electric car project model, 231-244
END, 39
EOQ model, 335-341, 350
Equal sign, 54-55
Equipment replacement, 353-359
Executive command, 24
Expand, 113, 122
EXPFORECAST, 304
Exponential functions, 89
Exponential smoothing, 304
F2 function, 305
FILE, 41-42
File, 33-35
Financial forecasting model, 255-261
Financial functions, 80-83
Financial planning languages, 3-4, 19
Financial ratios, 248-253
FOR, 52, 56
Forecasting, 14, 241-243, 255-261
Forecasting functions, 83-87, 292-293, 301-314, 326-327
FORMAT, 133-134
Formatting reports, 129-138, 248-249
Frequency table, 180, 269
FUTURE, 22, 55, 86, 248
Gauss-Seidel method, 260
GENDECBAL, 95
GENRAND, 165, 168-169,
GENREPORT, 129-131, 137, 149-151
Global search, 152-154
GOAL SEEKING, 22, 76-78
Goodness of fit test, 285-286
GRID, 108-110
Growth opportunities, 214-215
Guano project, 221-225
Headings, 54
HELP, 64-65, 367-371
Histogram, 175-179, 181-182, 190
HMMS model, 329-333
IF...THEN...ELSE, 114-115, 364
IFPS Users Manual, 4, 122, 123, 145
IFPS
  overview, 20-27
  structure, 24-27
  file processing, 73-74
  entering, 33-35
  making IFPS available, 32-33
Income statements, 255-261
INDENT, 104
Independence tests, 286-289
Index numbers, 312, 314-317
INSERT, 154-155
Interactive session, 23, 31-35
Internal Rate of return, 53, 81-83, 218-219, 324
INTERPOLATION ON, 89-92, 246-248
Interval halving, 211-213
Inventory, 63, 333-348
INVERT, 104, 112-113
Investment criteria, 205-219, 228-231
IRR, 53, 81-83, 218-219, 261, 324
Kurtosis, 181, 276-277
Laspeyres index, 317
Line length, 103, 118-119
Line numbers, 37, 38-39, 46-47, 71, 113, 119-120
Linear regression, 289-296, 306
LIST, 39, 113-124
Listing, 46-47, 48
Locating phrases, 152-153
Log on, 23, 31-32
Log out, 42-43
Logarithms, 89
Lot tolerance fraction defective, 362
Management information systems, 17
Management science model, 17
Market model, 9
Material requirements planning, 349-352
Mathematical functions, 87-93
MATRIX, 56, 84, 113-114, 268
MAXIMUM, 88, 253, 277, 312
MEAN, 83-84, 226-227, 267-271, 301-303
Mean, 83-84, 181, 267-271, 301-303
MEDIAN, 83-84, 271-273
Median, 83-84, 271-273
Miller-Orr Model, 253-254
MINIMUM, 88, 253, 277, 312
MIRR, 218-219
Mistakes, correcting, 44-46
Modeling, 4-14
  Building, 11-13
  Defined, 160
  Hierarchy, 6-7
  Language commands, 182
  Pitfalls, 14
  Subsystem, 27
Models, 5-11, 17-18, 33-34, 34-35, 41-42
Models (specific)

Capital asset pricing, 228-231
Cash management, 253-254
Economic lot size, 340
Economic order quantity, 337-339
Electric car, 231-239
Financial forecasting, 255-261
Guano, 221-225
HMMS, 329-333
Management science, 17
Market, 9
Miller-Orr, 253-254
Order point systems, 339-346
Pro-forma forecast, 255-261
Regression, 290-293
Simple IFPS, 36-40, 49-53, 170-171
Stock portfolio, 226-227
MONTE CARLO, 165, 242-244, 346-347
Model, 171-182
Options, 175
Pool, 182
Risk example, 187-188
Monte Carlo, 165, 174-182, 187-188, 242-244, 346-348
MOVAVG (moving average), 83, 85-86, 268-269, 301-304, 308-312
Moving Average, 267, 301-304, 309-312
Multiple Regression, 269-301
Myers, Stewart, 201
NATEXP, 88-89, 246
NATLOG, 88-89, 246
NEGOPT, 105
Net present value, 53, 80-82, 201, 326, 357
Net requirement, 349
New report creation, 130-131
New product model, 49-53
NOCOMMENTS, 104
NOINDENT, 104
Non-annual payments, 205
NONE, 175-179
NORRAND, 165, 167
NORM, 175-179, 277
Normal approximation table, 180-181
NPV, 202-203
NPVC, 53, 80-82, 202-203, 205, 219-220, 231-235, 261, 326
NTV, 81-82, 202-204
Operating characteristics (OC) curves, 359-361
OPT, 105-107
Order point systems model, 341-348
P-Chart, 364-366
Paasche index, 317
Payback period, 217, 236
PERIODS, 56, 83, 205
Permutations, 278-280
Pitfalls of modeling, 14
PLOT, 107-113
Plotting results, 107, 181-182, 231, 342-343, 345
Poisson distribution, 282-283
POLYFIT, 83, 87, 301-304
POOL, 182
POSOPT, 105
Postprocessing, 143-147
Prediction, 289
Present Value, 205-215, 216-217, 219, 261
PREVIOUS, 22, 38, 55, 219
Printer, 47-48
Pro forma financial forecasting, 255-261
Probability distributions, 165-169, 171-174, 187-188, 278-279, 346-347
Process average (for defectives), 362
Profit and loss (pro forma), 55-63, 135-138
Producers risk, 361-363
Quality control, 359-363
QUIT, 40-43
Random numbers, 160-161, 163-164, 169-170, 191-197
Random Variables, 160-161
RANGE, 112
Range, 277
Rate of return, 228-231
Ratio analysis, 248-253
RECORD,47-48
Regression, 86-87, 290, 296, 297
Regression coefficients, 290, 296, 297, 304
REMOVE, 154-155
Reports, 135-138, 145-151
RESEQUENCE, 113, 119-120
Risk analysis, 122,186-190, 228-231, 361-363
ROUND, 89
ROUNDUP, 89
ROWS, 104, 107-113
Sample statistics (in MONTE CARLO), 181, 189
Sampling, 160
SAVE, 39
SCALE, 112
Scatyter diagram, 289
Scenarios, 171-174, 239-244, 346-347
Search (for words or phrases), 152
Seasonal index, 63, 306, 308-312
Sensitivity, 73-76, 231, 238-239

Short-term forecastiong, 301-305
Simple IFPS model, 36-40, 49-53, 130-131, 170-171, 183-185
Simulation, 159-165, 174-179, 180-182, 187-190, 241-244, 346-348
Simultaneous equations, 259-260
SINGLE, 104
Skewness, 181, 276
Sobol, Marion G., 267
SOLVE, 39-40, 71, 101-105, 124, 129, 293
SOVER, 113
SPACE, 105, 130, 135
Spelling mistakes, 44-46
Standard deviation, 83-85, 181, 273-276, 364
Standard error of the estimate, 296, 297
Standard units of work, 327-328
Starr, Martin K., 267, 321, 362
Statistical functions, 83-87, 267-278
Statistical inference in regression, 295-296
STDDEV, 83-85, 273-276
STEP, 90-93
STLINE DEPR, 93-94, 225
Stock portfolio analysis model, 226-227
Stocks, 205-209, 226-227, 244-248
STORENT, 125, 145-147
Subsystems, 24-27
SUM, 115-116
SUM DEPR, 94-95
Switchover, 94-95
Symbols, 112, 113, 118-119, 152-153
T1090RAND,165-167
THRU, 103
Time (plotting), 112-113
Time-saving options, 120-121
Time series, 301-315
Timing for investments, 219-221
TITLE, 110-11
Tradeoffs, 328-331
TREND, 83, 86-87
Trend, 306
TRIRAND, 165-167, 242-245
TRUNCATE, 89
Uncertainty, modeling, 160, 346-348
UNDERLINE, 131
UNIRAND, 165, 166
Variable names, 122, 225
Variance, 226-227, 273-276
Variance analysis, 141, 226-227
Weighting, 85, 268-269, 270-271, 317
WHAT IF, 21-22, 70-73
WHAT IF CONTINUE, 72, 73, 79-80
WIDTH, 105-107, 132-133
XPOWERY, 89, 246
Year 1 vs. Year 0, 82, 203, 261-263
ZEROPRINT, 105
ZEROSUP, 105